W9-BWV-035

KENTUCKY,
Reduced from
ELIHU BARKER'S
Large Map.
W. Barker sculp.

of Guthrie's Geography improved.

The Voice
of the Frontier

The Voice of the Frontier

John Bradford's
NOTES ON
KENTUCKY

Thomas D. Clark, Editor

THE UNIVERSITY PRESS OF KENTUCKY

Frontispiece: Portrait of John Bradford by an unknown artist. Location and date unknown. Photograph in the Wilson Collection, courtesy of Special Collections, Margaret I. King Library, University of Kentucky.

Publication of this book has been assisted
by a grant from the John Bradford Society.

Copyright © 1993 by The University Press of Kentucky
Scholarly publisher for the Commonwealth,
serving Bellarmine College, Berea College, Centre
College of Kentucky, Eastern Kentucky University,
The Filson Club, Georgetown College, Kentucky
Historical Society, Kentucky State University,
Morehead State University, Murray State University,
Northern Kentucky University, Transylvania University,
University of Kentucky, University of Louisville,
and Western Kentucky University.

Editorial and Sales Offices: Lexington, Kentucky 40508-4008

Library of Congress Cataloging-in-Publication Data
Bradford, John, 1747-1830.
  The voice of the frontier : John Bradford's notes on Kentucky /
Thomas D. Clark, editor.
    p.   cm.
  Compilation of articles first published in the Kentucky Gazette
Aug. 25, 1826-Feb. 27, 1829.
  Includes bibliographical references and index.
  ISBN 0-8131-1801-8 (alk. paper) :
  1. Kentucky—History—To 1792—Sources. 2. Kentucky—
History—1792-1865—Sources. I. Clark, Thomas Dionysius, 1903-.
II. Title.
F454.B865   1993
976.9'03—dc20   92-28767

This book is printed on recycled acid-free paper meeting
the requirements of the American National Standard
for Permanence of Paper for Printed Library Materials.
∞

To my beloved
BETH
who has been a definite part of this enterprise

Contents

Preface

By 1826 John Bradford had grown old and reminiscent, having lived through the entire span of Kentucky's pioneer history and that of the borderland immediately beyond. In that year he began publication in his *Kentucky Gazette* of a series of sixty-six "Notes on Kentucky." In the next three years he selected topical materials from the file of the *Gazette*, covering a diversity of subjects and giving special emphasis to four or five.

As an important and respected player in the process of settling the central Kentucky region, and as founder and editor of the *Gazette*, John Bradford was in a cardinal position to make selections of materials detailing events and issues of the times. His rise to a position of influence in the western country was largely mandated by his official appointment as editor and publisher. His newspaper had been created primarily to serve as a publishing outlet for the proceedings of the official separation conventions that led to the creation of the Commonwealth of Kentucky, as well as to convey some notion of national and world events to western readers. Delegates to the Danville separation conventions after 1787 regularly requested that their proceedings be published in the *Kentucky Gazette*, which became a major repository of these historic documents.

Aside from the separation of the District of Kentucky from Virginia, the issues of foremost concern were the Indian menace and the development and execution of a national Indian policy. For two decades sporadic Indian raids and numerous retaliatory militia strikes were unsettling facts of life at villages north and south of the Ohio River. Possibly more disturbing in the long run of history was the proposed Jay Treaty, knowledge of which surfaced in 1786, by which Spain proposed to control navigation of the Mississippi River for twenty-five years. The very thought of such a restriction was anathema to westerners. The separation of the Kentucky District from Virginia, complicated by many complex questions and political manipulations, was obviously a matter of central importance, as reflected in the "Notes on Kentucky." The other issue of keen interest to John Bradford, a trustee of Transylvania University, was the rise and disintegration of that institution. The five notes relating to Transylvania seem almost non sequiturs to the rest of the "Notes." They are of value, nevertheless, in tracing the troubled and bigoted attacks against this early western institution of higher education.

That portion of the "Notes" that deals with events and issues after 1787 came almost wholly from the file of the *Kentucky Gazette*. There are handwritten marks of a contemporary nature in the Lexington Public Library file of the *Gazette* which were most likely placed on the pages by John Bradford as he selected the materials for his "Notes." In documenting the "Notes," references are made to other sources largely for purposes of corroborating Bradford's text as being faithful reporting. John Bradford had a habit of changing subjects almost without forewarning, a habit derived, no doubt, from the fact that in publishing the *Gazette* space was precious. He simply followed in the "Notes" the annalistic approach that characterized the *Gazette* itself. The "Notes" are strung together in a loose chronological order.

Once John Bradford got under way with the publication of the "Notes," the weekly deadline seems at times to have pushed him to production. For his subject matter, he turned to columns from the *Gazette*, stories of Indian attacks, and official materials, with little or no consideration for internal relationships. In some instances it is possible that the contents of documents and the news of events appeared nowhere else in near primary form.

An interesting interlude in the "Notes" is the two essays, or the essay in two parts, by H.H. Brackenridge of Pittsburgh. John Bradford had published this material earlier in the *Gazette* without identifying the author or giving any real reason for publication, and he did so again in the "Notes." Brackenridge no doubt was known either personally or by reputation to both John and Fielding Bradford. He had given Pittsburgh a slight literary reputation before he moved to practice law in Carlisle, Pennsylvania.

In the sections relating to Transylvania University, John Bradford more or less presented unedited the proceedings of the Transylvania Board of Trustees. That he did so is fortunate because one volume of the trustee minutes has since been lost, and the "Notes" now constitute the basic early record of Transylvania University.

In many other instances the file of the *Gazette* and the content of the "Notes" must be accepted as primary sources of information about pioneer Kentucky and the inception of the greater western movement. Interestingly, early historical collector Lyman C. Draper drew heavily on the *Gazette* for information, and even upon the "Notes." Any undertaking to document the *Gazette* material and the contents of the "Notes" can be only partially successful, leaving a generous amount of speculation in many instances. Attempts at documentation will run into a web of incestuous historical "cribbing." In all the contemporary Kentucky historical publications there is ample evidence that the authors drew heavily on the *Gazette*. Draper had access to G.W. Stipp's *Western Miscellany*, a fact documented in Draper's annotated copy of the book. Subsequent authors, such as Alexander Scott Withers in *Border Warfare*, John A. McClung in *Western Adventure*, Jacob Burnet in *Notes on the Early Settlement of the Northwest Territory*, James R. Albach in *Annals of the West*, and Lewis Collins and Richard H. Collins in their *History of Kentucky*—all drew information from the "Notes."

This book is the first in which all sixty-six of John Bradford's "Notes on Kentucky" are published in collective form. No doubt a question will arise as to the significance of the "Notes." Even without the privilege of examining some of the documents that John Bradford said he had in hand in 1826, it seems reasonable to assume that some of the contents of the "Notes" are original. In fact, some of the material in the "Notes" that was picked up from previous issues of the *Kentucky Gazette* exists nowhere else in any form.

Except for the proceedings of the first four Kentucky separation conventions, those appearing in the *Gazette* must be considered no more than quasi-official. Without in any way modifying the substance of fundamental debates in the conventions, Thomas Todd, the secretary of the conventions, published in the *Gazette* abbreviated reports free of procedural maneuverings. Both the *Gazette* and the "Notes on Kentucky" give insights into Kentucky's course to independent statehood during the years 1787-92, especially in relation to both Virginia and the young nation in the matter of political and procedural differences.

Through the collected "Notes" runs a vivid thread of emotionalism in reaction to Indian problems, Spanish efforts to assert control over the Mississippi River, the adoption of the United States Constitution, and the founding of the federal government. A historian may well cry out in anguish, however, that John Bradford, as editor of the *Gazette* and later as compiler of the "Notes," gave almost no attention to the social and economic process of pioneering and exploitation of the virgin land. There is almost no sense of the development of a distinctive regional culture, no flavor of human nature in reaction to the forces of the land.

John Bradford seems not to have overlooked a single Indian raid in the accounts he gathered in the "Notes." There are abundant references to this subject in other sources, but no other single source recounts the individual raids. It must be said, however, that the dust on the aged government documents has been too little disturbed by historians. John Bradford made generous use of much information published later in the *American State Papers* series, but there is no indication as to how he came by the facts. In the case of Indian wars in the Old Northwest, 1790-95, documents were published in the *Gazette* relating to correspondence between General Arthur St. Clair and Anthony Wayne that seem not to exist elsewhere, not even in Richard Knopf's excellent compilation of Wayne papers.

In John D. Shane's interview with Joseph Ficklin in 1853, Ficklin said that Allan B. Magruder had planned to write a history of Kentucky. This was an error. Magruder had collected material to write a history of the Indian wars. When he was appointed a land agent to work with establishing boundaries in the Louisiana Purchase in 1805 he turned over his notes on the Indian raids to John Bradford. No doubt Bradford made generous use of Magruder's notes. The notes, however, were lost and the fact of their use cannot now be determined. There is no indication of the volume or contents of Magruder's collection or from what sources he collected his information.

Once Kentucky had been securely admitted to the union of states, once the Indian menace had ended and free access to the Mississippi River had been assured in the Jay and Pinckney treaties, John Bradford seems, in the "Notes" at least, to have assumed that a particular era in frontier Kentucky history had concluded. It may have been the influence of old age and ill health that prevented him from publishing other notes to deal with the many basic issues that remained. Bradford surely was not oblivious to the great western debates over the Alien and Sedition laws, the Kentucky Resolutions, revisions of the first Kentucky constitution, the purchase of Louisiana, and the thunderous religious revivals that emotionally shook the whole western country. As editor of the *Kentucky Gazette* and then as an active Lexington official and citizen, he surely was aware of the rise of the new political leadership and the burning issues in politics and the domestic economy. The rising heat of the debates over slavery was to color Kentucky history for the next four decades. With the exception of the "Notes" sections relating to the rise and fall of Transylvania University, Bradford ignored the rich resources of educational topics in the first quarter of the nineteenth century.

The search for the complete file of John Bradford's "Notes on Kentucky" has over the years involved the interest and services of many individuals. Dr. Gerald Ham, subsequently of the Wisconsin State Archives, located five of the missing "Notes" when he prepared his two-part article on the materials contained in the McCalla Papers in the University of West Virginia Special Collections. James F. Hopkins and Burton Milward of Lexington have assisted me in comparative reading of the "Notes." Janet Marshall and Robin Rader of the Lexington Public Library staff gave me substantial assistance in the use of the files of the *Kentucky Gazette*. William B. Marshall, director of the Special Collections Division of the Margaret I. King Library, University of Kentucky, along with Claire McCann, Pamela Brackett, and Frank Stanger, were generous with their assistance. So was Carolyn Denton of the Special Collections Division of the Transylvania University Library. She made available to me the records of the board of trustees of that institution and the Horace Holley manuscripts. Joanne Hohler, reference archivist of the State Historical Society of Wisconsin, supplied me with a copy of Lyman C. Draper's annotated copy of G.W. Stipp's *Western Miscellany.*

Dr. Dwight Mikkelson, in doing research for his doctoral dissertation, *"The Kentucky Gazette:* Herald to a Noisy World" (University of Kentucky), discovered John Bradford's "Notes on Kentucky." He had these transcribed and spent many years in preparing and editing the "Notes" for publication. He located all sixty-six sections of the "Notes," and his mother, Clara Mikkelson, painstakingly and accurately transcribed the texts. She brought to the task a vast amount of experience, having been a secretary to two governors of North Dakota and then, for twenty-two years, the registrar of Asbury College in Wilmore, Kentucky. Her services were of tremendous importance in accurately transcribing this large volume of material. The late Jane Long Mikkelson did considerable typing of the "Notes" and of editorial materials prepared by Dr. Mikkelson. Great credit is due these three individuals for the preliminary work they did in the preparation of the "Notes," services which I wish to acknowledge with the fullest appreciation and admiration.

In October 1960 and January 1961, Gerald Ham published a two-part listing of the broadsides and newspapers contained in the McCalla Collection in the University of West Virginia. In doing this research he discovered the five missing sections and thereby corrected an oft-repeated error that there were only sixty-two "Notes."

Judge Samuel M. Wilson of Lexington, during the years 1916-1945, made a diligent search for documentary materials relating to John Bradford and the *Kentucky Gazette.* He catalogued and copied the "Notes." His manuscripts on this subject number a thousand pages, and his lecture before the American Bibliographical Society in 1937 was comprehensive. Judge Wilson, however, created a text too extensive and expensive to merit publication with the funds in hand. Most of the individuals mentioned by John Bradford will be too well known to require further identification. My own documentation is intended to identify the sources from which Bradford drew his information or corroborative sources. To attempt to identify all of Bradford's sources of information or all individuals mentioned would have been an exercise in futility. Clearly he drew heavily from the columns of the *Kentucky Gazette,* but the sources of information for those columns are often as fleeting as the word-of-mouth communication from which they were drawn.

I have added square brackets correcting the typographical errors of John Bradford's making which might otherwise cause confusion, rather than clutter the text with the ubiquitous *sic.* Quotation marks indicate that Bradford himself quoted sources. At the conclusion of the earliest "Notes" Bradford published a brief outline of the contents of the next section to appear. In time the outlines became materially shorter and eventually were discontinued. They are omitted here because they make no real contribution to the contents of the "Notes." The titles of the sixty-six "Notes" have been added to give some indication of the contents. Otherwise the "Notes" are reproduced as faithfully as possible in the form in which they appeared in the *Kentucky Gazette* from 1826 through 1829.

I alone am responsible for the research, documentation, bibliographical search, and introductory textual matter included here and for the tedious and often vexing task of preparing the text for publication. John Bradford's "Notes" are for the first time presented in their entirety with the belief that they add vastly to the understanding of one phase of the great American westward movement.

THOMAS D. CLARK

Introduction

John Bradford, a native of Prince William County, Virginia,[1] was frontier Kentucky's man for all seasons. There was scarcely an incident or activity that occurred in the area from 1775 through 1830 in which he was neither a participant nor an observer. In 1826, near the end of his life, he published the first series of newspaper columns that reflected both a personal and a general regional awareness that the Commonwealth of Kentucky had at last passed through its chrysalis stage of pioneering and had entered upon more advanced phases of economic, social and cultural, and political development.

As editor of the *Kentucky Gazette* from its founding in 1787 to 1802, and again in the latter half of the decade 1820-30, John Bradford was able to bring perspectives from two eras of Kentucky's history and to make his readers aware of their past. He had been an active participant in many phases of the pioneering era in the virgin land of central Kentucky.[2] He witnessed the phenomenal changes that occurred with the arrival of every new wave of settlers after the American Revolutionary War. Bradford was ever sensitive to the intensity of Indian resistance to the spread of white settlements and to the horrors inflicted upon the settler-victims of their raids. He had acute knowledge of the processes and frustrations associated with the separation from Virginia.[3]

By 1826, and the date of publication of the first "Notes on Kentucky," many of the old pioneers had either died or were too feeble of mind and body to give information about their personal experiences. They did not pass from the scene, however, without having made deep impressions on the land and its history. Like many of his pioneering contemporaries, John Bradford had a keen sense of the importance of the times. There prevailed among many of the pioneer Kentuckians an almost psychopathic yearning that future generations not be permitted to forget their ordeals. Nevertheless, those pioneers stood a fair chance of passing into oblivion unless some imaginative person among them collected and preserved their recollections and meager papers. John Bradford was fully aware of this fact and was the best qualified in the area to preserve the record for posterity. He was a man of broad experience as a land surveyor, Indian fighter, newspaper editor and printer, town trustee, legislator, university trustee, and president of the Lexington Democratic Society. Above all he shared the pioneer's pride of accomplishment. No other Kentuckian has made so complete a record of his generation.

With a profound sentimental commitment to his generation, John Bradford was determined to leave a record of how the land had been settled and passed on to the next generation in peace, after the trauma of the Indian raids, diplomatic entanglements, and oppressions from central government. Almost every entry of the "Notes" is laced with the thread of determination, challenge, and the sense of the settler's destiny in the western country. There is not a hint in the "Notes" that the land west of the Appalachians was not destined to be claimed and settled by pioneering Anglo-Americans.

By his eighty-first year John Bradford had assembled a considerable body of manuscripts, interview notes, recollections, and personal papers. Too, he had at hand the office file of the *Kentucky Gazette*. Whether or not he had been collecting these materials since he began publishing his newspaper in 1787 is not made clear in his editorial and biographical data. It is a tragedy in terms of Kentucky historical sources that Bradford's papers, including his file of the *Kentucky Gazette*, the collected "Notes" themselves, and possibly the papers of Allan B. Magruder were carelessly scattered and destroyed after his death.[4] No historian can determine how selective Bradford was in using manuscripts and oral recollections. Joseph Ficklin, newspaper editor and longtime Lexington postmaster, described for the Reverend John D. Shane in 1853 his purchase of Bradford's bound copy of the "Notes" for fifty cents, and said, "I have since lost sight of it. Do not know what has become of it."[5]

John Bradford wrote wholly within the context of his time, as can be corroborated by reference to a host of both official and reminiscent personal sources published after 1826. Since there exists no inventory of his library and manuscript holdings, one can only speculate on what information the author may have had in hand, or what data were readily available to him. At the outset of the publication of the "Notes on Kentucky," John Bradford informed his readers that he had in hand a considerable body of source materials relating to the pioneering era, no doubt including personal papers of early pioneers, which today exists only as excerpts in the "Notes on Kentucky."[6] Bradford gave no intimation, however, of what his source materials were or of the fact that he had available a copy of Thomas Jefferson's *Notes on Virginia*. It is inconceivable that this popular book, which went through so many editions, would have been overlooked by the Jeffersonian Republican Kentucky editor.[7] In fact, many of John Bradford's "Notes" bear some resemblance to those of Jefferson.

John Bradford obviously had access to Samuel Metcalf's *Indian Warfare* and to Allan B. Magruder's collected notes on the same subject, and he surely must have had in hand, in some form or other, much of the material that was later published in the *American State Papers* (*Indian Affairs*, 1834).[8] In discussing Indian affairs in the "Notes," Bradford obviously searched back files of his newspaper.[9] There is no doubt that he had in hand Humphrey Marshall's *History of Kentucky,* just as Marshall, conversely, consulted the files of the *Kentucky Gazette.* Marshall noted every Indian raid cited in the *Gazette.*[10] Generally, Bradford seems to have given credence to much of the contents of John Filson's *The Discovery, Settlement and Present State of Kentucke* and to Marshall's *History,* although he disagreed with Marshall in the political area.[11]

Bradford also had available a copy of Arthur St. Clair's *A Narrative of the Manner in which the Campaign against the Indians in the Year One Thousand Seven Hundred and Ninety-One Was Conducted under the Command of Major General St. Clair.* Both Henry Clay and John Pope were listed in this book as subscribers.[12] It is almost impossible to tell whether Bradford used these and other published materials as factual sources or for corroboration. Whatever sources Bradford may have consulted in the preparation of his "Notes," it is more important to speculate on what sources were used in the writing of news items for the *Kentucky Gazette.*

The sixty-six notes that Bradford compiled and published between August 25, 1826, and February 27, 1829, contain information gleaned from personal experiences and first-hand knowledge of many events, from the recollections of his contemporaries and notes supplied by others, and from the columns of the *Gazette.* In this connection it must be emphasized that he did not have access to any of the papers and correspondence of prominent frontier leaders that were published after 1829.[13]

John Bradford certainly knew and talked with many of the aging frontiersmen. Joseph Ficklin, the Lexington editor, postmaster, and raconteur, told John D. Shane, "I assisted Bradford in the preparation of his notes." He said the accounts of the "Battles of Bryan's Station and of the Blue Licks—in Bradford's *Notes*—were furnished by me." Ficklin also suggested that Bradford may have had access to the research papers of Allan B. Magruder, who had planned to write a history of Kentucky but who died a drunkard's death before he could do so.[14]

There appeared in almost every issue of the *Gazette* columns of the proceedings of the U.S. Congress. Bradford must have received at intervals copies of the *Annals of Congress.* In between times he copied accounts of the congressional proceedings from the *National Gazette* and other eastern newspapers that reached Lexington. When the mails failed to arrive in time, the Kentucky editor was hard-pressed to fill up the columns of his paper.[15]

At the state level of the government, John Bradford had access to all the minutes of the separation conventions that met in Danville. After the organization of the government of the Commonwealth of Kentucky, he had access to the records of the governor's office and to the proceedings of the General Assembly. As state printer, he produced the earlier *Acts* of the General Assembly and the *Journals* of both houses.[16]

The "Notes on Kentucky" reflect the author's capacity to gather and present facts in a clear, succinct form. With the long experience of an editor who had to produce a weekly newspaper with the most rigid conservation of paper, ink, and column space, John Bradford was skillful in composing a lean narrative. He was a self-disciplined historian who wrote from the outer edge of memory of the era he described, in a region where collected bodies of historical sources were nonexistent. Bradford, however, was one of those ingenious, clever natives who characterized the spread of the Anglo-American civilization across the continent. Personally, he embodied the experiences of a good portion of the first wave of settlers who penetrated the western mountain barrier of Virginia.

John Bradford was born June 6, 1749, in Prince William County, in the area that was later formed into Fauquier County in February 1759.[17] Many Kentucky immigrants came from this region, where at the time there was a rising interest in exploring and settling the western country. It was in the first year of John Bradford's life that Dr. Thomas Walker of Charlottesville led an exploring party through Cumberland Gap to "spy out the land."[18]

John Bradford's personal record is mute on the subject of his education. He doubtless received at least a rudimentary amount of schooling, perhaps in one of Virginia's famous "old field academies." Whatever his educational preparation, Bradford demonstrated as an adult a proficiency in both writing and mathematics. As a land surveyor he made generous use of the latter science, and as an editor he wrote with remarkable skill.[19] Strangely, none of the numerous biographical sketches of Bradford, including that of the famous newspaper historian James Melvin Lee in the *Dictionary of American Biography,* make any mention of education.[20]

Like thousands of other Kentucky pioneers, John Bradford was drawn westward by the availability of cheap land—cheap, that is, in monetary terms but often precious in terms of threats to life and peace of mind. He traveled west in 1775 to be an assistant to the official land surveyor, George May, in the future Kentucky County.[21]

Just as Daniel Boone had done six years earlier, John Bradford left behind in Fauquier County his wife, Elizabeth, whom he had married in 1771.[22] He did not move his family to Kentucky until 1784 or 1785.[23] Bradford did not spend all of the intervening time in Kentucky. Part of the time he served as an ensign in the Fauquier County militia and was engaged in the closing phase of the American Revolution. Following Lord Cornwallis's surrender at Yorktown, Bradford returned to Kentucky as a land surveyor in the newly created Fayette County.[24] He served as a deputy to Thomas Marshall of Prince William County, his uncle and the father of Chief Justice of the United States John Marshall.[25]

In 1783 John Bradford was an unsuccessful candidate for election to the Virginia General Assembly from Fayette County. The defeat may have been his good fortune, since it left him a surveyor in virginal Kentucky, where he was in a position to locate and make claims to much of the superior land along the Cane Run branch of the Elkhorn Creek. He also laid claim to a considerable portion of the site of the future town of Lexington.[26] Like most of his fellow Kentuckians, he had an insatiable land hunger.

John Bradford had the excitement of being a part of the many events he described in the "Notes on Kentucky" for the years 1775-1800. At some time in this tumultuous era he was at Harrodsburg, Bryan's Station, and elsewhere in the settlements. He was present at the sacking of Chillicothe,[27] an incident he was to write of forty-six years later in the "Notes" describing the war against the Shawnees.[28]

The pioneer Kentucky reflected in Bradford's "Notes" was almost solely confined to the central Bluegrass region, an area then tied to the older eastern states by the umbilical lashings of the Wilderness Trace and the Ohio River, and to the south by the Mississippi River. Spanish control of that stream was as threatening a menace to Kentuckians' future welfare as were the Indian raids,[29] as reiterated in many of the "Notes" that discuss the problems of the West.

The Commonwealth of Kentucky was conceived in a condition of political turmoil. As a matter of fact, it was the major political issue of separating the Kentucky counties from Virginia that brought John Bradford into a position of public prominence. When he returned to Kentucky to take up his Cane Run land claim, he had no more promising future than that of being a farmer-land surveyor and engaging in occasional raids against the Indians. When he brought Elizabeth Bradford and their children across the mountains in 1784 or 1785 to locate on a Kentucky homestead, he cut ties with Virginia and became a permanent resident on the western Kentucky frontier.[30]

The Bradford family arrived in Kentucky in an era of great social and political fermentation. By 1785 the immigrant entryways were crowded with settlers trudging their way westward to lay claim to land, build new homes, and establish fresh beginnings in the transmontane Eden. By that time the Wilderness Trace had been well trampled into a plainly marked highway, the boles of fallen trees and brush had largely been pushed aside, fording places of the streams had been established and stabilized, and safe camping sites located.[31] The Wilderness Trace, however, was still exposed to fierce Indian raids. To the Chickamauga of the South, the trace had become a galling symbol of the fact that their Kentucky hunting ground was slipping beyond their control. In retaliation they preyed upon immigrant parties all the way from Cumberland Gap to Boonesboro and Bryan's Station.[32]

On the northern immigrant route, the Shawnee and associated tribes attacked immigrant parties that drifted down the Ohio River and landed to make camp on bars at night. Too, the coming of settlers to central

Kentucky concentrated about the rising forts and stations droves of horses, animals highly prized by the Indians. Hardly an account of raids along the Wilderness Trace or the Ohio failed to mention the killing of settlers and the stealing of horses. Tomahawk wounds inflicted upon settlers became symbolical of Indian desperation over the loss of hunting grounds.

Much of central Kentucky by 1784 was well on the way to settlement, and the raids on Boonesboro, Ruddle's and Martin's forts, and Bryan's Station, and the bloody massacre at the Lower Blue Licks on August 19, 1782, had become history. There still occurred the sporadic firing on immigrant boats along the Ohio, the ambushes along the Wilderness Trace, and the horse stealing and murderous raids in the settlements. Such incidents were isolated and minor in comparison with those of earlier years, but they were serious enough to keep settlers in a constant state of apprehension, and they merited news items in the *Kentucky Gazette*.[33]

There prevailed in the Kentucky settlements a strong antagonism toward the British, whose northwest posts were looked upon as centers of stimulation of Indian hostilities. There was plenty of evidence to substantiate the belief that the raiders who came from north of the Ohio into Kentucky had the encouragement and blessing of the British.[34] To the south the Cherokee were perhaps an even greater menace because of their easy access to the Wilderness immigrant trace. Traveling parties on this road were seldom in a position to make a strong defense of their night camps or to protect the flanks of their processions. Immigrants unfamiliar with the long stretches of the trace subject to marauding Indians had no way of fending off surprise attacks.[35] For instance, in October 1784, Cherokee warriors set upon an immigrant party at the head of Skagg's Creek in present-day Laurel County, killed three of the McClure family's children, and captured the mother and an infant in arms. Colonel William Whitley led a militia company in pursuit of the Cherokee and Chickamauga and rescued Mrs. McClure and the baby. Within a fortnight there was a similar attack on the Moore family of immigrants at the famous old frontier stopping place, the Raccoon Spring.[36]

The most dramatic raid along the Wilderness Trace was that made upon the McNitt party on the night of October 1, 1786. This group of immigrants had made night camp on the side of the Wilderness Trace at the site of what is now Kentucky's Levi Jackson State Park, just south of the present-day town of London. A number of settlers were killed, others escaped into the woods, and the company's baggage was strewn over a large area. For years afterward the site of McNitt's Defeat was a reminder to Wilderness Trace travelers of the grisly incident that occurred there.[37] The incessant Cherokee raids provoked Benjamin Logan and William Whitley to organize local militiamen into a vigorous striking force, which they led against the Chickamauga villages along the great bend of the Tennessee River.[38] All of these incidents were noted in the *Kentucky Gazette*.

Kentuckians during the years 1781-92 were placed in a distressingly difficult and anomalous administrative situation. They lacked both the authority and the financial resources to organize and direct expeditionary forces beyond the boundaries of the Kentucky District. For Virginians east of the mountains, the Revolutionary War ended in October 1781, but in the aftermath Indian raids continued to threaten the western counties. The lack of authority to mount an adequate militia force and send it beyond district boundaries was central in setting in motion the process to separate the Kentucky District from Virginia. Lack of authority to deal with many local problems set off a veritable flood of petitions to Richmond by supplicating Kentuckians in the years before 1792.[39] Individuals could collect arms and ammunition to protect themselves, but the counties were unable to do so. Under prevailing Virginia law, organized Kentucky militiamen could not go at public expense north of the Ohio to attack the Shawnee villages or to raid those of the Chickamauga.[40]

By no means did all the Kentuckians' complaints after 1780 center on the Indian issue. Settlers of the western district were denied the power to act in many areas without the consent of the Virginia General Assembly and the governor.[41] One such matter was access to the Mississippi River. Despite Indian raids the central Kentucky lands and meadows had become so productive that the output demanded a fully accessible transportation artery to an outside market, primarily the Spanish port of New Orleans. By 1785 the question of access to the Mississippi had become as pressing as that of combatting Indians. In the succeeding separation conventions in Danville, this issue became as central as that of creating an independent state.[42]

Virginia's Kentucky counties were geographically too far removed from the seat of government in Richmond to permit timely communication or efficient administration. In many Kentucky petitions to the central government there was a note of frustration that officials in the East did not understand the pressures and dangers that bore upon the settlers in the West. Governors and legislators, it was felt, were too occupied with national and post-Revolutionary War problems to give attention to those of the backwoods.[43] In all the pleas for military and financial assistance there was an underlying expression of a desire for the separation of the western counties from the mother state.[44]

The combination of defense and administrative issues prompted Benjamin Logan to propose an assembling of representative delegates in Danville on September 27, 1784. As a county lieutenant, Logan was primarily interested in finding a way to mount a counterattack against the Chickamauga villages.[45] Humphrey Marshall correctly summarized the situation when he wrote in 1812: "To the people of Kentucky, forming a part of Virginia, and accustomed to look up to her, for acts of legislation, and grants of authority, it was as reasonable, as it was natural, to apply to her, for protection; and to demand as a right, the free exercise of the means, which God, and their own exertions, had put within their own grasp. This, to the extent of internal defense, was all legalized. Beyond that, it was forbidden. And this appeared an intolerable grievance."[46]

Delegates to the first Danville convention were selected by the district militia companies, thus giving a strong defense emphasis to the gathering. Virtually from the outset the central issue became that of separation from Virginia through creation of an independent state that could respond to its militia needs and adjudicate other public matters. Separation, however, became for the Kentucky District a much more complicated issue than anyone west of the mountains could readily have recognized in 1784. First, there was the tedious matter of achieving something approaching a consensus in the region. Because of the nature of the deep-seated state loyalties of the later eighteenth century, there was considerable reluctance on the part of many to sever ties with Virginia. This reluctance was a delaying factor in the move for separation. Relations with the central government of the Confederation were tenuous at best, bearing on the highly emotional issue of international diplomacy relating to free use of the Mississippi River. Finally, the thought of financing a state government was a sobering one in a region already resistant to taxes. It was not clear in 1784 whether there existed in the Kentucky counties the necessary political leadership to administer a state government.[47]

After 1781 the population of Kentucky had increased phenomenally. Despite lingering fears of Indian raids, Kentuckians in 1784 were too widely dispersed among forts, stations, and lonely homesteads to permit communication easily by either word of mouth or posted bulletin. In the second separation convention, in May 1785, the delegates "Resolved unanimously, That to insure unanimity of opinion of the people respecting the propriety of separating from Virginia, and forming a separate state government, and to give publicity to the proceedings of the convention, it is deemed essential to have a printing press."[48]

The second convention set the Kentucky District on a new political—and literary—course. The convention resolved unanimously "that it is expedient and necessary for this district to be separated from Virginia, and established into a sovereign state, to be known by the name of 'Commonwealth of Kentucky.'"[49] It then became necessary to arouse public opinion favorable to creating the Commonwealth, and to give publicity to future conventions.[50]

For whatever reason, there was no printer among the horde of Kentucky immigrants. Finding a printer was the specific assignment of a special committee composed of General James Wilkinson, Christopher

Greenup, and John Coburn.[51] The committee corresponded with John Dunlap of Philadelphia about the prospects of finding an editor in that city, which had established a considerable reputation in the newspaper field. The Kentucky committee was handicapped in its search because it could make no commitment as to potential financial support. No one in Philadelphia wanted to take such a chance on the Kentucky frontier. The committee then turned to Richmond, Virginia, where it undertook to entice Miles Hunter to move to Kentucky and begin publication of a newspaper, but because the committee could not promise income from public printing, and because of the fear of the Indian raids, Hunter refused the invitation.[52]

After the committee failed to attract a printer to move to Kentucky, John Bradford, then a land surveyor living in Fayette County, applied to General Wilkinson for the job of public printer, expressing a willingness to take such patronage as came his way. The committee accepted his proposal and submitted Bradford's name to the fourth separation convention in 1786.[53] Delegates to the convention concurred in the appointment of Bradford, and he became not only Kentucky's first newspaper editor and printer but a publisher as well.[54] On a much broader scale Bradford's print shop in time became a training ground for editors and printers who moved on with the expanding western frontier to found newspapers across the continent.[55]

In his description of how he came to be appointed editor of the *Kentucky Gazette*, Bradford gave no hint of the fact that he was without the basic editorial and mechanical experience essential to publish a semi-official journal. John and his brother Fielding had first to learn even the most elementary facts about printing and about the basic equipment for establishing a print shop. The closest source of instruction and supplies would have been Pittsburgh, up the Ohio River, but the Bradfords may in fact have had to search as far away as Philadelphia. There still remains a considerable historical haze as to where the Bradfords acquired their printing equipment and the first supplies of paper and ink. In his "Notes on Kentucky" John Bradford said he sent to Pittsburgh for equipment. In a later interview Fielding Bradford said he went there to secure supplies and to serve a very brief apprenticeship in John Scull's *Pittsburgh Gazette* shop.[56] Even though both Bradfords made statements about the acquisition of type and supplies, they were not specific about their acquisition or about the actual setting of the first issue of the *Kentucky Gazette*. Was this done while floating down the Ohio River aboard a flatboat, or at Limestone (now Maysville)?

Fielding Bradford is known to have spent approximately three months in Pittsburgh with John Scull, presumably learning the printer's trade.[57] Part of that time he was also awaiting the arrival of a press and type from Philadelphia. On his way home by flatboat, as indicated, he may have set the first issue of the *Kentucky Gazette*. However, he may even have set the type and locked the chace in John Scull's shop, but the flatboat seems to have been the more logical place. When Fielding Bradford landed at Limestone, the type may have been fully set. Between that place and Lexington the type fell into pi, meaning that it became scrambled through jolting. Not only did the type have to be reset in the crude one-room log hut that served the fledging printers, but a small hardwood block had to be carved to fit into an empty corner of the first four-page paper. The first issue of the *Kentucky Gazette*, which appeared on August 11, 1787, bore the apologetic note from John Bradford: "My customers will excuse my first publication, as I am much hurried to get an impression by the time appointed. A great part of the types fell into pi in the carriage to Lexington to this office, and my partner, which is the only assistant I have, through an indisposition of the body, has been incapable of rendering the smallest assistence for ten days past."[58]

The *Gazette* was produced in a small, four-page fold of approximately eight by ten inches. The front page universally carried advertising, the inside pages contained national, foreign, and a meager amount of local news. The back page contained public notices and official materials. There was no editorial column. The first issue had 180 subscribers.[59] The most sensational news appeared in the stories of Indian attacks and in notices that parties were being organized to meet at the Crab Orchard or Hazel Patch to return through the wilderness to the East.[60] The personality or strong political views of John Bradford are never clearly revealed in the columns of his paper. He served as editor of the *Gazette* from 1787 to 1802, and again from 1825 until his death in 1830.[61]

From the moment he opened his print shop in Lexington, John Bradford had to contend with grave shortages of paper and ink. In 1787 there was only one source of rag paper, and that was undependable: the newly established mill of Jacob Myers on the Dick's (now Dix) River.[62] Later the Craig-Parker mill in Georgetown would manufacture as much paper as Craig could find raw materials for in the form of rags.[63]

From 1787 to 1800 the editor of the *Gazette* had periods of serious difficulty in finding newsprint and supplies with which to produce more than even a single page of folio-size sheet. During the era of several of the separation conventions Bradford, unhappily, lacked paper on which to print the official proceedings. The reader who today turns through the files of the *Gazette* from those years would scarcely be aware that the separation process was under way in Danville except for some of the communications from individuals who engaged in philosophical political discussions and who concealed their identities behind veils of classical anonymity. Disappointing is the fact that there is no actual description of the process of drafting Kentucky's first constitution.[64]

The *Gazette* did carry the address by the notification committee that called on Isaac Shelby to inform him that he had been elected governor. The committee members were Christopher Greenup, Thomas Barbee, and Greenbury Darsey. The paper also printed Governor Shelby's response to his election.[65] On Monday, June 4, 1792, the new governor rode from Danville to Lexington, where he was joined by members of the General Assembly to begin the process of organizing the state government. The governor and legislators were welcomed in a brief address by John Bradford, who was then the president of the Lexington town trustees.[66] His remarks were less than a half column of newsprint in length. The *Gazette* contained no other description of this historic occasion.

In 1826 John Bradford seemed to look back over a half century of Kentucky's history, and his own mixed experiences, with some nostalgia. He had served as land surveyor, militiaman, and town trustee, real estate dealer, postmaster, legislator, and trustee of both the Lexington Public Library and Transylvania University.[67] Most important of all, however, was his secure place in journalistic history as a pioneer editor and publisher in the western country. Without having expressed his Jeffersonian views in strong partisan terms in editorials, he was an influential personal force in Kentucky politics. His avowed mission as editor was that of helping to formulate a public opinion favorable to separation from Virginia. His "Notes on Kentucky" must be viewed as an insightful contemporary view of Kentucky's pioneering era.[68]

Portrayed in the "Notes" is a panoply of pioneering personalities, including such major ones as Daniel Boone, George Rogers Clark, John Bowman, Isaac Shelby, Benjamin Logan, Simon Kenton, William Blount, Henry Hamilton, William Caldwell, John Floyd, and a host of Shawnee and Cherokee chiefs, among them Dragging Canoe, Cornstalk, Blackfish, and Hanging Maw. Perhaps the brief accounts of Indian raids and tomahawkings in the weekly editions of the *Gazette* were the only sensational bits of news published in the paper.[69]

Geographically, the "Notes" covered the region from western Virginia and eastern Tennessee along the Ohio from Pittsburgh to Fort Massac, and north to the Great Lakes. Locally the area covered by John Bradford in the "Notes" was almost wholly that of the central counties around Lexington, Danville, Harrodsburg, and Louisville. He and his contemporaries seem to have been wholly oblivious to the outlying western and Appalachian sections. Only the narrow corridor of territory along the Wilderness Trace and the scenes of bloody attacks by the Cherokee Indians attracted the author's attention.[70]

Almost never did John Bradford in the *Kentucky Gazette* give more than a general indication of the lapse of time between the occurrence of an event and the reporting of it in the newspaper.[71] Today's reader of the "Notes on Kentucky" who is familiar with the time intervals can only feel wonderment, nevertheless, at how quickly news and gossip passed by word of mouth among the settlements. Almost from the beginning of publication of the *Gazette* in 1787, the editor seems to have received via oral reports from unidentified persons a remarkable amount of information about what was happening in the western country, often in remote areas.[72]

In the "Notes on Kentucky," as in the columns of the *Gazette*, John Bradford gave little space to discussing the mode of everyday life in Lexington or the other frontier Kentucky communities. Occasionally an irate and abandoned husband used the newspaper to disavow further financial responsibilities for a faithless wife, or a disgruntled bondsman published the unreliability of a delinquent debtor. There was a veritable flood of "gone astray" notices, principally concerning horses that probably had been stolen. Indicative of the fear of traveling along the Wilderness Trace were the frequent notices that parties were being formed to make the journey eastward. Of special historical interest were the advertisements of the service of stallions. The emerging economy and the rise of towns and farms, however, went unnoticed Almost as silently as the settling of spring dew, the rising tide of immigration spread over the land. As far as John Bradford's "Notes" exhibited any interest in the flood of post-Revolutionary War immigrants, they might have been a mass of faceless human beings. There is missing any serious description of this horde as a society or in terms of its impact on the western country, including the institutions that settlers helped to establish. Bradford did, however, express genuine concern for the safety of immigrants traveling along the Wilderness Trace and up and down the Ohio.[73]

Except for Bradford's description of John McKinney's traumatic encounter with a wildcat in his Lexington fortress schoolroom, or occasional advertisements of academy masters, or his notes on Transylvania University, there is no mention of education. Bradford also ignored the activities of the various religious groups, including the experiences of the Traveling Church congregation, which crossed the mountains in 1781 to found a string of Baptist churches across central Kentucky.[74] There is no mention of Lewis or Elijah Craig, the congregation's leaders, despite the *Kentucky Gazette*'s dependence on the Craig-Parker mill for paper. Early Bradford made the decision that the *Gazette* would not become involved in the theological disputes that raged in Kentucky in the early period.

The *Gazette* frequently named women as members of migrating families, as fighters against Indian attacks on forts and families, and as heroic defenders of their homes. Writing thirty-five years after the incident, John Bradford confirmed the fact that the women in Bryan's Station, on the morning of August 15, 1782, British-Indian attack, risked their lives by leaving the besieged fort to bring back water from the spring.[75]

In no "Note" did John Bradford give specific attention to agriculture and the development of the livestock industry, but he made indirect reference to the subject in his observations on the rapidly increasing population, on the federal government's irritating excise tax on distilled spirits, and on the bitter international dispute over free use of the Mississippi River by Kentucky farmer-traders.[76] Agricultural concerns are also implicit in his discussion of the special land court created by the Virginia General Assembly to bring a semblance of order out of the chaotic land claims and titles that were plastered haphazardly over the face of the central area.[77]

Throughout the "Notes" there are references to the horse. This animal, in almost ancient Grecian fashion, became a symbol of pioneering. The *Gazette* made recurring statements of the number of horses stolen by Indians. As a matter of fact, horse stealing seems to have been one of the major objectives of many of the raids by both northern and southern Indians. Quoting Harry Innes, John Bradford said that over two decades the Indians had stolen 20,000 horses. The animal was an essential beast of burden. Every overland immigrant party arrived in Kentucky mounted and leading packhorses. In time there appeared professional packhorse train transporters of goods to and from Kentucky. Those immigrants who drifted down the Ohio River aboard flatboats brought horses aboard. Occasionally Bradford noted that Indians concealed along the river banks had shot and killed horses.[78] Militiamen relied on their mounts to pursue Indians and on pack animals to transport their military supplies. After 1788 the advertisement columns of the *Kentucky Gazette* carried notices of stallions available for breeding service.

The social and cultural development of frontier Kentucky was viewed by Bradford and many of his contemporaries as only incidental to the basic problems of pioneering and establishing a foothold on the land. Bradford repeatedly returned to the theme of pioneering, but solely in terms of establishing a state, defending the border, and removing political and international barriers to expansion.[79]

The Indian problems in the western country became a near obsession with Bradford, both as editor of the *Kentucky Gazette* and as author of the "Notes on Kentucky." In the case of many of the incidents, Bradford had access in 1826 to information that he had gathered in 1788 or earlier. For instance, he was a member of Col. Robert Patterson's command in John Bowman's raid against the Miami villages in 1778 and had first-hand knowledge of what was happening. As a matter of fact, Robert Patterson wrote a good part of one of the "Notes" (section 23, February 16, 1827). Bradford had knowledge of other raids and incidents that beset the Kentucky settlements and of expeditions from the Kentucky settlements against the British and Indians in the Old Northwest in 1775-94. One of the most important of these was George Rogers Clark's campaign against Kaskaskia, Cahokia, and Vincennes. Then there were the attacks on Boonesboro, Bryan's Station, and the disaster at the Lower Blue Licks.[80]

Most shocking of all the British-Indian raids, however, was Col. Henry Byrd's bloody assault against Ruddle's and Martin's forts on June 22, 1783. Byrd led a force of six hundred Canadians and Indians down the Miami River and up the Ohio and Licking rivers to assault the Kentucky settlements. He lost control of his Indian warriors, who inflicted brutal injuries on men, women, and children.[81] To the South, no immigrant party was safe from the marauding Cherokee attacks that led to the highly destructive expedition of Benjamin Logan and William Whitley.[82]

Possibly no Indian raiding party crossed the Ohio River and attacked settlers and forts without becoming a news item in the *Kentucky Gazette*. There were few bits—perhaps none—of western country news more intriguing or more disturbing to the Kentucky frontiersman than those detailing raids, ambushes, killings of settlers, and theft of horses. At times these occurred so frequently that John Bradford inserted a special section in the *Gazette* entitled "Indian News."[83] The more brutal and ghastly the incident, the more currency the editor gave it. For instance, at least four stories of Indian encounters became classically interwoven with the broader aspects of the westward movement itself: the harrying adventures of Robert Benham and John Watson, members of a flatboat immigration party on the Ohio River that was set upon by Shawnee raiders in October 1779 (section 7); the capture and daring escape of Alexander McConnell (section 11); the Davis, McGuire, and Cafree encounter with Cherokees on the Wilderness Trace (section 19); and the assault on the Shanks family (section 26).[84]

Benham and Watson's boat crew had landed their craft on the north bank of the Ohio in the belief that they could surprise a small party of Indians they had spotted. As it turned out, however, a larger band of warriors had spied the boat earler, and when its crew landed the Shawnee fired on its crew from ambush. The hail of bullets broke both of Watson's arms and pierced Benham's hips. The two disabled men, left isolated after the ambush, were individually helpless, vulnerable to the least threat. They did not starve, however. Benham, with the free use of his arms, was able to shoot a raccoon that came near him. Watson, who could walk, kicked the dead animal up to Benham, who skinned, dressed and cooked it. Watson, in turn, waded into the river and, by manipulating his hat with his mouth, scooped up water that he carried to Benham. Cooperating in this manner, the two men survived to hail a passing flatboat and to reach safety.[85]

In 1771, Alexander McConnell, a resident of the Lexington Fort, killed a deer some distance away in the woods. He returned to the fort for a horse to bring the carcass home. While he was away Indians discovered the carcass and awaited in ambush for McConnell to return. He was captured and led away toward the Ohio and the Shawnee villages. During a night encampment he planned a daring escape. He was able to reach an

Indian's knife and cut his wrists free of their bindings. By manipulating the five loaded and primed Indian guns, McConnell was able to shoot and kill four of his captors, while the fifth was so frightened that he ran away. McConnell returned to the fort unharmed and lived to be further immortalized in Kentucky history as the plaintiff in the famous land case *McConnell v. Kenton,* which was one of the earliest lawsuits heard by the newly formed Kentucky Court of Appeals.[86]

In the spring of 1784 three men from Logan's Fort, McClure, Davis, and Cafree, pursued a party of Cherokee horse thieves southward toward their Tennessee River villages. The three came upon a small party of apparently friendly Indians and traveled with them some distance, until the latter stepped aside to confer. At the same time the whites schemed to kill the Indians. McClure killed his target, but Davis's gun misfired. Cafree was killed by the Indians, and Davis ran into the woods, pursued by one of the Cherokees. McClure was left with three dead men at his feet. He picked up his gun and started back to the fort, but along the way he came on an elderly Indian and a boy. The old man found great amusement in telling McClure he would be captured, and sat astride a log to demonstrate how the prisoner would be tied on a horse upside down. McClure shot his tormentor, but he was still not free of danger. He was set upon by a pack of Indian dogs that threatened to tear him apart.[87]

In Robert Patterson's account of how Indians attacked his party at a night camp on the Ohio River in 1776, the ordeal of men wounded in the skirmish almost defies belief. How human beings withstood the serious wounds and fractured bones—and the infections that followed from primitive methods of treating gunshot wounds and extracting bullets—remains a miracle. Patterson described an incident on the river that had occurred twenty-eight years before, a narrative that he no doubt gathered some color in the telling and retelling.[88] Nevertheless, George Rogers Clark recorded similar graphic descriptions in his brief diary in 1776, when he told of the wounding and killing in Indian raids against the new Kentucky settlements.[89]

An account of Indian atrocities that circulated among the Kentucky pioneers was the April 11, 1787, night attack on the Shanks family, who lived on Cooper's Run in Bourbon County. There were eight family members, two males and six females. Their double log cabin was hailed in the night with the customary frontier enquiry, "Who keeps house?" The family matriarch, wise to Indian tricks, forbade the opening of the cabin door. In the following assault, one of her daughters killed an Indian with a knife and in turn lost her own life. Two other daughters were slaughtered, and so was one of her sons as well as the older woman herself. The following morning a company of neighbors followed the Indians north, overtaking them near the Licking River. One Indian was killed and the other fled.[90]

In that same season there occurred a bizarre incident that stained the humanity of the Kentuckians. There appeared before a Bourbon County door a young man in Indian garb. He explained that he was in fact a white who had been taken prisoner early in life by a Lake Erie Indian tribe and had been adopted by a chief. That spring the old man had taken him and two sons by blood on a hunt in the Miami Valley. They had then crossed the Ohio River to hunt in Kentucky. The night before they reached the settlements, the old chief had been aroused from his sleep by a strange cry of an owl that he interpreted as an evil omen. That and a strange dream had prompted him to withdraw from the Kentucky hunting ground. The captive son had left the others to return to his people. When he revealed himself to the settlers, however, their suspicions were aroused, and they forced the young man to reveal the campsite of the Indians. The settlers then killed the Indian chief, tracked the sons to the Ohio, and killed them also. The white adopted son pleaded for the victims but was forced to witness the atrocities.[91]

In publishing the accounts of these incidents, John Bradford perhaps only mirrored his readers' major concerns. Not only did he record the details of what seems to have been every attack made on the forts and cabins and along the trails, but his "Notes" almost make the adventures of Daniel Boone seem secondary to the real conquest of the western country. Though Bradford showed genuine respect for Boone, Kenton, and the earlier trail-breaking heroes, his favorites were George Rogers Clark, Benjamin Logan, William Whitley, and Anthony Wayne. These were the warriors who finally wrested the western country from the Indians and put an end to their raids.

In some of his news accounts of the Indian attacks, John Bradford debunked several myths about the Indians. Although they had a well-developed capability to penetrate heavily wooded country, they appear not always to have had the skill to track their victims as tradition would have us believe. They demonstrated repeatedly their unbelievably poor marksmanship, although they wounded many of their antagonists. Their poor effectiveness with guns may have been caused partly by the inferior type of English trade guns with which they were armed, or by their stinginess in the use of powder and lead.[92]

Though Indians killed and maimed many Kentucky settlers, they no doubt suffered much greater pains and losses. The Bradford "Notes," as a matter of course, give only one side of the history of the struggle to possess the Kentucky hunting ground. There is no hint from the author that the Indians may have had some legitimate claim to the area as their traditional hunting ground.

When Alexander Scott Bullitt negotiated with the Shawnee in their Miami villages for permission to plant a settlement at the Falls of the Ohio in 1776, he acknowledged that the Indians had ancient hunting claims on the territory. He offered this as a persuasive argument to secure their granting his request.[93] Yet throughout the "Notes on Kentucky" a prevailing theme is that the flood of white settlers had claim to the land virtually by divine right or manifest destiny.

In all the contemporary published sources, the brutalities of the Indian resistance were presented as highly criminal acts. None of the sources, however, recognized the griefs and hardships inflicted on the tribes by the destructive raids of backwoods militiamen beyond the point of stating the nature of destruction wrought on villages and cornfields. A case in point was the destruction of the Piqua towns of the Shawnee when John Bowman's militiamen not only set fire to the huts in the villages but also slashed a phenomenal acreage of growing corn to the ground when it was still in the roasting ear stage, leaving Indian families to face a grim winter on short rations. In many respects Bowman's actions made the surprise assault on Ruddle's and Martin's forts seem small-scale by comparison.[94]

John Bradford viewed the Indian policy and treaty-making activities of the United States government with open suspicion. When he prepared his "Notes" on those subjects, he most certainly had available government documents and the texts of the various treaties.[95]

One can only speculate on what a literate "Indian Bradford" might have written had he published a series of notes on settler-Indian relations in the last quarter of the eighteenth century. He no doubt would have viewed the great in-rush of white settlers onto the Kentucky hunting ground with anger. He would have recorded, too, numerous incidents of the horrors wrought by white spies and militiamen on the Indian men, women, and children, of destroyed villages, and of the cornfields they laid waste. Surely the Indians had their own horror stories of surprise raids, of maimings and loss of life, and of humiliating defeats. In reality they had more to fear from the "Long Knives" than the Long Knives had to fear from the "Braves." What might an Indian chronicler have written describing the sufferings of seriously wounded warriors, like Benham and Watson, or captives trapped amidst a snoring host, as Alexander McConnell was? Too, his notes would have had to include an extra chapter describing a primitive people caught between the British forces in the Old Northwest and the Kentucky militiamen and subsequently confronted by the U.S. armed forces.[96]

One reads John Bradford's accounts of the Indian menace and the exploits of white militiamen and settlers with the feeling that this was the dramatic raw material that later dime novelists dredged to produce their lurid accounts of border warfare.[97] In fact, descriptions of the heroics of many of the individual Kentucky frontiersmen have been published and republished many times over.[98]

The inhabitants of the Kentucky District of Virginia faced more politi-

cal problems than they had legal authority to solve. Aside from legal au-
thorization to finance and send militiamen beyond the local boundaries
for purposes of defense, the Kentucky District lacked the power of immediate adjudication of its complex land disputes and other cases as well as
power over grants and privileges and the issuance of licenses. For instance, no stream could be blocked by a mill dam without the consent of
the state government in Richmond. From the beginning of settlement in
Harrod's and Logan's forts, there was a growing feeling in the western
counties that the Virginia governors and legislators were too much occupied with immediate local matters to be properly concerned with those
that agitated the Kentucky backwoodsmen.[99]

It was the increasing Indian menace that prompted Benjamin Logan
to call for an assembly of county representatives in Danville in December
1784. He had been told that the Cherokees had under way a massive
campaign to invade the Kentucky settlements. The purpose of the assembly in Danville, then, was to discuss how the Kentucky militia could be
used to defend the settlements under the restrictive laws of Virginia, and
how to raise funds to pay the militiamen.[100]

The 1784 convention reached no conclusions except to provide for a
second convention to gather in May 1785. It was in the May assembly that
the delegates settled on two major issues: separation from Virginia and
the establishment of a newspaper press to disseminate information and
unify public opinion favorable to creation of independent statehood.[101]
By transcribing the resolutions and debates in the "Notes" Bradford left
an objective source of information that is vital to an understanding of the
complex issues that delayed the creation of the Commonwealth of Kentucky.[102]

The Virginia General Assembly responded to the various resolutions
submitted by the Danville conventions by enacting, on January 6 and 10,
1786, the first of the Virginia Enabling Acts.[103] This act gave real impetus
to the separation of the Kentucky District from Virginia. Aside from laying
out the political formula and fiscal arrangements for separation, the act
contained the famous reservation clause governing future access to and
use of the Ohio River as an open channel of travel and commerce and as
the northern and northwestern boundary of the new state. For two
centuries this reservation has sent batteries of engineers, lawyers, and
judges in search of those elusive levels on the river's bank called "the low
water marks in 1786, 1789, and 1792."[104]

In "Note 20" John Bradford clarified many of the reasons why the
conventions were so handicapped in responding to Virginia's enabling
acts.[105] Though the fifth convention, one of the most important, was
scheduled to meet in Danville in 1787, the delegates present did not make
up a quorum. George Rogers Clark was absent while leading an expedition against the Wabash tribes, and Benjamin Logan was leading a strike

against the Shawnee.[106] No doubt the biggest problem at the moment, however, was that of unifying local public opinion to favor separation from Virginia and to accept the responsibilities of operating a separate state government.[107] The nearer the Kentucky District approached to independent statehood, the more discussion of many points of view on the subject appeared in the *Kentucky Gazette.*

In the *Gazette* and later in his "Notes" John Bradford filled in the intervals between conventions with brief accounts of the lingering Indian invasions, or with interminable letters discussing the processes of democratic government sent by correspondents who signed their letters with classical Greek and Latin names as if this gave their communications a greater weight of authority.[108] Occasionally glimpses of what was happening in the country crept into the columns of the paper. In detailing the Danville debates, John Bradford digressed to publish the story of a wildcat attacking the schoolmaster John McKinney in his schoolroom in Lexington. This bit of folksy educational history has become a popular anecdote related by nearly everyone who has written on the subject of Kentucky education.[109]

Nothing in the political arena—not even the process of separating Kentucky from Virginia and establishing an independent government—excited the old editor more than John Jay's proposed treaty with Spain, the excise tax on whiskey, and the general western policies of the federal government. The news of Jay's treaty in the spring of 1787 stirred hot fury of condemnation.[110] This treaty proposed to close the Mississippi River to free American access for twenty-five years, an act that would have made the Kentuckians subservient to the whims and will of the Spanish. Kentuckians first learned of the treaty from a communication by a western Pennsylvanian.[111]

The proposal to close the Mississippi River to western Americans threatened devastation to the economic and political expansion to the Kentucky settlements at the moment their fertile lands were beginning to yield bountiful crops and herds of livestock. Equally frustrating was the convention that the central government was dominated by the merchants and shippers of the eastern seaboard, who were willing to sacrifice the interests of the West for their own advantage. Fortunately the Kentuckians had the influential support of the Virginia General Assembly, which sent Congress a strongly worded resolution opposing ratification of the treaty.[112]

The broader Spanish issue became a subject of extensive, sometimes furious, debate in the fifth and sixth Danville conventions. Sometimes it almost obscured the main question of separation from Virginia.[113] In the "Notes on Kentucky" John Bradford gave little or no attention even to the great debate in Virginia at this time over ratification of the United States Constitution.[114]

In the fifth through the seventh Danville conventions personalities became almost as significant as the questions under discussion. This was the period when the old Indian-fighting, trail-breaking pioneers retreated into the background, leaving a new group of leaders to decide the destiny of the region.[115] Among the latter were John Brown, James Wilkinson, Samuel McDowell, George Müter, George Nicholas, Caleb Wallace, and Benjamin Sebastian.[116] It was in the fifth convention that the delegates adopted the positively worded resolution "That it is expedient for, and the will of the good people of the District, to be erected into an independent state on the terms of conditions specified in the two acts of assembly." Under the terms of the acts the new state of Kentucky was to come into official existence on December 31, 1788.[117]

In the meantime John Brown had been elected to Congress. He presented to that body an address or petition from the Danville conventions soliciting sanction of the creation of the Commonwealth of Kentucky. Kentucky sought admission at a most complex moment in early American history, at a time that required formulation of a policy on addition of new states to the Union. The Articles of Confederation granted no authority to enlarge the Union of States beyond the original thirteen. The Constitution of 1787, which provided for such additions, had not yet been ratified. Despite the lack of authority under the Articles of Confederation, the Congress may have been on the verge of admitting Kentucky when New Hampshire ratified the Constitution and the matter was dropped until the new Congress could act.[118] In his "Notes" John Bradford laid the blame for congressional failure to admit Kentucky on Congressman "Dane," by whom he surely meant Nathan Dane of Massachussetts, who was active in the organization of the Northwest Territory. The implication was that out of prejudice "Dane" had held up the admission of Kentucky.[119] There was a pronounced opinion in the West that easterners saw a danger in the admission of new states as shifting the center of political power in the Union.

There was disappointment in Kentucky when Congress referred the admission question back to Virginia and the Kentucky District to draft a constitution that would conform with the recently ratified U.S. Constitution. In his "Note" on the subject John Bradford showed how Kentucky residents viewed the delay as further obligating them to help pay for the defense of the frontier, with no help from Virginia and too little from the central government.[120]

At the point when congressional action delayed separation from Virginia, delegates had already been elected to Kentucky's seventh convention, to meet in April 1788 to draft a constitution. In the local political arena, ironically, the attention John Bradford gave to the last seven of the separation conventions was more or less the product of a sense of duty. He published the resolutions that the conventions generated and otherwise noticed the Danville debates. The columns of the *Gazette* occasionally contained philosophical discussions of the political needs of the Kentucky District.[121] When the tenth convention, in April 1792, set about drafting a constitution, Bradford in his role as editor, and subsequently as the author of the "Notes on Kentucky," seems almost to have been oblivious to the serious business that was under way in Danville. A reader of the "Notes" is left uninformed about the actual process by which the first constitution was drafted, and about the personalities of the framers. For instance, the name of George Nicholas, the constitution's principal framer, does not appear in either the *Gazette* or the "Notes."[122]

Except for the organization of the Kentucky state government in Lexington on June 4, 1792, the occasion of Kentucky's becoming an independent state got no other printed notice from John Bradford. As president of the Lexington town trustees, he served as chairman of the welcoming committee that greeted Governor Isaac Shelby and members of the General Assembly. Surely this event must have represented something more than a lull in the fight to drive the Indians as far beyond the Ohio River as possible and to wrest the control of the Mississippi River from Spain.[123] Yet it would be hard to imagine more matter-of-fact news reporting than Bradford's description of the events on June 4, 1792.

Throughout his newspaper career, three subjects were of basic interest to John Bradford: the Indian conflicts, free access to the Mississippi River, and the creation of state government, which demanded printed materials.[124] Bradford had a demonstrated sense of history and definitely had posterity in mind when he prepared his "Notes on Kentucky." In the 1930s Samuel M. Wilson wrote that the "Notes on Kentucky" were "promptly recognized and acclaimed as most valuable documents for the preservation and interpretation of Kentucky's earliest annals, and as a consequence that 'sections' were widely copied, as they successively appeared by the newspaper press of the country."[125] One of the newspapers that copied the earlier sections was the *Ohio State Journal*. This was done, no doubt, at the urging of Col. Robert Patterson, who, as noted earlier, contributed directly to the preparation of one section of the "Notes."

In 1827 G.W. Stipp of Xenia, Ohio, published the first twenty-three sections of the "Notes" in a book entitled *The Western Miscellany, or, Accounts Historical, Biographical, and Amusing.* Later Lyman Copeland Draper acquired a copy of this book and annotated it with material that he gathered in interviews with many of the old Kentucky pioneers.[126] His annotations had to do largely with corrections of dates and typographical errors, with some corroboration of Bradford's narratives. There is little or no evidence that anyone made as much use of "Notes" 23-66. As a matter of fact, both Samuel M. Wilson and J. Winston Coleman assumed there were only sixty-two, not sixty-six sections.[127] Subsequent scholars who have dealt with the historic beginnings of Kentucky and the Ohio Valley have made generous use of the earlier published "Notes."[128]

In the case of the organization of the government of Kentucky there exists a reasonable volume of contemporary documents. The papers of Isaac Shelby do not exist in a single collected volume,[129] however, nor do those of John Brown, Thomas Todd, Samuel McDowell, and George Nicholas. Documentation is more complete for George Rogers Clark, Arthur St. Clair, and Anthony Wayne.[130] The records of the Kentucky land grants have been preserved in relatively complete form.[131] The records of the two houses of the Kentucky General Assembly are represented in the published journals and the *Acts,* as are the proceedings of the Congress. The treaties made with the Indians are collected in published volumes, and so are the Territorial Papers.[132] The manuscripts, documents, and recorded interviews collected by Lyman Copeland Draper both corroborate and modify Bradford's "Notes." In the case of the "Kentucky Papers" in the Draper Papers, many of the entries were extracted from the *Kentucky Gazette.* Nevertheless, the "Notes on Kentucky" must be considered classic and basic to the study of the early phase of western American pioneering history.

Modern historians of the early westward movement would be denied a window onto the past without access to the "Notes on Kentucky," even though modern archival holdings have been enormously expanded and contemporary scholarship has greatly broadened the perspective on this particular segment of the early West. This collection assembles the "Notes" in a single published volume for the first time. Because the files of the *Kentucky Gazette* are broken and widely dispersed, the task of collecting and verifying the texts of the "Notes" has demanded diligent search. How useful it would be if John Bradford's clipped and bound copy of his "Notes" had survived the indifference of a fifty-cent bidder for them.

John Bradford's
NOTES ON
KENTUCKY

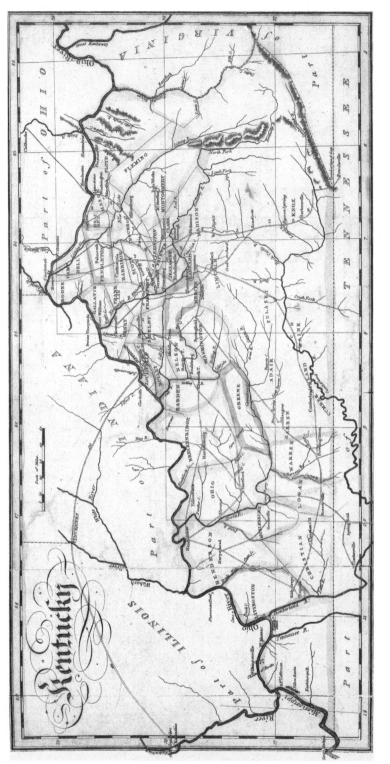

"Kentucky." In John Melish, *Travels through the United States of America* (Philadelphia, 1812). Courtesy of Special Collections, Margaret I. King Library, University of Kentucky.

Opening the Way West

[August 25, 1826]

This country was well known to the Indian traders many years before its settlement. They gave a description of it to Lewis Evans, who published his first map of it as early as 1752.

In the year 1750,* Dr. Thomas Walker, Colby Chew, Ambrose Powell and several others from the counties of Orange and Culpepper, in the state of Virginia, set out on an excursion to the Western Waters; they travelled down the Holstein river, and crossed over the Mountains into Powell's valley, thence across the Cumberland mountain at the gap where the road now crosses, proceeded on across what was formerly known by the name of the Wilderness until they arrived at the Hazelpatch: Here the Company divided, Dr. Walker with a part continued north until they came to the Kentucky river which they named Louisa or Levisa river: After travelling down the excessive broken or hilly margin some distance, they became dissatisfied and returned and continued up one of its branches to its head,[1] crossed over the mountains to New River at the place called Walker's Meadows.[2]

In the year 1754, James McBride with some others, passed down the Ohio River in canoes, and landed at the mouth of the Kentucky river, where they marked on a tree the initials of their names, and the date of the year. These men passed through the country and were the first who gave a particular account of its beauty and richness of soil to the inhabitants of the British settlements in America.[3]

No further notice seems to have been taken of Kentucky until the year 1767, when John Finlay with others (whilst trading with the Indians) passed through a part of the rich lands of Kentucky. It was then called by the Indians in their language, the Dark or Bloody Grounds Some difference took place between these traders and the Indians, and Finlay deemed it prudent to return to his residence in North Carolina, where he communicated his knowledge of the country to Col. Daniel Boone and others. This seems to have been one of the most important events in the history of Kentucky, as it was the exciting cause which prompted Col. Boone shortly afterwards to make his first visit to the Dark or Bloody Grounds.[4]

---

*Marshall in his History Vol. 1, says, it was 1758. Mr. H. Taylor thinks Dr. Walker informed him it was in 1752, but Col. Shelby states implicitly, that in 1779 in company with Dr. Walker on Yellow creek a mile or two from Cumberland mountain, the Doctor observed "upon that tree" pointing to a beach across the roade to the left hand "Ambrose Powell marked his name and the date of the year."—I examined the tree and found *A. Powell*, cut in legible letters.

The Long Hunters

[September 1, 1826]

The report made by Columbus of his discovery of America, did not produce greater excitement in the Court of Spain, than that made by Finlay did in the people of Carolina, in the vicinity of his residence, of the discoveries he had made in the valley of the Ohio.

In consequence of the information given by Finlay, Col. DANIEL BOONE, in company with John Finlay, John Stewart, Joseph Holden, Jas. Monay and William Cool, set out from his residence on the Yadkin river, in North Carolina, on the 1st day of May 1769, under the direction of Finlay as their guide, and steered westwardly. After a long and fatigueing march over a mountaneous and pathless wilderness, they on the 7th day of June following, arrived on Red river, at a place recognised by Finlay, where he had formerly been whilst trading with the Indians. Here, from the top of an eminence, they first obtained a distant view of the beautiful level of Kentucky.[5]

At this place they erected what they called their station camp, and from thence made excursions, either for the purposes of hunting or exploring the country; and where they agreed to rendezvous, in case of being at any time separated from each other.[6]

On the 22d day of December following, whilst Boone and Stewart were traversing the forest near the Kentucky river, late in the evening, they were surprised by a party of Indians, who rushing out of a thick Canebrake, made them both prisoners.—They continued in the possession of the Indians until the seventh night, when in the dead of night, whilst the Indians were sound asleep, they effected their escape, and returned to the camp, which they found plundered and all their companions gone.[7]

At this inauspicious moment, Squire Boone, (brother of Col. Daniel Boone) with one other, who had penetrated into this unexplored region in search of his brother, by mere accident, arrived at this camp. This meeting, notwithstanding the untowardness of the circumstances attending the parties, was productive of mutual joy.

A short time after the arrival of Squire Boone at the station camp of these adventurers, John Stewart was killed and scalped by a party of Indians, which so frightened the man who accompanied Squire Boone, that he immediately set out on his return to North Carolina, leaving the two Boone's without any other company.

At this camp Col. Boone and his brother erected a hut, to protect them from the inclemency of the approaching winter, and where they continued until the succeeding spring, during which time no occurrence took place worthy of notice.[8]

On the first day of May 1770, Squire Boone left his brother, and returned home to Carolina for a supply of ammunition and horses, leaving him entirely alone, who as the summer approached, extended his excursions, whereby he obtained an extensive knowledge of all the lands in the country North of the Kentucky river.

On the 27th day of July 1770, Squire Boone returned with the necessary supplies of ammunition and horses, after which it was but a short time before they set out homeward; examining the country as they proceeded to Cumberland river, giving names to the different rivers and creeks as they passed, and in the month of March 1771, arrived at their respective places of residence in N. Carolina.[9]

Col. Shelby in one of his notes, says: "In May 1772, I met Daniel Boone below the Holstein settlement alone; he informed me that he had spent the two years preceding that time, in a hut on Louisa river, (now Kentucky) so called by all the long hunters; that he had been robbed the day before by the Cherokee Indians, of all the proceeds of his hunt."[10]

The same year that Daniel Boone first visited Kentucky, viz. in 1769, Hancock Taylor, Richard Taylor, Abraham Hapdenstall and others, from Orange county, Virginia, descended the Ohio river, visited its shores, passed the Falls, and into the Mississippi. At the mouth of either White river or Arkanza, Richard Taylor and Barbour left the others, and went through the Creek nation of Indians, to their residence in Virginia. Hancock Taylor and Abraham Hapdenstall went on to Red river, explored the country in that quarter, descended the Mississippi to New Orleans, and from thence went round to New York, and home.[11]

In the same year also, (1769) James Knox, (afterwards Col. Knox) Henry Skegs, and seven others, came through the wilderness, and made a hunt on Dick's river,* and the head waters of Green river, South of the Kentucky river. This party confined themselves to that portion of country bordering on the Cumberland mountains, and what was then called the *Brush*, and afterwards the Wilderness.[12]

The country South of the Kentucky river was explored by James Smith, (afterwards Col. Smith) in the year 1766, the following is the account given of his excursion, written by himself:—

"In the year 1766, I heard that Sir William Johnson, the King's agent for settling affairs with the Indians, had purchased from them all the land west of the Appalachian Mountains, that lay between the Ohio and the

*Dicks river was named after an Indian whose name was Dick, and who had a hunting camp on that river.

Cherokee river; and as I knew by conversing with the Indians in their own tongue that there was a large body of rich land there, I concluded I would take a tour westward, and explore that country.

"I set out about the last of June, 1766, and went in the first place to Holstain river, and from thence I travelled westward in company with Joshua Horton, Uriah Stone, William Baker, and Jas Smith, who came from near Carlisle. There was only four [five] white men of us, and a mulatto slave about eighteen years of age, that Mr Horton had with him. We explored the country south of Kentucky, and there was no more sign of white men there then, than there is now west of the head waters of the Missouri. We also explored Cumberland and Tennessee rivers, from Stone's† river down to the Ohio.

"When we came to the mouth of Tennessee, my fellow travellers concluded that they would proceed on to the Illinois, and see some more of the land to the west:—this I would not agree to. As I had already been longer from home than what I expected, I thought my wife would be distressed, and think I was killed by the Indians; therefore I concluded that I would return home. I sent my horse with my fellow travellers to the Illinois, as it was difficult to take a horse through the mountains. My comrades gave me the greatest part of the ammunition they then had, which amounted only to half a pound of powder, and lead equivalent. Mr. Horton also lent me his mulatto boy, and I then set off through the wilderness, for Carolina.

"About eight days after I left my company at the mouth of Tennessee, on my journey eastward, I got a cane stab in my foot, which occasioned my leg to swell, and I suffered much pain. I was now in a doubtful situation—far from any of the human species, excepting black Jamie, or the savages, and I knew not when I might meet with them—my case appeared desperate, and I thought something must be done. All the surgical instruments I had, was a knife, a mockason awl, and a pair of bullit moulds; with these I determined to draw the snag from my foot, if possible. I stuck the awl in the skin, and with the knife I cut the flesh away from around the cane, and then I commanded the mulatto fellow to catch it with the bullit moulds, and pull it out, which he did. When I saw it, it seemed a shocking thing to be in any person's foot; it will therefore be supposed that I was very glad to have it out.—The black fellow attended upon me, and obeyed my directions faithfully. I ordered him to search for Indian medicine, and told him to get me a quantity of bark from the root of a lynn tree, which I made him beat on a stone, with a tomahawk, and boil it in a kettle, and with the ooze I bathed my foot and leg:—what remained

†Stone's River is a south branch of Cumberland, and empties into it above Nashville. We first gave it this name in our journal in May 1767, after one of my fellow travellers, Mr. Uriah Stone, and I am told that it retains the same name unto this day.

when I had finished bathing, I boiled to a jelly, and made poultices thereof. As I had no rags, I made use of the green moss that grows upon logs, and wrapped it round with elm bark: by this means (simple as it may seem) the swelling and inflamation in a great measure abated. As stormy weather appeared, I ordered Jamie to make us a shelter, which he did by erecting forks and poles, and covering them over with cane tops, like a fodder house. it was but about one hundred yards from a large buffaloe road. As we were almost out of provision, I commanded Jamie to take my gun, and I went along as well as I could, concealed myself near the road, and killed a buffaloe. When this was done we jirked†† the lean, and fryed the tallow out of the fat meat, which we kept to stew with our jirk as we needed it.

"While I lay at this place, all the books I had to read, was a Psalm Book, and Watts upon Prayer. Whilst in this situation I composed the following verses, which I then frequently sung.

> Six weeks I've in this desert been,
>   With one mulatto lad,
> Excepting this poor stupid slave,
>   No company I had.
>
> In solitude I here remain,
>   A cripple very sore,
> No friend or neighbour to be found,
>   My case for to deplore.
>
> I'm far from home, far from the wife,
>   Which in my bosom lay,
> Far from my children dear, which used
>   Around me for to play.
>
> This doleful circumstance cannot
>   My happiness prevent,
> While peace of conscience I enjoy,
>   Great comfort and content.

"I continued in this place until I could walk slowly, without crutches. As I now lay near a great buffaloe road, I was afraid that the Indians might be passing that way, and discover my fire place, therefore I moved off some distance, where I remained until I killed an elk. As my foot was yet sore, I concluded that I would stay here until it was healed, lest by travelling too soon it might again be inflamed.

††Jirk is a name well known by the hunters, and frontier inhabitants, for meat cut in small pieces and laid on a scaffold, over a slow fire, whereby it is roasted till it is thoroughly dry.

"In a few weeks after, I proceeded on, and in October I arrived in Carolina. I had now been eleven months in the wilderness, and during this time I neither saw bread, money, women, or spirituous liquors; and three months of which I saw none of the human species, except Jamie."[13]

SECTION 3

The Beckoning Land

[September 8, 1826]

In the month of September 1773, Col. Daniel Boone with his family, accompanied by five other families set out from North Carolina, with the purpose of making a permanent settlement in Kentucky. In Powel's Valley they were joined by forty men. On the tenth of October this party were attacked by a large party of Indians; and notwithstanding the Indians were finally repulsed, Boone's party lost six men killed and had one wounded, among the slain was the eldest son of Col. Boone.

This encounter discouraged Boone and his party from prosecuting their intended journey, and they retreated forty miles to Clinch river, where the family of Boone remained until the year 1775.[14]

By the proclamation of the King of Great Britain in the year 1763, all the officers and soldiers who had served in America either in the army or navy, were entitled to a bounty in lands for their services the quantity proportioned to their respective ranks, and to be located on any vacant land in his majesty's dominions in America. In consequence of the reputation which the lands of Kentucky had obtained generally throughout the different states at this time, those who were entitled to bounty lands, became anxious to have them located there, and therefore most of the military warrants were in this year (1773) put into hands of the surveyor of Fincastle county, which at that time included the whole of the present state of Kentucky. To hasten the surveying business, a number of deputy surveyors were commissioned by the governor of Virginia, and sent to make the surveys.[15]

In this year (1773) Capt Thomas Bullitt with a party of men from

Virginia, descended the Ohio and landed at the falls, their object was the surveying of land and making a settlement in the country.

Captain Bullitt on his way down the Ohio visited Chillicothe a shawonee town of Indians, in order to obtain the consent of the Indians to his intended settlement. He left his party on the Ohio river, and went to the town alone. He was not discovered until he entered the town, where he displayed a white flag in token of peace. The Indians astonished at this unexpected ambassador, flocked around him, and the following dialogue between him and a principle chief took place.

Indian Chief.—What news do you bring?—are you from the Long Knife?— If you are an ambassador why did you not send a runner?

Bullitt.—I have no bad news.—The Long Knives and the Redmen are at peace, and I have come among my brothers to have a friendly talk with them about settling on the other side of the Ohio.

Indian Chief.—Why did you not send a runner?

Bullitt.—I had no runner swifter than myself, and as I was in haste, I could not wait the return of a runner.—If you were very hungry and had killed a deer, would you send your Squaw to town to tell the news, and wait her return before you would eat?

This reply of Bullitt put the byestanders into high humour; they relaxed from their native gravity and laughed heartily. The Indians conducted Bullitt into the principle wigwam of the town and regaled him with venison, after which he addressed the chiefs as follows:

"*Brothers*—I am sent with my people whom I left on the Ohio, to settle the country on the other side of that river, as low down as the falls. We came from Virginia. I only want the country to settle and to cultivate the soil. There will be no objection to your hunting and trapping in it as heretofore, I hope you will live with us on terms of friendship."

To this address the principal chief made the following reply:

"*Brother*—You have come a hard journey through the woods and the grass. We are pleased to find that in settling in our country, your people are not to disturb us in our hunting; for we must hunt to kill meat for our women and children, and have something to buy powder and lead, and to procure blankets and other necessaries. We desire you will be strong in discharging your promises towards us, as we are determined to be very strong in advising our young men to be kind, friendly and peaceable towards you."

Having finished his mission, Capt. Bullett returned to his party, and with them descended the river to the falls.[16]

On the arrival at the falls, Capt. Bullitt and his party proceeded to erect a hut or place to protect himself and men from the weather, and as a place of deposit for their stores.

Shortly after his arrival, he made some surveys in the neighbourhood, and extended his researches to a remarkable salt lick on what is now called Salt River, which was so called on account of the lick, and the lick was called Bullitt's lick after Captain Bullitt who included it in a survey made for himself.[17]

In the same year (1773) James Douglas a Scotchman, with a party, also descended the Ohio river. They landed first at the mouth of a creek which they called Landing Creek, near the mouth of the Big Bone creek, and went to the Big Bone lick, so called on account of the extraordinary large bones found there. The rib bones were so long, that Douglas and his party used them instead of poles, over which they stretched their blankets to shelter themselves from the weather.

After spending some time at this lick, Douglas and his party went down the Ohio river to the falls from whence they explored the country some distance, and returned to Virginia.[18]

In the same year James Harrod from Monongehely, headed a party whose object it was to improve land (as they termed it) in Kentucky, under an expectation of obtaining 400 acres for every cabbin they should build, and plant corn or make other improvement at such cabbin.[19] They built a cabbin at what is now Harrodsburgh, in 1774 by which name it was then called after the leader of the party, and by which it has been known ever since. This was the first permanent settlement made in the country, and served as a rallying point or place of refuge for all who visited the country at that period. The first corn ever planted in Kentucky was in this year at a place called Fountain Blue, by David Williams, John Shelp and James Sodowsky, near Harrodsburgh.

In the year 1774 several surveyors arrived in Kentucky, amongst whom were Col. John Floyd, Hancock Taylor, James Douglass, Isaac Hite and Willis Lee; Taylor and Lee were both killed by the Indians.[20]

Early in the summer of this year, (1774) the Indians fell on the surveyors and their assistants, killed several and the remainder made their escape, some through the wilderness, and some down the Ohio river and Mississippi, and thence round to the Eastern states.

The defeat of the combined forces of the Northern tribes of indians at Point Pleasant by General Lewis in the following October, and the subsequent treaty made with them by Lord Dunmore, the then governor of Virginia,[21] induced many of the surveyors to return to Kentucky early in the spring 1775.

In the month of March 1775, Col. Richard Henderson of North Carolina, formed a company, and entered into a treaty with the Cherokee Indians at Wataga, by which they obtained a grant for all the lands lying on the South side of the Kentucky river and within the present limits of the State, and although it was contrary to the established laws, for private individuals, to purchase and hold lands of the Indians in their own right, yet the company pursued their original intention of establishing a colony of their own and actually took possession of the land, surveyed and made deeds to part of it.[22] However in the year 1778 the nature of Henderson's claim was inquired into by the Legislature of Virginia, and notwithstanding it could not be maintained, the party having acted in contempt of the authority of the state, and the country having been previously purchased from the Cherokees on behalf of the State of Virginia at the treaty of Long Island by Col. Donaldson; yet the Legislature of Virginia as an indemnification for the expence and trouble Col. Henderson & co. had incured, and in consequence of their purchase having reconciled the war-like spirit of the Cherokees against Virginia, made them a grant of twelve miles square of land at the mouth of Green river.[23]

Notwithstanding the Indian claims were thus fairly and completely extinguished by purchase, yet the first settlers were not permitted to occupy the country in peace.

SECTION 4

Opening the
Great Western Road
[September 15, 1826]

About the 1st of March 1775, Col. Boone with forty choice woodsmen from Powell's valley, together with Col. Richard Henderson, Capt. N. Hart, John Lutrel and Maj. Wm. B. Smith, again attempted to brave the terrors of a savage wilderness, with the view of making a permanent settlement in the fertile regions of Kentucky. They prosecuted their journey until within 15 miles of where Boonsborough now stands, unmolested, when [on the 20th of March, a little before daybreak] they were attacked by a party of Indians, who fired into their tents, and wounded a Capt. Twitty through both knees, and his servant mortaly. The Indians rushed forward to Twitty's tent to scalp him, when a faithful bull dog of his, laid hold of one of them by the throat and put him down; he cried out for help to his companions, when one of them tomahawked the dog, and the whole made a precipitate retreat. Boone's party lost two men killed and had one wounded. Notwithstanding the enemy were repulsed, on the 23d they returned again and made a second attack, in which three white men were killed and two wounded and the enemy again repulsed. Having arrived on the back of the Kentucky river, the party on the 1st day of April 1775 began to erect a fort, and called it Boonsborough (after Col. Boon) and the place has retained that name from that to the present time.[24]

On the 4th day of April the Indians killed one of Boone's party—on the 14th the fort was finished, when Col. Boone set out on his return for his family whom he had left on Clinch river, and as soon as the journey could be accomplished returned with them to Boonsborough. Mrs. Boone and her daughters, were the first white women that migrated to Kentucky. On the 24th day of December following, the Indians killed one white man and wounded another near Boonsborough.[25]

In the spring of the same year (1774) [1775] Benjamin Logan (afterwards Gen. Logan, and a conspicuous character in the history of Kentucky) set out from his residence near Abingdon Virginia, for this new country. On his arrival in Kentucky, he, with William Gillespie, planted and raised a small crop of corn. Logan returned to his family, and on the 8th of March 1776 he arrived again at his camp in Kentucky, with Mrs Logan and the rest of his family. This place was afterwards known by the names of Logan's station and St. Asaphs.

Logan endeavored to prevail on some adventurers in the neighbourhood of the Crab Orchard, to make a stand with him at his place, but without effect; he was therefore compelled for the safety of his family, which he considered in great danger to remove them to Harrodsburg, after which he returned home himself and attended to his crop. His family remained at Harrodsburg until February 1777 when they also joined him at St. Asaphs.[26]

During the year 1775, Boonsborough and Harrodsburg were places of general rendezvous and considered the only places of safety in the country; those therefore who removed their families to Kentucky, made choice of one of these places for a temporary residence. About the month of September in that year, Harrodsburg was first honoured with the presence of a white woman. Among the first were Mrs. McGarey, Mrs. Denton and Mrs. Hogan.[27]

On the 14th day of July 1776, being a fine pleasant evening, Jemima

Boone, a daughter of Col Boone, and Betsey and Fanny Calloway, daughters of Col. Calloway, took a walk from the fort at Boonesborough down the margin of the Kentucky river; they had gone but a short distance before they were surprised by a party of Indians who lay in ambush, taken prisoners and hurried off as fast as possible. It was no sooner known that the young women were missing, than Col. Boone, Maj. Wm. Smith and six other men on foot pursued them and on the 16th a little below the upper Blue licks, over took them, killed two of the Indians, recovered the young women without losing a man or having one wounded.—Col Calloway and family had arrived at Boonsborough but a short time previous to this event.[28]

Capt George Rogers Clark (afterwards General Clark) arrived in Kentucky early in 1775, left Leestown in the fall, went to Pittsburgh and returned early in 1776.[29]

In 1773 Col Thompson from the state of Pennsylvania, came down the Ohio and made a number of surveys on the Ohio and Licking rivers, the latter they called Salt lick creek.[30]

The company of which Col Henderson was principal, assumed the title of the Transylvania Company, and a number became attached to them during the early part of this year, after which they conceived the project of establishing a proprietary government, south of the Kentucky river, by the name and style of TRANSYLVANIA. For this purpose a convention was held at Boonsborough, the members like the ancient States General, sat under the noted large elm at that place, where all the civil officers of the proposed government were appointed.[31]

The adventurers on the south side of Kentucky were very much divided, on account of the claim set up by the Transylvania company, within the chartered limits of Virginia, some claiming under Henderson and Co, and some under Virginia.[32]

In consequence of this division, a meeting of the people was called at Harrodsburg on the 1st of June, when a considerable number assembled and George Rogers Clark, (afterwards Gen. Clark) and John Gabriel Jones were elected delegates to represent the state of the country to the Legislature of Virginia. The Transylvania company used every means in their power to prevent the election of delegates to Virginia, but failed.[33]

Through the representation of Clark and Jones to the legislature of Virginia, the county of Kentucky, was stricken off from the county of Fincastle, and to enable the inhabitants of Kentucky to defend themselves against the Indians, Clark and Jones were furnished with a quantity of ammunition. They took charge of the ammunition and with it descended the Ohio river to an island near the mouth of Lawrence's or Limestone creek, when for the want of horses to carry it on they deposited it on the island.

A few days after the arrival of Clark and Jones, at McClelland's station, the latter with nine others set out on horseback to bring on the ammunition from the island. On the 26th of December they were met on Johnson's fork of Licking by a party of Indians, and were routed with the loss of four of their party. Joseph Rogers was taken prisoner, John G. Jones and William Graden killed, and Josiah Dixon missing who was never after heard of.[34]

On the 29th of the same month, between 40 and 50 Indians commanded by a noted Mingo warrior named Pluggy attacked McClelland's fort, in which at that time there were about 20 men; after a few hours the Indians withdrew, having received considerable injury as it was afterwards understood, with the loss of Pluggy their principal warrior. The loss of the whites were John McClelland and Charles White mortally wounded, and Robert Todd (afterwards General Todd) and Edward Worthington wounded who recovered.[35]

After the attack made on McClelland's fort, a party from Harrodsburg made a second attempt to bring the ammunition from the island, and succeeded and deposited it in Harrodsburg. This was considered not only a relief at that moment, but an important means of saving the country. As by it the people were not only enabled to procure food for themselves, but to defend their forts against the attacks of the indians. As there were not more than from 20 to 30 men who were materially interested in keeping possession of the posts on the north side of the Kentucky, they were considered too few to maintain their standing in the Spring, they therefore on the 30th January 1777 broke up and removed some to Boonesborough, and the rest to Harrodsburg. Thus the whole population of Kentucky were in these two forts, and did not exceed 150 men fit for duty, and about 40 families who were to be supported by meat from the woods and corn from the fields.[36]

The perilous situation of the country at this time, pointed out the necessity of forming the militia into companies, and their submitting to some kind of authority. George Rogers Clark, who shortly after was commissioned a Major, was appointed to command at Harrodsburg—Cols. Calloway and Boone at Boonesborough.[37]

On the 28th of March 1777 a large body of Indians laid siege to Harrodsburgh. They began their operations by dividing into small parties, and waylaying every path and avenue to the fort from the fields or forest; concealing themselves behind trees bushes, &c. and they also attempted to cut off all supplies by killing the cattle. Unable however to accomplish their purpose, they retired from Harrodsburg and made a descent on Boonesborough. During the attack on Harrodsburg, Garret Pendegrass was killed, and Peter Flinn either killed or taken, as his body was never found.

Kentucky having been formed into a county;[38] on the 18th day of April, Richard Calloway, and John Todd were elected to represent the people in the General Assembly of Virginia.

On the 20th April Benj. Lynn and Samuel Moore, two active woodsmen set out from Harrodsburg for Illinois; their business was only known to Major Clark and a few others until after their return, which was on the 22d of June, and not then to many. Maj. Clark's arrangements with the executive, and his expedition the next Spring best explains the errand of Lynn and Moore to Kaskaskias.[39]

On the 20th of May 1777, whilst the women at Logan's station were milking early in the morning, having a guard of men with them, a large party of Indians who had been concealed, made a sudden attack upon them, in which one man was killed, and two wounded, one of which mortally, the other with the women and the rest of the men got into the fort.

The man who was mortally wounded, was left on the ground, as the party were unable to bring him off; his name was Burr Harrison. The Indians were afraid to attempt to approach the wounded man, as he was within rifle shot of the fort and in open view. After some time he was discovered attempting to rise, when Logan who had in vain endeavoured to excite a party to aid him in bringing in the wounded man, made the attempt alone and succeeded in the midst of a shower of Bullets discharged at him by the Indians without receiving any injury.[40]

On the 4th of July Boonesborough was besieged by about 200 Indians; they killed one white man and wounded two.[41] At that time there were only 22 men in the fort. The siege lasted two days, during which the Indians had seven of their party killed.

About this time all the stations in the country were besieged, for the obvious purpose of preventing the people from aiding each other.

On the 19th July 1777, Logan's station was again besieged by about 200 Indians; there was at that time only 15 men in the fort, two of whom were killed and one wounded.

One of the men killed was shot down at the fort gate and scalped, and a large bundle of papers laid on his breast. These papers were proclamations from Sir Guy Carleton (Lord Dorchester) at that time Commander in Chief of all the British forces in Canada, and addressed to the people of Kentucky generally, and to Clark and Logan by name. They were kept secret by Gen. Logan for many years afterwards, for what reason is not know.[42]

About this time Col. John Bowman arrived from Virginia at Logan's station with 100 men, most of whose time of service had expired on the road, and was not considered as a permanent protection.[43]

A Wilderness Ordeal

[September 22, 1826]

On the 6th day of March 1777 a large party of Indians fell in with three men, about four miles from Harrodsburgh, on their march to that place; one of the men William Ray was killed at Shawonee spring and Thomas Shores taken prisoner, and the third (James Ray, since Gen. Ray) escaped, and apprised the people at the fort of their danger. On the next day (the 7th) the fort was compleatealy invested, in the unusual form of an Indian siege. Many shot were exchanged during the day between the besiegers and the besieged, and some execution done on both sides. The Indians when they retired left their dead on the field, a thing never done if they can avoid it, and is the best evidence of defeat. On the part of the besieged, four men only were wounded, three of whom recovered; among the wounded was Col. M'Gary, who was afterwards a leader. Harrodsburgh at that time contained only 65 men.[44]

On the 15th day of April 1777, a party of about one hundred Indians attacked Boonesborough; they killed one man Daniel Goodman and wounded four others, viz: Cap. Daniel Boone, Cap. John Todd, Isaac Hite and Michael Stoner; the loss on the part of the Indians was not known, as they carefully removed and concealed their dead and wounded.[45]

On the 25th of July 1777 Boonesborough was strengthened by the arrival from North Carolina of forty-five men; and about the 20th of August Logan's fort was also strengthened by an accession of part of the men ordered from Virginia under Col. Bowman, the remainder of Bowman's men went to Harrodsburg.

About this time the people of the country assumed an entire new attitude. Whenever a party of Indians were known to be on the South side of the Ohio river they were sought for by the inhabitants rather than avoided, from which circumstance the Indians instead of calling them the *Longknife* a name by which the Virginians were known, they called them *Close* or *Sharpshooters*.

It is due to the memory of Gen. Benjamin Logan and Col. James Harrod, to state, that at the most perilous time in Kentucky, in the year 1777 that these two intrepid woodsmen went alone from Kentucky through the wilderness more than two hundred miles into the settlements on Holstein, and there obtained for Col. Isaac Shelby two small kegs of powder, with an equivalent of lead, from a small store of public ammunition, then in the care of Shelby. They returned with it to Kentucky after this most hazzardous trip, in perfect safety; and from the great scarcity of ammunition in Kentucky at that time, it is believed that the distribution of this amongst the people, was the salvation of the country.[46]

The British government occupied not only the military posts of Detroit and Niagara on the lakes, but also St. Vincennes, Kaskaskias and other places on the Wabash and Mississippi. From these posts the Indians obtained supplies of arms and ammunition, and were thereby enabled to continue their hostilities against the Kentucky settlements.[47]

Virginia, satisfied of the advantages of defending her western frontiers, projected the reduction of the British posts situated within the limits of her charter, to effect which, her Legislature voted the raising of a regiment of state troops and the command and was given to Col. George Rogers Clark, whose military reputation and acquaintance with the country, fitted him admirably for that purpose, the sending Lynn and Moore to Illinois the preceding April, was to obtain information respecting the situation and strength of the country, and on their report the expedition of Col Clark was predicated.[48]

On the first day of January 1778 Col. Boone with thirty men went to the Lower Blue Licks for the purpose of making salt. On the 7th of February whilst hunting in the neighborhood of the licks, he was met by a party of 102 Indians and two French men on their way against Boonesborough, they made Boone prisoner, who knowing that his companions at the licks could not possibly escape them, and being too weak to oppose the Indians, he entered into a treaty for them, they were twenty-seven in number, three having returned home with the salt that had been made.[49]

Boone remained a prisoner with the Indians until the 16th day of June following, when he made his escape, and arrived safely at Boonesborough on the 20th a distance of 160 miles, during which he eat but one meal. He made choice of this particular moment, on account of information received, that 450 of the choice Indian warriors, had collected for the purpose of going against Boonesborough, and fearing that the people of that place would have no information of the intention of so formidable a force coming against them, would be taken by surprise and entirely unprepared; he was therefore determined at all hazards to endeavour to apprize them of their danger.

In consequence of the escape of Col. Boone, the Indians knowing he would apprize the whites of their meditated attack, postponed their march for three weeks. This information was given by one who was a prisoner with Boone and who made his escape after him.

On the arrival of Boone at Boonesborough, the inhabitants immediately set about repairing their fort, which was in a very bad state for defence, but in the course of ten days finished the necessary repairs.

Some time in June (1778) Maj. Smith with 17 men followed a party of Indians from Boonesborough to the Ohio river when coming up with them killed one, the rest having crossed over. As they returned, about 20 miles from the Ohio, they met another party of about thirty Indians. They discovered the Indians by a loud laugh, and immediately prepared to receive them. They tied their horses and left nine men with them, with directions that if they heard an attack to rush forward to it. Smith with the other eight men crept forward until they came near the Indian lying in the grass; one of the Indians passed by Smith partly and went on towards the horses, and was shot by one of the whites; he cried out;—his friends raised a great laugh thinking he himself had killed a fox; at that moment the eight men with Smith fired on the Indians and rushing up routed them. The Indians notwithstanding returned the fire before they ran off, and wounded John Martin, one of Smith's men.[50]

About the last of July Hancock who had been taken prisoner with Boone at the Blue Licks made his escape from the Indians and came home, and gave notice that a large party of Indians were preparing to make an attack on Boonesborough.

On the first day of August 1778, having no further news of the intended invasion, Col. Boone with nineteen men, set out from Boonesborough, with the intention of surprising an Indian town on Paint creek a branch of the Sciota river, with the view of taking prisoners, in order to discover the intention of the Indians with respect to Kentucky. Within four miles of their town they fell in with a party of 30 Indians, who had just started to join in with the combined Indian forces, who were at that time on their march against Boonesborough. A skirmish ensued, in which the Indians had one of their party killed and two wounded; three horses and all their baggage was taken by Boone's party, who sustained no injury whatever.

Satisfied that this party of Indians were on their way to join the main body destined for Kentucky, Boone and his party set out immediately for home, and on the 6th of August 1778, passed the main body of Indians undiscovered, and on the 7th arrived at Boonesborough.[51]

The day after Boone and his party got home, (August 7) the Indian army consisting of from 5 to 700 men, commanded by Cap. DuQuesne and eleven other Frenchmen, Moluntha a king and Black-Fish a war chief arrived at Boonesborough; they marched up in open view of the fort, with English and French colours flying. A flag was sent into the fort by two men who announced letters from Governor Hamilton, and demanded in the name of his Britannic majesty a surrender of the fort. The bearers of the flag were directed to return and bring the letters;—to this message the commander replied, that Boone must come out to him;—and as a token of good faith sent Boone seven roasted Buffaloe tongues. Upon this Boone and one or two others went out, and when they came near the Indians about twenty of them laid down their arms, and introduced Boone to Moluntha and Black-Fish. Black-Fish delivered the letters from Governor Hamilton to Col Boone, and asked him how he liked them? Boone answered he would consider their contents,—Black-Fish then said "brother there is a heavy cloud hanging over this country.—This is called the *Bloody land*, you know;—we have had much war, and whoever gets the first fire, always beats.—Now I am come to take you away easy."—Then Moluntha spoke and said "you killed my son the other day over the Ohio river." Boone answered no, I have not been there—Moluntha replied "it was you, I tracked you here to this place."

The parties now entered into a conversation about the nature of the war, when Black-Fish observed "I have brought forty horses and mares for the old people and women and children to ride," and pressed the delivery up of the fort. Boone demanded two days to read the letters of Governor Hamilton to his people and to consider their contents, which was agreed to. Boone returned with his party to the fort and read the letters of Governor Hamilton to the people calling on those who were in favor of surrendering, to turn out; but they unanimously declined.

During the two days of the truce, the people collected into the fort through private ways, all the cattle and horses they could, having determined to defend the place to the last extremity, and on the evening of the night [ninth—*Ed.*], Col. Boone returned the following answer to the summons: "We laugh at all your formidable preparations; but thank you for giving us notice, and time for us to prepare for our defence. Your efforts will not prevail, for our gates shall forever deny you admittance."

In order to deceive Boone, the commander of the Indians assured him, that he had it in orders from Governor Hamilton, to take them prisoners, and not to kill any, and therefore proposed that nine men from the fort, should come out and treat with them. This proposition was finally agreed to, and after some altercation about the place where the parties should meet, it was finally concluded that they should meet at the lick, about sixty yards from the fort, and on the morning of the 10th the meeting took place.

Col. Boone suspected treachery in this pretended treaty, and therefore before he left the fort, directed that every part should be strictly guarded, and the walls nearest the place of holding the treaty, he manned with the best marksmen, with orders, that if any attempt should be made by the Indians, on those ingaged in the treaty, to fire on them immediately, which would cover their retreat to the fort.

The treaty continued the whole day, during which time Squire Boone, (the brother of Col. Boone) mentioned that an army was on their march from Virginia under the command of Maj. George R. Clarke; this information excited manifest uneasiness. After the council closed in the evening, Black-Fish walked round the fort and viewed it. The next morning Boone and five men went down to the lick, and perceived that the chiefs had brought with them young men to the council.—He mentioned it to Black-Fish, but he denied it and said they were the same.

After a considerable discussion on the subject of the treaty on the 11th, the treaty was agreed to and each party signed. The Indians then observed, that it was a custom among them on all such occasions, for two Indians to shake hands with every white man in the treaty, which being consented to, every white man was seized by two Indians, with evident intention to detain him; but the whites broke forcibly from them and escaped towards the fort. At this moment the marksmen on the walls of the fort, by a timely and well directed fire, checked the immediate pursuit by the Indians; and notwithstanding the greater part of them were concealed in the high weeds for that purpose near where the treaty was held, and immediately on the escape of the whites opened a tremendous fire on them, all the injury they sustained was one man wounded.[52]

During the siege the Indians made use of the following method to set fire to the houses in the fort, they collected the long dry loose bark of the shell bark hickory, and bound it into taper bundles of an inch at the small end and four or five at the large, which was loose, the binding extending only about half the length from the small end—there whole length were about 18 inches or 2 feet. These small faggots or bundles of dry bark were lighted at the large loose end; thrown on the roofs of the houses, when a constant fire was kept at the place where it lay on the roof, smaller bundles of this lighted bark were tied to arrows and shot on to the tops of the houses; but they were all extinguished in time to prevent their taking effect.

The inhabitants had no water, but what was brought from without the fort, therefore all their vessels were filled with water during the two days taken to consider of the propositions made by the enemy, but in consequence of having many cattle and horses to furnish, and the siege being lengthened far beyond their expectation, they became seriously alarmed, and set about digging a well; about the same time the Indians had commenced digging on the outside in order to undermine the fort, which had not been discovered before they commenced the well. The Indians who could hear the digging on the inside of the fort called on them to know what they were digging for and were answered to countermine them, upon which they ceased digging.[53]

At this time fortunately for the besieged, there came a heavy rain and continued wet weather until the siege was raised, by which means they were sufficiently supplied with water.

The siege lasted until the 20th of August, during which time only two white men were killed and four wounded.—Thirty-seven Indians were killed and a great number wounded.

Clark of the Ohio

[September 29, 1826]

It has been noticed (Sec. 4) that General Clarke had procured a supply of amunition, from Virginia, and that some arrangements with the executive of that state had been made for an expedition against the enemy on the waters of the Mississippi, the ensuing spring. To effect this object, a regiment of state troops were at the succeeding session ordered to be raised, and the command given to Gen. Clarke, who descended the Ohio river in the spring of the year 1778 with about 150 men, all that he had been able to enlist; and early in June sent expresses to Harrodsburgh, requesting his friends and acquaintances in Kentucky, to raise as many as possible and immediately join him at the falls. The whole number from Kentucky did not exceed 80; so that the force mustered on the island at the falls on the 24th day of June, did not exceed 230 men.[54]

About 10 o'clock on the 24th day of June 1778 whilst the sun was totally eclipsed,[55] Clarke and his little army passed through the fall of the Ohio, and on the evening of the 28th landed at a creek about three leagues below Tennessee river, and a little above Massac, and by sun rise on the morning of the 29th took up the line of march for Kaskaskia.

They had with them no horse or other four footed animal; each man, both officers and soldiers carried his own baggage, arms and amunition on his back—their clothing consisted in a shirt, breech cloth leggins and moccasons; and their arms a rifle, tommahock and large knife. The pretended guides who undertook to pilot the army through the woods, proved to be entirely unacquainted with the country, until they approached the town; the calculation was, that from the place of landing, they could reach the town of Kaskaskia in four days, but it took them six; and having provisions for only four, most of the men were intirely without for nearly the two last days.

About dark on the fourth of July, this little army crossed Kaskaskia creek about half a mile above the town; and without the inhabitants having any intimation that any such enterprize was on foot, or ever contemplated. They lay by, and entered the town about midnight undiscovered, took the governor (Rochblave) in his bed, got from him the keys of the magazine, and took also the entire possession of the Artillery, before the least alarm was given, and before a single inhabitant knew they were there, except about half a dozen whom they took up in the street, and put immediately under guard, and thereby prevented the alarm being given.

The inhabitants were all disarmed before day, and their arms secured in the fort: and to oblige every one to deliver up his arms, an order was issued, that any inhabitant on whom a firelock should be found after a few hours, should suffer death. The arms were detained only until about the middle of the next day: previous to the delivering them back the inhabitants took the oath of allegiance to the state of Virginia, and were enrolled as militia of that state under suitable officers appointed for that purpose.

Ten or twelve of the citizens who were considered dangerous, were ordered to be ironed the next morning. When brought out for that purpose, they asked to see the commander;—when General Clarke was pointed out to them they appeared to be much confused; and although they were handcuffed, the irons did not remain long on before the General ordered them off again.

The inhabitants furnished the troops plentifully with provisions, together with horses to carry a detachment to Coho, on the credit of the state of Virginia, and declared themselves well satisfied with the change that had taken place. It was estimated that there were in the town at least four hundred men who were furnished with arms.

Kaskaskia was a handsome village, and contained a considerable number of very decent respectable inhabitants, both male and female, extremely polite and agreeable; they were principally French.[56]

On the morning of the 5th of July 1778 Cap. Joseph Bowman, an active vigilent officer, was detached with a party of men on horseback to take Coho,[57] a village said to be about twenty leagues from Kaskaskia; they arrived at the village the same evening, and before information had reached it of the fate of Kaskaskia, or of their being an enemy in the country; Coho was therefore taken in the very same manner that Kaskaskia had been the night before, without the knowledge of a single individual that an enemy approached them, until they were in possession of their town. The inhabitants of Coho like those of Kaskaskia immediately took the oath of allegiance to the state of Virginia, and claimed the protection of that government.

As soon as it was known to the tribes of Indians in the vicinity of Kaskaskia, that Gen. Clarke was in quiet possession of that place, several of their chiefs paid him a visit and tendered him the right hand of friendship which he reciprocated; so that in a very short time there was peace and submission throughout that entire section of country.[58]

Matters being arranged at Kaskaskias, Gen. Clarke paid a visit to Coho, where he met with Battisse, who it seems was an Indian chief (but it does not appear of what nation) also some of the chiefs of the Socks; their object appears to have been to settle some difference between their respective nations. Gen. Clarke attended the conferences of the chiefs— Battisse first rose and made a speech, giving the history of his fathers and of the Socks for many hundreds of years back, showing how their wars had wasted away both nations &c The Sock chief rose and in his speech confirmed all that Battisse had said, took the blue belt and confirmed a treaty of peace, to continue as long as trees grow or waters run.[59]

At Post St. Vincennes, sometime called O'Post and sometimes St. Vincennes, and which was situated on the banks of the Wabash, when Clarke took Kaskaskia, there was a British Lieutenant with a few troops, who immediately on hearing of Clarke's success and movements, abandoned the place and went to Detroit; of which fact Clarke was shortly after apprised by one of his Indian spies.

To influence the people of St. Vincennes in favor of the government of Virginia father Gibeaux a popular priest, & Doctor Lefong were engaged to visit that place [and] prepare them for a quiet peaceable submission, which they in a very short time effected. As soon as Gen. Clarke was informed of this fact, he sent Cap. Leonard Helm to that place as a civil Governor & commandant of the militia. Cap Helm had not long the honour of his appointment before Governor Hamilton of Detroit with five hundred British, Canadians and Indians, descended the Wabash to St. Vincennes, and disrobed Cap. Helm of all his new made honours, and held him a prisoner of war. This force under Gov. Hamilton set out from Detroit with the purpose of attacking Clarke at Kaskaskia, but on their way, hearing that St. Vincennes was in possession of Helm, together with the lateness of the season and difficulty of marching by land and taking with them the necessary baggage, he changed the determination to St. Vincennes. Considering himself intirely safe for the winter, Gov. Hamilton discharged all his Indians, and sent his white forces back to Detroit to remain until wanted, keeping only about one hundred soldiers.

Gen. Clarke was a sore thorn in the side of Governor Hamilton; he therefore left no mean unessayed to get him under his control. Among the inducements held out to the civillised part of the inhabitants, was a reward of $30,000 to any person or persons who would place Clarke in his power. He also engaged eighty warriors to waylay and take Gen. Clarke on his way between Kaskaskia and Coho. The plan was laid by Hamilton himself, and was as follows: Eight of the party were to conceal themselves near the road at the foot of a small hill, whilst the remainder were to lie a little beyond the top of the hill, and to join them immediately on the approach of the General, so as to enclose him and any small party that might accompany him. This party was apprised of the day the General was to pass, but not the hour, and from the promptitude of his movements, he arrived at the place of ambuscade early than was expected with twelve men, who discovered the eight Indians and routed them, before they had time to give the signal to those beyond the hill, who were also unprepared for the attack.[60]

Another project to entrap the General was attempted by a party of Valsavan Indians. They came to Coho under the pretence of a friendly visit to the General, and had laid a plot to take him and his escort prisoners in the fort: to effect which thirty or forty were to go into the fort after dark and before the gate was closed and conceal themselves, and when a certain signal was given by those without the fort they were to open the gate and let in the whole party, who were encamped near the town. This project was defeated by the vigilence of the guard, who when they attempted to enter the fort gate challenged them, and they for fear of being identified ran off to the camp.[61]

After the General returned to Kaskaskia, from Coho whilst standing by the side of a garden fence conversing with an officer, an arrow shot from a bow with great force passed between them, and stuck deep into one of the posts of the garden, evidently aimed at one of them. A party of men was immediately ordered to surround the square, and examine every house or other suspected place for the person who shot the arrow; dilligent search was made but without effect.

As soon as Gen. Clarke understood that Gov. Hamilton had taken St. Vincennes and discharged all his men except about one hundred, he determined to dislodge him before he obtained a reinforcement, which he knew was intended as soon as the winter was so far gone [as] to make it practicable for them to come from Detroit. Although it was in the middle of the winter the waters were not frozen, and the season was very wet; he therefore manned a boat with upwards of forty men, with a piece of Connon, with directions to descend the Mississippi, and ascend the Ohio and Wabash rivers and meet him at a point a little below Vincennes. The General then with about one hundred marched across by land from Kaskaskia to St. Vincennes, a great part of the way was covered with water, and many places more than knee deep. They arrived on the Wabash at the time appointed late in the evening, but there was no appearance of the boat. Knowing that he was undiscovered, and that delay would jeopardize success, he determined to attack the town that night, and not attempt to wait for the arrival of his artillery. He therefore marched his men up and so placed them as to be able to shoot into the bastions and port holes, and so near as to kill or wound every centinel if he attempted to show himself above the works or at a port hole. As soon as he got his men placed, a tremendous fire commenced, and so efficient was the attack, and so many of the centinels wounded that they could not be kept at their posts.

When the first fire was given Governor Hamilton, Cap. Helm and several other gentlemen, were seated at a game of Whist, (of which Helm was remarkably fond;) the instant he heard the fire, he jumped to his feet and exclaimed aloud "By G—— that's Clarke."

Finding that there was no probability of getting possession of the town that night he drew off his men to where they could encamp comfortably, leaving as many as would keep the town on the watch during the night.

In the course of the night, Clarke procured a trusty Canadian, who was well acquainted with the town, to endeavour to get admittance as a friend, under the pretence of giving information of Clarke's approach: he succeeded and informed the Governor (before whom he was immediately taken,) that it was not the intention of Clarke to have made the attack with small arms, but with cannon, which was on the way up the river, and was to have met him there that evening, and had not arrived, but was confidently expected the next day, with an addition of fifty or sixty more men. This information seemed to produce a considerable damp on the spirits of the whole town; the Canadian was immediately ordered into the guard house, to be carefully watched.

It was an understanding between the General and Cannadian that if he could not obtain admittance that he was to return; but if he could then he would certainly give the information agreed on. Nothing having been heard from the Cannadian, early the next morning, Clarke as soon as it was light paraded his men on the side of a small eminence within cannon shot of the fort, and so marched and countermarched them as to expose them to the view of the people of the fort, only as they marched one way, in order that their number should appear to be double what they really were; he also exhibited the appearance of a cannon, and of planting it on the top of the rise from whence the fort could be battered.

About ten o'clock all motion ceased, and Clarke sent in a flag demanding a surrender of the fort forthwith. Three flags passed before the terms were agreed on, when Hamilton surrendered to Clarke, a garrison well furnished with every thing necessary for its defence, including a greater number of efficient men than were opposed to him.

In a very few days after the surrender of Vincennes Clarke received notice, that a Mr. De Jean was descending the Wabash from Detroit, with eight or ten boats, in which were clothing, money and military stores for Vincennes. Immediately on receiving this information, Clarke dispatched Helm with a party to intercept this flotilla. Helm so managed as to come on De Jean and his party in the night encamped on the bank of the river,— surprised and took the whole, consisting of eighty-five men, and every thing in their possession, and returned to Vincennes without the fire of a gun.[62]

The principal officers taken prisoners on this expedition were sent to Williamsburg in Virginia, by the way of Harrodsburgh, especially Governor Hamilton, Mr. De Jean and Maj. Rocheblave governor of Eastern Illinois under British authority, and who had in his possession when taken $13,000 worth of British goods to trade with the Indians.[63]

Raiding the Chillicothe Villages

[October 6, 1826]

In the month of May 1779 Col. John Bowman, with 160 men marched against the Indian town called Chillicothe, situated about 60 miles from the mouth of Little Miami, and near the head of that river. The party rendezvoused at the mouth of Licking, and on the second night got in sight of the town undiscovered. It was determined to wait until day light in the morning before they would make the attack; but by the imprudence of some of the men whose curiosity exceeded their judgment, the party were discovered by the Indians, before the officers and men had arrived at the several positions assigned them. As soon as the alarm was given a fire commenced on both sides, and was kept up, whilst the women and children were seen running from cabin to cabin in the greatest confusion, and collecting in the most central and strongest. At clear day light it was found that Bowman's men were from 70 to 100 yards from the cabins in which the Indians had collected, and which it appeared they intended to defend. Having no other arms than rifles and tomahawks, it was thought imprudent to attempt to storm strong cabins well defended by expert warriors. In consequence of the warriors collecting in a few cabins contiguous to each other the remainder of the town was left unprotected, therefore whilst a fire was kept up at the port holes which engaged the attention of those within, fire was set to 30 or 40 cabins which were consumed, & a considerable quantity of property consisting principally of kettles and blankets were taken from those cabins. In searching the woods near the town, 130 horses were collected.

About 10 o'clock, Bowman and his party commenced their march homeward, after having nine men killed. What loss the Indians sustained was never known except their principal chief Black-Fish, who was wounded through the knee and died of the wound. After receiving the wound, Black-Fish proposed to surrender, being confident that his wound was dangerous and believing that there were among the white people, surgeons that could cure him, but that none amongst his own people could do it.

The party had not marched more than 8 or 10 miles on their return home, before the Indians appeared in considerable force in their rear, and began to press hard on that quarter. Bowman selected his ground and formed his men in a square; but the Indians declined a close engagement, and only keeping up a scattering fire, it was soon discovered that their object was only to retard their march until they could procure reinforcements from the neighbouring villages.

As soon as a strong possition was taken by Col. Bowman, the Indians retired, and he resumed the line of march, when his rear was again attacked; Col. Bowman again formed for battle, again the Indians retired and the scene was acted over several times; at length John Bulger, James Harrod and George Michael Bedinger, with about 100 or more mounted on horseback, rushed on the Indian ranks and dispersed them in ever direction, after which the Indians abandoned the pursuit. Bowman crossed the Ohio at the mouth of Little Miami, and after crossing, the men dispersed to their several homes. Col. Bowman had nine men killed and one wounded. The loss sustained by the Indians was never ascertained except the death of Black-Fish.[64]

In the month of October 1779, as two keel boats were assending the Ohio river some small distance above the mouth of Licking, the men on board discovered Indians standing on a sand bar on the South side of the river, and a canoe coming across to them with 3 or 4 in it. Capt. Rogers who commanded the boats, ordered the men to land and make their boats fast to the same shore near which they were, which was immediately done, when the party consisting of about 70 marched through the woods up until opposite to the sand bar where they had seen the Indians, with the expectation of killing or taking the whole; or driving them into the river, believing they were undiscovered by the Indians, and that their number did not exceed 12 or 15. When Rodgers and his party turned towards the river, the Indians who were fully aprised of their motions and from which they judged of their intentions, had so secreted themselves in the bushes, that Rodgers' party were within a few paces of them before they discovered them, upon which the Indians to the amount of several hundreds rose and poured on them a deadly fire. All who were not killed or disabled by this tremenduous fire made a precipitate retreat and aimed to get to their boats but the Indians pressed them so close, that many of them were at the boats as soon as the whites, and several whites were tomahawked in the attempt to get on board. Before the Indians got so close as to prevent it, one of the boats with five men on board cut loose and pushed off into the river, and soon floated out of reach of the Indians, (who were busily engaged with the other,) and thereby escaped. Rogers was himself killed, and the whole of his party consisting of 60 or 70 either killed or taken, except seven. Among those who were taken prisoners were Col. John Campbell, and Major Abr. Chaplin.

The following most singular circumstance attended this defeat. A man whose name was Robert Benham was wounded through the hips, in such manner as to render him unable to walk, he crawled into the brush of a fallen tree, taking his rifle with him, and so secreted himself that the Indians passed him unnoticed. He lay concealed two days without a mouthful of sustenance, when a Raccoon came near him, and he shot it: immediately after his gun fired he heard somebody call, but suspecting it was Indians, he reloaded his gun determined to sell his life dear; by the time his gun was charged he heard the voice again very near and calling in plain English, "Whoever you are I bet you will answer me, for I am in the utmost distress." Upon this Benham answered him & immediately appeared John Watson one of his unfortunate companions with both his arms broken; mutual congratulations were exchanged, when Benham pointed to the Raccoon where it lay, & directed Watson to kick it to him with his feet which he according did. Having good use of both his hands, Benham was able to skin and prepare the Raccoon for the spit, as well as to procure fire, whilst John Watson having the full use of his feet, could with them kick and drag pieces of broken wood to Benham who could make the fire and cook the meat. Before the Raccoon was eaten up, a flock of wild turkeys came in view, Benham directed John Watson to go round them and induce them to come near him which was done by which means he killed a large turkey. Happily the weather was mild, & the man with broken arms could wade into Licking river (near where they lay) so deep into the water as to stoop down and drunk, but Benham unable to move from the spot where he lay was likely to die of thirst, when this project occured to John Watson he desired Benham to put his hat into his mouth in such manner as that the hollow part of the crown should be upwards, which was done, and he went into the water and filled it by stooping down, and by that means furnished his friend with water. Benham dressed and splintered up the broken arms of John Watson, as well as dressed his own wounds; to enable him to do which he tore up both their shirts. They remained in this situation fifteen days, whilst their wounds healed very fast, insomuch that with the use of a crutch Benham began to be able to move a little during which time he killed plenty of game to support them whilst John Watson was able to bring wood with his feet and water with the aid of the hat. About four weeks after they were wounded, Benham and his companion went to the Ohio river at the mouth of Licking, and about a mile from where they were wounded, and from whence they were taken by a boat descending the river which they hailed, and were taken on board.[65]

Virginia having passed a law opening a land office for the sale of land warrants, to be located on any waste and unappropriated lands within the state (with a few exceptions,) together with the success of Gen. Clarkes expedition in reducing the military posts North West of the Ohio river, and on the waters of the Mississippi river, induced a very great number of families to remove to Kentucky, and especially from the states of North Carolina and Virginia. They had to pass through an uninhabited wilderness of more than two hundred miles, with no other road than that made by the feet of the animals passing over it; in many places this road was crossed by logs, many of them nearly three feet high, over which the animals were obliged to leap, there being no way round them. The narrowness of the way and the many obstructions in it, very much retarded the passage of families, insomuch, that many days they could not advance more than 10 miles; these circumstances, added to the quantity of provisions necessary to support families so great a distance, so fatigued their horses, who had no other sustenance than what they could obtain in the woods after a fatiguing days march that many gave out and were left on the road.

Notwithstanding the winter did not set in very severe until nearly Christmas, yet many hundreds of men women and children were overtaken by the bad weather, and were, in consequence of the extreme coldness of the winter, forced to remain where they were until the winter broke, which was not until early in February. The weather was so severe, and continued so long, that it obtained the name of the hard winter, and has been known to those who were in Kentucky at that time, by that name ever since. A very great number of people wintered on Cumberland river and Richland creek, and when the winter broke up, the waters in both rose to such a height, that almost the whole of their stock were drowned, and it was with great difficulty the families escaped drowning. In addition to their other calamities, the weather was so cold and the snow so deep that hunters could not procure food, so that many were compelled to use carcasses of their dead cattle; and from the poor children there was a perpetual cry for bread, which it was out of the power of the parents to furnish.[66]

Claiming the Land, Safeguarding the Frontier
[October 13, 1826]

The law providing for the appropriating the vacant lands in the state of Va. passed at the May session of the Legislature of that state in the year 1779.—By this law no land office treasury warrant was to be issued by the Register until the 15th day of October 1779; and the manner in which entries were to be made on the warrants when issued, was provided for as follows,—"If several persons shall apply with their warrants at the office of any surveyor at the same time to make entries, they shall be preferred according to the priority of the *dates* of their warrants." This provision prompted every person desirous of obtaining lands, to endeavour to procure his warrants on the 15th of October 1779, (the first day on which Land office treasury warrants were permitted to issue,) on account of the preference of entry in favour of the oldest warrant. No entries on treasury warrants could by law be made until the first day of May 1780, therefore a very great number of people visited Kentucky, previous to that day, with the view of exploring the country, so as to enable them to locate their warrants to the greatest advantage.[67]

On the 1st day of May 1780, the Surveyor's office for the County of Kentucky [for] receiving Warrants and making entries, was opened according to law, at Wilson's Station, on a branch of Salt River and about two miles from Harrodsburgh; but so numerous were the applicants on that day with their Warrants, that it took the surveyor, with the assistance of two or three deputies, several days to receive and receipt for the warrants; after which he was engaged 15 or 20 days more in arranging them, before any entries were permitted to be made.

The claims adjudged to those who had settled in the country and raised corn or made improvements called Preemption, or Settlement and Preemption claims, were so numerous, that all the most noted and valuable situations were secured by them; so that strangers had little chance of distinguishing between the lands claimed and those unclaimed, and were therefore unable to make entries with any reasonable prospect of securing the land; consequently early in June, most of the owners of warrants, confided them to the experienced Hunters and Woodsmen of Kentucky to make entries on them and returned to their respective homes.[68]

The great influx of people into Kentucky in the latter part of the year 1779, and the early part of 1780, occasioned a scarcity of provisions in the country, bordering on a famine. Many families never tasted bread, until the corn was fit to make meal of, their dependance was entirely on the game, of which the Buffalo was the principal; but the settlements were so closely watched by the Indians, and the game having retired from the neighbourhood of the stations, it was with great labour and hazard, that provisions could be procured. All the traces* contiguous to the stations were waylayed by the Indians, therefore the hunters found it necessary to start early enough to get out in the woods 3 or 4 miles before day; and on their return, to travel a like distance after night to their homes.[69]

In the spring 1780, more families came to Louisville than to any other point in the country, by means of the Ohio River, from whence they moved out to Bear Grass and Salt River stations; and as there was a very great intercourse between those two stations and Louisville, and especially the former, it was almost impossible to pass without being attacked by Indians. The danger became so great at last, that none attempted to pass in the day time without a party sufficiently large to protect themselves against any enemy that would likely assail them. As it was not convenient to make up a party at all times, strong enough to be safe, they adopted the practice of travelling in the night. No sooner did the Indians discover this than they made choice of suitable ground, where they tied grape vines across the road, so as to check both man and horse attempting to pass, who therefore fell an easier prey than in the day time.[70]

Early in the same year Gen. Clark with a party of upwards of two hundred men went down the Ohio river from Louisville to a place on the Mississippi below the mouth of the Ohio called the Iron Banks, where he erected a fort and called it Fort Jefferson. At the mouth of the Ohio he fell in company with Doc. Walker, who had descended the Ohio for the purpose of ascertaining the point on the Mississippi, where the line between the States of Virginia and North Carolina would intersect that river which he effected.

After fixing fort Jefferson, Gen. Clark left at that place about 100 men and with the remainder of his force ascended the Mississippi, to relieve Coho and St. Louis, which were besieged by a considerable force of French and Indians, assisted by the British, and who before he arrived had killed 53 of the inhabitants.[71]

When Gen. Clark arrived at Coho, he was informed that the number of men at St. Louis, collected from Kaskaskia and other places, was

---

Trace means a path, or road made by the travelling of animals, & which has not been made by art; such were all the ways in Kentucky at that time.

between three and four hundred. He went over to St. Louis to review the troops as well as the works of defence. The Spanish commandant at St. Louis had built a blockhouse† and strengthened other parts of the place, and on the arrival of Clark, offered him the command on both sides of the Mississippi river, but General Clark declined taking the command, until he could ascertain where the assault would be made; he continued only about two hours in St. Louis, before he returned to Coho.

The Commandant at St. Louis was disappointed in Clark's leaving him so soon; he expected he would have staid to dinner with him, and to entertain him the better, he had sent out a hunter to kill some ducks for that purpose. This hunter fell in with a spy from the invading army near the margin of the river, who entered into conversation with him, and asked him a great many questions, and amongst others, who commanded at Coho? The hunter answered Montgomery had heretofore commanded, but that Clark had just arrived with a great force, and that Coho was now commanded by him. The spy replied that was impossible, as he knew Clark was in Kentucky; for an express from the Governor of Virginia with despatches to Gen. Clark, addressed to him at Louisville, had lately been killed by the Indians, and therefore he knew Clark could not be at Coho. The hunter said it was immaterial about the despatches, but that Clark was at that moment in St. Louis, and that he had come out to kill some ducks for his dinner.[72]

In the evening an attack was made on the town of St. Louis by the invading enemy, and shortly after a similar attack was made on Coho— Clark drew out his forces at Coho, but only a slight skirmish took place before the enemy retreated; he had two men killed. Immediately after the enemy withdrew, Clark sent over 300 men to the relief of St. Louis, and on their approach the enemy retired from that place also. This invading army had come from Michilimackinack.[73]

Whilst Gen. Clark was at Coho, several French deserters came in and gave him the information of the intended expedition against Kentucky under the command of Col. Byrd from Detroit. He sent three or four hundred men up the Illinois, and to Rock river who destroyed several towns.

Soon after receiving certain intelligence of Byrd's intentions, Gen. Clark, Major Harlan, and Capt. Consola with a few others set out from St. Louis for Fort Jefferson and sent 50 men up to Louisville with ammunition for the purpose of carrying an expedition into the enemy's country, and if possible intercept Byrd on his march for Kentucky.[74]

From Fort Jefferson, Clark, Harlan and Consola set off on foot for Harrodsburgh in Kentucky. It was a remarkable wet season, all the rivers

---

† *Blockhouse*, a strong log house the second story of which overjuts or protrudes beyond the first 18 inches or more all round.

were very full so that they were obliged to make rafts to cross both the Tennessee and Cumberland rivers, and smaller rivers they swam. A short distance from the Tennessee river they were discovered by a party of Indians and pursued and very narrowly escaped, the Indians having crossed the Tennessee above them, and waited to meet them on their landing; but fortunately they discovered the Indians in time to make their landing below the mouth of a wide and deep creek, and immediately on landing were out of sight; not long after leaving the Tennessee they came across a boar [bear], and being almost out of provisions they killed it, but did not want [wait] to skin it, but cut off each a piece with the skin on and pushed on till night, when they found a sinkhole in which they made a fire, and cooked and slept until morning. They crossed the Cumberland river not far below Nashville, and fell into the path from that to Kentucky and arrived at Wilson's station near Harrodsburgh, about one hour before the express which brought the news that Ruddle's & Martin's Stations†† were taken.[75]

The plan of this expedition was laid by the British at Detroit, and with the aid of the Northern tribes of Indians, calculated on breaking up the settlements in Kentucky, and bringing the whole country under their control. To effect this project the whole Indian force under the influence of the British were collected, with Simon Girty and McKee and joined by Col. Byrd with some British regulars and Canadian volunteers; and besides small arms were provided with six pieces of artillery.

The original design of this expedition, was first to have gone to Louisville and taken that, and established their headquarters at that place; but on their approach to the Ohio, received information that the waters of Licking river were sufficiently high to admit their boats to ascend that river, and from the unwillingness of the Indians to come in contact with a place where there was cannon, the project was changed.[76]

The first intimation the people of Kentucky received of this meditated attack was from Major A. Chaplin who was taken prisoner by the Indians when Capt. Rodgers was killed in an attempt to ascend the Ohio the preceding fall, as has been noticed. Upon receiving information of the meditated attack on Kentucky, Maj. Chaplin determined to apprize his country of their danger or perish in the attempt; he therefore made his escape and safely arrived at Harrodsburgh, early in the month of May, and gave the information.[77]

Immediately on the arrival of Maj. Chaplin, the information he gave was sent to every station in the country, and consultations were held to devise the best mode to defeat them. From the best calculations that could be made, it was considered impossible that they could arrive with such an

††Station is understood to be a place where many families settled together for mutual safety and defence.

army, earlier than the last of July or first of August, and all arrangements for defence were made agreeably to that calculation; nor was that opinion changed until about the first of June, when a party of 25 men attempted to cross the Kentucky river at the ford below Frankfort, on their way from Bryan's station to Louisville to purchase corn. As this party descended the bank they were fired on by a party of Indians with muskets, charged with ball and buck shot. These were arms not generally used by Indians; it was therefore immediately conjectured, that it was an advance party of the army that was expected.

The information of the taking of Riddle's [Ruddle's] and Martin's stations, entirely changed the project that had been conceived, of intercepting the army on its way to Louisville, where Major Chaplin informed was the place on which they designed to make their first attack. Gen. Clark therefore recommended, that the whole force that could possibly be raised, should pursue the Indians to their towns, and destroy all their provisions at least. This proposition was unanimously agreed to by all the officers of the militia; and as there were a considerable number of men on a visit to the country, immediate orders were given to enroll every man—and to prevent any from leaving the country, an officer with a sufficient force was stationed at the Crab Orchard the only outlet from the settled parts, with orders to stop all who attempted to leave the country; and if they refused to return and join the expedition, to take from them their arms and ammunition. Drafts were immediately made in all the stations in the country, and four-fifths of all the men able to bear arms, ordered to hold themselves ready to march as soon as arrangements could be made at Louisville for the transportation up the river of a field piece, ammunition and provisions.[78]

The Horrors at Ruddle's and Hinkston's Forts

[October 20, 1826]

It has already been noticed, that the summer 1780 was exceedingly wet, and that all the water-courses were full. This circumstance induced Colonel Byrd to change his original purpose of attacking Louisville first. He therefore decided to ascend Licking river into the heart of the country, by which means he would be enabled to take with him his artillery to Ruddle's Station, and would easily take it by land from Ruddle's to Martin's and Bryan's Stations, and Lexington, the ground being level, and the roads easily made passible. Col. Byrd landed his artillery, stores and baggage on the point of Licking, where he put up some huts to shelter them from the weather; and from thence marched by land, a few miles, to Ruddle's Station, where he arrived on the 22d day of June, at the head of 1000 men. In consequence of the extreme wetness of the weather, which had continued for many days, the men at Ruddle's and Martin's Stations, who were accustomed to be in the woods, had all come in, and therefore, Byrd taking advantage of that circumstance, arrived within gun shot of the fort undiscovered, and the first information the people received of the approach of an enemy, was the report from a discharge of one of the fieldpieces. Byrd sent in a flag and demanded a surrender at discretion—to which demand Capt. Ruddle answered, that he could not consent to surrender but on certain conditions, one of which was: that the prisoners should be under the protection of the British, and not suffered to be prisoners to the Indians; to these terms Col. Byrd consented, and immediately the gates were opened to him. No sooner were the gates opened, than the Indians rushed into the Station, and each seized the first person they could lay their hands on, and claimed them as their own prisoner. In this way the members of every family were separated from each other; the husband from the wife, and the parents from their children. The piercing screams of the children, when torn from their mothers—the distracted throes of the mothers when forced from their tender offspring, are indescribable. Ruddle remonstrated with Colonel Byrd against this barbarous conduct of the Indians, but to no effect. He confessed that it was out of his power to restrain them, their numbers being so much greater than

that of the troops over which he had controul that he himself was completely in their power.

After the people were entirely stripped of all their property, and the
prisoners divided among their captors, the Indians proposed to Colonel
Byrd, to march to and take Martin's Station, which was about five miles
from Ruddle's; but Col. Byrd was so affected by the conduct of the Indians
to the prisoners taken, that he peremptorily refused, unless the chiefs
would pledge themselves in behalf of the Indians, that all the prisoners
taken should be entirely under his control, and that the Indians should
only be entitled to the plunder.—Upon these propositions being agreed
to by the chiefs, the army marched to Martin's Station and took it without
opposition. The Indians divided the spoil among themselves, and Colonel Byrd took charge of the prisoners.[79]

The ease with which these two stations were taken, so animated the
Indians, that they pressed Col. Byrd to go forward and assist them to take
Bryan's Station and Lexington. Byrd declined going, and urged as a
reason, the improbability of success; and besides, the impossibility of
procuring provisions to support the prisoners they already had, also the
impracticability of transporting their artillery by land, to any part of the
Ohio river—therefore the neceissity of descending Licking before the
waters fell, which might be expected to take place in a few days.

Immediately after it was decided not to go forward to Bryan's Station,
the army commenced their retreat to the forks of Licking, where they had
left their boats, and with all possible dispatch got their artillery and
military stores on board, and moved off. At this place the Indians separated from Byrd, and took with them the whole of the prisoners taken at
Ruddle's Station. Among the prisoners were Capt. John Hinkston, a
brave man and an experienced hunter and woodsman. The second night
after leaving the forks of Licking, the Indians encamped near the river;
every thing was very wet, in consequence of which it was difficult to
kindle a fire, and before a fire could be made it was quite dark. A guard
was placed over the prisoners, and whilst part of them were employed in
kindling the fire, Hinkston sprang from among them and was immediately out of sight. An alarm was instantly given, and the Indians ran in
every direction, not being able to ascertain what course he had taken.
Hinkston ran but a short distance before he lay down by the side of a log
under the dark shade of a large beach tree, where he remained until the
stir occasioned by his escape had subsided, when he moved off as silently
as possible. The night was cloudy, and very dark, so that he had no mark
to steer by, and after travelling some time towards Lexington, as he
thought, he found himself close to the camp from which he had just
before made his escape. In this dilemma he was obliged to tax his skill as a
woodsman, to devise a method by which he should be enabled to stear
his course without light enough to see the moss on the trees, or without
the aid of sun, moon or stars. Captain Hinkston ultimately adopted this

expedient: he dipped his hand in the water, (which almost covered the whole country) and holding it upright above his head, he instantly felt one side of his hand cold; he immediately knew, that from that point the wind came—he therefore steered the ballance of the night to the cold side of his hand, that being from the west he knew, and the course best suited to his purpose. After travelling several hours he sat down at the root of a tree and fell asleep.

A few hours before day, there came on a very heavy dense fog, so that a man could not be seen at twenty yards distance. This circumstance was of infinite advantage to Hinkston, for as soon as day light appeared, the howling of wolves, the gobling of turkeys, the bleating of fawns, the cry of owls, and every other wild animal, was heard in almost every direction. Hinkston was too well acquainted with the customs of the Indians, not to know that it was Indians, and not beasts or birds that made these sounds—he therefore avoided approaching the places where he heard them, and notwithstanding he was several times within a few yards of them, with the aid of the fog he escaped, and arrived safe at Lexington. It was the 8th day after Ruddle's Station was taken, when Hinkston arrived in Lexington, and brought the first news of that event.

The Indians not only collected all the horses belonging to Ruddle's and Martin's Station, but a great many from Bryan's Station and Lexington, and with their booty, crossed the Ohio river near the mouth of Licking, and there dispersed. The British descended Licking river to the Ohio, down the Ohio to the mouth of the Big Miami, and up the Miami as far as it was then navigable for their boats, where they hid their artillery and marched by land to Detroit. The rains having ceased, and the weather being exceedingly hot, the waters fell so low, that they were able to ascend the Miami but a short distance by water.[80]

The great panic occasioned throughout Kentucky by the taking of Ruddle's and Martin's Stations, caused the people to look up to General Clarke as their only hope. His counsel and advice was received as coming from an oricle. He advised that a levy of four-fifths should be made of all the men in the country capable of bearing arms, whether inhabitants or strangers, and to meet at the mouth of Licking on the 20th of July. Those from Lincoln and Fayette under the command of Col. Logan, were to march down Licking—those from Jefferson under Gen. Clarke, were to march up the Ohio.[81]

As soon as it was decided that an expedition should be carried on against the Indians, General Clarke gave orders to have a number of small skiffs built at Louisville, capable of taking 15 or 20 men, which together with batteaus, the provisions and military stores, were taken by water from Louisville to the mouth of Licking. These vessels were under the direction of Col. George Slaughter, who commanded about 150 troops raised by him in Virginia for the Western service.[82]

In ascending the river, it was necessary to keep the vessels close to the shore, some of which were on one side of the river, and some on the other; it happened whilst one of these skiffs was near the north side of the river, a party of Indians ran down the water's edge, and fired into it and killed and wounded several before assistance could be obtained from the other boats.

That part of the army commanded by Col. Logan, assembled at Bryan's spring, about eight miles from Lexington, and on the following night a man by the name of Clarke, stole a valuable horse and went off. It was generally believed that he intended to go to Carolina. When the army arrived at the mouth of Licking, the horse was found there, when the conjecture was, that he had been taken prisoner by the Indians; but it was afterwards discovered that he had gone to the Indians voluntarily, in order to give them notice of the approach of an army from Kentucky.

The army rendezvoused and encamped on the ground whereon Cincinnati now stands, and the next day built two block-houses, in which was deposited a quantity of corn, and where several men who were sick were left, with a small guard, until the return of the army.

The division of the army commanded by Col. Logan, took with them generally provisions only sufficient to last them to the mouth of Licking, as it was understood a sufficient quantity for the campaign would be brought up from Louisville to that place; but when the army were about to march, the provisions were distributed among the men, and was only *six quarts of Indian corn*, measured in a quart pot, for each man, most of whom were obliged to carry it on their backs, not having a sufficiency of pack-horses to convey the whole, together with the military stores and other baggage of the army.[83]

Clark's Raid against
the Piqua Towns
[October 27, 1826]

On the 2d day of August 1780, Gen. Clarke took up the line of march from where Cincinnati now stands, for the Indian towns. The army consisted of 970 men, and were formed in two divisions. The line of march was as follows: the first division, commanded by Gen. Clarke, took the front position; the center was occupied by the artillery, military stores and baggage; the second, commanded by Col. Logan, was placed in the rear. The men were ordered to march in four lines, at about 40 yards distance from each other, and a line of flankers on each side, at about the same distance from the right and left lines—these flankers just kept in sight of each other. There were also a front and rear guard, who only kept in sight of the main army. In order to prevent confusion in case of an attack by the enemy on the march of the army, a general order was issued, that in the event of an attack in the front, the front were to stand fast, and the two right hand lines were to wheel to the right, and the two left hand lines to the left, and form a compleat line, whilst the artillery was to advance forward to the center of the line—and in case of an attack on either of the flanks or side lines, these lines were to stand fast, and likewise the artillery, whilst the opposite lines wheeled and formed on the two extremes of those lines; and in the event of an attack being made on the rear, similar order was to be observed as in an attack in front.

In this manner the army moved on without encountering any thing worthy of notice, until they arrived at Chillicothe, (situated on the Little Miami river) about two o'clock in the afternoon, on the 6th day of August. They found the town not only abandoned, but most of the houses burnt down and burning, having been set on fire that morning. The army encamped on the ground that night, and on the following day, cut down several hundred acres of corn, and about four o'clock in the evening, took up their line of march for the Piqua towns, which was about 12 miles from Chillicothe.—They had not marched more than a mile from Chillicothe, before there came on a very heavy rain, with thunder and lightning, and considerable wind. Without tents or any other means of shelter from the rain, which fell in torrents, the men were as wet as if they had been plunged into the river; nor had they it in their power to keep their guns dry. It was nearly dark before the rain ceased, when the army were ordered to encamp in a hollow square, with the baggage and horses in the center, and as soon as fires could be made to dry their clothes &c., they were ordered to examine their guns, and to be sure that they were in good order, to discharge them in the following manner:—one company was to fire, and time given to reload, when a company at the most remote part of the camp from that which had fired, was to discharge theirs, and so on alternately, until all the guns were fired. On the morning of the 8th, the army marched by sunrise, and having a level, open way, arrived in sight of Piqua, situated on the west side of Mad river, about 2 o'clock P.M. The Indian road from Chillicothe to Piqua, which the army followed, crossed Mad river about a quarter of a mile below the town, and as soon as the advance guard crossed the river into a prarie of high weeds, they were attacked by the Indians, who had concealed themselves in the weeds. The ground on which this attack was made, as well as the manner in which it was done, left no doubt that a general engagement was intended. Col. Logan was therefore ordered, with about 400 men, to file off to the right and march up the river on the East side, and continue to the upper end of the town, so as to prevent the Indians from escaping in that direction, whilst the remainder of the men, under Colonels Lynn, Floyd and Harrod, were ordered to cross the river and encompass the town on the West side, whilst Gen. Clarke, with the troops under Col. Slaughter, and such as was attached to the artillery, marched directly towards the town. The prarie in which the Indians were concealed who commenced the attack, was only about two hundred yards across to the timbered land, and the division of the army destined to encompass the town on the west side, found it necessary to cross this prarie, to avoid the fire of a concealed enemy. The Indians evinced great military skill and judgment, and to prevent the Western division of the army from executing the duties assigned them, they made a powerful effort to turn their left wing—this was discovered by Floyd and Lynn, and to prevent being outflanked, extended the line of battle west more than a mile from the town, and which continued warmly contested on both sides, until about 5 o'clock, when the Indians disappeared every where unperceived, except a few in the town. The field-piece, which had been entirely useless before, was now brought to bear upon the houses, when a few shot dislodged the Indians which were in them.[84]

A nephew of Gen. Clarke, who had been many years a prisoner with the Indians, and who attempted to come to the whites, just before the close of the action, was supposed to be an Indian, and received a mortal wound; but he lived several hours after he arrived among them.

The morning after the battle, a Frenchman, who had been taken by the Indians a short time before on the Wabash, and who had stole away from them during the action; was found in the loft of one of the Indian cabbins. He gave information, that the Indians did not expect the Kentuckians would have reach their town that day, and if they did not, it was their intention to have attacked them in the night in their camp, with the tomahawk and knife, and not to fire a gun. They had intended to have made an attack the night before, but were prevented by the rain, and also by the vigilance evinced by the Kentuckians in firing off their guns, and re-loading them, the reasons for doing which they comprehended when they heard the firing. Another circumstance showed that the Indians were disappointed in the time they expected Clarke; they had not dined. When the men got into the town, they found considerable quantities of provisions ready cooked in large kettles and other vessels, almost untouched. The loss on each side was nearly equal. Twenty Indians were killed, and about the same number of whites.[85]

The Piqua town was built in the manner of the French villages. It extended along the margin of the river for more than three miles, the houses in many places are more than 20 poles apart. Col. Logan, therefore, in order to surround the town on the East, as his orders were, marched fully three miles, whilst the Indians turned their whole force against those on the opposite side of the town, and Logan's party never saw an Indian during the whole action. The action was so severe a short time before the close, that Simon Girty, a white man who had joined the Indians, and who was made a chief among the Mingoes, drew off 300 of his men, declaring to them, that it was folly in the extreme to continue the action against men who acted so much like madmen as Gen. Clarke's men did, for they rushed into the most extreme danger, with a seeming disregard of consequences. This opinion of Girty, and the withdrawal of his 300 Mingoes so discouraged the others, that the whole body soon after dispersed.[86]

It is a maxim among the Indians, never to encounter a fool or a madman, (in which terms they include a desperate man) for they say, that with a man that has not sense enough to take a prudent care of his own life, the life of his antagonist is in much greater danger than with a prudent man.

It was estimated that at the two towns, Chillicothe and Piqua, more than 500 acres of corn was destroyed, as well as every species of vegetables cultivated for the purpose of food. In consequence of the destruction of the corn and vegetables at those towns, the Indian warriors were obliged, for the support of their women and children, to employ their whole time in hunting, which gave quiet to Kentucky for a considerable time.

The day after the battle, viz: the 9th, was occupied in cutting down the growing corn, and destroying the cabbins and fort &c and collecting horses On the 10th of August, the army began their march homeward, and encamped in Chillicothe that night—and on the 11th cut a field of corn, which had been left for the benefit of the men and horses on their return. Nothing remarkable transpired on the march to the mouth of Licking, except a man killed by one of the centinels who supposed him to be an Indian. At the mouth of Licking the army dispersed, and each individual made the best of his way home.[87]

Thus ended a campaign, in which most of the men had no other provisions for 25 days, than six quarts of Indian corn each, except the green corn and vegetables found at the Indian towns, and one gill of salt—and yet not a single complaint was heard to escape from the lips of a solitary individual. All appeared to be impressed with the belief, that if this army should be defeated, that few would be able to escape, and that the Indians would then fall on the defenceless women and children in Kentucky, and destroy the whole.—From this view of the subject, every man was determined to conquer or die.[88]

SECTION 11

Bravery under Siege
[November 3, 1826]

In consequence of the destruction of the corn at the Chillicothe and Piqua towns, the Indians were reduced almost to a state of famine, and the warriors were not only obliged to attend to the immediate wants of their women and children, but to provide for them habitations for the approaching winter—hence all their time was so occupied, that Kentucky enjoyed considerable repose until the ensuing spring.[89]

Many of the disaffected to the cause of the American Revolution, had removed to Kentucky from North Carolina, as well as from other parts of the United States, to avoid being compelled to take up arms against Great Britain, who in consequence of the flattering success of the British arms in the South, in the taking of Charleston, and other successes, together with the gloomy prospects in Kentucky, immediately after the return of the army from chastising the Indians, made ready and removed back to North Carolina in the autumn of 1780, some of whom entered the British service.

A great number of those who had been considered permanent settlers in the country, removed to the old settled country in the autumn of the year 1780, which so discouraged the remaining inhabitants, that if the Indians had not, by stealing their horses, deprived them of the means of removing the women and children, the country would have been abandoned; but owing to the impossibility of removing them, the men resolutely determined to protect and defend them. The gloomy prospects in Kentucky checked the emigration to it until the spring of the year 1781, and even then it was by no means equal to what it had been the preceding year.[90]

About the first of March 1781, Col. Wm. Lynn and Captains Tipton and Chapman, were killed by parties of Indians who waylaid the paths on Beargrass. In pursuit of one of these parties, Capt. Aquilla Whitaker, with 15 men, followed them to the Ohio river at the foot of the Rapids, where they found some canoes, in which they embarked in order to cross the river in the pursuit: but as soon as they were fairly on board, the Indians, who lay concealed under the bank of the river, fired on them, and killed one and wounded nine others—they instantly relanded, rushed on the Indians and defeated them.[91]

In the month of April, in the year 1781, a Station settled by Squire Boone, (brother of Col. Daniel Boone,) near the place where Shelbyville now stands, was so exposed, and had so suffered by the Indians, that the inhabitants determined to break up and remove to Beargrass. Whilst they were on their way, incumbered with women and children, and their household goods, they were attacked by a party of Indians near Long run, defeated and dispersed with great slaughter. Col. John Floyd receiving information of this defeat, collected together 30 men, and went in the immediate pursuit of the Indians. Calculating on being pursued, the Indians formed an ambuscade, into which Floyd and his party were unsuspectingly drawn, and one half their number killed. Col. Floyd would himself have fallen into the hands of the Indians, but for the manly intrepidity of Capt. Samuel Wells, who seeing the Col. on foot, nearly exhausted and hard pressed by the army, nobly dismounted himself from his own horse, assisted Col. Floyd into the saddle, and accompanied him on foot. Such illustrious acts ought never to be forgotten. But what adds greatly to the magnanimity of the act is, that at that time Capt. Wells and Colonel Floyd were at variance.[92]

On the 9th of May 1781, M'Afee's Station on Salt river, about seven miles from Harrodsburg, was attacked by a party of Indians. One of the M'Afee's and another man were on their way from the Station to a plantation in the vicinity of the place, on whom the Indians fired and pursued them to the station. The siege lasted only about three hours when the Indians withdrew, and shortly after, men from different places in the neighborhood collected to the amount of forty, and pursued the Indians, and within a mile of the station, overtook and defeated them. The

Indians in this affair lost six men killed, and several wounded, as appeared by the bloody trails the whites had one killed only, and one mortally wounded who died in a few days after.[93]

In the spring of the year 1781, it appearing that Fort Jefferson afforded no security to the Western settlements, it was evacuated.

About the same time a party of men on their way from Harrodsburgh to Logan's Station (St. Asaphs) were attacked by Indians near the former place; two of them were mortally wounded, one of whom was notwithstanding enabled to escape to the Fort. The other hid himself behind a log and was carried into Harrodsburgh by a party who went immediately to the place where the attack was made. Col. Logan raised a party of men and went in pursuit of the Indians, but did not come up with them: On their return home they were fired on by the same or another party of Indians, and one of his men wounded; as soon as the Indians fired they dispersed.[94]

Montgomery's station in Lincoln county was in the course of this year taken by Indians, where the father and a brother of Mrs. Logan (wife of Col. Logan) were killed, and a sister, sister-in-law with four children taken prisoners. Col. Logan immediately raised a company of men, quickly pursued, overtook and defeated the Indians, retook the two women and three of the children; the fourth was murdered during the action which was for some time doubtful. In this action William Montgomery killed three Indians, and wounded a fourth.[95]

In the month of May 1782, a party of Wyandot Indians attacked Estill's Station, destroyed a number of cattle, killed a white man, and took a negro prisoner. The Indians were 25 in number. Capt. Estill hastily raised the same number of white men, pursued and overtook them, when a bloody conflict ensued, the victory was contested for two hours—the Indians ultimately prevailed. In this action Capt. Estill and seven of his men were killed, and four mortally wounded. The loss on the part of the Indians, it was afterwards understood, was equal to that on the part of the whites.

On the 10th of August 1782, the Indians took two boys from Hoy's Station in Madison county. They were immediately pursued by Col. John Holder with 17 men, who overtook the Indians, when an action ensued, in which Holder and his party were defeated, having four men killed and one wounded.[96]

Early one morning in the year 1781, Mr. Alexander M'Connell,* who resided in the neighborhood of Lexington, wandered into the woods on foot in pursuit of game. Having succeeded in killing a deer at some distance from home, he found it necessary to return for a horse on which

---

*This account of the very extraordinary exploit of Alexander M'Connell, may be seen in the Western Review for April 1820, and was furnished by himself. [See *Western Review* 2:177-79.]

to carry it off. While he was gone five Indians came to the spot where the deer lay, and naturally concluded that some one would soon return thither for it. Three of them remained to watch it, and two placed themselves in ambuscade near the path, along which they rightly supposed the huntsman would pass. As he rode, therefore, near their place of concealment, they shot at him, killed the horse under him, and consequently took him prisoner. For several days he travelled quietly with them, and as he had a good rifle, and was an excellent marksman, they required him to shoot deer, buffaloe &c. for them. At night however, they used the precaution of having him tightly bound by each arm, and the rope attached thereto carefully passed under their bodies as they lay on each side of him. For some time he quietly submitted to this treatment, but at length he ventured to complain that he was bound too tight, and to beg that the cords might be tied about him more loosely. The confidence of the savages increasing, and their apprehension of his escape diminishing, they yielded to his request, but still continued to bind him at night in the same manner, though not so closely as at first.[97]

One night when the party had reached the banks of the Ohio, and when he thought it necessary if possible, to make his escape, he observed a knife lying near his feet as he was fixed in his position for the night.— With considerable difficulty and the imminent hazard of awakening the savages who were snoring around him, and who were connected to the rope by which he was bound, he at length succeeded in drawing the knife with his feet until he could reach it with his hand, when he cut the cord that confined him, and was enabled to rise. His first thought then was to run off, leaving the Indians asleep; but upon reflection he concluded that it would be impossible for him to escape in this way, as they would probably soon awake and rapidly pursue him. He came therefore to the heroic and almost desperate resolution, to endeavor to kill the five Indians, or as many of them as he could. With the utmost coolness he proceeded to examine their guns, which he perceived lying together, primed them and put them in good order for service. He then disguised himself by putting on a coat belonging to the Indians and fixing a tomahawk and scalping knife in his belt; and placed his own rifle at a little distance off, where the savages would not be likely to observe it, but where he himself could instantly find it. All these preparations were made at a moment when five Indians were sleeping by him, and when the waking of either of them would have been to him instant death.

All things being ready, he proceeded to make the assault. He took two guns, one in each hand, and placing their muzzles at the breasts of two Indians who were lying on each side of the spot where he had been, shot them both at once. The others, as he expected, being awakened by the noise, sprang up and stared in amazement. With a third gun he instantly shot at two of them who were close together, killed one, as he afterwards had reason to believe, and mortally wounded the other. The fifth Indian, seeing his companions lying dead about him, and not knowing where to find his arms, and probably in the confusion of the scene; uncertain by how many he was assailed precipitately fled. Mr. M'Connell therefore, was left in quiet possession of the field. Not feeling inclined however, to fight any more such battles, he took his rifle and proceeded expeditiously towards home, where, after a tedious and painful journey, he safely arrived, to the great joy of his friends, who had began to despair of ever seeing him again.

Some little time afterwards, Mrs. Dunlap, a lady of respectability, who had been taken by the Indians, and retained a prisoner among them on Mad river in the state of Ohio, made her escape and returned home to the neighborhood of Lexington. She stated that shortly after the time when Mr. M'Connell made his desperate and successful assault, one Indian, out of five who had made a journey towards Lexington, returned with an account that they had taken a white man prisoner, and had brought him as far as the Ohio river, when in the night, while they were asleep, they were suddenly attacked by a party of whites, who killed all his companions, and probably likewise the poor defenceless prisoner, who was lying on his back, tightly bound with cords.[98]

SECTION 12

Death on the Elkhorn

[November 10, 1826]

The first permanent settlement made at Bryan's station was in 1779, principally by emigrants from North Carolina, the most conspicuous of whom were the family of Bryans, from whom the place took its name. There were four brothers viz: Morgan, James, William and Joseph, all respectable men in easy circumstances, with large families of children, and mostly grown. William, though not the eldest brother, was the most active and considered their leader. His wife was a sister of Col. Daniel

Boone, as was also the wife of Mr. William Grant who likewise settled in Bryan's station in 1779.[99]

In the spring of the year 1780, all the paths near the different stations, were almost perpetually watched by small parties of Indians, so that if a few men attempted to pass, they scarcely ever escaped being fired on; in consequence of which it became necessary, that the hunters should go in parties equal in number at least to the parties of Indians which usually watched their paths.

In the latter part of the month of May 1780, William Bryan with 15 or 20 men set out on a hunting party down Elkhorn creek. After going beyond the point where the paths were usually watched by Indians, in order to secure success in hunting, they divided, one part of the company was to cross Elkhorn Creek, and travel down on the north side, the other to go down on the south side, with an understanding that they all should meet at the mouth of Cane run, and encamp together the following night. The party who crossed the creek were headed by James Hogan, and had with them a led horse; the other party was headed by William Bryan. Hogan's party had travelled but a short distance after crossing the creek, before they heard the voice of some body cry out "boys stop!" on looking back they discovered several Indians closely pursuing them; they therefore laid whip to their horses and for several miles when in open woods, could see the Indians in their rear. The led horse was left behind early in the pursuit; one of the party had his hat pulled off by the brush, but the Indians were so close he could not take time to pick it up, but pushed on bare headed. Late in the evening Hogan and his party determined to recross the creek and come home that night, as they could not discover what was the number of the Indians in pursuit; and if they continued on to the mouth of Cane run, would probably lead them to where the other party were, and might by that means, sacrifice the whole. They accordingly recrossed the creek, and as soon as Hogan ascended the bank, he dismouted, and waited until the foremost of the Indians had got to about the middle of the creek, when he fired on him, which produced a great splash in the water, but whether he killed or wounded him was not known, but the Indians ceased their pursuit.

Hogan and his party returned to Bryan's station that night, and before the next morning with an additional number, started for the mouth of Cane run, to apprise Bryan's party of their danger. When they came within about a mile of the camp, they heard a number of guns near the place and concluded Bryan's party had fallen in with a gang of Buffaloe; they therefore pushed forward with great speed in the hope of participating in the sport, but before they came up, the firing ceased, and it being a little foggy, the smoke from the guns which had been fired settled down, and produced so great a darkness that Hogan and his party came within a few steps of a party of Indians before they discovered them; the Indians were setting down on their packs, having but a few minutes before fired on Bryan's party, which firing led Hogan to that point. As soon as Hogan's party discovered the Indians, they dismouted and commenced an attack; it was met by the Indians with firmness, and continued about half an hour, when the Indians being hard pressed gave way, and were ultimately and entirely defeated. Hogan lost one man killed and three wounded, the loss of the Indians were not known.[100]

William Bryan and his party met at the mouth of Cane run the preceding evening agreeable to appointment, and encamped there. A little after day that morning, it (being foggy) they heard a bell at some distance, which they recognised to be the bell of the horse led by one of Hogan's party, the day before, and thinking they could not find the mouth of Cane run the over night, had stoped [stopped] a little distance short, the bell sounded by seeming jirks as if on a horse that was hobbled. Bryan, to ascertain the fact, mounted his horse and with Israel Grant rode to where the bell was heard; when they came near the bell, which was among low cane, they were fired on by a number of Indians and both wounded; Bryan through the hip and knee (of which wounds he died) and Israel Grant across the back; they rode off and both escaped falling into the hands of the Indians, and were taken home after the action.[101]

A short time after the above transaction Col. Daniel Boone and his brother Edward, went out to hunt on the waters of Licking. They came across a bear which the Col. shot, the bear run off and Boone followed it down a branch, leaving his brother with the horses; the bear ran but a short distance and fell, Boone had but just got to it before he heard several guns about the place where he had left his brother, and immediately after the yelp of a small dog, coming towards him. Satisfied that his brother was killed, and that the Indians were pursuing him by means of a dog, he betook himself to a cane break, in the hope they would not pursue him further, but he was mistaken. He had not gone far into the cane, before the dog came up with him; upon his turning on the dog he ran back to the Indians when he heard them encourage him forward, and the dog again pursued yelping, by which means he was so closely pursued by the Indians, that he thought his chance doobtful if he could not by some means get clear of the dog; and more especially as he had on a pair of new shoes, which became so slippery that he could scarcely keep his feet when he came on dry leaves. He therefore determined that when the dog approached him again he would endeavour to shoot him, (having loaded his gun before he pursued the bear) accordingly when the dog came up again, he approached nearer to Boone than at any former time, he therefore fired at the dog and luckily killed him; when the Indians came to the dead dog, they gave a horrid yell, and from that moment he heard no more of them; he therefore proceeded more leisurely until he arrived at home. The next day Boone with a party went to the place where he supposed his brother was killed, and found his body which they burried.[102]

Bryan's Station

[November 17, 1826]

Early in August 1782, large detachments of Indian warriors from the Cherokee, Wyandots, Tawas and Pottowatomies, as well as from several other tribes bordering on the lakes, assembled in grand council at Chillicothe, where they were met by Simon Girty and M'Kee, two renegado white men, unprincipled in disposition, and stained with the blood of innocent women and children, their lives were assimilated to the customs and habits of the Indians, from which, and their general knowledge of the white people, they had acquired the confidence of the Indians, were faithful to their interests, and assisted at and were conspicuous in their councils.

Girty in order to inflame the minds of the young warriors against the Kentuckians, took an elevated stand, when he disengaged his arm from his blanket, assumed the attitude of an Orator, and to the painted savage assembly, equipped in all the habillaments of war, delivered the following address:

"BROTHERS.—The fertile region of Kentucky, is the land of cane and clover—spontaneously growing to feed the buffaloe, the elk and the deer; there the bear and the beaver are always fat—the Indians from all the tribes, have had a right from time immemorial, to hunt and kill unmolested these wild animals, and bring off their skins, to purchase for themselves clothing.—To buy blankets for their backs and rum to send down their throats, to drive away the cold and rejoice their hearts after the fatigues of hunting and the toil of war. (great applause from the crowd.) But
"Brothers,
The long knives* have overrun your country, and usurped your hunting grounds—they have destroyed the cane—trodden down the clover—killed the deer and the buffaloe, the bear and the raccoon:—The beaver has been chased from his dam† and forced to leave the country." (palpable emotion among the hearers.)
"Brothers,
The intruders on your lands exult in the success that has crowned

---

*Long knife A name by which the Virginians were designated by the Indians from other white people.
†The beaver builds dams to catch fish, and to secret the avenue to their houses.

their flagitious acts.—They are building cabbins and making roads on the very ground of the Indian camp and war-path.—They are planting fruit trees and ploughing the lands where not long since were the cane break and clover field.—Was there a voice in the trees of the forest, or articulate sounds in the gurgling waters, every part of this country would call on you to chase away these ruthless invaders, who are laying in waste.—Unless you rise in the majesty of your might, and exterminate their whole race, you may bid adieu to the hunting ground of your fathers—to the delicious flesh of the animals with which it once abounded, and to the skins with which you were once enabled to purchase your clothing and your rum."

Inflamed to frenzy with this harrangue, the young warriors expressed their approbation, and evinced their determination to comply with the recommendations of the speaker, by extending an outstretched arm towards Kentucky, (grasping the tomahawk) and sticking it into the ground with a hedious yell. The old warriors signified their approbation by a loud sonorous *Grunt!*[103]

No sooner had Girty concluded his harrangue than the Indians took up the line of march for Kentucky, with the determination first to take Bryan's station, after which to act as circumstances should direct.

Bryan's station contained about forty cabbins, built so as to form a parallelogram of about 200 yards long and 50 wide, and where the houses did not join, the vacancy was filled up with pickets. The angles were strengthened by bolckhouses which answered the purpose of bastions.

On the 15th day of August in the year 1782, this formidable savage army appeared in hostile array before Bryan's station; the inhabitants immediately on the discovery of their approach, closed the gates and made every preparation in their power to defend the place.

Bryan's station or fort,[104] five miles North East from Lexington, became the most exposed point in Kentucky, after the destruction of Ruddle's and Martin's stations in the year 1780. The death of William Bryan who died of a wound received near the mouth of Cane run, so discouraged his friends that they returned to North Carolina, and the greater part of the population from that state, left the fort about the same time, which would have so reduced the strength, as to compel the remainder also to remove, if the fort had not acquired new strength in a number of families from Virginia.—Robert Johnson Esq. the father of the Hon. Richard M. Johnson, with several families of his connexions from the same section of Virginia, removed to Bryan's station, and kept up the strength of the place at what it had been, if not greater than at any former period.[105]

It has been stated that Bryan's station was at that time the most exposed of the settlements in Kentucky, and that was to be ascribed to the residence of the hostile tribes and the guide they found in the Miami rivers on the north west side, and the Licking and Kentucky rivers on the south east of the Ohio. The former served to pilot them to the shores of the Ohio, and the latter served the same purpose to bring them to the vicinity of Bryan's station.—Lexington, Bryan's station, Boon's station, M'Gee's and Stroud's were the only places occupied on the north side of the Kentucky river at the period of the formidable attack on Bryan's,[106] which was conducted so secretly by Simon Girty and his brother James, that the fort was completely surrounded on the night of the 15th of August 1782, while the men, women and children slept quietly, not dreaming of danger until alarmed by the fire of the savages before sun rise, on those who first opened their doors.[107]

The night before, news had been received that Capt. Holder with a party of men from M'Gee's and Stroud's stations, had been defeated, and the greater part of the force from Bryan's were preparing to march to that quarter; and if the Indians had delayed the fire one hour longer, the fort would have been reduced to a mere handful, as the men were on the eve of departing. The greater danger at home now called for united exertions of the whole country. Two men, Nicholas Tomlinson and Thomas Bell, were mounted on good horses, and sent off at the first fire to Lexington, on arriving there the force of that place had gone to Boon's station, on the way to Holder's assistance. Thomlinson and Bell followed and overtook them at Boon's station, where a force of 16 mounted men and about 30 on foot immediately started to the aid of the beseiged fort.—The Indians agreeably to their mode of warfare, attempted to take the fort by a stratigem of the following nature:—It has already been stated, that the fire commenced early in the morning, this firing was by a party of 100 Indians on the south east side or angle of the fort, where the road from Lexington to Paris now passes, about 200 yards from the spot where Mr. Joseph Rogers resides at present.—The great body of the enemy (500) lay concealed in high weeds on the opposite side of the fort, within pistol shot of the spring, from which the supply of water was drawn.

The former practice of this fort was known, and the Indians expected every man to run to the spot where the firing commenced, which would leave it undefended on the side where the main body lay; but the number of guns discharged, and the near approach of the party, convinced the people of the fort that it was a plan to draw the men out, and instead of falling into this trap, every man went to work in reparing the fort, which required picketing in several places, and the women commenced supplying water from the very spring near the ambuscade of the enemy.—And although the Indians lay so near the spring, the women ventured to it from the assurance, that the enemy would remain concealed until the men from the fort fired on the party on the south east side, which was perceived at once to be the plan; accordingly, when a sufficient quantity of water was drawn the fort put in order, and the men at their posts, a party of 13 went out on the direction of the first fire, and soon were convinced of the force of the enemy, by a fire from about 100; and at that moment the ambuscade rushed on the fort, believing the men were engaged on the other side. How they must have been disappointed to find every thing ready to receive them.

A heavy well directed fire from the fort, put the savages to flight, a small body of the most daring reached the fort, and set fire to a few houses and stables, which were consumed; but the rest of the fort and the lives of the people were saved by an easterly wind, which drove the flames from the houses. This defeat about two hours after the first fire in the morning, drove the Indians to a respectful distance.[108]

The enemy, encamped on the bank of the creek where the road now crosses, convenient to the spring, at a place out of sight of the fort.

It was known to the savages that two men had been sent early in the morning on the direction to Lexington, and they formed a party of about 300 of their best warriors at the upper end of the lane leading to Lexington, to intercept the expected reinforcement, on the south east side of the fort. On the right of the present road to Paris, grew a field of more than 100 acres of corn, through which the Indians passed and repassed, from the encampment on the bank of the creek to the party at the head of the lane. At about 2 P.M. the men from Lexington and Boon's station arrived in sight of the fort, at a moment that the firing had ceased, and no indications of danger appeared; this reinforcement believed it had been a false alarm, and the 16 mounted men approached the fort the usual rout along a narrow lane, which was lined for more than 100 yards by the enemy on both sides, who commenced a fire unperceived at a few feet distance. It is believed the great dust which was raised by the horses feet, in a considerable degree protected the party; they got safe into the fort without the slightest wound on man or horse, but the party on foot were less fortunate. They were approaching through the large corn field on the right and could have passed into the fort unseen by the savages, but on hearing the firing at the head of the lane on their comrades, they ran to their aid without reflecting that from the number of guns that the force was an over match for them. When they reached the head of the lane, the mounted men were gone, and the enemy were in great force between them and the fort, augmenting every moment from the camp on the bank of the creek. A sharp firing commenced, and nothing but the thickness of the corn saved this party of 30 brave men from destruction; two only were killed and four wounded. The white men separated & sought safety in flight and the force of their rifles, in many instances where parties of 6 or 8 Indians were pursuing one man, they were kept off by a knowledge of the danger of approaching a man with a gun in his hand, supposed to be loaded. James Girty, with half a dozen savage brethren, pushed on one of the white men so hard, that he fired, and Girty fell, which stopped the rest of the party, and saved the man from certain death. Unfortunately for many suffering victims who fell by the hands, or by the influence of this monster, he had bound to the strap of his powder horn, a piece of leather, just stolen from the tan vats, the folds of which saved him—and he only received a severe shock, which brought him to the ground. Mr. John Sharp, the father of the present jailor of Fayette, was of this party, and too infirm to make his escape, if he had not been able to keep the Indians in pursuit at bay, from fear of his rifle, until he reached a thicket of cane.

In the evening the cattle and stock attempted to return, as usual, to the fort, and were mostly killed; the few sheep were totally destroyed.

A little after sun set, Simon Girty approached under cover of a thick growth of hemp, to a large stump of a tree, which stood about the spot where the dwelling house of Mr. Rogers now stands, and hailed the fort— demanding a surrender, stating, that the forces were commanded by him, and enquired if he was known to the people of the fort.—He declared that the prisoners should be protected if they would surrender, which was out of his power if the place was taken by storm, as it would be that night, on the arrival of his cannon and strong reinforcements, which were hourly expected. This language from Girty, and the recollection by the people in the fort, that cannon were employed in the reduction of Ruddle's and Martin's stations, was calculated to create considerable alarm. It was so handsomely parried by Aaron Reynolds, a young man remarkable for wit and sprightliness, that in justice to this individual his name is mentioned, as it will be hereafter, in a noble act at the battle of the Blue Licks, a few days after. Mr. Reynolds observing the discouraging influence of Girty's lofty commanding address, took the liberty of replying to him. In the first place Mr. Reynolds admitted the name of Girty was so well known, and held in such detestation, that he had named a worthless dog after him; and as to reinforcements, that the fort would receive a strong one in time to meet the cowardly army commanded by him. For his part, he felt so little concern or apprehension from such an enemy, that he considered it disgraceful to use fire-arms in repelling him, and should in the event of any of his party breaking into the fort, resort to switches, which he had no doubt would be sufficient to drive the naked rascals from the country. Girty took great offence at the levity and want of politeness of his adversary, and pretended to deplore the consequences resulting from such obstinacy, and left his position very quickly. During the night a small party was left to keep up occasional firing, but the main body marched off in great haste to the lower Blue Licks, where a battle the most distressing that Kentucky had ever witnessed, occurred in a few days.[109]

In recapitulating the preceding attack, there are some very singular circumstances, worthy of attention. The firing in the morning was in time to prevent the march of nearly all the men to a distant point, & the enemy so far overrated their plan, that instead of drawing the men out, every one prepared for a siege, and although there were more than one hundred guns discharged, not a solitary person was touched; the singular circumstances of the wind springing up from the east and saving the place from the flames; the fortunate passing out and return of Tomlinson and Bell, the two expresses; and the passage of sixteen mounted men through a fire of several hundred Indians unhurt—all these things are singular. There were 560 Indians and about 60 Cannadians and tories, forming an army of more than 600, to fight 42 men. The whole number in the fort was 44 men, but two were sent off as expresses, and two were killed in the fort. The persons killed were Mitchell and Atkinson; and ††Tomlinson slightly wounded in the arm, after his return from the express. The loss of the Indians was very considerable, but the precise number not known.[110]

SECTION 14

Tragedy at the Blue Licks
[November 24, 1826]

The Blue Licks, remarkable for the sanguinary battle fought in its vicinity, is situated about 40 miles from Lexington, and about 35 from Bryan's Station. The Licking river at this place is about 300 feet wide, at common water, and forms a semi elipsis, which embraces on its N E side, towards Limestone, a great ridge of rocks which had been made bare by the stamping of buffaloe and other game, drawn together from time immemorial, to drink the water and lick the clay.—Two deep ravines, heading in this ridge near each other, and extending in opposite directions, formed the longest diameter of this elipsis. This ridge had very little timber on it, and what it had was very indifferent, and exhibited a dreary appearance;

††Nicholas Tomlinson continued one of the most active defenders of this country, and was employed in Harmer's expedition in 1790, as a spy—at the defeat of a detachment of the army under Col. John Hardin, on the Oglaze, Tomlinson being in advance, was literally shot to pieces by an ambuscade of more than one thousand Indians.

but the ravines were furnished not only plentifully with timber, but with thick brushwood also.[111]

Shortly after the Indians left Bryan's Station, the men at Lexington, Harrodsburgh, and Boonsborough, assembled at that place, to the number of 160, and determined to pursue them immediately—and on the 18th of August, Col. John Todd of Lexington, and Colonel Stephen Trigg, took the command. These men, well armed and accoutered, were skilful marksmen, and animated with an ardent desire to chastise the insolence of these savage invaders of their settlements.—Col. Boone encouraged the expedition by his presence. This force was very small, compared with the number of the enemy; but so eager were they in the pursuit, that they could not be prevailed on to await the arrival of Col. Logan, who was known to be collecting all the force at his station to join them.[112]

It requires no strong effort of the imagination, to pourtray the affecting scene produced by the departure of these brave men. The forebodings of the mother—the misgivings of the wife—the sighs of the parents—the solicitude and tears of congenial affection, strongly marked the feelings of almost every individual.

Every preparation having been made, the army commenced their march on the route the Indians had taken, but had not proceeded more than nine or ten miles, before the lynx-eyed Boone discovered certain signs on their route indicating a willingness on the part of the Indians, that they should be pursued, which was plainly evinced by their leaving a plain trail. Notwithstanding, they evidently used every means in their power, to conceal their number, for which purpose they marched in single file, treading in each others footsteps.

After a very fatiguing march, this gallant band reached the South bank of Licking river, at the lower Blue Licks, without having seen a single Indian. On the arrival of the front of the party at the river, they discovered Indians on the ridge on the opposite side, who without manifesting any symptoms of fear, retired leisurely over the hills out of their sight. Upon this discovery, a halt was ordered, and a council of the principal officers held, in order to determine the most prudent course to be pursued. In this critical moment, the age and great experience of Col. Daniel Boone in Indian warfare, insensibly attracted the attention of every one present, to solicit his advice at this perilous moment, to obtain which, Col. Todd addressed Col. Boone as follows:

"Skilled in Indian warfare, and familiar with the ground in the vicinity of this place, we require your opinion on the expediency of attacking the enemy in their present position." To which Col. Boone replied: "I am of opinion, and indeed fully persuaded, that the enemy exceed us in number fully three hundred—that their main body is at no great distance, and that they are lying in ambush. Their position is equal to an host, should we continue our march, and be drawn in between the ravines they occupy.—I therefore advise, that we divide our gallant band—that one half march up the river on this side and cross over at Elk creek, fall upon the upper side of the ravine—whist the other half take a position (to co-operate with them) in another quarter. By this means the great advantage of their position will be changed effectually in our favour. But gentlemen, "continued Boone, "whatever may be your ultimate decision, I caution you against crossing the river at any rate, before spies have reconnoitered the ground." [113]

A deep silence ensued, and the superior officers seemed to acquiesce in the salutary advice of Colonel Boone, when Maj. Hugh M'Gary, remarkable for the impetuosity of his temper, exclaimed, "Delay is dastardly! Let all who are not cowards follow me, and I will show them the Indians," so saying he spured his horse forward into the river. [114]

The rashness of M'Gary was contagious. He was followed in quick succession by the whole party, who crossed the river in great disorder and confusion, whilst the officers were reluctantly borne along in the tumult. After crossing the river, no authority was exercised, nor any order observed in the line of march, but every one rushed forward tumultuously pursuing the road over the bare rocks, to the end of the ridge of hills, where a forest of oaks, deep ravines with underwood, concealed the enemy from view, who waited in their ambuscade to receive them.

M'Gary led the van of the army, closely followed by Major Harlan, and Capt. Wm. M'Bride, supported by the men on horseback, when Girty, with a chosen part of his tawny host, rushed forth from their covert, and with horrid shrieks and yells, attacked them with great impetuosity. The conflict instantly became hot and sanguinary. The advantageous position occupied by the Indians, enabled them to assail the whole of the whites at the same moment, and from the confused manner in which the approach was made, soon turned their right wing, and a retreat was the inevitable consequence, and that too, under the immediate edge of the tomahawk. Cols. Todd and Trigg, and Maj. Harlan, fell early in the action, whilst many brave officers and men fell under them. [115]

The survivors attempted to gain the river at the ford, some on foot and some on horseback; but the Indians so managed, as to prevent a great part of them, by getting between them and the ford, forcing them into the river below, where it could only be crossed by swimming. As most of the fugitives aimed to gain the ford, the Indians pressed their principal force to that point, where the greatest carnage took place, and where many were tomahawked in the river. It was at this moment that Benjamin Netherland,* whose personal bravery had by some been doubted, not only gave evidence to the contrary, by assuming the office of a commander, called aloud to his flying companions, as they arrived on the

*Major *Netherland* now living in Nicholasville.

South side of the river, to HALT! and fire on the enemy; which order many obeyed, and thereby arrested the pursuit for a few moments, which enabled many who were almost exhausted, to escape from the hatchet suspended over their devoted heads.

Brave or benevolent actions should never be permitted to pass unnoticed by the historian: It is therefore with pleasure this opportunity is embraced to perpetuate the conduct of the gallant AARON REYNOLDS. He was a young, active man, in the prime of life, and when the retreat took place, was on horseback; on his way to the ford, he overtook Col. Robert Patterson, who though not an old man, was infirm, having suffered very much from wounds which he had received from the Indians on a former occasion. When Reynolds overtook him, he was entirely exhausted, and the Indians in close pursuit—Reynolds, with a greatness of soul which will forever redound to his honour, dismounted from his horse, and assisted Patterson into the saddle, and risked his own safety on foot. He crossed the river by swimming, some distance below the ford, when he discovered many Indians had also crossed. He had on a pair of buck-skin overalls, which became so heavy from the water they had absorbed in crossing the river that on getting on shore, he sat down to pull them off, and whilst in the act of doing so, three Indians came to him and took him prisoner. At that moment several white men passed in sight, when Reynolds was left in the possession of one of his captors, whilst the other two pursued the white men. One of the moccasins of the Indian with whom Reynolds was left, became untied, and the Indian stooping down to tie it, Reynolds sprang from him, and being an active man, was soon out of danger.[116]

It is supposed that one fourth at least, of the men who fought the battle of the Blue Licks on the 19th day of August, 1782, were commissioned officers. The whole number was 176, out of whom 61 were killed, and 8 taken prisoners. Among the most prominent who fell, were Colonels John Todd, Stephen Trigg; Majors Silas Harlan, Edward Bulger; Captains John Gordon, and Wm. M'Bride, together with Isaac Boone, a son of Col. Daniel Boone, &c. &c. The loss on the part of the Indians, was never rightly ascertained. By some it was said to be 90, but that calculation is very improbable, as the whites stood but a very few minutes before they were compelled to retreat.

Despatches had been sent to Col. Benj. Logan in Lincoln county, during the siege at Bryan's Station, which preceded the battle of the Blue Licks only two days. Col. Logan hastily collected about 300 men and marched for the relief of that place; but before Col. Logan reached Bryan's Station, the Indians had raised the siege and were gone.[117] Col. Logan followed as fast as possible, with the hope of coming up with those who marched from the neighborhood of Lexington, before they overtook the Indians; but met them not far from Bryan's on their return. Logan continued on to the battle ground, with the view at least of burying the dead, if he could not chastise the enemy. Col. Logan was joined by many of the friends of the killed and missing from Lexington and Bryan's Station, and arrived on the fatal ground on the 25th. A solemn silence pervaded the whole party as they approached the field of battle. No sound was uttered but the cry of the gorged vulture hovering over their heads. Those who were drawn by affection to the horrid spectacle, with the hope of saving some relic of hair or garment from a lost father, brother or friend, were denied this favour. The remains of the mangled bodies were so distended by the excessive heat of the weather, or so disfigured by the tomahawk, vultures and wild beasts, that it was impossible to distinguish one individual from another.

The solemn rites of sepulture were performed in a very rude manner. The ground was so rocky, that without spades or shovels, it was with great difficulty a quantity of earth could be collected sufficient to cover the mangled remains of the slain.[118]

SECTION 15

Retaliation and a Step toward Statehood

[December 1, 1826]

The Kentuckians were not long in making preparations to revenge their loss at the Blue Licks. All seemed to breathe the same spirit of revenge, and determination of carrying ruin and devastation into the Indian settlements. Gen. Clarke was vested with the chief command, and Col. Logan was chosen the second of the forces about to be raised, and who were to rendezvous at the mouth of Licking, on the Ohio river.[119]

About the last of September, 1782, Gen. Clarke with about 1000 men, took up his line of march from the Ohio opposite the mouth of Licking, for the Indian towns situated on the Miamies. On their march, they fell on the camp of Simon Girty and his party, who would have been taken completely by surprize, but for a straggling Indian, who discovered the Kentuckians in time to give the Indians notice of their approach, upon which Girty and his party evacuated their camp and fled in every direction, spreading the alarm of the appearance of any army from Kentucky. As the Kentuckians approached the town, the Indians retreated into the woods, declining an engagement. All the cabbins at the Chillicothe towns, Piqua and Wills, were burnt. During this expedition, some skirmishing took place, in which five Indians were killed and seven made prisoners, without the loss of one man, and but one, (William M'Cracken) slightly wounded in the arm, of which wound he died. During this expedition an Indian warrior of distinction surrendered himself a prisoner, who was afterwards inhumanly murdered by one of the Kentuckians, much to the mortification of Gen. Clarke.[120]

In the month of October a party of Indians approached a house near the Crab Orchard, in which there was a negro man, a white woman and three small children: one of the Indians rushed into the house and made at the negro, a little girl instantly shut the door, which she fastened so as to prevent another from entering. The negro seized the Indian who had entered, and threw him down, when the white woman seizing an axe which happened to be in the house, beat out his brains. The Indians on the outside of the house attempted to break through the door with their tomahawks, but could not effect it, before a party of armed men who accidently saw the Indians going towards the house, followed them, and came up in time to prevent them from breaking the door. As soon as they discovered the white men approaching they ran off.[121]

On the night of the 1st of September, 1782, a party of Indians broke into Kincheloe's Station on Salt river, whilst the people were asleep, and killed seven, and no doubt would have killed or taken the whole, had not the darkness of the night favoured their escape. A man by the name of Thompson Randolph defended his family with great bravery, and it was believed killed several Indians. His wife with an infant in her arms were killed by his side—with their remaining child he got into the loft of his cabbin, and made his escape through the roof; but as he jumped from the roof to the ground, he was attacked by two Indians, one of which he stabed, and the other he struck with his empty gun, upon which they both left him.[122]

Several women and children, after they were made prisoners, were tomahawked. A Mrs. Bland, who was made a prisoner, escaped from the Indians the second day after she was taken, and rambled through the woods for 18 days, subsisting on grapes and walnuts. She was accidently found by some hunters, and taken to Lynn's station. A Mrs. Polk, with four children, were taken prisoners at the same time—she was far advanced in pregnancy, and was compelled to walk until she became entirely exhausted, when her captor was about to kill her—she was saved by another Indian, who took her and two of her children to Detroit, where she was kindly used, and where by the influence of the officers, she obtained her other two children. Her husband, who was not at home when she was taken, and to whom she wrote from Detroit, went for her, and brought her and her five children safe back to Kentucky.[123]

The first political arrangements made in Kentucky, and which were afterwards so matured as to produce a separation from the State of Virginia, originated with Colonel Benjamin Logan, afterwards Gen. Logan.[124]

In 1784, there were only three counties in Kentucky, viz: Fayette, Jefferson and Lincoln. Lincoln county comprized in its limits all the lands lying South of the Kentucky river, and East and South of a line beginning on the Kentucky river at the mouth of Benson's Big Creek; running up the same and its main fork to its head; thence South to the nearest waters of Hammond's creek; thence South to Green river, and down the same to its junction with the Ohio.[125] Col. Benj. Logan then held the first military appointment in that county, under the title of County Lieutenant. In the November of this year he received intelligence from the Cherokees, that some hostile tribes meditated and were preparing for the invasion of Kentucky. It may be proper here to mention, that this project was afterwards abandoned by the Indians, nothing having been done in pursuance of it, except the murder of a few emigrants on the wilderness road. But the intelligence as received by Col. Logan, was sufficient alarm to authorize the most vigorous measures. He therefore convened a number of the inhabitants of the district at Danville, which was then the principal town in Kentucky, and communicated to them the information he had received. To them as well as him it seemed to demand the immediate undertaking of an expedition. But from adopting such a measure they were prevented by difficulties utterly insurmountable. No man or set of men in the district were invested with the authority to call the militia into service. Ammunition sufficient for the expedition was not in the district: what was there was private property, and there existed no authority to purchase on the behalf of government—no funds to pay for it, and no power to take it for the public use. There was the same want of power as to procuring provisions; and if the militia would have served voluntarily, and could have furnished themselves with arms, ammunition, and every thing necessary, no person was authorized to assure them that government would ever pay them for their services, or ever reimburse their expenditures; for as it would be an expedition unwarranted by law, government might thereafter censure it as an act of merit or criminality, as sympathy might dictate or prejudice suggest.[126]

In this crisis of anarchy within and hostility without, the citizens convened at Danville, recommended to the people at large to elect one representative from each militia company in the district, to meet on the

27th of December at that place, to devise if possible, some means of preserving their country from that immediate destruction which seemed then impending.[127]

The measure thus recommended was adopted. Elections were held; and the persons elected convened at the time and place appointed; and after deliberating on the state of the country for about ten days, resolved that many inconveniences under which they labored might be removed by the Legislature of Virginia. But that the great and substantial evils to which they were subjected, arose from causes beyond the power or controul of that government, viz: from their remote and detached situation, and could never be redressed until the district had a government of its own. The constitution of Virginia had made provision for the erection of one or more governments in the western territory, when occasion might require.[128]

In pursuance of the above resolution, the convention recommended the election of members in every county, to meet in another convention to be held at the same place on the 23rd of May following, whose deliberations were to be directed peculiarly to the propriety of making application to the legislature of Virginia, for permission to become an independent state. The time fixed on for holding these elections, was the court days in the month of April, as this was likewise the legal election day for members of assembly. It was considered that the people would be generally collected, received full information of the question to be discussed, and be completely represented in the convention.[129]

Members were elected pursuant to the recommendation, who met in Danville at the time appointed; and on the ninth day of their deliberations, passed the following resolutions:

"*Resolved unanimously, as the opinion of this Committee,* That a petition be presented to the Assembly, praying that the said district may be established into a state, separate from Virginia.

"*Resolved unanimously,* That this district, when established into a state, ought to be taken into union with the United States of America, and enjoy equal privileges in common with the said states.

"*Resolved,* That this Convention recommend it to their constituents, to elect deputies to their respective counties, to meet at Danville on the second Monday in August next, to serve in convention, and to continue by adjournment till the first day of April next, to take further under their consideration the state of the district.

"*Resolved unanimously,* That the election of deputies for the proposed convention, ought to be on the principles of equal representation.

"*Resolved,* That the petition to the assembly for establishing this district into a state, and the several resolves of the former and present convention, upon which the petition is founded, together with all other matters relative to the interest of the district, that have been under their consideration, be referred to the future convention, that such further measures may be taken thereon as they shall judge proper." [130]

SECTION 16

The Resolution to Achieve Statehood
[December 8, 1826]

"To the Honourable the General Assembly of Virginia.
    "The petition of a convention of the inhabitants of the District of Kentucky, begun and held at Danville, in Lincoln county, on Monday the twenty-third day of May, 1785:
    "HUMBLY SHEWETH,
    'That your petitioners having been deputed by the people, pursuant to the recommendation of a late convention, to take into consideration the propriety and expediency of making application to the legislature for having this district established into a separate state, to be taken into union with the United States; (as also the several grievances stated by that convention; and to adopt such measure, thereon, and whatever else might come before them) as should appear most conducive to its interests are unanimously of opinion—that the remote situation of the district from the seat of government, together with sundry other inconveniences, subjects the good people thereof to a number of grievances too pressing to be longer borne, and which cannot be remedied whilst the district continues a part of the state of Virginia; conceiving it to be not only the privilege, but the duty of all men to seek happiness by entering into any form of civil society, not injurious to others, that they may judge most conducive to this great end; at the same time being anxiously desirous to cultivate the most perfect harmony with our brethren in the other parts of the state, and when we are under the necessity of being separated from the parent, whose fostering hand we gratefully acknowledge, has for-

merly been extended to our infant settlements; wishing nothing more devoutly, than that her blessing may ever attend us: therefore, we are induced to pray, that agreeable to the provisional clause in the constitution, the district of Kentucky may be established into a separate and independent state, to be known by the name of the Commonwealth of Kentucky; which we wish to take place under the following regulations, to wit:

That as soon as may be after the said state is established, a convention be authorized to assemble and adopt a constitution and form of government; that the several acts of assembly which may be in force at the time of separation, together with the common law of England, all statutes or acts of Parliament, made in aid of the common law, prior to the fourth year of the reign of James the first, which are of a general nature, not local to that kingdom nor repealed or altered by the legislature of Virginia, continue to be the rule of decision, and be considered as in full force, so far as they are applicable to the district until the same shall be altered by the legislative power of the commonwealth of Kentucky; and that as soon as conveniently may be, after the district is established into a state, an equal number of commissioners from Virginia and the said state, be appointed and authorised to settle and adjust the proportion of the state debt to be paid by each; and if the commissioners cannot agree, that the difference be referred to and settled by Congress, as provided by the articles of confederation and perpetual union.

Finally, we hope and expect that our representatives will cheerfully grant a request justified by the principles of our government, as well as by the necessities of our condition; and that by an act of separation we shall be placed in the situation best adapted for attaining the advantages of a free and well regulated government; and that we shall likewise be recommended to Congress to be taken into union with the United States of America, to enjoy equal privileges in common with them.

"And your petitioners shall ever pray, &c."[131]

> "To the inhabitants of the District of Kentucky.

"Friends and Fellow Citizens,

"We your representatives, met in convention, in consequence of our appointment, beg leave to address you on a subject which we consider of the last importance to you, to ourselves, and to unborn posterity. In every case where it becomes necessary for one part of the community to separate from the other; duty to Almighty God, and a decent respect to the opinions of mankind, require that the causes which impel them thereto, should be clearly and impartially set forth.

We hold it as a self evident truth, that government is ordered for the ease and protection of the governed: and whenever these ends are not attained by one form of government: it is the right, it is the duty of the people, to seek such other mode, as will be most likely to ensure to themselves and their posterity, those blessings to which by nature they are entitled.

"In the course of our enquiries, we find that several laws have passed the legislature of Virginia, which, although of a general nature, yet in their operation are particularly oppressive to the people of this district; and we also find, that from our local situation, we are deprived of many benefits of government, which every citizen therein has a right to expect; as a few facts will sufficiently demonstrate.

"We have no power to call out the militia, our sure and only defence to oppose the wicked machinations of the savages, unless in cases of actual invasion.

"We can have no executive power in the district, either to enforce the execution of laws, or to grant pardons to objects of mercy; because such a power would be inconsistent with the policy of government, and contrary to the present constitution.

"We are ignorant of the laws that are passed until a long time after they are enacted; and in many instances, not until they have expired: by means whereof penalties may be inflicted for offences never designed, and delinquents escape the punishment due to their crimes.

"We are subjected to prosecute suits in the High Court of Appeals at Richmond, under every disadvantage, for the want of evidence, want of friends, and want of money.

"Our money must necessarily be drawn from us, not only for the support of civil government, but by individuals, who are frequently under the necessity of attending on the same.

"Nor is it possible for the inhabitants of this district, at so remote a distance from the seat of government, ever to derive equal benefits with the citizens in the eastern parts of the state; and this inconvenience must increase as our country becomes more populous.

"Our commercial interest can never correspond with, or be regulated by theirs, and in case of any invasion, the state of Virginia can afford us no adequate protection, in comparison with, the advantages we might, (if a separate state,) derive from the *Federal union*.

"On maturely considering truths of such great importance to every inhabitant of the district, with a firm persuasion that we were consulting the general good of our infant country, we have unanimously resolved, 'that it is expedient and necessary for this district to be separated from Virginia, and established into a sovereign independent state, to be known by the name of the "commonwealth of Kentucky," and taken into union with the United States of America.' In order to effect this purpose we have agreed on a petition, to be presented to the Legislature of Virginia, at their next session, praying that a separation may take place; in which petition are fully set forth such terms as we thought beneficial to our infant country, and not inconsistent for Virginia to grant.

"It is generally admitted that this district ought at some period not for [far] distant, to be separated from the government of Virginia.

"The only question then is, whether we are now of sufficient ability, either to fill the different offices of government, or to provide for its support? In answer to the first part of this objection, examples have taught us, that sound principles and plain sense suffice for every laudable purpose of government; and we generally find that the liberty of the subject and the laws of the land, are in the highest reverence, at the foundation and rise of states, before the morals of the people have been vitiated by wealth and licentiousness, and their understandings entangled in visionary refinements and chimerical distinctions: and as to the latter part, we have now in our power several valuable funds, which, if by *procrastination* we suffer to be exhausted, we shall be stripped of every resource but internal taxation and that under every disadvantage: and therefore we do not hesitate to pronounce it as our opinion, that the present is preferable to any future period.

"By an act of the last session of assembly, we find, that the revenue law is now fully and immediately to be in force within the district, so that we shall not only pay a very considerable part of the tax for supporting the civil government of Virginia, but also be obliged to support our supreme court, and every other office we need in the district, at our own charge; and we are of opinion, that the additional expence of the salaries to a governor, council, treasurer and delegates to congress, will for a number of years be more than saved out of the funds before alluded to, without any additional tax on the people.

"To impress you still more with a sense of our regard to your interests, as a free people, we have determined not to proceed in [a] matter of such magnitude, without a repeated appeal to your opinions; we have therefore recommended the election of another convention, to meet at Danville on the second Monday in August next, to take further into consideration the state of the district, and the resolves of this and the preceeding convention. In this election we hope you will be actuated by a serious sense of the important objects, which the proposed election is designed to promote.

"Ordered, That the clerk of the convention transmit one copy of the petition and one copy of the address now agreed on, to the clerks of the several courts in the district, with a request that they be set up at their respective court-house doors.

"Ordered, That the resolve of this convention, fixing the time of holding the several elections in the district, be annexed at the foot of the copies of the two addresses which are to be transmitted to the clerks of the several courts.

"Resolved, That the number of members for each country, be as follows; for the county of Jefferson, six—for the country of Nelson, six—for the county of Lincoln, ten—for the county of Fayette, eight: and that the elections be held on the July court day of each county, at the courthouse."[132]

Extracts from the Journals of the Conventions held on
Monday, the 8th day of August, 1785.

"The convention, according to the order of the day, resolved itself into a committee of the whole on the state of the district, and after some time spent therein, Mr. President resumed the chair, and Mr. Muter reported that the committee had had under consideration the matters to them recommitted, and had made several amendments, which having read in his place, and afterwards delivered in at the clerk's table; where the same were again read and agreed to, as follows, viz.

"Your committee having maturely considered the important subject to them referred, are of opinion that the situation of this district, upwards of five hundred miles from the seat of the present government, with the intervention of a mountainous desart of two hundred miles passable only at particular seasons, and never without danger from hostile nations of savages, precludes every idea of a connection on republican principles, and originates many grievances; among which we reckon the following:

"1st. It destroys every possibility of application to the supreme executive power, for support or protection in cases of emergency, and thereby *subjects the district to continued hostilities and depredations of the savages;* relaxes the execution of the laws, delays justice, and tends to loosen and dissever the bonds of government.

"2nd. It suspends the operation of the benign influence of mercy, by subjecting condemned persons, who may be deemed worthy of pardon, to tedious, languishing and destructive imprisonment.

"3rd. It renders difficult and precarious the exercise of the first and dearest right of freemen—adequate representation—as no person properly qualified, can be expected, at the hazard of his life, to undergo the fatigue of long journies, and to incur burthensome expences, by devoting himself to the public service.

"4th. It subjects us to penalties, and inflictions which arise from ignorance of the laws, many of which have their operation and expire before they reach the district.

"5th. It renders a compliance with many of the duties required of sheriffs and clerks, impracticable; and exposes those officers, under the present revenue law, to inevitable destruction.

"6th. It subjects the inhabitants to expensive and ruinous suits in the High Court of Appeals, and places the unfortunate poor, and men of mediocrity completely in the power of the opulent.

"Other grievances result from partial and retrospective laws, which are contrary to the fundamental rights of freemen:—such are, 1st, the laws for the establishment and support of the district court, which, at the same time that we are subject to a general tax for the support of the civil list, and the erection of public buildings, oblige us to build our own court-houses, jail and other buildings by a special poll-tax imposed upon the inhabitants of the district, and leaves several officers of the court without any certain provision.

"2d. The law imposing a tax of five shillings per hundred acres, on lands previously sold, and directing the payment thereof into the regis-ter's office at Richmond, before the patent shall issue: the same principles which sanctify this law, would authorise the legislature to impose five pounds per acre on lands previously sold by government on stipulated conditions, and for which an equivalent hath been paid; and is equally subversive of justice as any of the statutes of the British parliament, that impelled the good people of America to arms.

"3d. General laws, partial and injurious in their operation: such are the laws. 1st.—concerning entries and surveys on the western waters. 2d. Concerning the appointments of sheriffs. 3d. For punishing certain offences injurious to the tranquility of this commonwealth,—which last law prohibits, while we experience all the calamities which flow from the predatory incursions of hostile savages, from attempting any offensive operation: a savage, unrestrained by any law, human or divine, despoils our property, murders our fellow-citizens, then makes his escape to the north-west side of the Ohio is protected by this law.

"Whereas all men are born equally free and independent, and have certain natural, inherent and unalienable rights; among which are the enjoying and defending life and liberty, acquiring, possessing and pro-tecting property, and pursuing and obtaining happiness and safety.

"Resolved therefore, That it is the indispensible duty of this conven-tion, as they regard the prosperity and happiness of their constituents, themselves and posterity, to make application to the general assembly, at the ensuing session, for an act to separate this district from the present government forever, on terms honourable to both and injurious to nei-ther; in order that it may enjoy all the advantages, privileges and immu-nities of a free, sovereign and independent republic.

"Unanimously agreed to by all the members present, whose names are hereto annexed: Mr. Saml. M'Dowell, President, Mr. George Muter, Mr. Christopher Irvin, Mr. William Kennedy, Mr. Benjamin Logan, Mr. Caleb Wallace, Mr. Harry Innes, Mr. John Edwards, Mr. James Speed, Mr. James Wilkinson, Mr. James Garrard, Mr. Levi Todd, Mr. John Coburn, Mr. James Trotter, Mr. John Craig, Mr. Robert Patterson, Mr. Richard Terrell, Mr. George Wilson, Mr. Benjamin Sebastian, Mr. Philip Barbour, Mr. Isaac Cox, Mr. Isaac Morrison, Mr. Andrew Hynes, Mr. Mathew Watson, Mr. James Morrison, and Mr. James Rogers."[133]

"To the Honorable General Assembly of Virginia"

[December 15, 1826]

The Convention which met on the 8th day of Aug. 1785, recommended to the officers of the militia, to meet in their respective counties, and concert such plans as they should deem expedient for the defence of the country. They also drafted a memorial to the Legislature of Virginia, on the state of the country, and another to the inhabitants of the District of Kentucky, of which the following are copies:

"To the Honourable General Assembly of Virginia.
"GENTLEMEN—The subscribers resident in the county of Jefferson, Fayette, Lincoln and Nelson, composing the district of Kentucky, being chosen at free elections held in these counties respectively by the free men of the same, for the purpose of constituting a convention to take into consideration, the general state of the district, and expressly to decide on the expediency of making application to your honourable body, for an act of separation—deeply impressed with the importance of the measure, and breathing the purest filial affection, beg leave to address you on the momentous occasion.

"The settlers of this distant region, taught by the arrangements of Providence, and encouraged by the conditions of that solemn compact for which they paid the price of blood, to look forward to a separation from the eastern parts of the commonwealth; have viewed the subject leisurely at a distance, and examined it with caution on its near approach:— irreconcileable as has been their situation to a connexion with any community beyond the Appalachian mountains other than the federal union; manifold as have been the grievances flowing therefrom, which have grown with their growth and increased with their population; they have patiently waited the hour of redress, nor even ventured to raise their voices in their own cause until youth quickening into manhood, hath given them vigour and stability.

"To recite minutely the causes and reasoning which have directed, and will justify this address, would, we conceive, be a matter of impropriety at this juncture. It would be preposterous for us to enter upon

the support of facts and consequences, which we presume are incontesti-
ble; our sequestered situation from the seat of government, with the
intervention of a mountainous desert of two hundred miles, always
dangerous, and passable only at particular seasons, precludes every idea
of a connexion on republican principles: The patriots who formed our
constitution, sensible of the impracticability of connecting permanently in
a free government, the extensive limits of the commonwealth, most
wisely made provision for the act which we now solicit.

"To that sacred record we appeal.—'Tis not the ill-directed or incon-
siderate zeal of a few, 'tis not that impatience of power to which ambitious
minds are prone; nor yet the baser considerations of personal interests,
which influences the people of Kentucky; directed by superior motives,
they are incapable of cherishing a wish unfounded in justice; and are now
impelled by expanding evils, and irremediable grievances, universally
seen, felt and acknowledged, to obey the irresistible dictates of self-
preservation, and seek for happiness by means honorable to themselves,
honorable to you, and injurious to neither.

"We therefore, with the consent, and by the authority of our constituents, after the most solemn deliberation, being warned of every consequence which can ensue, for them, for ourselves, and for posterity
unborn—do pray that an act may pass at the ensuing session of assembly,
declaring and acknowledging the sovereignty and independence of this
district.

"Having no object in view but the acquisition of that security and
happiness which may be attained by scrupulous adherence to principles
of private justice, and public honor; we should most willingly at this time
enter into the adjustment of the concessions which are to be the condition
of our separation, did not our relative situation forbid such negociation,
the separation we request being suggested by necessity and being con-
sonant to every principle of reason and justice, we are persuaded will be
cheerfully granted, and that we shall be as cheerfully received into the
continental union on the recommendation of our parent state.

"Our application may excite a new spectacle in the history and politics
of mankind. A sovereign power solely intent to bless its people, agreeing
to a dismemberment of its parts, in order to secure the happiness of the
whole; and we fondly flatter ourselves, from motives not purely local, it is
to give birth to that catalogue of great events which we persuade ourselves
are to diffuse throughout the world, the inestimable blessings, which
mankind may derive from the American revolution.

"We firmly rely that the undiminished lustre of that spark which
kindled the flame of liberty, and guided the United States of America to
peace and independence, will direct the honorable body to whom we
appeal for redress of manifest grievances, to embrace the singular occasion reserved for them by divine providence, to originate a precedent

which may liberalize the policy of nations, and lead to the emancipation of enslaved millions.

"In this address we have discarded the complimentary style of adulation and insincerity. It becomes freemen, when speaking to freemen, to employ the plain, manly, unadorned language of independence, supported by conscious rectitude.

"*Resolved*, That two commissioners be appointed to have the address now agreed on preferred to the next general assembly, and to use their endeavors to give it success."

George Muter and Harry Innis, Esqs: were unanimously appointed commissioners to have the address now agreed on preferred to the next general assembly.

"To the inhabitants of the District of Kentucky.
"Friends and Countrymen—Your representatives in Convention having completed the important business for which they were specially elected, feel it their duty before they rise, to call your attention to the calamities with which our country appears to be threatened; *blood has been spilt from the eastern to western extremity of the District;* accounts have been given to the convention from Post St. Vincennes, which indicate a disposition in the savages for general war; in the meantime if we look nearer home, we shall find our borders infested, and constant depreadations commited on our property. Whatever may be the remote designs of the savages, there are causes sufficient to rouse our attention, that we may be prepared not only to defend, and punish those who unprovoked offend us. God and nature have given us the power and we shall stand condemned in the eyes of Heaven and mankind, if we do not employ it, to redress our wrongs and assert our rights. The Indians are now reconoitering our settlements in order that they may hereafter direct their attacks with more certain effect, and we seem patiently to await the strike of the tomahawk; strange indeed it is that although we can hardly pass a spot, which does not remind us of the murder of a father, a brother or a deceased friend, we should take no simple step for our own preservation, have we forgot the surprise of Bryan's Station, destruction of Kinchloe's Station, let us ask you? Ask yourselves, what there is to prevent a repetition of such barbarous scenes? Five hundred Indians might be conducted undiscovered, to our very threshold, and the knife may be put to the throats of our sleeping wives and children. For shame—let us rouse from our lethargy, let us arm, associate and embody—let us call upon our officers to do their duty, and determine to hold in detestation and abhorence, and to treat as enemies to the community, every person who shall withhold his countenance and support of such measures as may be recommended for our common defence;—let it be remembered that a stand must be made somewhere; not to support our present frontier would be the hight of

cruelty as well as folly; for should it give way, those who now hug themselves in security, will take the front of danger, and we shall in a short time be huddled together in stations; a situation in our present circumstances, scarcely preferable to death—let us remember that supineness and inaction may entice the enemy to general hostilities—whilst preparation and offensive movements will disconcert their plans, drive them from our borders, secure ourselves and protect our property.

"Therefore *resolved*, That the convention in the name and behalf of the people, do call on the lieutenants or commanding officers of the respective counties of this district, forthwith to carry into execution the law for regulating and disciplining the militia.[134]

"*Resolved*, That it be recommended to the officers to assemble in their respective counties, and concert such plans as they may deem expedient for the defence of our country, or for carrying expeditions against the hostile nations of Indians."

In the month of March 1785 the Indians attacked a family who had settled at the mouth of the Kentucky river, killed a part and the remainder escaped.

In the month of October, a Mr. M'Clure and family, together with several other families, on their passage through the wilderness, were attacked by a party of Indians on Skegg's creek, and defeated—six of the whites were killed, and Mrs. M'Clure and one of her children made prisoners, together with a number of others. Captain William Whitley, with 21 men pursued and overtook the Indians, and killed two of them— and retook Mrs. M'Clure and a negro woman and the scalps of the six persons that were killed when Mrs. M'Clure was taken.[135]

Ten days after the retaking of Mrs. M'Clure, a Mr. Moore, with a party of whites, were attacked and defeated by the Indians, about two or three miles from Raccoon creek, nine of whom were killed. On Capt. Whitley receiving information of this event, he raised 30 men, and went immediately in pursuit of the Indians, and on the sixth day came up with them, killed three and took from them eight of the scalps they had taken at the defeat of Moore, together with all the booty and horses taken at the defeat. In November two men by the name of Sloan, were killed by the Indians on Salt river.[136]

Resisting a Persistent Enemy
[December 22, 1826]

The convention that met on the 8th of August 1785, recommended it to the officers of the militia to meet in their respective counties and adopt such plans as should be deemed most expedient for the protection and defence of the country. To effect this end, an expedition was set on foot against the Wabash Indians, who was at that time considered the most troublesome, and the command given to Gen. Clarke.

About one thousand men were soon raised, who rendezvoused at the Falls of Ohio, and from thence marched towards the Indian towns. In consequence of the delay in the boats which were to take the provisions up the Wabash, as well from the scarcity of provisions, the men when within two days march of the Indian towns, became mutinous upon which General Clarke called a council of his officers; they were rather tumultuous, and they therefore concluded to return home.[137]

After crossing the Ohio river, Col. Benj. Logan returned to Kentucky, for the purpose of raising a party to march against the Shawnee Indians, who lived on the Scioto. It was expected that the attention of these Indians would be attracted by the march of Gen. Clarke to the Wabash, and that their towns would be left defenceless—to accomplish which, several weeks elapsed before Col. Logan crossed the Ohio with his forces. As was expected, Col. Logan surprised an Indian town, killed several warriers, and took most of the women and children prisoners.[138]

During this year [1785] frequent intelligence was received of the hostile designs, machinations and war-like preparations of the Indians; but they were not actually very troublesome. To the nations north of the Ohio, overtures of peace had been made by the general government, and Gen. Clarke with Gen. Parsons from New England, and Gen. Butler from Pennsylvania, attended as Commissioners at the mouth of the Great Miami, in September or October, but they were met by no tribe except the Shawnees, and even as to them the meeting answered no beneficial purpose.—It is true that they entered into a treaty in the January following, but did it in such a manner as afforded no reason to believe that they would abide by it, and their future conduct confirmed the apprehensions then entertained. General Butler was agent in behalf of the United States for Indian affairs, and as a Pennsylvanian, had no favourable, impression for the Virginia character. General Parsons in all probability, had no small share of that strong aversion which his countrymen have uniformly manifested towards the people of Virginia. Certain it is, that they both entertained great prejudices against the Kentuckians, and Gen. Butler represented them to Congress as the aggressors; and fostered the sentiment then but too readily entertained by that body, that to the white people of the Western country, and not the Indians, ought the continuation of hostilities to be imputed.[139]

Some intelligence had been lately received from Vincennes, which in the opinion of the Convention rendered it necessary for them to address the people on the subject of Indian affairs. This address the members undertook to promulgate; and from that and the two resolutions which were immediately entered into, the reader will judge of the apprehensions then entertained.[140]

The commissioners appointed to present the memorial of the convention to the legislature of Virginia, attended at Richmond in November, presented and supported it, and procured the passage of the 'act concerning the erection of Kentucky into an indepent state.' This act authorized the people of the district in the month of August 1786, on the respective court days of the counties at the court-houses, to elect representatives to compose a convention, to be held at Danville on the fourth Monday in September, according to the proportions therein specified, and as soon as two thirds of the members elected should convene, they were directed to consider, and by a majority of votes to determine whether it be expedient for, and the will of the good people of the said district, that the same be erected into an independent state on terms and conditions specified in said act.[141]

The temperate perseverance, patience, and moderation with which these matters were conducted, I am covinced equals any thing which the reader could be prepared to expect. The repeated considerations and reconsiderations had on the subject—the efforts which were made to communicate information to the populace, and to obtain their deliberate consent, display the genuine characters of those who took the lead in this business. The transactions speak for themselves, and require neither apology or comment.[142]

Converting the District
to Statehood
[December 29, 1826]

*"An Act concerning the erection of the District of
Kentucky into an independent State.*

"Whereas it is represented to be the desire of the people inhabiting the district known by the name of the Kentucky District, that the same should be separated from this commonwealth whereof it is a part, and be formed into an independent member of the American confederacy, and it is judged by the General Assembly that such a partition of the Commonwealth is rendered expedient by the remoteness of the more fertile, which must be the more populous part of the said district, and by the interjacent impediments to a convenient and regular communication therewith.[143]

"*Be it enacted by the General Assembly,* That in the month of August next, on the respective court days of the counties within the said district, and at the respective places of holding courts therein, representatives to continue in appointment for one year, and to compose a convention, with the powers, and for the purposes hereinafter mentioned, shall be elected by the free male inhabitants of each county in like manner as delegates to the general assembly have been elected within the said district, in the proportion following:—In the county of Jefferson shall be elected five representatives; in the county of Nelson 5 representatives; in the county of Fayette five representatives; in the county of Bourbon five representatives; in the county of Madison five representatives; and in the county of Mercer five representatives. That full opportunity may be given to the good people, of exercising their right of suffrage on an occasion so interesting to them, each of the officers holding such elections, shall continue the same from day to day, passing over Sunday, for five days, including the first day, shall cause this act to be read on each day, immediately preceding the opening of the election, at the door of the courthouse, or other convenient place, and shall fix up two copies at least of this act, in the most public situations at the place of elections, twenty days before the commencement thereof. Each of the said officers shall deliver to each person duly elected a representative, a certificate of his election, and shall moreover transmit a general return to the clerk of the supreme court of the district, to be by him laid before the convention. For every neglect of any of the duties hereby enjoined on such officer, he shall forfeit one hundred pounds, to be recovered by action of debt, by any person suing for the same. The said convention shall be held at Danville, on the 4th Monday of Sept. and as soon as two thirds of the representatives shall be convened, they shall and may proceed, after choosing a president and other proper officers, and settling the proper rules of proceeding, to consider, and by a majority of voices to determine, whether it be expedient for, and be the will of the good people of the said district, that the same be erected into an independent state, on the terms and conditions following:

"1st. That the boundary between the proposed state and the state of Virginia, shall remain the same as at present separates the district from the residue of the Commonwealth.

"2d. That the proposed state shall take upon itself a just proportion of the public debt of this Commonwealth.

"3d. That all private rights and interests in lands with in the said district, derived from the laws of Virginia prior to such separation, shall remain valied and secure under the laws of the proposed state, and shall be determined by the laws now existing in this state.

"4th. That the lands within the proposed state of non-resident proprietors, shall not in any case be taxed higher than the lands of residents at any time prior to the admission of the proposed state to vote by its delegates in Congress, where such non-residents reside out of the United States, nor at any time either before or after such admission, where such non-residents reside within this Commonwealth, within which this stipulation shall be reciprocal; or where such non-residents reside within any other of the United States, which shall declare the same to be reciprocal within its limits; nor shall a neglect or cultivation or improvement of any land within either the proposed state of this Commonwealth, belonging to non-residents, citizens of the other, subject such non-residents to forfeiture or other penalty, within the term of six years after the admission of the said state into the Federal Union.

"5th. That no grant of land, nor land warrant to be issued by the proposed state, shall interfere with any warrant heretofore issued from the land office of Virginia, which shall be located on land within the said district now liable thereto, on or before the first day of September, one thousand seven hundred and eighty-eight.

"6th. That the unlocated lands within the said district, which stand appropriated by the laws of this Commonwealth to individuals or descriptions of individuals, for military or other services, shall be exempt from the disposition of the proposed state, and shall remain subject to be disposed of by the Commonwealth of Virginia, according to such appropriation, until the first day of September, 1787 and no longer; and thereafter the residue of all lands remaining within the limits of the said district, shall be subject to the disposition of the proposed state.

"7th. That the use and navigation of the river Ohio, so far as the territory of the proposed state, or the territory which shall remain with the limits of this Commonwealth, lies thereon, shall be free and common to the citizens of the United States, and the respective jurisdictions of this commonwealth, and of the proposed state, on the river as aforesaid, shall be concurrent only with the states which may possess the opposite shores of the said river.

"8th. That in case any complaint or dispute shall at any time arise between the commonwealth of Virginia and the said district, after it shall be an independent state, concerning the meaning or execution of the foregoing articles, the same shall be determined by six commissioners, of whom two shall be chosen by each of the parties, and the remainder by the commissioners so first appointed.

"Be it further enacted, That if the said convention shall approve of an erection of the said district into an independent state, on the foregoing terms and conditions, they shall and may proceed to fix a day, posterior to the first day of September, 1787, on which the authority of this common-wealth, and of its laws, under the exceptions aforesaid, shall cease and determine [terminate] forever, over the proposed state, and the said articles become a solemn compact, mutually binding on the parties, and unalterable by either without the consent of the other. *Provided however,* that prior to the 1st day of June, 1787, the United States in Congress, shall assent to the erection of the said district into an independent state, shall release this commonwealth from all its federal obligations arising from the said district, as being part thereof; and shall agree that the proposed state shall immediately after the day to be fixed as aforesaid, posterior to the 1st day of September, 1787, or at some convenient time future thereto, be admitted into the Federal Union. And to the end that no period of anarchy may happen to the good people of the proposed state, it is to be under-stood that the said convention shall have authority to take the necessary provisional measures for the election and meeting of a convention at some time prior to the day fixed for the determination of the authority of this commonwealth, and of its laws over the said district, and posterior to the first day of June, 1787 aforesaid, with full power and authority to frame and establish a fundamental constitution of government for the proposed state, and to declare what laws shall be in force therein, until the same shall be abrogated or altered by the legislative authority, acting under the constitution so to be framed and established.

"This act shall be transmitted by the executive to the delegates repre-senting this Commonwealth in Congress, who are hereby instructed to use their endeavours to obtain from Congress a speedy act to the effect above specified

"Jan. 6, 1786—Passed the House of Delegates JOHN BECKLEY, C.M.D
"Jan. 10, 1787—Passed the Senate   H. BROOKE, c."[144]

In the spring of the year 1784,* three men, whose names were M'Clure, Davis and Cafree, pursued some Indians who had stolen horses from Lincoln county, and were resolved, that if they did not overtake them, to proceed as far as their towns on the Tennessee river, and make reprisals. They had advanced as they supposed, to within a few miles of an Indian town called *Chickamauga*, when they fell in with three Indians, who were travelling in the same direction with themselves. By signs they agreed to travel together; but they had not gone far, before the Indians turned aside evidently to consult, whereupon the whites decided on the course they would pursue. It was determined that M'Clure and Davis should each shoot an Indian, whilst Cafree declared he would take the other prisoner. He accordingly seized him, which was the signal for M'Clure and Davis to fire on the others—M'Clure killed his man, but Davis's gun missed fire, and he, the Indian at which he fired, and M'Clure, each took to a tree, whilst Cafree was on the ground endeavouring to tie the Indian he had seized. At length the Indian at whom Davis attempted to fire, shot Cafree and gave him a mortal wound—he was immediately shot dead himself by M'Clure. Cafree growing faint, called to Davis to come to him, and at the same instant falling from the Indian, instantly expired—the Indian then picked up Cafree's gun and turned towards Davis who ran off, and was pursued by the Indian; they were neither of them ever heard of any more. M'Clure being now left with the three dead men, made the concerted signal, which had been previously agreed on which not being answered, he took up Davis's gun and proceeded homewards, with the hope of meeting with him on the way. He had traveled but a short distance before he met two Indians, a man and a stout boy. Dropping the extra gun, which he conceived would have excited suspicion, he marched boldly up to them, and after making signs indicative of a friendly disposition, they all sat down on a log. In a few minutes they heard the sound of a number of bells approaching, and the grown Indian gave M'Clure to understand, that as soon as that party came up, they would get horses to ride; at the same time putting his legs under the log to shew he would be tied under the horse's belly. M'Clure now began to dread passing the late scene of action in company with the Indians, knowing it would indicate to his savage companions, the part he had acted in the recent conflict. When the large Indian rose and looked towards the place where the bells appeared to be, as if he felt impatient of their delay—M'Clure, improving the opportunity, shot him dead, and the boy ran off—M'Clure likewise ran the contrary way, but was instantly pursued by a number of dogs, which frequently ran between his legs and threw him down. At length he became totally blind and fell down, expecting every moment to be as-

*This narrative ought in point of time, to have appeared in Section 15. It was published in the *Western Review* for March 1820, page 120.

sailed by the stroke of an Indian tomahawk. In this situation he remained some time—at length his sight and strength returning he ventured to rise, and to his great astonishment neither Indian nor dog was to be seen. He then proceeded slowly and sorrowfully towards home, where he arrived in four days. Such was the heat of the weather and fatigue he experienced, that the whole of the cuticle or scarf skin came off.[145]

[The writer of this article received it from M'Clure's own mouth.]

SECTION 20

"The Obstinate Inattention of Congress"

[January 19, 1827]

In the spring of the year 1786, the Indians on the north side of the Ohio became very troublesome to the people of Kentucky. Representations were made on the subject to the executive of Virginia, and an answer to the following effect was received from Gov. Henry, viz: That he had addressed Congress on the business, and urged the adoption of such measures as might ensure protection to the district. This was his *public* answer. But he informed the county lieutenant of Lincoln, Col. Benjamin Logan, in a *private* letter, that congress had paid no attention to his representation. In consequence of which he had again called their attention to the subject, and had demanded of that body a categorical answer to the following question, *"will you give the people of Kentucky protection?"* [146]

The obstinate inattention of Congress to these representations induced the executive of Virginia to give some very general directions to the county lieutenants of the district. Under these instructions, two expeditions were carried on against the Indians north of the Ohio; one under the command of Gen. Clarke against the Wabash tribes, the other by Col. Benjamin Logan against the Shawanese.[147]

In the month of August, elections were held in the several counties conformably to the act of separation; and a number of the members convened at Danville on the day appointed in that law. But so many of the members had marched with the two armies, that a number sufficient to proceed to business could not be had.

On the 26th day of September, the members present formed themselves into a committee, prepared a memorial to the Legislature of Virginia, starting the reason why the convention could not proceed to business, and requesting that some alterations might be made in the act of separation, and after appointing John Marshall, the present Chief Justice of the United States, to present the memorial, the committee was dissolved. But in order to prevent the extinction of the powers delegated to the convention, and the consequent delay of a separation, some members with the clerk, attended regularly and adjourned from day to day until some time in January, 1787.[148] At this time the members who had marched with the army having returned, a quorum was had, and the convention proceeded to business, and determined *"that it was expedient for, and the will of the good people of the District to separate from the State of Virginia and become an independent state."* But at this stage of the proceedings a letter was received by the president of the Convention from a member of the Assembly, enclosing an act repealing that law under which the convention were then acting, and authorising the people in the August following to elect another Convention, to be held at the same place in September 1787. The reasons assigned for this measure were 1. That the time contemplated in the repealed act was not sufficient to enable congress to determine on proper deliberation as to the propriety of admitting the proposed state into the union.

2. That twelve months had been given for purposes which could not now be complied with in that time.

3. That the people of the district were represented as being much divided respecting the propriety of a separation.

Hitherto the question relative to a separation had been conducted with much coolness and moderation. But the disappointment and mortification produced by this conduct in the government of Virginia, strongly affected the public mind.[149]

The people saw in this measure the much desired separation placed on the same footing which it stood twelve months before. The object in view was now at least as remote as it appeared then, and might be more so, for the same legislature which had repealed the former law, might in the same stage of proceedings repeal the present, and pretences equally plausible for so doing could readily be found. But while the separation was postponed to an indefinite period the evils and inconveniences which had suggested the necessity of it and produced the application for it, were hourly increasing, and it was obvious must continue to increase.

The members of the Convention solicitous to soothe the popular mind, and preserve peace in the country, discontinued their deliberations, and returned to their respective counties. But they were far from being satisfied with the defeat of a measure on which they were convinced that the prosperity and probably the existence of their country eminently depended.[150]

In June 1782, about sunrise one morning, Mr. John M'Kenney an instructer of youth, was sitting in his school house, on the public square in the town of Lexington, and near the west corner of the present iron railing, when a Wild Cat of uncommon size, made its appearance at the door, and without seeming to notice him, suddenly leaped into the room, snapping its jaws and foaming at the mouth. On observing it, Mr. M'Kinney's first thought was, what fine sport it would afford him; if he had but a good dog, and the door closed; but to his great surprize the cat, on casting his eyes around and seeing him, instead of precipitately retreating, as he had expected, it advanced towards him in a menacing manner. He instantly reached forward to a table near him, and attempted to grasp a ruler, but before he had obtained it, the animal was upon him, and seized him with its teeth on the collar bone near the throat. With much difficulty, by striking at it upwards, under his jacket, he released himself from this grasp, but the enraged animal instantly caught him by the right side, and its long crooked tusks pierced through his clothes and penetrated between the ribs, and held him so fast that he found it impossible to disengage himself. At the same time the sharp claws of the animal were applied with astonishing activity, in tearing off his clothes as well as the flesh on his side. From its situation, he was unable to strike it with any considerable force, and in his efforts, only injured his hand by striking it against the table. Finding he could do nothing in that way, he seized the animal with both his arms, brought down its hinder parts between his legs, and pressed with his whole force against the table. It struggled violently, and fearing that it might escape from his grasp, and again attack him with its claws, he now for the first time, made an exclamation, in the hope that some one might come to his relief. The women who were engaged near the place in milking their cows, were alarmed at his cries, and ran precipitately into the fort, exclaiming, that something was killing Mr. M'Kinney in the schoolhouse. Three of them however, (Mrs Masterson, Mrs Collins and Miss Thompson,) being less timid than the rest, ran towards the schoolhouse, and after some deliberation among themselves who should venture to look in first, they entered nearly together. Mr M'Kinney perceiving they were females, and knowing Mrs Masterson to be in a peculiar delicate state of health, was fearful of alarming them, and notwithstanding his own painful situation, assumed an air of composure and with a smile observed, "don't be alarmed, it is only a cat I have caught, and I want some person to assist me in killing it." He was then careful not to inform them, as he might have done with more truth, that *the cat had caught him!!* The women then boldly advanced towards him, and one of them stooping down and observing the size of the animal exclaimed *what a monster!* ran to the door and called a man who was at that time passing by—He came in, and first proposed cutting off the claws of the cat, but Mr. M'Kinney perceiving it to be perfectly still, concluded it was dead, which on rising he found to be the fact. They then endeavoured to disengage the teeth of the animal from Mr. M'Kinney's side, which they were unable to do, in consequence of their having hooked in between the ribs. The whole party then left the school-house, and went into the fort, M'Kinney carrying the cat in his arms, where, from the alarm, the people were rushing in crowds. After getting into the fort, another effort was made to relieve Mr. M'Kinney from the tusks of the cat, which was effected by placing its head in the same position it was when it made the attack.[151]

Notwithstanding his wounds, Mr. M'Kinney attended his school that forenoon, but found himself so exhausted and in so much pain, that he was obliged to dismiss the school at noon and retire to his bed. By proper applications, he was relieved from pain, his wounds healed rapidly, and his usual health speedily restored.[152]

It was the general opinion, that it was a rabid or mad cat, but if it was, it did not communicate the disease to him, as he is now (1820) in good health, living in Bourbon county, and has never exhibited any symptoms of madness.[153]

SECTION 21

The Downing Caper
[January 26, 1827]

In the month of August 1786, Mr Francis Downing* then a lad, lived in a fort, where soon afterwards an Ironworks was erected by Mr Jacob Myers, which is now known by the Slate creek works, and owned by Col. Thos. Dye Owings.[154]

*Mr Downing is a respectable citizen, now living in Lexington

One morning, a young man by the name of Yates, together with Mr Downing, went out in search of a horse that had strayed away from the fort. After travelling six or eight miles in search of the horse, Downing began to be alarmed at the idea of danger from Indians, and observed to Yates, (who was much older than himself, and to whom he looked up for protection) that he thought he heard a noise like sticks cracking behind them. Yates laughed at him and told him not to be a coward—that it was only his immagination, and that there was no danger whatever. Downing, however, was not convinced, but embraced the first favourable opportunity afforded him for concealment, to stop in a thick cluster of whortleberry bushes, while Yates went on. In a few minutes an Indian was seen by Downing, running towards him, until he was within about one hundred yards, when he suddenly stopped. Downing, to use his own expression, was as it were, *thunderstruck*. He resolved however, as he had a gun, to fire and then run; but unfortunately his gun having a double trigger, before he had raised her to his face, she went off, and, as he remarks, *he instantly went off too!* After running some distance, he met Yates, who having heard the report of the gun, had turned to ascertain what was the matter, and learning that they were closely pursued by Indians, they ran together. At length they reached a declivity, and were compelled, in following the path, to descend into a valley surrounded with hills. Here they soon saw two Indians, who had taken a shorter course, and were running by another route towards the bottom of the valley. There was no alternative: it was absolutely necessary to keep the path, and to run with the utmost possible rapidity, although from the superior knowledge possessed by the Indians of the different roads, they had gained considerably on the pursued, and seemed likely soon to overtake them. Both parties ran on until they reached a dry gutter in the middle of the valley, about six feet deep, and of considerable width. The Indians had, by this time approached very near them, and attempted to leap across the gutter at about the same time with the whites. All got across safe, except Mr. Downing, who just reached the edge of the gutter, against which striking his foot, he fell upon his breast, rebounded and fell backward into the gutter. The violence of the fall almost deprived him of breath for a time, but fortunately the Indians were too intent upon the chase to observe his remaining behind, and both happening to direct their attention solely to Mr Yates, continued to pursue him. Mr. Downing at length recovering from the shock, walked along the gutter, which grew shallower as he advanced, and soon ceased to serve the purpose of concealing him from the sight of the Indians. At length he discovered one of them returning in search of him—he instantly dropped his gun, left the gutter, and ran back the same way he had came.—The injury he had received from his fall, affected his speed, and the Indian gained upon him rapidly. After running a considerable distance, considering his case a desperate one, and his being overtaken inevitable, he came to a large poplar tree, which had been blown down by the wind. It so happened that whilst he ran along one side of the tree, the Indians pursued him on the other. At this critical moment, he felt himself caught by the leg, and was compelled to make a momentary pause, when he perceived that he had been stopped by a small dog, which instantly ran away from him. This pause had given to the Indian a considerable advantage, and he perceived himself likely to be caught at the root of the tree. Most fortunately however, just at that spot a large she bear had taken up her abode with several cubs. Not being pleased with the violence with which the Indian approached her young, she instantly attacked him, when Mr. Downing, taking advantage of the interference of this unexpected coadjutor, suddenly wheeled around, and left the savage engaged in a most violent struggle with his new adversary. What was the result of the rencounter, we are not informed.[155] It had however the happy effect of preserving Mr Downing from almost inevitable destruction; and as no remains of the Indian was ever afterwards found, at or near the place, it is probable he escaped with his life, if not with considerable injury.

Mr Yates likewise succeeded in getting off unhurt. After running several miles, he concealed himself amidst trees or in a canebrake, and thus eluded the pursuit, and returned home safe.

It was a custom with Mr Downing, in the summer, about the time referred to above, to go out of the fort every afternoon, to a cluster of hickory trees, several hundred yards distant, for the purpose of shooting squirrels, which at that place were very numerous. Near his path, (as he afterwards discovered) fifteen Indians lay concealed for three days, behind a large log, where they had placed a number of bushes to serve as a blind, there waiting for a favourable opportunity to kill some one or more men, and obtain plunder. The two first days he passed as usual to the hickory grove and back again without molestation, the Indians probably being aware, that little if any thing could be obtained from him, and fearing that an attack upon him would lead to immediate detection and pursuit. On the third day he observed that the bushes around the log were apparently dying, and being unable to conjecture the cause, was attracted by curiosity towards the spot, and had advanced to within about ten feet, for the purpose of ascertaining what was the matter, when his attention was caught by the fluttering of a beautiful bird, entangled in some burs just by him. He instantly turned and caught the bird, which drew off his curiosity about the dying bushes, and he returned to the fort, and spent the remainder of the day in making a cage for his bird. Had he not been interrupted, he would inevitably have been taken by the Indians without the firing of a single gun. So completely were his thoughts occupied with his little bird, that he forgot to mention the circumstances of the dying bushes. The next morning early, a pack-horse driver and his son went out to see after their horses, when the concealed Indians shot them both, scalped and stripped them before the people of the fort who heard the guns, could get to the place. They having previously stolen and secured a number of horses, they instantly made off.[156]

One Sunday morning, three men, one by the name of Poor, another named Wade, the name of the third not recollected, who had been in the habit of reconnoitering the country in the capacity of spies, proposed to Mr Downing to go with them to Mud Lick, now the Olympian Springs, seven miles distant from the fort. They accordingly set out together on foot, and travelled unmolested until they came in sight of the Lick. As they ascended a hill, they discovered several hundred buffaloes, elks and deer, which they considered an indication that there were no Indians there; but whilst they were surveying the prospect, and were descending the hill, Poor and Wade, who were some distance in advance of Downing and his companion, suddenly turned round and gave notice, that there were ten or fifteen Indians sitting and endeavouring to conceal themselves in the drain that proceeded from the Lick and that it was necessary that they should fly for their lives. They immediately started and ran with all possible speed, but soon heard the Indians behind them. The pursued took one path and the pursuers took another, but after a short distance the two paths came together—the whites however reached the point of junction before the Indians, although the latter had gained by the choice of paths. Young Downing being small, and not like his companions accustomed to running, was unable to keep up with them, and was advised as the only chance of escape, to embrace the first opportunity when the situation of the road should throw them out of sight of the Indians, to step behind a log and lie concealed, whilst the rest of the party ran on. Reluctant as he felt to be left in the woods surrounded by savages, he considered it the only alternative, and followed the advice.—Accordingly, the first opportunity that presented itself, he jumped aside from the path, and lay close behind a log. The Indians soon came along and eager in the pursuit to overtake those whom they still saw before them, passed by Downing, who lay trembling by the way side. About ten minutes after they passed, he ventured to rise and leave his place of concealment—for some time however, he was utterly at a loss what course to pursue. To go back towards the Lick was his first thought, but it was abandoned almost as soon as conceived. In this state of uncertainty, he slowly walked along the path in the direction the Indians had taken. A little reflection, however, convinced him of the danger of this course as it was very probable they would soon turn and come the same direction back—he therefore left the path, and, after wandering thro' the woods, reached the fort in safety, several hours after his companions, who had outrun their pursuers and returned likewise.[157]

On another occasion Mr Downing fell in company with Wade and

Poor at Stroud's Station,[158] and set out with them to return to the fort. On their way it was proposed and agreed to go about three miles from the road to a place called Cassidy's Station, (where a settlement had been made and abandoned on account of its exposure to the Indians) in order to get watermelons, which were in great abundance at that place. When they came near the enclosure, Wade and Poor told Downing to sit on his horse and hold their horses, whilst they went to reconnoitre and ascertain whether they could enter the water-melon patch in safety—charging him on no account to leave the horses, or move from the spot until they returned, unless the Indians should appear, or he should hear a signal agreed on, by a sound made on corn blades, in which last case he should repair immediately to a corner of the fence, and there wait for them. They accordingly went, leaving him alone; and having been absent a considerable time, he began to be uneasy, and regardless of the positive injunctions he had received, determined to go and see what was the matter. With this view he dismounted, and tied his horses to the poles which formed the fence of the enclosure, jumped over and began to make his way through the high broom-corn which concealed the houses from view. When he had almost reached the extremity of the cornfield, he caught a glimpse of the cottages, and saw a man whom he took to be an Indian, run from one house to another, and at the same instant heard the signal agreed on, given by his companions. He was now aware of the imprudence of which he had been guilty, and ran with all possible speed towards the fence. Unfortunately however, the violence with which he jumped over it, he alarmed the horses, and they ran off, each with a pole hanging to its bridle. Wade and Poor went to the corner of the fence according to agreement, but, not finding Downing or the horses, were exceedingly alarmed, and ran to ascertain the cause, when they saw the horses running off and Downing running after them.—With the utmost expedition they caught their horses, cut away the poles, sprang on them and rode several miles in full speed without uttering a single word. At length, having recovered their self-possession, they discovered they were not pursued, and proceeded on deliberately home, censuring Downing in the most pointed language, for his imprudent conduct, which had put to hazard the lives of the whole party.[159]

SECTION 22

The "Infamous Jay Treaty"

[February 9, 1827]

Sometime in the month of April, in the year 1786, Col. William Christian with a party of men, pursued some Indians (who had stolen horses from Bear Grass) across the Ohio river, and overtook them about twenty miles from the river, and totally defeated them. Col. Christian and one of his men were killed in this rencountre.[160]

In the same year, Simon Kenton, with thirty-six men, surprised and defeated a party of Indians on Bullskin, on the North side of the Ohio river.

In the month of October, 1786, a number of families known by the name of M'Nitt's company, were defeated and totally routed by Indians, between Big and Little Laurel rivers, on the wilderness road, in which twenty-one persons were killed, and the remainder dispersed or taken prisoners.[161]

About the same time, Capt. Hardin, from the south western section of the state, and from what is now Breckinridge county, crossed the Ohio river, with a party of men, and on the Saline, surprised a party of Indians encamped—he routed them, killed four, and dispersed the remainder, without the loss of a man.[162]

In December, the same year, a Mr. Hargrove with several others, were defeated by Indians at the mouth of Buck creek on Cumberland river—one of the party was killed, and Hargrove was wounded. This attack was made in the night.[163]

Some time in March 1787, a communication was made from a corresponding committee in the western part of Pennsylvania, to the people of Kentucky, informing them that John Jay, the American Minister for foreign affairs, had made a proposition to Don Gardoque, the Spanish Minister, to cede the navigation of the Mississippi to Spain, for twenty-five or thirty years, in consideration of some commercial advantages from which the people of the western country could never derive any benefit. It will not be supposed, that this information tended to soothe the minds of the people, already labouring under innumerable inconveniencies, and deprivations, neglected by the general government, and tantalized by their own. It was very evident that this measure had nothing less in view, than the absolute sacrifice of every interest of the western country, to promote the prosperity of the eastern states. But if the thing did not speak for itself, some members of Congress spoke sufficiently explicit for it, one in particular from Massachusetts, who held a high rank in political life, and possessed the confidence of government in an eminent degree, had declared on the floor of Congress, that it would give him real pleasure to see the ocean wash the western foot of the Allegany. And the account of the proposition, was accompanied with information that seven states approved. It was received in Danville during the sitting of the Supreme Court for the District of Kentucky, where a considerable number of people were attending. They took the matter into immediate consideration, and appointed a committee to communicate the information to the people at large, and recommended to them to elect five representatives from each county, to meet at Danville in the May following, and take into consideration the proposed cession of the Mississippi. Several members elected in consequence of this recommendation, attended at Danville on the day appointed, and after a conferrence of several days, adjourned without adopting any measures respecting the matter. The reason was, because the legislature of Virginia had entered into several resolutions on the subject, expressed in strong language, and had instructed her delegates in Congress, to oppose the cession.[164]

These resolutions were couched in the following terms:

"RESOLUTIONS IN THE HOUSE OF DELEGATES, 29th Nov. 1786.
"*Resolved*, unanimously, That the common right of navigating the Mississippi, and of communicating with other nations through that channel, be considered as the bountiful gift of nature to the United States, as the proprietors of the territory watered by the said river and its eastern branches.

"*Resolved*, unanimously, That the confederacy having been formed on the broad bassis of equal rights in every part thereof, to the protection and guardianship of the whole, a sacrifice of the rights of any one part, to the supposed or real interest of another part, would be a flagrant violation of justice, a direct contravention of the end for which the Federal Government was instituted, and an alarming innovation of the system of the union.

"*Resolved*, therefore, That the delegates representing this state in Congress, be instructed in the most decided terms, to oppose any attempt that may be made in Congress, to barter away or surrender to any nation whatever, the right of the United States, to the free and common use of the river Mississippi: and to the protest against the same as a dishonourable departure from that comprehensive and benevolent policy, which constitutes the vital principles of the confederacy, as provoking the just resentments and reproaches of our Western brethern, whose essential rights and interests would be thereby sacrificed and sold, as destroying that confidence in the wisdom, justice and liberality of the federal councils, which is so necessary at this crisis, to a proper enlargement of their authority, and finally as tending to undermine our prosperity and our union itself, and that the said delegates be further instructed to urge the proper negociations with Spain, for obtaining her concurrence in such regulations, touching the mutual and common use of the said river, as may secure the permanent harmony and affection of the two nations, and such as the wise and generous policy of his Catholic Majesty will perceive to be no less due to the interests of his own subjects than to the just and friendly views of the United States."[165]

But the defeats of the object they had nearest at heart by the Legislature of Virginia, and the dismal prospect held out to them by Jay's projected treaty, were only a part of the troubles of the people of Kentucky, at this time. In the spring of this year, the Indians infested and seemed likely to overrun the whole country—Great depredations were committed in almost every quarter. Congress, though repeatedly urged by the executive of Virginia, pertinaciously refused to afford the people any protection, and without assigning any reason for the measure, disbanded the troops which had apparently been raised for that purpose.

The following extract of a letter from Harry Innes to John Brown, a member of Congress dated Danville, April 4th, 1788, evinces that fact:

"The representations of Gov. Henry, were strengthened and supported by Col. Harmer of the continental troops, in consequence of which Congress resolved, on the 20th October, 1786, to increase the army to 2040 non-commissioned officers and privates: the quota of Virginia was 60 horse, who were recruited and marchen to Winchester in the spring of 1787, and there soon after disbanded."

And the executive of Virginia now censured the officers who had projected and conducted the two expedetions formerly mentioned, as conducted by General Clarke and Col. Logan, in consequence of orders received from the executive. But to render their situation still more distressing, the Cherokees, who in 1785 had entered into a treaty with Congress, now commenced hostilities. A party of that tribe came to Fishing Creek, in Lincoln county, and murdered a man of the name of Luttrell. Information was given to Col John Logan, then second in command in that county. He embodied some of the militia; went with them to the house where the murder had been committed, and near it discovered the route which the Indians had taken. He pursued them several days; crossing the Cumberland river into the Indian territory, the party was overtaken, several of them killed, a quantity of skins and furs and all their horses taken. Those of his party of Indians who escaped, attempted to avail themselves of the treaty, by complaining to the Indian agent, that the people of Kentucky had intruded[166] on their hunting ground, and murdered some of their peacable hunters. The agent communicated this complaint to the executive of Virginia, and the Governor thereupon directed the attorney general of the district to "institute the proper legal inquiries for vindicating the infraction of the treaty." This vague and indefinite direction the attorney general refused to act under, and no further direction was given. The people were conscious of their innocence in all matters relating to the Indians, and extremely exasperated on receiving intelligence of the instructions to prosecute: as they were directly intended to stigmatize a highly meritorious officer, for doing what the laws of nature and God required of him. The following is Governor Randolph's letter to the attorney general:

"RICHMOND, Va. May 1st, 1787
"Sir—I have reason to believe that the late hostilities committed by [against] the Indians, have aroused their resentment. It is the duty of government to prevent and punish, if possible, all unjust violations. I beg leave, therefore, to urge you to institute the proper legal inquiries for vindicating the infractions of peace.
      "I am, sir, your most obedient serv't.   EDM: RANDOLPH.[167]
"Mr HENRY INNES, Attorney General."

"KENTUCKY, July 21st, 1787
"Sir—Your excellency's letter of the 1st of May, was delivered to me on the 6th inst. and after reflecting on the contents, I feel myself constrained to ask of the executive in what capacity they view me? because from the tenor of your letter, it would be construed that I was vested with some executive powers; your letter directs me 'to institute the proper legal enquiries for vindicating the infractions of the peace'—how am I to proceed on the business from so vague a direction, I know not. In my official capacity I cannot do it—in a private capacity it would render me odious; but of whom I am to enquire, or against whom your excellency wishes a prosecution to be instituted, your letter is silent.
      "If your excellency calls upon me in a private capacity, I shall be very ready and willing to give you such information as far as may come to my knowledge of any matter in which the weal of the state may be interested; and shall now give you the information on the subject which your letter refers viz: Col. John Logan's excursion in February last, and some others.
      "Indians had made their appearance upon our south eastern frontiers at several different times in the fall and winter;[168] some of our hunters had been attacked, and early in February one of our citizens killed at his own house; this induced Col. John Logan, the then commanding officer of Lincoln, to raise his corps to range on the waters of Cumberland, and to rendezvous at or near the place where the person had been killed, which was on a branch of Green river. Within a few miles of the place of

rendezvous, Col. Logan came upon the trail of the Indians, who it was supposed had committed the murder; he followed and overtook them, killed seven and got possession of the skins and horses they had along, among which was a valuable mare of mine and a horse belonging to a Mr. Blain, of Lincoln, also a rifle gun which was well known to belong to a person who was murdered in the wilderness in October last on his journey to this district. Judge from these facts of the innocence of the Cherokees.

"Since the excusion by Col. Logan, one hath been made by some volunteers from Fayette and Bourbon under the command of Col. Robert Todd, to the Scioto, in consequence of information received from the Shawnees of the hostile conduct of a small tribe said to be Cherokees; who had settled on Plant [Paint] creek, upon this occasion three were killed and seven taken, who have since made their escape.

"Last fall an excursion was made to the Saline by some volunteers from Nelson, under Capt. Hardin, who fell in with some Indians, three or four of whom he killed and put the others to flight.

"Another hath been made from Jefferson in June last, under Maj. Oldham, upon the waters of the Wabash, but nothing was done.

"The Indians have been troublesome on our frontiers, and still continue to molest us, from which circumstance I am decidedly of opinion that this western country will in a few years act for themselves and erect an independent government; for under the present system we cannot exert our strength, neither does congress seem disposed to protect us, for we are informed that those very troops which congress directed the several states to raise for the defence of the Western country, are disbanded. I have just drop'd this hint to your excellency for matter of reflection. If some step is not taken for our protection a little will prove the truth of the opinion.

"I have the honor to be, &c. &c.   HARRY INNES" [169]
"Governor Randolph"

SECTION 23

Robert Patterson's Memoir
[February 16, 1827]

[To the *Ohio State Journal*] "SIR—It is well known that Mr Bradford, the editor of the "Kentucky Gazette," has been for some time engaged in collecting and publishing, "Notes and Anecdotes" relating to the first settlement of Kentucky.[170] To me Mr Bradford's Notes have a peculiar interest, by recalling to my recollection, incidents, that the unsparing hand of time had obliterated, and by awakening emotions which none can feel who have not known Kentucky as I have. I emigrated to that state in 1775, and resided there until 1804, when I moved to my present residence in this county [in Ohio]. Very few of those with whom I was called to act and to suffer at the early period of our settlement, are spared to witness the astonishing changes which have been made in that state as well as in this, which we often visited in a hostile manner, and I find myself standing as it were, on a promontory almost alone.

"Some time since, a friend of mine in that state, requested me to furnish Mr Bradford with any information I might be in possession of, upon the subject alluded to, but more particularly with accounts of such events as transpired within my own observation, and of such transactions as I might have been engaged in. In compliance with the above request, I had prepared the following narrative to place at Mr Bradford's disposal; but believing the same object will be promoted if it is published here, and trusting as I do, that it will not be altogether uninteresting to many of your readers. Instead of sending it to him as I had intended, I now send it to you with permission to publish it if you think proper. I will here state, (and I take a pleasure in making it) that as far as my knowledge and recollection extends, the facts related by Mr Bradford, are substantially correct.

"Very respectfully,   R. PATTERSON[171]

"*Dayton, Jan.* 16, 1827.
    "In the fall of 1776, I started from M'Clellan's station, (now George-town Ky.) in company with Jos. M'Nutt, David Perry, James Wernock, James Templeton, Edward Mitchell and Isaac Greer, to go to Pittsburgh. We procured provision for our journey, at the Blue Licks, from the well known store-house the Buffalo. At Limestone we procured a canoe, and

started up the Ohio river by water. Nothing material transpired during several of the first days of our journey. We landed at Point Pleasant, where was a fort commanded by Capt. Arthur Arbuckle. After remaining there a short time and receiving despatches from Capt. Arbuckle to the commandant at Wheeling, we again proceeded. Aware that Indians were lurking along the banks of the river, we travelled with the utmost caution. We usually landed an hour before sunset, cooked and ate our supper, and then went on till after dark. At night we lay without fire, as convenient to our canoe as possible, and started again in the morning at day-break. We had all agreed that if any disaster should befall us by day or by night, we would stand by each other as long as any help could be afforded. At length the memorable 12th of October arrived. During the day we passed several new improvements, which occasioned us to be less watchful and careful than we had been before. Late in the evening we landed opposite the Island then called the Hockhocking, and were beginning to flatter ourselves that we should reach some inhabitants the next day. Having eaten nothing that day, contrary to our usual practice, we kindled a fire and cooked supper. After we had eaten, and made the last of our flour into a loaf of bread and put it into an old gallon brass kettle to bake, so that we might be ready to start again in the morning at day-break, we lay down to rest, keeping the same clothes on at night that we wore during the day. For want of better, I had on a hunting shirt and brich clout (so called) and flannel leggings. I had my powder horn and shot pouch on my side, and placed the butt of my gun under my head. Five of our company lay on the east side of the fire and James Templeton and myself on the west; we were lying on our left sides, myself in front, with my right hand hold of my gun. Templeton was lying close behind me. This was our position and all asleep when we were fired upon by a party of Indians. Immediately after the fire, they rushed upon us with tomahawks as if determined to finish the work of death they had begun. It appeared that one Indian shot on my side of the fire. I saw the flash of the gun and felt the ball pass through me, but could not tell where, nor was it at first painful. I sprang to take up my gun, but my right shoulder came to the ground, I made another effort and was half bent getting up, when an Indian sprang past the fire with savage fierceness, and struck me with his tomahawk. From the position I was in, it went between two ribs just behind the back bone, a little below the kidney, and penetrated the cavity of the body. He then immediately turned to Templeton, (who by this time had got to his feet with his gun in his hand) and seized his gun. A desperate scuffle ensued, but Templeton held on and finally bore off the gun. In the meantime I made from the light, and in my attempt to get out of sight I was delayed for a moment by getting my right arm fast between a tree and sapling, but, having got clear, and away from the light of the fire, and finding that I had lost the power of my right arm, I made a shift to keep it up, by drawing it through the straps on my shot pouch. I could see the crowd about the fire, but the firing had ceased, and the strife seemed to be over. I had reason to believe that the others were all shot and tomahawked. Hearing no one coming towards me, I resolved to go to the river, and if possible, to get into the canoe and float down, thinking by that means I might possibly reach Point Pleasant, supposed to be about 100 miles distant. Just as I got on the beach a little below the canoe, an Indian in the canoe gave a whoop, which gave me to understand that it would be best to withdraw. I did so. And with much difficulty got to an old log, and being very thirsty, faint and exhausted, I was glad to sit down. I felt the blood running, and heard it dropping on the leaves all around me. Presently I heard the Indians board the canoe and float past. All was now silent and I felt myself in a most forlorn condition. I could not see the fire, but determined to find it, and see if any of my comrades were still alive. I steered the course which I supposed the fire to be, and having reached it, I found Templeton alive, but wounded nearly in the same way that I was. Jas. Wernock was also dangerously wounded, two balls having passed through his body; Jos. M'Nutt was dead and scalped; D. Perry was wounded, but not badly, and Isaac Greer was missing.—The miseries of that hour cannot well be described.

"When day light appeared, we held a council, and concluded, that inasmuch as one gun and some ammunition was saved, Perry could furnish us with meat, and we would proceed by slow marches, up the river to the nearest settlement, supposed to be 100 miles. A small quantity of provision, which was found scattered around the fire, was picked up and distributed among us, and a piece of blanket which was saved from the fire, was given to me to cover the wound on my back. On examination it was found that two balls had passed through my right arm a little above the joint, and that the bone was broken; to dress this, splinters were taken from a tree near the fire that had been shivered with lightning, and placed on the outside of my hunting shirt and bound tight with a string. And now being in readiness to move, Perry took the gun and ammunition, and we all got to our feet except Wernock, who on attempting to get up, fell back to the ground. He refused to try again—said that he could not live— and at the same time desired us to do the best we could for ourselves. Perry then took hold of his arm and told him if he would get up we could carry him—upon this he made another effort to get up, but falling back again as before, he beged us in the most solemn manner, to leave him. At his request the old kettle was filled with water, and placed at his side, which he said was the last and only favour he required of us, and then again conjured us to leave him and try to save ourselves, assuring us, that should he live to see us again, he would cast no reflections of unkindness upon us.—Thus we left him. When we had got a little distance, I looked back, and distressed and hopeless as Wernock's condition really was, I felt to envy it. After going about one hundred poles, we were obliged to stop and rest, and found ourselves too sick and weak to proceed. Another consultation being held, it was agreed that Templeton and myself should remain there with Edward Mitchell, and Perry should take the gun and go to the nearest settlement and seek relief.—Perry promised that if he could not procure assistance, he would be back himself in four days. He then returned to the camp, and found Wernock in the same state of mind as he was when we left him, perfectly rational and sensible of his condition, replenished his kettle with water, brought us some fire, and started for the settlement.

"Alike unable to go back or forward, and being very thirsty, we set about getting water from a small stream that happened to be near us, our only drinking vessel was an old wool hat, which was so broken that it was with much difficulty made to hold water; but by stuffing leaves into it, we made it hold so that each one could get a drink from once filling it. Nothing could have been a greater luxury to us than a drink of water from the old hat. Just at night Mitchell returned to see if Wernock was still living, intending if he was dead, to get the kettle for us—he arrived there just in time to see him expire; but not choosing to leave him till he should be certain that he was dead, he stayed with him till dark came on, and when he attempted to return to us, he got lost and lay from us all night. We suffered much that night for the want of fire, and through fear that he was either killed, or that he had run off; but happily for us, our fears were groundless, for next morning at sunrise he found his way to our camp. That day we moved about two hundred yards up a deep ravine and farther from the river. The weather, which had been cold and frosty, now became a little warmer and commenced raining. Those that were with me could set up, but I had no other alternative but to lie on my back on the ground, with my right arm over my body. The rain continuing, next day Mitchell took an excursion to examine the hills, and not far distant he found a rock projecting from the cliff sufficient to shelter us from the rain, to which place we very gladly removed. Mitchell kept a station on the river, in hopes of seeing some boat pass which might be brought to our relief. He also gathered paupaus for us, which were our only food, except perhaps a few grapes.

"Time moved slowly on until Saturday. In the mean time we talked over the danger to which Perry was exposed, the distance he had to go, and the improbability of his returning. When the time had expired which he had allowed himself, we concluded that if he was alive he would return, and that we would wait for him until Monday, and if he did not come then, and no relief should be afforded, we would attempt to travel to Point Pleasant. The third day after our defeat, my arm became very painful. The splinters and sleves of my shirt were so cemented together with blood, and stuck so fast to my arm, that it required the application of warm water nearly a whole day to loosen them so that they could be taken off; when this was done, I had my arm dressed with the white-oak leaves, which had a very good effect. On Saturday about twelve o'clock, Mitchell came with his bosom full of paupas, and placed them convenient to us, and returned to his station on the river. He had been gone about an hour, when to our great joy, we beheld his coming with a company of men. When they approached us, we found that our own trusty friend and companion, David Perry, had returned to our assistance, with Capt. John Walls, his officers and most of his company. Our feelings of gratitude may possibly be conceived, but words can never describe them—suffice it to say, that these eyes flowed down plenteously with tears, and I was so completely overwhelmed with joy, that I fell to the ground. On my recovering, we were taken to the river, and refreshed plentifully with provisions which the captain had brought, and had our wounds dressed by an experienced man who came for the purpose. We were afterwards described by the Captain to be in a most forlorn and pitiable condition, more like corpses beginning to putrify than living beings.

"The cliff which sheltered us from the rain, is situated on a ridge about one hundred poles from the ridge, south about five feet from the opening or cavity below, which might have been twenty feet from east to west. While we remained there, the howling of the wolves in the direction of the fatal spot, whence we had so narrowly escaped with our lives, left no doubt that they were feasting on the bodies of our much lamented friends, M'Nutt and Wernock. While we were refreshing ourselves at the river, and having our wounds dressed, Captain Walls went with some of his men to the place of our defeat, and collected the bones of our late companions, and buried them with the utmost expedition and care. We were then conducted by water, to captain Walls' station at Grave creek on the Ohio river, ten or twelve miles below Wheeling.[172]

After the declaration of American Independence, application was made to the Court of Spain, to acknowledge the United States as an independent nation, and treat them as such. But that government, foreseeing that the independence of those states might prove prejudicial to her colonies, refused.[173] At a particular period of the war, when the Southern states were overrun by the British—the governments of Georgia and South Carolina prostrated, and all resistance at an end; when North Carolina could make but a feeble and ineffective opposition—when the British forces were embodied in the heart of Virginia, the finances of the government exhausted, and France weary of the war, and wishing for peace; at this period of desperation, it was suggested, that if the Mississippi should be relinquished to Spain, it might remove her jealousies; induce her to acknowledge our independence, and prove the basis of a treaty under which we might avail ourselves of her assistance. Upon this suggestion, the Legislature of Virginia passed a resolution, recommending its relinquishment—and Congress passed an act authorising the American Minister at the Spanish Court to cede it, on condition that Spain would acknowledge our independence, and exert herself in support of it. But no such treaty was made, and Spain seemed to set no value on the right which was proposed to be relinquished in her favour, and never until the close of the war acknowledged our independence. As soon as the war terminated, the power to make such treaty was revoked, and the resolution on which it was predicated was rescinded.[174]

Some time after this, Spain sent a minister to the United States (having now acknowledged their independence) to have the boundaries of her claims and ours settled by treaty. She now claimed in her own original right the exclusive navigation of the Mississippi, and by an extension of West Florida northwardly, about half the state of Georgia and a large part of the state of Kentucky. John Jay, the then Minister for Foreign Affairs, was authorized by special commission to make a treaty adjusting and settling this question; but even this special commission was so restricted as to prohibit him from relinquishing our right to the Mississippi *on any consideration whatever.*[175]

After about ten months spent in this negociation, the American minister wrote a letter to Congress, stating that difficulties had arisen, which in his opinion should be so managed, that even their existence should remain a secret for the present; and therefore proposed that a committee should be appointed to direct and instruct him in every case relative to the proposed treaty. After considerable debate about appointing a committee, the minister was called before Congress itself, and directed to explain the difficulties which he had mentioned. It now appeared that instead of adjusting the boundaries of land, which his commission had confined him to, he had been planning a project of a commercial treaty, which he strongly urged congress to adopt, and invest him with authority to carry into effect. The features of the treaty were such as might be expected. Spain was to grant to the United States some commercial preivileges, from which Jay's own state and the states of New England, might derive advantages; and in consideration of this, all the interests and prospects of the western states were to be sacrificed by a relinquishment of the Mississippi for twenty years.[176] Seven states voted for acceding to the minister's proposition. This was a majority—but here a constitutional question arose. By the confederation the assent of nine states was requisite to enter into a treaty. Congress had hitherto considered the instructions to the minister as the basis of the treaty, and had required the assent of nine states to such instructions. That number had assented to the instructions already given to Jay; the motion now was to revoke one part of the instructions, and to vary the other; and the question, was whether this could be done by less than nine states, or whether if seven states could and would take off the restriction, the authority to make any treaty, would not be thereby repealed. This question was debated at great length, and with much animosity; but the majority decided that they had a constitutional authority to unfetter the minister and vary his instructions. The minority protested, and entered their protest on the journals; and the vote and decision of the majority was transmitted to the minister for his instructions, and authority to enter into a treaty on the plan he had projected.

But happily about this time the question respecting the adopting of the present Federal Constitution, engrossed the attention of all parties: in the magnitude of that, minor considerations were lost. The execution of the project was consequently delayed, and the project itself ultimately abandoned.[177]

SECTION 24

Founding of the *Kentucky Gazette*
[March 2, 1827]

To ensure unanimity in the opinions of the people, respecting the propriety of separating the District of Kentucky from the State of Virginia, and forming a separate government, by exhibiting to public view, the situation in which the country was placed, both as it regarded its then perilous condition, as well as its future prospects. To give general publicity to the proceedings of the Convention &c. it was deemed essential to the interests of the country, that it should be furnished with a printing press. To accomplish this end, the Convention in their session of 1785, appointed Gen. James Wilkinson, Colonel Christopher Greenup, and Mr. John Coburn, a committee to use their best endeavours to induce a printer to settle in the country, and publish a weekly newspaper.[178] Wilkinson and Coburn applied by letter to Mr. John Dunlap of Philadelphia, to aid them in procuring a printer, but as no assurances of a competent salary could be given by the committee, no printer could be obtained in Philadelphia. Col. Greenup wrote to a Mr. Miles Hunter in Richmond, Va. a young printer of that place. From the flattering prospects held out by the Colonel of future advantages to the printer who should first establish himself in Kentucky, Mr. Hunter at first consented to remove to Kentucky, but being afterwards informed of the many difficulties likely to intervene before Kentucky would become a separate state, and the uncertainty of a competent support from the printing business, until that event should take place, declined altogether.[179]

The attempts of the committee having failed entirely, Mr. JOHN BRAD-FORD, then a resident of Fayette county, called on Gen. Wilkinson and informed him, that if the Convention would give any assurance, that he should enjoy public patronage when the printing business should become so profitable, as to induce one or more printers to settle in Kentucky, that he would, as soon as an office could be procured, establish a newspaper in Kentucky. The reasonableness of this proposition induced the committee in their report to recommend to the Convention, to accede to it—in consequence of which, the Convention at their session in 1786, when the committee reported, passed a resolution concurring in the report, and promising the patronage required, as far as they from the nature of the appointment were authorised.[180] In consequence of this resolution, Mr. Bradford sent immediately to Pittsburgh, where he procured a printing press and other materials for a small printing establishment, and in the month of August 1787, presented to the world the first number of the "KENTUCKE GAZETTE." [181]

Indian hostilities increasing, the county Lieutenants of Lincoln, Fayette and Jefferson counties, held a meeting on the 17th day of May 1787, and forwarded by express a memorial on the subject to the Executive of Virginia. In June the following answer was returned:—

"IN COUNCIL—JUNE 5, 1787.
"The Lieutenant Governor laid before the board letters which came to him by express from the county Lieutenants of Lincoln, Jefferson and Fayette, giving information that the Western Indians had lately and at different times, committed hostilities on the inhabitants of Kentucky.

"Whereupon it is ordered, that copies of the several letters and papers, be forwarded to the delegates of this state in Congress.

"That Col. Benj. Logan be directed immediately to convene the County Lieutenants or commanding officers of the different counties composing the District of Kentucky, and with their advice, to form some system for the defence of that district—cautiously avoiding offensive operations, and taking care that the troops, which it may be necessary to embody, for carrying into execution any plan of defence that may be adopted, *do on no occasion go without the limits of the state, except in the immediate pursuit of an invading enemy."* [182]

    "Attest.   A. BLAIR, c.c."

As early as the year 1780, the people of Kentucky had discovered, that the only effectual way of repeling attacks from the Indians, was to obtain intelligence of their intended movements, and surprize or divert them by an expedition into their own country. This has been the settled mode of defence ever since; but independent of this, the directions of the executive were in the last degree preposterous and absurd—Kentucky exhibited a frontier of almost as many miles as there were people in it. To keep a perpetual watch on such a frontier, would have been impracticable, if every man in the district had been furnished with arms, ammunition and provisions, and had no other business to attend to.

By virtue of these orders, the people were compelled to remain inactive, even if they knew that a dozen nations of Indians were collecting and embodying themselves within five miles of their residence. They were obliged to wait until they had collected and united all their strength, arranged their mode of attack, and made every possible provision therefor, and made an attack; but when the Indians thus embodied, organized and arrayed, had marched *into* their country, they were allowed the privilege of driving them *out*—if they could. This restriction, excited very unpleasant sensations in the minds of the people.[183]

In consequence of the representations made by the Executive to Congress, that body on the 21st of July, passed the two following resolutions, *professedly* with the view of giving protection to this remote and afflicted portion of the United States, but which in reality, were merely an insult and mockery of their distress:

    "By the United States in Congress assembled, JULY 21st, 1787.
"Resolved, That the Secretary at War place the troops of the United States in such position as shall afford most effectual protection to the frontier inhabitants of Pennsylvania and Virginia, from the incursions and depredations of the Indians, for preventing intrusions on the federal lands, and promoting a favourable issue to the intended treaty; to this end, one company and an half shall remain at Venango, Fort Pitt and Fort M'Intosh; one be posted on the Muskingum; one on the Miami; three at Post St. Vincennes, and the remaining troops at the Rapids of the Ohio, subject however, to such changes and alterations as the commanding officer shall judge the good of the service may require.

    "Resolved, That the Executive of Virginia be requested to give orders to the Militia of the District of Kentucky, to hold themselves in readiness to unite with the federal troops in such operations as the officer commanding them may judge necessary for the protection of the frontiers, and that

on the application of the commanding officer of the federal troops, the said Executive be requested to give orders that a part of the said Militia, not exceeding one thousand, be embodied and take such portions as the said commanding officer shall direct, for acting in conjunction with the federal troops in protecting and defending the frontier inhabitants, and in making such expeditions against the Indians, in case they continue hostile, as Congress shall hereafter order and direct.[184]

"CHA. THOMPSON, Sec'y"

In conformity to the requisition made on the Executive of Virginia, the following proceeding was had:

"IN COUNCIL—Aug. 14, 1787.
"SIR—Inclosed is a copy of the act of Congress, providing for the defence of the Western frontier.

"You will in conformity to this act, hold your militia in readiness at all times to united with the federal troops in such operations as the officer commanding them shall judge necessary.

"You are not, however, to consider yourself at liberty to embody any part of your militia for the purpose of carrying into execution the above mentioned act, until you receive special orders from the Executive for that purpose.

"I am sir your obedient servant,   BEVERLY RANDOLPH.
"To the county Lieut. or commanding officer of Lincoln."

By the first of these resolutions, Congress declared that it was their intention with the regular troops consisting of one regiment, to give effectual protection to the frontier inhabitants of Pennsylvania and Virginia, from the incursions and depredations of Indians, to prevent intrusions on the federal lands, and promote a honourable issue to their intended treaty. The frontier proposed to be *effectually* protected with one regiment, was 700 miles in length, and infested with Indians in its whole extent. One company and a half was to remain at Venango, Fort Pitt and Fort M'Intosh, for the protection of the western part of Pennsylvania; these were between three and four hundred miles from the nearest settlements in Kentucky; one at Muskingum, about 150 miles lower down; one at the mouth of the Miami; three at the Post St. Vincennes, 100 miles from the nearest part of Kentucky, and the remainder at the Rapids of the Ohio. It is manifest that the primary object of this measure, was more hostile to the whites than to the Indians; to prevent intrusion on the public lands, and not to protect the people of Kentucky. All troops except those at the Falls of the Ohio, were stationed at such a distance from the then settled parts of the country, as to be of no service to the people.

The second resolution requested the Executive of Virginia, to order the militia in the District of Kentucky to hold themselves in readiness to unite with the federal troops in such operations as the officer commanding the same might deem necessary for the future protection of the frontiers; and that on application of said commanding officer, one thousand of said militia should take such position as he should direct, for acting in conjunction with the federal troops against the Indians.

This resolution might have been productive of great advantage, but the Executive of Virginia restricted and embarrassed it in such a manner as to render it entirely nugatory. The Governor enclosed the act of Congress in a letter dated the 14th of Aug. to Colonel Ben. Logan, and directed that the "militia be in readiness at all times to unite with the federal troops in such operations as the officer commanding them shall judge to be necessary. *You are not however* (continued he) *to consider yourself at liberty to embody any part of the militia for the purpose of carrying into execution the above mentioned act, until you receive official orders from the Executive for that purpose.*" [185]

Nothing could have been more preposterous and absurd than this order; the nearest county lieutenant in the district to the seat of government, was more than 500 miles distant, 200 of which was through a dangerous uninhabited wilderness, constantly infested with hostile Indians. If the officer commanding the federal troops should on any emergency want the co-operation of the militia, he must make the requisition on the county lieutenant—*he* must send a messenger through the wilderness to the Governor of Virginia; if this messenger by accident (for it would indeed have been an accident) escaped being murdered on the way, and have reached the Governor, *he* must call in his council and they decide the question whether the officer had in reality any occasion for the assistance of the militia, or whether the requisition originated in conceit, whim or caprice; if they determined that the requisition was reasonable, the messenger might return alive (if he could) convey the intelligence, and the county lieutenant begin to embody his troops; but by this time the white inhabitants might have been all massacred and putrified, or the Indians, if an attack was the object, have fled to Canada. [186]

"A Melancholy Experience at Statemaking"

[March 9, 1827]

The conduct of the United States and of the Executive of Virginia, added to the large stock of melancholy experience which the people of Kentucky had already acquired, was sufficient to confirm them in the belief that all their hopes of happiness or safety, if not of existence itself, must depend on a separation from the parent state. They therefore proceeded under the second act of separation, to elect members of a convention, once more to decide on the propriety of a separation.[187]

A majority of the members so elected, met at the time [September 17, 1787] and place appointed, and proceeded to business. The two acts of separation, and the several papers already mentioned relative to Indian affairs, were referred to a committee of the whole on the state of the District. After maturely considering the conditions imposed in the two acts of assembly, and all the calamities and inconveniencies resulting from local causes, the Convention on the eighth day, decided *nemine contradicente*, "That it was expedient for, and the will of the good people of the District, to be erected into an independent state, on the terms and conditions specified in the two acts of assembly." Conformable to this determination, an address was prepared, requesting admission into the Union as an independent state. This, with the resolution respecting the expediency of a separation, and another resolution fixing on the 31st day of December 1788, as the period when the authority of Virginia over the proposed state should terminate, were forwarded to the delegates in Congress from Virginia; copies of the two resolutions were likewise transmitted to the Executive of Virginia, to be by him laid before the Legislature—and that nothing might be wanting to ensure success to the measure, the president of the Convention was directed to address the representatives from the District to the General Assembly, requesting them to use their best endeavours to have an inhabitant of the District appointed a member of Congress.[188] The following are copies of the resolutions and address above alluded to:

Extracts from the Journals of a Convention, begun and held at Danville in the county of Mercer, on Monday the 17th of September 1787.

"RESOLVED, *nemine contradicente,* by the representatives of the good people of the District of Kentucky in convention assembled, that it is expedient for, and the will of the same, that the said district be erected into a separate and independent state, on the terms and conditions specified in the two acts of assembly, one entitled 'An act concerning the erection of the District of Kentucky into a separate and independent state'—the other entitled 'An act making further provision for the erection of the District of Kentucky into an independent state.'

"*Resolved,* That this Convention do fix the 31st day of December 1788, to be the time on which the authority of the Commonwealth of Virginia and of its laws, over the District of Kentucky shall cease and determine [terminate] forever, under the exceptions specified in the act entitled 'An act concerning the erection of the district of Kentucky into an independent state.' "

"*To the hon. the Congress of the United States of America,*

"The representatives of the good people of Kentucky in Convention assembled, pursuant to an act of the General Assembly of Virginia, entitled 'An act concerning the erection of the District of Kentucky into an independent state,' having determined that it is expedient that the said District should be erected into a sovereign independent state, on the terms and conditions specified in the said act, and that the jurisdiction and authority of Virginia and her laws, shall cease and determine [terminate] forever, over the said District, on the 31st day of December 1788, do therefore beg leave to address your honourable body on the important subject.

"Happiness we all eagerly and incessantly pursue—this is the mark to which our aim is, and while we continue to be rational creatures, will forever be directed. If the inhabitants of the District of Kentucky, connected with the Commonwealth of Virginia, cannot from the peculiarity of their situation, obtain this great object; it is natural, it is reasonable to wish for a change.

"This separation we anxiously desire to effect in the regular constitutional mode prescribed by the law under which we act; but so great are our present sufferings, which must grow with our growth, and increase with our population, that should we be unsuccessful in this application, we shall not consider ourselves in any manner answerable for the future conduct of our constituents.

"We assure your honours that our wish to separate from our parent state, does not proceed from any impatience under restraints of her government, which we think wisely organised and well administered: but our remote situation from the seat of that government, and the many interjacent natural impediments, prevent our enjoying equal advantages with our eastern brethren, and preclude the idea of a connection on republican principles.

"Therefore, implicitly confiding in the justice and liberality of Congress—conscious that their cares are equally extended to every part of the confederacy—Sensible that, as it is their duty, it is their inclination to relieve the distresses and to communicate happiness to all the citizens of America.

"We in conformity to the acts of assembly, before referred to, and agreeable to a subsequent act entitled 'An act making further provision for the erection of the District of Kentucky into an independent state,' apply to your honours to ratify the compact solemnly entered into between the state of Virginia and the district of Kentucky, by declaring your assent to the erection of the said district into an independent state, on the terms and conditions stipulated in the said acts, and that the said district when erected as aforesaid, be permitted to enjoy equal privileges with the other of the United States of America, and be styled the Commonwealth of Kentucky.

"As it is of great consequence to the good people of Kentucky, to have the earliest information of the decision of your honours, to this important and to them deeply interesting subject, we most earnestly entreat you to enter on the consideration thereof, as soon as the other great affairs of state, which demand your attention, will permit; and that when decided, you will be pleased to transmit to us the result of your deliberations, in order that the convention to be elected to form a constitution of government, may have time to accomplish that arduous and momentous business, before the expiration of the period fixed on by us, when the authority of the Commonwealth of Virginia and of its laws, under certain exceptions, shall cease and determine [terminate] forever."[189]

As the assent of Virginia to this measure had twice been obtained, as it was in itself reasonable, and as proper means had been adopted for impressing on the minds of Congress the necessity and propriety of the measure, the Convention calculated on the undoubted assent of that body to it; they therefore recommended to the people, to elect representatives in the month of April following, to meet in Danville on the 4th Monday in July 1788, to form a constitution for the proposed state.[190] That full notice might be given of the time of holding these elections, the printer of the Kentucky Gazette was requested "to print the resolutions respecting the elections, six weeks successively immediately preceding the time." The resolutions were as follows:

"*Resolved*, as the opinion of this Convention, that a convention shall be elected, with full power and authority to frame and establish a fundamental Constitution of government for the proposed state, and to declare what laws shall be in force therein, until the same shall be abrogated or altered by the Legislative authority, acting under the constitution so to be framed and established.

"*Resolved*, That in the month of April next, on the respective court days of the counties within the said District, and at the respective places of holding courts therein, Representatives to continue in appointment until the 31st day of December 1788, to compose the said Convention, shall be elected within the said district, by the free male inhabitants of each county, in the like manner as delegates to the General Assembly have been elected, in the proportions following:—In the county of Jefferson shall be elected five representatives; in the county of Nelson five representatives; in the county of Fayette five representatives; in the county of Bourbon five representatives; in the county of Lincoln five representatives; in the county of Madison five representatives, in the county of Mercer five representatives. That full opportunity may be given to the good people of exercising their right of suffrage on an occasion so interesting to them, each of the officers so holding the elections, shall continue the same from day to day, and cause these resolutions to be read, immediately preceding the opening the election, at the door of the court-house, or other convenient place, and that Mr. Bradford be requested to publish the same in his Kentucky Gazette, six weeks successively, immediately preceding the said election." [191]

SECTION 26

The Enemy at the Door

[March 16, 1827]

During these political struggles and difficulties, the Indians continued their depredations on the defenceless inhabitants of Kentucky.

On the 11th of April, in the year 1787, a party of 15 Indians attacked a family by the name of *Shanks*, on Coope's Run, Bourbon county. The family consisted of an old lady, her two sons from 18 to 22 years of age, a widow daughter, with a small child in her arms, who occupied one end of a double cabin—while two other single, grown daughters, and a third of about 10 years of age, occupied the other end.[192]

A little after night a knocking at the door of the room occupied by the old lady was heard, and a call, in good English *"who keeps house."* One of the family was about opening the door, when the old lady forbid it, saying they were Indians. The young men sprang to their guns, and the enemy fled to the door of the three daughters, which opened on the side of the house, out of reach of the guns from the other part, the door of which opened at the end in the passage formed by the cabins. The Indians finding the young women unprotected, beat down the door with a rail, and attempted to take the three girls prisoners, one of whom they secured; the little girl broke out, and might have escaped by making off in the dark, but the poor thing ran around the house calling for help, and such was the feelings of the unhappy brothers, that they would have flew to her aid, if they had not been prevented by their aged mother, who forbid the door being opened, and in an instant the *tomahawk* of an Indian finished the cries of this little girl, in the hearing of her mother and brothers. While a part of the enemy were engaged in securing one of the girls as a prisoner, and tomahawking the other, the third and eldest, defended herself with a knife used by her at her loom, where she was engaged at the moment of the attack. The defence of this heroine deserved a better fate. She stabbed an Indian who fell dead at her feet; but she was overpowered and murdered.* Thus ended the conflict in one part of the house: of the three sisters, two were killed and one made prisoner—had the old lady permitted her two brave sons to take off at this moment, the night was so dark, and the dread of the enemy so great in approaching a rifle, the probability is, that all the other part of the family would have escaped. The Indians when in possession of the room occupied by the three sisters, set fire to it, and the flames soon extended to the other end, and spread a light around to a considerable distance. The Indians posted themselves in the dark in the angles of the yard fence, and waited for the flames to drive their prey from the house. The old lady, too infirm to run, placed herself under the protection of one of her sons, while the other took charge of his widowed sister, who had her infant in her arms—under this arrangement they all left the house at the same time, and attempted to pass the yard fence at two different points. The old lady was shot dead in crossing the fence—and at the point where the others attempted to cross, several Indians rose upon them and the young man fell in gallantly defending his sister and her infant. Of those in the room containing 5 persons, two only fell, viz: the old lady and the youngest of the two brothers, while the rest escaped to the neighboring farms, and alarmed the country.

---

*There was no doubt that the Indian was killed by the young woman in the manner stated—the wound fitted the knife, and his death could be accounted for in no other way.

Early on the next day, Col. John Edwards, with about thirty men were on the spot, and witnessed a scene too shocking for description. Every thing was either destroyed or carried off. The Indian killed by the young lady with her weaving knife, was found in the hollow of a tree, sunk in a branch near the house—While the massacre was going on and during the night, a snow fell much deeper than usual at that season.

Col. Edwards, with the number of men above mentioned, started in pursuit of the Indians, who were on foot, and made for the most hilly part of the country, formed by the waters of Eagle creek on the left, and Licking river on the right. The trail of the Indians was so plain, that the men, who were all mounted, could push on as fast as the nature of the ground would permit, and late in the evening on the same day, found the young woman lying tomahawked and scalped, only a few minutes before—they having been notified of the pursuit by the cries of a dog, which had been permitted to follow the men from the house. A few friends were left to take charge of the expiring victim, while the rest of the party pursued on in full speed, and on the point of a narrow ridge, saw the Indians passing and repassing from one tree to another so quickly, that it was believed the whole party had prepared for battle. The men dismounted and approached cautiously from tree to tree, flanking to the right and left. The Indians continued one steady yell, to induce a belief of great strength. When the whites approached near enough, a fire commenced; one Indian was killed and another fled badly wounded. It appeared that these two were all that remained who had no doubt agreed to sacrifice their lives for the safety of the rest of the party, by which means they gained so great a start as to enable them to reach a long branch, which was muddy by the melting of the snow, and night coming on, no further traces of the savages could be found. Before the next morning the snow had disappeared, and the men returned home. From the blood on the blanket left by the wounded Indian, it was believed he could not survive; and as he threw away his gun, he would not be able to make fire until he should meet with his party, which could not take place that night.[193]

In the summer of 1787, a person of savage appearance, hailed a house in Bourbon county, near the late residence of the unfortunate widow Shanks, who had been killed and her house burnt the preceding spring. The person was answered from the house, and invited by signs, as well as words, to come in—the invitation was accepted after a little hesitation, and the stranger, who appeared to be about 20 years of age, made the following narrative of himself in broken English, which he spoke very imperfectly.

He stated that he was taken prisoner when too small to recollect his name or the place from where he was taken; the rest of his family, he believed were killed. The Indians into whose hands he fell, gave him to one of the party who had recently lost a son, and he was adopted instead of the lost child, and treated with all the tenderness of which his adopted parents were capable. He was instructed in the art of war and hunting, and partook of those pleasures near the Indian town on the waters of Lake Erie, where he resided until the present spring, when his adopted father took him and an only son, to hunt on the Miami river, about 40 miles from where Cincinnati now stands. After a considerable quantity of meat was secured, the old man proposed to indulge his white and red sons, in a war trip to the settlements of Kentucky, where they were both anxious to display their skill in the art taught them by their warlike father. They prepared a bark canoe, and crossed the Ohio river a little below the mouth of Licking river, and secured their barque in some thick bushes on the Kentucky side, to prevent injury from the sun, which quickly destroyed such frail craft, if exposed.

There remained some feelings of civil life in the bosom of this adopted son of the forest, and as he approached the settlements, he formed a plan of leaving his companions, but the thought of betraying them never entered his mind. The night before they reached the settlements, the old man heard an owl scream in a manner which he considered the forerunner of misfortune, he was about retracing his steps, when his white son remonstrated against it, and being joined by his red brother, the fond father submitted to the entreaties of his children, and agreed to persevere in the previous plans of war. They went to sleep, and were soon roused by the old man, whose dreams had disturbed his sleep, which warned him of certain danger. The entreaties of the young men again prevailed over him, and he consented to continue the trip, but would by no means agree to remain any longer in the place they then occupied, but removed some distance, for the remainder of the night. The next day they reached the settlements, and at night were approaching a house, when this young man escaped in the dark, which frustrated all further attempts of the father and red son. All the signals agreed on to collect the party, were in vain. He remained concealed in the thick weeds until morning, when he hailed the house as before stated.

The neighbourhood was alarmed, and the timid stranger was examined over and over again. Strong suspicions arose, that he was a spy employed by the enemy, and to remove all doubts, he was required to conduct his countrymen to the spot where the canoe had been concealed on the bank of the Ohio river. He remonstrated against this measure, and was greatly distressed at the idea of assisting in the death of his father and brother, whom he still loved. Nothing would satisfy the white men, short of some evidence to support his account of himself, and he was ultimately compelled to conduct a body of 15 men in search of the canoe.—He stated, that on their way, his father had hid a kettle and some provisions, fifteen miles on this side of the Ohio, to which place he would first conduct them—they were all mounted on good horses. Such had been the speed of the Indians, that they were found seated by a fire cooking in the kettle when the whites arrived where it had been hid. At the request of the adopted son, an attempt was made to take the two Indians prisoners; but their exertions to get off were found to be such, that they were fired at and the old man was mortally wounded, and did not expire until he saw his distressed son who had betrayed him.—The other Indian escaped unhurt, and the white men ordered their guide to conduct them to the canoe. In the deepest anguish he beged to be spared from another sight so distressing, as to be the cause of the death of his brother, the partner of all his former amusements—urging that he had now convinced them of the correctness of his first statement, and hoped they would require no further act so afflicting to his feelings—but they were not to be appeased, they mounted their guide again and continued the pursuit. It was fifteen miles to the canoe, and so precise was the skill of this son of the forest in finding his way to the spot, that he steared directly to it, without the aid of the slightest trace of any sort. The men halted some little distance from the river bank, concealed their horses and then placed themselves in some thick bushes near the canoe. In about ten minutes the unfortunate Indian arrived, and was about launching his canoe into the river, when he fell dead, pierced with several balls, and never experienced the pang which a sight of his treacherous brother must have produced. This adopted son of the forest was not required to assist in killing his father and brother. He suffered greatly—and the writer of these notes has not been able to learn whether he still lives.[194]

[If any additional information exists among the early settlers of this country, on this or any other subject, it would be most thankfully received.]

EDITOR [Bradford]

SECTION 27

Horse Stealing
[March 23, 1827]

In the Spring of 1787, the Indians took the horses from a waggon on the road near the Blue Lick, and a man by the name of Scott. Simon Kenton with a party immediately pursued them across the Ohio river about 30 miles, overtook them and retook Scott, and the horses.[195]

About the same time the Indians killed a man on Fishing creek Lincoln county, by the name of Lutrell. Col. John Logan with a party of men pursued them across Cumberland river, overtook and routed them, killed three and took all their plunder.[196]

On the 3d of December 1787, three Indians stole horses near the Great Crossings, Scott county; they were immediately pursued by a party of men under Jacob Stucker. The Indians were overtaken at their camp on the following night, fired on and two killed and the third wounded, who made his escape; all the horses were recovered.[197]

A small station on Drennon's lick was about this time taken by the Indians and two men killed.

On the 4th Dec. 1787 an Indian fired on a whiteman on Bear Grass near Louisville, who being wounded fell; with his loaded rifle in his hand, which he laid across his breast; the Indian ran up to scalp him, when the wounded man fired and wounded the Indian in turn. The Indian was so badly wounded that he dropped his gun and blankett and ran off. The whiteman lived but a short time.[198]

About the 28th January 1788, the Indians stole twenty five horses from Col. Johnson's at the Great Crossings, Scott County, and made their escape with them.[199]

On the night of the 21st of February 1788, five men who were encamped at the Sinkhole Spring on the road from Lexington to Nashville, were fired on whilst asleep by a party of Indians, two of them were killed, two escaped unhurt, and one ran off and was not heard of afterwards. The two who escaped came to the nearest settlements in Kentucky, when a party of men immediately collected and went in persuit of the Indians. After several days travel they overtook the Indians in the night at their camp, and fired on them, at which they were so alarmed, that they ran off naked, without their guns or any part of their baggage.[200]

About the same time three boats, in descending the Ohio river, were taken by Indians near the mouth of the Big Miami, and the whole of the crews as well as passengers indiscriminately murdered.[201]

On the 25th June 1788, five Indians stole a number of horses from the mouth of Cane run in Scott county. They were quickly pursued by eight men, and overtaken the next evening, when one of them was killed and one badly wounded, and all the horses retaken.[202]

On the 31st day of Oct. 1788, a man driving a waggon near the Blue Licks, was killed by a party of Indians and six horses taken off. The next day, the same party of Indians killed a man near Limestone.[203]

The legislature of Virginia, desirous of manifesting to the people of Kentucky, a disposition to accelerate a separation, so ardently wished for; at their November session 1787, elected John Brown, esq. then a senator in the state legislature from the district of Kentucky, a representative to

Congress.[204] The address of the convention was presented to Congress on the 29th February 1788, and referred to a committee of the whole, who made the following report, "That it was in their opinion expedient that the district of Kentucky, should become an Independent State," and therefore a committee of one member from each State was appointed to prepare and report a bill on the subject.[205]

This committee from motives which will be explained, delayed reporting until the 2d of June, when on their own request they were discharged without having done any thing. On the day after their discharge, Mr. Brown made a motion to the following effect, after reciting the Virginia acts of separation, and the resolutions of the convention on the subject: "That the congress do ratify and confirm the compact entered into by the state of Virginia, with the district of Kentucky; and that the said district be admitted into the union as an independent federal member, on the first day of January 1789, and be styled the Commonwealth of Kentucky; and that congress release Virginia from all federal obligations arising within said district after the first day of January 1789, and that the said district be admitted to a representation in Congress, provided it contains sixty thousand inhabitants."

A motion was then made by Mr. Dana, a member from Massachusetts, to postpone the consideration of Mr. Brown's motion, which passed in the affirmative. Congress then entered into the following resolution: "As the Constitution of the United States is now ratified, congress think it unadvisable to adopt any other measure for admitting the District of Kentucky into the federal union; but thinking it expedient that the said district should become an independent state, and a member of the union, as soon as convenience will permit, under the constitution, recommend it to the legislature of Virginia, and the inhabitants of the district, to alter their acts and resolutions, so as to make them conformable to the provision of the constitution."[206]

During the pendency of this business before congress, the inhabitants of Kentucky had cherished the most sanguine hopes of success. Intelligence had been received that the committee of the whole had decided in favor of a separation, and that a committee had been appointed to draught a bill for admission into the union. The people had considered this an an absolute determination, both as to the right and policy of the measure, and viewed all that was to come as mere formality. They consequently concluded that their safety and prosperity were settled on a basis firm and indubitable.

In the meantime elections were held in the month of April 1788, for representatives to a convention to form a constitution. The members elected met at Danville on the 4th Monday in July, with a view of entering on the task; but on that day and at that place, they had the mortification to receive the dispatches forwarded by the secretary of Congress, to the

President of the Convention, giving intelligence of the fate of the application to Congress. The mortification and chagrin produced by this disappointment, was intense. The submissive patience, the undeviating moderation and respect with which this great object had been pursued, was within the recollection of all. The dangers in which they had been exposed, from a surrounding, ferocious, relentless enemy, were brought afresh to their view, and the great disadvantages resulting from their local situation, increased the agony of their feelings. Their request for the active interposition of Government in their defence had been obtained, and the natural right of exercising their own strength in defending themselves, constantly circumscribed, restrained and embarrassed. But above all, the disgraceful project of sacrificing the western country at the shrine of Eastern America, by relinquishing to Spain the navigation of the river Mississippi, had not been abandoned. Seven states had assented to that disgraceful act, and the subject might again be revived, whenever it was known that another state could be brought over. [207]

SECTION 28

"Sinister Political Design" at Work?
[March 30, 1827]

The conduct of congress on the application of the district for a separation, evinced the existence of some *sinister political design.*—Two months after the address had been referred to a committee of the whole, had nearly elapsed, before any further notice was taken of it, and one more month occupied with the pretence of draughting a bill, but without effecting anything, when the committee at their own solicitation were discharged, and the business in effect *thrown out of the house.* [208]

What the design alluded to was, and the motives which produced it, had been explained in the debates in the Virginia Convention to adopt the Federal Constitution. Col. Grayson, (who was a member of Congress from Virginia, when the Mississippi project was discussed) told them that the language and policy of the eastern states had been and ever would be—*"Let us prevent any new states from arising in the western world, or they will out vote us; we will lose our importance and become as nothing in the scale of nations. If we do not prevent it, our countrymen will remove to those places instead of going to sea, and we will receive no particular tribute or advantage from them."*—Deb. Vir. Con. vol. 2, page 134.[209]

This unforeseen and unexpected disaster, involved the members elected to form a convention, in great difficulties, but it was ultimately determined to convene and organize themselves into a deliberative body, and to take into consideration the proceedings of Congress. Several days were occupied in deliberating on the situation in which the district was placed. It was finally determined to recommend to the people the election of five representatives from each county the ensuing October, to meet in Danville on the first Monday in November following, and to delegate to these representatives full power to take such measures for obtaining admission into the union, as a separate and independent state, and the navigation of the Mississippi river, and also to form a constitution of government for the district, and organize the same when they shall judge it necessary, or to do and accomplish whatever, on consideration of the state of the district, may in their opinion be necessary to promote its interests. To give sufficient notice to this measure, the printer of the Kentucky Gazette was requested to publish the resolutions which has been agreed to, until the first day of October, with which he complied; and to prevent surprize the persons who were to conduct the elections, were requested to keep open five days, and to cause the resolutions to be read every day, previous to opening the polls.

It may be proper to notice, that during the session of this convention, they entered into a resolution, that Col. M'Dowell the President, wait on Mr. Brown, when he should return to the district, and in the most respectful terms, express to him the obligations which the convention and their constituents were under to him, for the faithful attention to their interests.[210]

In the year 1788, the northern and southern frontiers of Kentucky, were infested by the Indians; and whilst its inoffensive citizens were bleeding under the tomahawk and scalping knife, inflicted on the road to the interior counties, butchered on their farms, and in their houses, could obtain no protection from their government; Congress on the first day of September entered upon the following resolution:

"Resolved, that the secretary at war, be and he is hereby directed, to have a sufficient number of troops in the service of the United States in readiness to march from the Ohio to the protection of the Cherokees, whenever congress shall direct the same; and that he take measures for obtaining information, of the best routs for troops to march from the Ohio to Chota, and for dispersing all the white inhabitants settled upon or in the vicinity of the hunting grounds, secured to the Cherokees by the treaty concluded between them and the United States, November 28th 1785, and the proclamation of congress of this date.

"Resolved, that copies of the said proclamation, and of these resolutions, be transmitted to the executive of Virginia and North Carolina, and that the said states be, and they are hereby requested to use their influence that the said proclamation may have its intended effect, to restore peace and harmony between the citizens of the United States, and the Cherokees, and to prevent any further invasions of their respective rights and possessions; and in case congress shall find it necessary to order troops to the Cherokee towns to enforce a due obedience of the said treaty, that the said states be and they are hereby requested to co-operate with the said troops for enforcing such observance of that treaty."

This measure was designed to give protection to the Cherokee Indians, the notorious robbers and murderers of the people of Kentucky. The sensibility which it excited, may be conceived—it cannot be expressed. But it afforded additional inducement to the citizens of the district to persevere in their exertions to obtain a separation, and thereby the privilege of protecting themselves.[211]

Elections were held agreeably to the recommendations before mentioned, and on the first Monday in November a convention, vested with the extensive powers above stated, convened at Danville.[212] This was an important crisis in the affairs of Kentucky. On the third day it was resolved, once more to address the legislature of Virginia, and request them to pass another act respecting the independence of Kentucky. A committee was accordingly appointed to draught and report an address, which was done. On the address being reported, an amendment was proposed, and both that and the address ordered to lie on the table. The reason of this was, that some objection had been made to the substance of the address, and several members disapproved of the proceedings *in toto*.[213]

The people of Kentucky had in full convention four several times solemny declared their wish to separate from Virginia. Virginia had twice announced her assent; and Congress had once expressed their approbation of the measure; that this assent of Congress, had proved abortive was well known to have been owing to the malign influence of an eastern politician, whose talents for intrigue have been famous throughout the civilized world. To repeat the process of again applying to Virginia for her assent; again referring it to the people, and then again to Congress, would be a tedious parade of mere formality, and tend only to increase the difficulties under which the district then laboured. A considerable time must elapse, before the new Federal Government could come into operation, and experience had furnished them no cause to believe, that the protection of Kentucky would engross its earliest care. On the other hand, there was much reason to fear, that bartering away the navigation of the Mississippi would be among its first acts. But whatever the disposition of the government might be, delay must be inevitable. From these considerations, some were of opinion, that it was the duty of the convention under the power delegated to them, to proceed to form a constitution; that measures should be taken to organize the district under it, and as soon as affairs of the general government would permit, Kentucky should present herself in that organized state, for admission into the Union, on the conditions contained in the compact with Virginia. Under these impressions the following resolution was submitted to the consideration of the convention.

"Resolved, that it is the wish and interest of the good people of this district, to be separated from Virginia, and that the same be erected into an independent member of the Federal Union." This resolution resulting from necessity, contemplated no violent measures; nor did it exceed the powers delegated, but was expressly authorized by the people under the recommendation of the convention of July, in these words: "And also to form a constitution of government for the district, and organize the same when they shall judge necessary."[214]

The propriety and necessity of adopting this resolution, was advocated on the following principles. By acceding to the compact stipulated by Virginia, the contract, as far as related to the state and district, would be closed. The rights of individuals and of the district, would be so far ratified, as would preclude Virginia from hereafter imposing new conditions, or varying the terms offered and acceded to. The strength of the district might under this organized form, be called into action, the attacks of the Indians repelled, and they reduced to the necessity of suing for peace. Migrations would increase, and the country be thereby enriched and strengthened. The inconvenience resulting from locality would terminate.

These considerations were enforced by the reflection, that Virginia, viewing Kentucky as on the eve of separation, would pay little or no attention to her interests in any laws which she might thereafter pass.[215]

A Quest in New Orleans
[April 6, 1827]

As a further inducement to adopt the foregoing resolution, it was stated that there was a prospect of obtaining from Spain permission to export the produce of the country by the way of the Mississippi; and in consequence of information which Gen. Wilkinson had given to some friends on that subject, the General was requested, from the chair, to state to the convention his opinion on this matter. In compliance with this request, the General informed the house, that he had descended the Mississippi in the summer 1787, with a view of obtaining commercial advantages for himself, and with a prospect of opening a communication for commercial purposes between New Orleans and the country bordering on the Ohio. On his arrival at New Orleans, he informed the Governor of the object which he had in view; represented the rapid increase of the population in the western parts of the United States, the fertility of the soil, the extensive navigable rivers with which the country was watered, the abundance of produce already raised for exportation, which would increase with the increasing population of the country; the great advantages which the Spanish government might derive by cultivating an amicable intercourse; the extensive monopoly of the trade; the certainty of obtaining supplies of flour and pork for the inhabitants of their islands and the country bordering on the Gulf of Mexico &c.—That he had addressed the fears as well as the hopes of the Spanish natives—that he had inferred from the rapidly increasing population of the western country; from the sentiments universally entertained by the inhabitants, that they had a right, by the laws of God and nature, to the free use of that river—that the time might not be remote, when they would claim as a right, what they would now accept as a favour. Gen. Wilkinson mentioned further, that Governor Mero requested him to commit to writing, his sentiments on this interesting subject, which he complied with by way of memorial. A copy of this he produced and read in convention, and concluded by observing, that the memorial had been received by the Governor, with expressions of approbation, with a promise to transmit it to his Catholic Majesty.[216]

This memorial was much admired by the literary gentlemen present in convention, for its manly and dignified style, the copious and comprehensive view which was taken of the subject, the elegance of the composition, and its peculiar adaption to operate on the fears and avarice of the Spaniards.

The convention, in order to manifest their gratitude to Gen. Wilkinson for the exertions he had made towards obtaining permission for the western country, to export their produce to New Orleans, resolved unanimously, that the convention highly approve the address presented by Gen. Wilkinson to the Governor intendant of Louisiana; and that the President be requested to present him with the thanks of the Convention for the regard which he therein manifested for the interests of the western country.[217]

This communication brought to recollection, information received by the president of the convention on the same subject, in a letter written by Mr. John Brown, while in congress, after the application of Kentucky to that body had been defeated, as before mentioned. A motion was then made, that the president request Mr. Brown (who was then present and a member of the convention) to make such communication on the subject, as he should think proper.—Mr. Brown then stated in a concise manner, the substance of what he had written Col. M'Dowell; but in doing this Mr. Brown merely stated, that "in a conversation he had with Mr. Gardoque the Spanish minister to the United States, relative to the navigation of the Mississippi, he stated that if the people of Kentucky would erect themselves into an independent state, and appoint a proper person to negotiate with him, he had authority for that purpose, and would enter into an arrangement with them for the exportation of their produce to New Orleans on terms of mutual advantage"; without recommending the adoption of any measures in consequence of it, or suggesting a single sentiment of approbation.[218]

About the 1st of August 1787, Col. Ben. Logan received an express from Col. James Robinson, commanding officer of the settlements on the Cumberland river, containing the following intelligence: That he was informed by express from the chief of the Chickasaw nation, and also by some Indians who had escaped from that country, that the Creek, Chickamawga and some other tribes of Indians, had in a grand counsel held at Mobile, declared war against the settlements on Cumberland river, and were to invade that country in the course of the present month, with all the force they could raise; that in consequence of this determination, M'Gilvray, superintendant of the Creek nation had sent a party of Creeks to the Chickasaw nation, with orders to kill Mr. Turnbull, Capt. Davenport and every other white man they could find in that country. Turnbull having information by an Indian of their design, made his escape, but Davenport and four others were killed in the Chickasaw town, and the whole settlements of Chickasaw Bluff cut off, except three.[219]

The Chickasaws (though mortal enemies of the Creeks,) were unable to protect these people from their cruelty being destitute of ammunition; but assured Col. Robinson, that as soon as they receive a supply from Cumberland or Kentucky, they will declare open war against that nation. Col. Robinson wrote in the most pressing manner for assistance from Kentucky; urging that unless immediately reinforced, the whole country was in danger of falling a sacrifice to the superior force of the enemy, that an attack was hourly expected, from the sign which had been discovered of large parties within a few miles of Nashville.[220]

Intelligence was received, that two days after the express had left Col. Robinson, the contemplated attack was made; that four families were destroyed, that a party of white men who had given the Indians battle were defeated, and that a great deal of corn had been cut down by the enemy.

The following speech was delivered to Col. Logan at Limestone on the 20th of August 1787, by Capt. Jonny (chief commander in the Shawanee nation).

"We have sent for Logan to let him know our opinion. He shall soon know our opinion from our hearts. I heard your words, by which I was informed not to be afraid to come and exchange for my prisoners. I was not afraid, but our people is scattered so far apart, that it took me a great deal of trouble, in which I made all industry I could to collect all the prisoners from our young brothers, to do which I was two months out at the Wabash towns, among the rest of our younger brothers. I found out their opinions, all those who had prisoners said they could not give them up to the big knife, which was one half the town. Those who had not prisoners, plead to take pity on the women and children, to give them up to get their prisoners from the white people. When I was there, I looked back to the place where I had lived, where our old towns were, I seemed to be alone, or like a man among children. I could by no means obtain prisoners from the others. I heard our brothers word and believed it, & meant to come myself. All my town is for peace, the one half of Picakway town, one half of Chillicothe town, one half of Cespeco town also, and the half of Wacatomaca; of which all say let us take pity on our women and children, and agree to make peace with our brother the big knife, which our brother the big knife have always said was in our power. If we want peace we shall have peace, to which we are agreed, to come back to where our old town was burnt and live like brothers. These Indians who are for war, they will be always out on the Wabash, and we will make a destinction between them and ourselves, to let our brother the big knife know we are really for peace. Here will be five little towns of us that will be for peace, and will trade with our brother big knife, and use all industry we can, to get as many prisoners as possible. Our women have talked to us to take pity on them and to make peace, that they may live in peace and plenty. When we listened to them, we took pity upon all that are now for peace. The others who are for war, took no pity on their women and children. We want to let our women and children live in peace and plenty. Now we took it upon ourselves to be as poor people as the rest of our brothers would take no pity on us, to get our prisoners; but we hope through time, we will be able to redeem them all, then will we live in peace and plenty like brothers. All our young main chiefs are for peace. Of the other towns, there are none but some wild young men who will be out on the Wabash, who will be for war; we can do nothing with them.[221]

"Paper and time is scarce, for which I am in hopes of being excused."

"Col. Logan's Answer:
"I now speak to the head chiefs and warriors of the Shawanee nation.
"*Friends & Brothers,*

"I hope we have met here in peace,—and in the first place, to consider the tedious and bloody war we have been engaged in with each other— You may well remember, that ten years ago we were all governed by one king, over the great waters. But it has so happened, that our father the King, engaged you on his part, and the Congress engaged us on their part. And you and us living nearly in one country, it hath been our fortunes to attack each other and have spilt much blood in our land— many of our people have fallen into your hands, and some of your people have fallen into our hands.
"*Brothers,*

"You may see plainly, how your father over the water, who engaged you in so long and bloody a war, has treated you; that although you lost many brave warriors, yet when he got beaten by the great men of the United States, he made peace and gave your country away, and said nothing about you, but left you to the discretion of the Americans, to treat you as they pleased.
"*Brothers,*

"You and all the red people may plainly see, that when your father and all his forces added to all yours, could not conquer the Americans, that it will be in vain for you (the red people) to continue a war yourselves alone; it is true you may kill a few old men and old women in different parts of the country, but this will do you no service, but harm; for we can go to all the towns in your country and destroy all your living.
"*Brothers,*

"Let us not think of those bloody designs any longer; let us live at peace and prevent your old father the king from laughing at us, when we are fighting and destroying one another, and think that he will get our country for his own people.
"*Brothers,*

"There are a great many designing men in this country, and some may encourage you to go to war, because they know if you do, that you will be driven out of the country you now inhabit, and then they can live where you now live, and laugh to think how they have fooled you. This will surely be the case, and it is you and us that must fight the battle. When your country shall lie waste, then will the Americans sell it; but if you will live at peace and keep possession of it, it will not be taken from you, and you can be a happy people and continue to live on your own land.

As to the prisoners, I am sorry you have not got the young prince, but he lives very well. I hope this is not the last time we are to see each other, or to exchange prisoners.—Our desire is to have our prisoners whose names we gave you, and after they are exchanged, the remainder must be purchased from you by their friends, upon such terms as you may be agreed on. The names of those prisoners that we gave you, their friends assisted in taking the prisoners from you—they shewed themselves like men and warriors, for which reason they now have the preference.— When I transact business of this kind, I call on the great spirit above to judge me, that I do all things right. I have considered your request in returning the young Pickaway woman, and your getting the young Prince; it appears to me it was their fortune to be both taken at the same time, they were equal to me, and I not knowing that you wished one more than another, it has been her fortune to be brought here and not his; now for me to send her back, and bring the young prince away from his mother, would be giving me a great deal of trouble, and I think the great man above will not think it just; and for that reason I cannot do it. But you may rest assured, your prince shall be well treated, and be delivered at the next exchange, and you need be at no trouble, only send the prisoners to Limestone, where Mr. Jacob Boone will receive them, and send yours to you. I have no more to say to you, only advise you to go home and live at peace; and I will assure you no army will march against you from Kentucky.

"I am not authorised to treat any further with you, only to wish a friendly trade could be carried on between us.—I hope what I have said will be agreeable to you, and that you and I will subscribe our names thereto.   BENJAMIN LOGAN, *Com.*[222]

"Aug. 20, 1787

    Test. ISAAC RUDDELL   CAPT JONNY, c.c.s.n.
           JOHN CROW   PEMENAWAH,
           DANIEL BOONE,   MANEMSECHO,
                                LATHENFECCHO."

The Lurking Enemy
[April 13, 1827]

On the night of the 3d of Sept. 1787, a Mr. Schooler, at Harrison's Station on Licking, hearing something in his garden which he supposed to be horses, went out to see, when an Indian fired at him, but fortunately missed him—he instantly ran at the Indian and seized his gun, which the Indian let go and made his escape, leaving the gun in the hands of Schooler.[223]

In the latter part of March 1788, three boats descending the Ohio river, were captured by a party of Indians near the mouth of the Big Miami. Among the passengers on board these boats, were Samuel Purviance of Baltimore, a Mr. Ridout of Maryland, Mons: Ragaut and two other French gentlemen, one a mineralogist, the other a botanist, destined to explore the natural products of the Western country—a Mr. Pierce of Maryland and a Mr. Ferguson, a trader: besides these there was a Mr. Gray, Garland, Simpson and five others, and a negro woman. The three French gentlemen and Mr. Pierce who occupied one boat, were attacked on the 26th of March, the others passed Limestone on the 19th. The Indians had in their possession a flat boat, in which eight or ten of them gave chase to the boat of Mr. Pierce and the three Frenchmen, who finding they could not escape, hoisted a white handkerchief as a token of peace, and surrendered without resistance. When the Indians approached near enough, Ragaut who displayed the flag, posted himself at the stern of the boat, and offered them his hand, and in return received the barbarians tomahawk in his skull; the botanist at this instant was shot dead, and the mineralogist badly wounded. Whilst the Indians were butchering and rifling these, the boat had drifted near the shore, when Pierce and the surviving Frenchman jumped overboard, and the rapidity of the current carried them past the Indians; they both fortunately got on shore, and by means of the darkness of the night which at that time closed in, evaded pursuit. They made a circuit, and struck the river some distance below, where they continued until daylight, when they were taken into a boat descending the river, and conveyed to Louisville that evening. None of the passengers in the other boats were ever heard of afterwards, and were no doubt all killed.

The few hours before these boats were attacked, two boats under the direction of Capt Ballard Smith and a Mr Hinds, were attacked at the same place, from the shore; but Smith and his party returned the fire, and thereby effected an escape with no other injury than having two horses wounded.[224]

About the 12th of May 1788, two lads on Licking Creek, who were going to a Lick, fell in with two Indians riding on one horse. They fired on the Indians and wounded both mortally, who dropped one of their guns and baggage, and ran off. The lads went home and raised a party of men and went in pursuit of the wounded Indians and killed them both.

On the 25th of May 1788, five Indians stole some horses on Cane Run, a branch of Elkhorn. They were pursued immediately by eight men, who followed them that day and night, and late in the evening of the next day overtook them within twelve miles of the Ohio, fired on them and killed one on the spot and wounded another, who with the remainder made their escape, leaving all their baggage and the horses they had stolen.

About the same time, a boat was taken up adrift at the mouth of Goose Creek near Louisville, in which were several barrels that had been lately emptied of whiskey and flour. There was much blood in the boat, and several balls sticking in its sides. It was supposed to have belonged to Col Mitchell, from Berkley county Virginia, and that all on board had been killed by the Indians.[225]

On the 26th of Nov. 1788, a number of packhorses and several teams, that were on their way from Lexington to Limestone, were attacked by a party of about five Indians, about two and a half miles from the Blue Licks. One of the party, a Mr. Lata, was killed and six horses taken. The same party of Indians killed a man the next day near Limestone.

On the 10th day of November 1788, in the Convention then setting, Gen. Wilkinson from the committee appointed to draught an address to Congress, requesting immediate and effective measures to be taken, to obtain the navigation of the Mississippi river; made the following report, which was twice read and agreed to as follows:[226]

"To the United States in Congress assembled.
"The people of Kentucky, represented in Convention as freemen, as citizens and as part of the American republic, beg leave by this humble petition, to state their rights, and call for protection in the enjoyment of them.

"Fathers!—Fellow citizens!—and Guardians of our rights!—As we address you by the endearing appellation of fathers, we rely on your paternal affection to hear us. We rely on your justice, as men and citizens to attend to the wrongs done to men and citizens; and as a people recognized by the solemn acts of the union, we look for protection to the federal hand.

"When the peace had secured to America that sovereignty and independence for which she had so nobly contended, we could not retire with our Atlantic friends, to enjoy in ease the blessings of freedom—Many of us had expended, in the struggle for our country's rights, that property which would have enabled us to possess a competence with our liberty.

"On the western waters the commonwealth of Virginia possessed a fertile but uninhabited wild.

"In this wilderness we sought, after having procured liberty for our posterity, to provide for their support. Inured to hardships by a long warfare, we ventured into almost impenetrable forests, without bread or domesaic cattle—we depended on the casual supplies afforded by the chase; hunger was our familiar attendant, and even our unsavoury meals were made upon the wet surface of the earth, with the cloud-deformed canopy for our covering. Though forced to pierce the thicket, it was not in safety we trod. The wily savage thirsted for our blood, lurked in our paths and seized the unsuspecting hunter. Whilst we lamented the loss of a friend, a brother, a father, a wife, a child became a victim to the barbarian tomahawk; instead of consolation, a new and greater misfortune deadened the sense of former afflictions. From the union, we receive no support—but we impeach not their justice. Ineffectual treaties, often renowned, and as often broken by the savage nations, served only to supply them with the means of our destruction. But no human cause could controul that Providence, which had destined this western country to be the seat of a civilized and happy people. The period of its accomplishment was distant, but it advanced with rapid and incredible strides. We derived strength from our falls and numbers from our losses; the unparalleled fertility of our soil made grateful returns, far disproportioned to the slight labour which our safety would permit us to bestow. Our fields and herds afforded us not only sufficient support for ourselves, but also for the emigrants who annually double our numbers, and even a surplus still remains for exportation. This surplus would be far greater, did not a narrow pollicy shut up our navigation, and discourage our industry.

"In this situation we call for your attention. We beg you to trace the Mississippi from the ocean—survey the innumerable rivers which water your western territory, and pay their tribute to its greatness—examine the luxuriant soil which these rivers traverse: then we ask, can the God of wisdom and nature have created that vast country in vain? Was it for nothing that he blest it with a fertility almost incredible? Did he not provide those great streams which empty into the Mississippi, and by it communicate with the Atlantic, that other nations and climes might enjoy with us the blessings of our fruitful soil? View the country, and you will answer for yourselves. But can presumptuous madness of man imagine a policy inconsistent with the immense designs of the Deity? Americans cannot.

"As it is the natural right of the inhabitants of this country to navigate the Mississippi, so they have also the right derived from treaties and national compacts.

"By the treaty of Peace, concluded in the year 1763, between the crowns of Great Britain, France and Spain, the free navigation of the river Mississippi was ascertained to Great Britain: the right thus ascertained was exercised by the subjects of that crown, till the peace of 1783, and conjointly with them by the citizens of the United States.

"By the treaty, in which Great Britain acknowledged the independence of the United States, she also ceded to them the free navigation of the river Mississippi. It was a right naturally annexed to the possession of this western country. As such it was claimed by America, and it was upon that principle she obtained it; yet the court of Spain, who possess the country at the mouth of the Mississippi, have obstructed your citizens in the enjoyment of that right.

"If policy is the motive which actuates political conduct, you will support us in this right, and thereby enable us to assist in the support of government. If you will be really our fathers, stretch forth your hands to save us. If you would be worty guardians, defend our rights. We are a member that would exert any muscle for your service. Do not cut us off from your body. By every tie of consanguinity and affection, by the remembrance of the blood we have mingled in the common cause, by a regard to justice and policy, we conjure you to procure our right.

"May your councils be guided by wisdom and justice, and may your determinations be marked by decision and effect. Let not your beneficience be circumscribed by the mountains which divide us; but let us feel that you are really the guardians and asserters of our rights: then you will secure the prayers of a people, whose gratitude would be as warm as the vindication of their rights will be eternal; then our connection shall be perpetuated to the latest times, a monument of your justice, and a terror to your enemies." [227]

The Fine Hand
of James Wilkinson
[April 20, 1827]

On the 10th day of November 1788, in the Convention, Gen. Wilkinson from the committee, appointed to draught an address to the people of this district, reported that the committee had taken the matter into considera-tion, and prepared an address, which he read in his place, and ordered to be referred to a committee of the whole convention.[228]

The Convention, according to the order of the day, resolved itself into a committee of the whole, to take into consideration the state of the district.

Mr Innis was elected to the chair. After some time spent therein, the President resumed the chair, and the chairman reported that the commit-tee had taken into consideration the address to the Assembly of Virginia, and made an amendment thereto, which he read in his place, and then delivered in the same at the clerk's table, where it was again twice read, and again amended, and then agreed to *namine contradicente,* as follows:

"*To the Hon: the General Assembly for the Commonwealth of Virginia.*
GENTLEMEN—The representatives of the good people inhabiting the sev-eral counties composing the district of Kentucky, in convention met, beg leave again to address you on the great and important subject of their separation from the parent state, and being made a member of the federal union.

"To repeat the causes which impel the inhabitants of this district to continue their application for a separation, will in our opinion, be unnec-essary. They have been generously acknowledged and patronized in former Assemblies, and met the approbation of that august body, whose consent was necessary towards the final completion of this desirable object, and who resolved that the measure was expedient and necessary, but which from their peculiar situation, they were inadequate to decide on.

"As happiness was the object which first dictated the application for a separation, so it has continued to be the ruling principle in directing the good people of Kentucky to that great end, upon constitutional terms, and they conceive the longer that measure is delayed, the more will they lie exposed to the merciless savage, or (which is greatly to be feared) anarchy, with all the concomitant evils attendant thereon.

"Being fully impressed with these ideas, and justified by frequent examples, we conceive it our duty as freemen, from the regard we owe to our constituents, and being encouraged by the resolutions of Congress, again to apply to your honourable body, praying that an act may pass at the present session, for enabling the good people of the Kentucky district, to obtain an independent government and be admitted into the confederation, as a member of the federal union, upon such terms and conditions as to you may appear just and equitable; and that you transmit such act to the president of this convention with all convenient despatch, in order for our consideration and the final completion of this business. This we are emboldened to ask, as many of the causes which produced former restrictions, do not now exist. Finally, relying on the justice and liberality of your honourable house, so often experienced, and which we are even bound to acknowledge, we again solicit the friendly interposition of the parent state, with the Congress of the U. States for a speedy admission of the district into the federal union, and also to urge that honourable body, in the most express terms, to take effectual measures for procuring to the inhabitants of this district the free navigation of the river Mississippi, without which the situation of a large part of the community will be wretched and miserable, and may be the source of future evils.

"*Ordered*, That the president sign and the clerk attest the said address, and that the same be enclosed by the president to the speaker of the House of Delegates."[229]

The calamities anticipated from procrastinating the separation were soon realized by melancholy experience. Virginia had hitherto manifested a disposition to separate from the district on terms honourable and generous; but her temper was now changed. A third act respecting the separation was passed on the 29th day of December 1788, in consequence of the address of the Convention, in which the second and eighth articles of the compact were materially altered to the prejudice of Kentucky: lst by fixing on the proposed state a part of the *domestic debt*. 2d. By reserving a right to unappropriated lands after the district should be erected into an independent state.[230]

This law authorised elections to be held in the several counties for members of a convention to decide *again* on the expediency of a separation, and directed that the convention should convene at Danville on the 20th day of July 1789. Elections were held accordingly, and a number of representatives sufficient to proceed to business convened at the place appointed, and on the third day adopted a resolution to the following effect.

That it was the opinion of the convention that the terms now proposed by Virginia, on which the separation of the district should be effected, were materially different from those agreed on in 1785, *and were inadmissible.* That therefore a memorial ought to be presented to the general assembly, requiring the necessary amendments to the act.

But another consequence of the delay more immediately alarming, was now experienced. The executive of Virginia had heretofore authorized the lieutenants of the several counties to call into service scouts and rangers for the purpose of giving to the inhabitants the earliest intelligence of an invasion. This measure promised to produce the most salutary effects. But the governor now [June 1st, 1789] wrote to the county Lieutenants, immediately to discharge all the scouts and rangers, and in future in case of depredations to make communication to the continental officer on the Ohio, stationed nearest to the place of attack, the defence of the country being in the hands of the general government.[231]

This was no trivial cause of alarm. The district presented a frontier of more than six hundred miles, and the regular troops, from the smallness of their number, and the manner in which they were stationed could afford no efficient protection. The troops were all stationed beyond the extreme northern limit of the district; whereas the Southern Indians were equally hostile as the Northern. Not only this, but there were in all but about six companies, and even part of them artillery; the remaining part were infantry, and on that account wholly incompetent to any effectual pursuit of the Indians, or even a safe retreat from them; as they generally made their escape on the horses which they had stolen from the inhabitants.[232] But if these circumstances would not have rendered their aid inefficient, their distance from the settlements would; two thirds of the troops were stationed at Fort Washington, opposite the mouth of Licking: this was then more than 60 miles from the nearest settled part of Kentucky.—Discharging the scouts and rangers, deprived the people of the means of obtaining previous intelligence of danger. They must wait until the tomahawk and scalping knife were actually on their heads, *then* give information of it to the county lieutenant, and he make a formal communication to an officer sixty or perhaps an hundred and fifty miles distant, who as soon as convenient would send a party of men to their relief. The objection which Kentucky had to this mode of protection was, that long previous to the arrival of the troops, the citizens who had been attacked would all have been murdered and the enemy who had made the attack would have fled beyond the reach of pursuit. But this had been deemed by Virginia a matter worthy of no consideration. The remaining part of the regular troops were stationed on the North side of the Ohio, just above the rapids, nearly 200 miles distant from the former, so that all idea of cooperation on any emergency was excluded.

The convention thoroughly convinced that no aid could be derived from *this system of protection*, appointed a standing committee to draw up and forward a remonstrance to the executive of Virginia against discharging the scouts and rangers, and to address the president of the United States on the defenceless state of the frontier, the impracticability of the projected mode of protection, and to report their proceedings to the next convention.[233]

SECTION 32

The Bloody Ordeal of the Kentucky Frontier

[April 27, 1827]

During these political operations the Indians continued to harrass the frontier settlements.

On the 14th of March 1789, three Indians killed a man and wounded another, on the road from Lexington to Limestone, near May's Lick, and the same day they took a prisoner and a number of horses, near Limestone. They were pursued by about forty men, overtaken at the Ohio river, and the whole killed in attempting to cross.

On the 29th of May 1789, two boys were killed on the N.W. side of the Ohio, about three miles above Limestone; and about the same time a woman and child were killed at their own spring on Beargrass, where the woman had gone for water.

On the 3d of June, two men and three boys who were fishing on Floyd's Fork of Salt river, were attacked by a party of Indians; the two men were killed, and the boys taken prisoners. After travelling some distance, the Indians gave one of the boys a tomahawk and kicking him, ordered him to return to his people and inform them what had become of his companions.

On the evening of the 14th of June, three Indians stole Capt. Jacob Stucker's horses; and on the next day a party of about twelve killed a lad near Captain Herndon's on Elkhorn. They were immediately pursued by Capt. Herndon with fifteen men; but crossing the trail of the party that had stolen Stucker's horses, and which was much easier to follow, pursued it, and in a short time came up with the Indians, killed two and wounded another, and recovered all the horses. On the following day two men were killed by the Indians near the Crab Orchard, and a number of horses taken. And on the 17th, a hunter was killed near Bullitt's Lick. A few days afterwards the Indians fired on a man on Licking creek, in Bourbon county, and wounded him in two places.

On the 27th of December, Col. Robert Patterson with three others, on their way to the mouth of Licking, were fired on by a party of Indians in the night whilst encamped on the head waters of Eagle creek—two of the party were killed/ the Colonel and the other escaped unhurt.

About the 15th of January 1790, the Indians killed two men on the waters of Dick's river in Lincoln county. On the 23d, the Indians killed three men at Fox's station on Lee's creek, near Limestone, and wounded another. An Indian attempted to tomahawk the wounded man, who seized the tomahawk and succeeded in getting it out of his hands, and made his escape, carrying off the tomahawk. About the 21st of March, a boat descending the Ohio river, was decoyed to the shore by a party of Indians, and Mr John May and a young woman who were on board killed, and the remainder of the passengers taken prisoners.

On the 23d of June, as a company were returning home from meeting on Brashear's creek, they were fired on by a party of Indians, and a man killed and a woman taken prisoner. They were immediately pursued, and when likely to be overtaken, they killed the woman and dispersed, so that they could be followed no further.

On the 17th of June, two spies were ranging near the Bigbone Lick, fell on the trail of six Indians, which they followed some distance, and coming within gun shot, fired on them—four of the Indians returned the fire, and rushed on the spies, who retreated. After running some distance, one of the spies fell behind, the other pushed on and left him. Shortly after, he heard two guns fire and the Indians give the war whoop. He was closely pursued himself, but he made his escape. About the same time two men went to a deer lick on Cox's creek to watch for deer; they had not been long at the lick, before they discovered an Indian coming up the creek to the lick—they both made ready and fired at him at the same instant, and killed him dead on the spot.

On the 19th of June, the Indians fired on two men at Baker's station on the head waters of Licking, killed and scalped one, and wounded the other. On the 26th of the same month the Indians fired on nine men at Morgan's station in the same neighbourhood, and wounded three of them, one of which mortally. On the same day, a boat descending the Ohio river, on board of which were six men, three women and six children, were attacked by sixteen Indians in four bark canoes, at the lowest of the Three Islands. The Indians got around the boat and near it before a single shot was fired, when the whites discharged their guns, upon which the Indians rushed up and boarded them without further resistance, and made prisoners of the whole. No lives were lost—no Indian was slightly wounded. All the property they could not carry off with them was sunk in the river. The evening after, one of the women was delivered of a child, and was the next day compelled to march on foot. The second day after the capture one of the men made his escape, from whom these particulars were obtained.[234]

The legislature of Virginia at their October session, 1789, reconsidered their last act of separation, and on the 18th day of December passed a fourth act, repealing the obnoxious clauses, and authorising the people again to elect Representatives to meet at Danville on the 26th day of the ensuing July, to determine a *fifth time* on the inclination of the people to separate from Virginia, and the expediency of the measure. If the Convention should decide in the affirmative, they were authorised by this act, to fix on some day posterior to the 1st day of November, 1791, on which the authority of Virginia was to cease, provided the general government should assent thereto; and to take the necessary measures for the election of a Convention to form a Constitution, which convention was to meet posterior to the first day of November, and prior to the day to be fixed on for the determination of the authority of Virginia.[235]

Elections were held in conformity to this act, and the representatives chosen met at Danville on the 26th of July 1790, and on the third day decided on the expediency and propriety of a separation on the terms now offered by Virginia. They then prepared an address to Congress in the following words:[236]

"To the President and the Honorable the Congress of
the United States of America.

"The Memorial of the representatives of the people of Kentucky in convention assembled, pursuant to an act of the legislature of Virginia, passed the 18th day of December, 1789, entitled "an act concerning the erection of the district of Kentucky into an independent state."

"Humbly sheweth that the inhabitants of this country are as warmly devoted to the American union, and as firmly attached to the present happy establishment of federal government, as any of the citizens of the United States.

"That, migrating from thence, they have with great hazard and difficulty effected their present settlements.

"The hope of increasing numbers could alone have supported the early adventurers under those arduous exertions; they have the satisfaction to find their hope verified. At this day the population and strength of this country render it fully able in the opinion of your memoralists, to form and support an efficient domestic government.

"The inconveniencies resulting from its local situation, as a part of Virginia at first, but little felt, have for some time been objects of their most serious attention; which occasioned application to the legislature of Virginia for redress.

"Here your memorialists would acknowledge with peculiar pleasure the benevolence of Virginia in permitting them to remove the evils arising from that source by assuming upon themselves a state of independence.

"This they have thought expedient to do in the terms and conditions stipulated in the above recited act; and have fixed on the first day of June 1792, as the period when the said independence shall commence.

"It now remains with the president and the congress of the United States to sanction these proceedings by an act of their honorable legislature prior to the first day of November 1791, for the purpose of receiving into the federal union the people of Kentucky, by the name of the state of Kentucky.

"Should this determination of your memorialists meet the approbation of the general government, they have to call a convention to form a constitution, subsequent to the act of Congress and prior to the day fixed for the independence of this country. When your memorialists reflect on the present comprehensive system of federal government; and when they also recollect the determination of a former congress on this subject, they are left without a doubt that the object of their wishes will be accomplished. And your memorialists as in duty bound shall forever pray."[237]

The Convention also passed the following resolution:

"*Resolved*, Therefore that in the month of December, 1791, on the respective court days of the counties within said district, and at the respective places of holding courts therein, representatives to continue in appointment for seven months, shall be elected by the free male inhabitants of each county above the age of twenty one years, in like manner as the delegates to this present convention have been elected in the proportions following: In the county of Jefferson shall be elected five representatives, in the county of Nelson five representatives, in the county of Mercer five representatives, in the county of Lincoln five representatives, in the county of Madison five representatives, in the county of Fayette five representatives, in the county of Woodford five representatives, in the county of Bourbon five representatives, and in the county of Mason five representatives. Provided, that no person shall vote in any county except that in which he resides, and that no person shall be capable of being elected unless he has been resident within the said district at least one year. Each of the officers holding such elections shall continue the same from day to day, passing over Sunday, for five days including the first day, and shall cause this resolution to be read each day immediately preceding the opening of the election at the door of the court house or other convenient place. Each of these officers shall deliver to each duly elected a representative, a certificate of his election, and shall transmit a general return to the clerk of the supreme court, to be by him laid before the convention. For every neglect of any of the duties hereby enjoined on such officers, he shall forfeit one hundred pounds, to be recovered by action of debt by any person suing for the same. The said convention shall be held at Danville, on the first Monday in April, and shall and may proceed after choosing a president and other proper officers, and settling the proper rules of proceeding, to frame and establish a constitution or form of government, and also to declare what laws shall remain in force until altered or abrogated by legislative authority acting under the constitution to be framed and established. Provided however, that five members assembled shall be a sufficient number to adjourn from day to day, and issue writs for supplying vacancies which may happen from deaths, resignations or refusal to act of any of the officers appointed by this resolution to hold the said election, any magistrate who shall chuse to act in any county where such absence, death, resignation or refusal to act shall happen, may proceed to hold such election under the same rules as such officer should or might have held it."[238]

SECTION 33

Governor Randolph's Message
[May 4, 1827]

The increased population, and consequent expansion of the settlements, and the diffusion of the settlers, increased the calamities arising from Indian depredations. This had been foreseen and expressed in the November session of 1788. In these two years a greater number of persons were murdered, and more horses stolen, than in any two preceding years. Yet at this time, the Governor of the territory North West of the Ohio, was by some means, induced to complain to the executive of Virginia, that the inhabitants of Kentucky had made incursions into the territories of the Indian nations, who were in amity with the United States. In consequence of this, the Governor of Virginia wrote to the County Lieutenants, to issue the most positive orders, that no party ordered out to repel the attack of an enemy, should under any pretence whatever, enter into the territory of the United States, or of any Indian tribe. The following is a copy of the Governor's letter:

"RICHMOND, *March* 10th, 1790.
"Sir—The Governor of the Continental Western Territory, has given the executive information of incursions having been made by parties from this state, upon the tribes of Indians in amity with the U. States.

As conduct like this is higly dishonorable to our national character, and will inevitably draw upon individual delinquents the punishment due to such offenders, it becomes our duty to enjoin you to exert your authority to prevent any attempt of this kind in future. Should it be necessary, on any occasion to order out parties to repel attack of an enemy within the limits of the state, you will issue the most positive orders, that no such party shall, under any pretence whatever, enter into the territory either of the United States, or of any Indian tribe.

"I am sir, your most obedient servant, BEVERLY RANDOLPH."[239]

The absurdity and cruelty of this mandate, would need no comment, even if the premises on which it was predicated had been true, but it is presumed this was not the case. There is no reason to believe that the incursions mentioned by the territorial Governor, had ever been made. The Kentucky Gazette was published weekly during all those years, and as intelligence respecting either the invasion or pursuit of the Indians, was to the citizen, of all other the most interesting, it is believed it was never neglected. The files of that paper have been carefully examined, and no notice is taken of any expedition at or near the time alluded to by the Governor. Whether he received his information from the Indians themselves, or from white men, does not appear—but however received (if received at all) it is believed not to be true.

But happily, by this time the President of the U. States became better informed, and discovered that it was necessary to adopt some general decisive system respecting the Indian tribes, and whilst these regulations were carrying into effect, he devised temporary means to give partial relief to sufferers from savage hostility. An incipient measure was, to employ scouts to range in the frontier counties. To effect this, the Hon. Harry Innis, then Judge of the Federal District Court, and afterwards attorney general, was commissioned by the Secretary at War, to authorise the county Lieutenants to call forth the scouts in certain cases. The following is an extract of the secretary's letter to Mr. Innis:

"*WAR OFFICE, April* 13, 1790.

"SIR—By some recent information from the Ohio, it appears that the Indians still continue their depredations on the frontiers.

"The President of the United States is exceedingly desirous that the inhabitants of the frontier counties, should experience the benefits of the said orders to the commanding officer, he has directed me to make this communication to you, &c.

"And he has further directed me to empower you that in case any of the counties of Kentucky should not have already availed themselves of said provision, and should in your judgment stand in need thereof, that you should, under your hand and seal, authorise the Lieutenants of such counties to call forth the scouts precisely as to the numbers, and under the regulations directed in the instructions to the Governor of the Western Territory, or in his absence, to the commanding officer of the troops.

"I have the honor to be, sir, your most obedient humble servant,

"H. KNOX, *Sec'y. of War*.[240]

"HARRY INNIS, Esq. *District Judge of Ky.*"

Judge Innis embraced this opportunity of making an official statement to the Secretary at War, by a letter dated July 7, 1790, of the depredations which had been committed by the Indians since he became acquainted with the district, which embraced a period of some months less than seven years; in this time the Indians had murdered in the district, on the wilderness road, and on the Ohio, about 1500 persons, and stolen upwards of 20,000 horses, and had destroyed or carried away other property to the value of at least fifteen thousand pounds.

The following is an extract of a letter from Judge Innis, dated

"*DANVILLE, Ky, July 7th*, 1790.

"I have been intimately acquainted with this district from November 1783. I can with truth say, that in this period of time the Indians have always been the aggressors—that any incursions made into their country have been from reiterated injuries committed by them; that by the depredatory war and plundering carried on by the savages, it is rendered difficult and almost impossible to discriminate what tribes are the offenders; that since my first visit to this district, which was the time above named, I can venture to say, that fifteen hundred souls had been killed and taken in the district, and migrating to it; that upwards of twenty thousand horses have been taken and carried off, and other property, such as money, merchandize, household goods and wearing apparel, have been carried off and destroyed by these barbarians, to at least fifteen thousand pounds.

"I am with great respect, sir, your most obdt. servt.

"HARRY INNIS.[241]

"Maj. Gen., KNOX, *Secretary of War.*"

Employing scouts and rangers, was calculated to produce a particular and determinate effect. It impressed on the minds of the Indians a belief that the whites were on their guard, and they might have concluded that a sufficient force was in readiness to take advantage of any discoveries which these sentinels should make. This persuasion operating on ignorance and fear, would repress or divert an intended invasion; and however limited and restricted in the right of self defence, the people were by their own government, there was still convenience in having intelligence when it was necessary to assume a defensive attitude. But beyond these incidental advantages, the establishment was of no use. The militia to whom these scouts were to convey intelligence, were prohibited from going in quest or pursuit of an enemy—and in effect prohibited from every effort to self defence, unless in cooperation with an army far distant from the theatre of attack, and to which the existence of an attack might be utterly unknown.

The people were not so infatuated, as to feign themselves secure under such a system of defence; and if they had been, the events which soon followed, would have undeceived them. A continuation of Indian depredations produced a meeting of the citizens at Danville, on the 2d day of July 1790, at which the following resolution was entered into:

"*Resolved* as the opinion of this meeting, that from the frequent depredations of the Indians on the people and property of this district, a meeting of the several field officers within the same, is highly advisable.

"And therefore it is requested, that the said officers give their attendance at Danville on Monday the 26th inst. to consider of the best mode of defence for the inhabitants of the district.

"*Resolved*, That the above resolutions be transmitted to the printer of the Kentucky Gazette, and to request him to insert the same. A copy.

CHRIST. GREENUP, *Clerk.*"

But notwithstanding the incursions of the Indians were frequent, and often attended with fatal consequences; yet the want of legitimate power in the officers, and the apprehension of again incurring the censure of government prevented them from doing anything under this resolution.

SECTION 34

The Stalking Enemy
along Road and River
[May 11, 1827]

About the 1st of March 1790, the Indians killed a man at Kennedy's bottom on the Ohio river, and tied a handkerchief around his head.

On the 21st, three boats descending the Ohio river, were attacked by a party of Indians about three miles above the mouth of the Scioto. The Indians were in possession of a boat which they had taken the day before, which they manned with about fifteen men, together with a large canoe, which they also manned and gave chase to the three boats. Those in the boats finding that they would be overtaken, abandoned two of them and fixing three oars to each side of the other, double manned them, by which means they escaped. The Indians pursued the boat nearly twenty miles. All the property on board the two boats that were abandoned, (supposed to be worth 2,500£) fell into the hands of the Indians.

A few days previous to the attack above related, the Indians took a large canoe that was ascending the Ohio river, near the same place, and killed three men on board.

On the 8th of August, about ten miles above the mouth of the Scioto a boat was attacked by a large party of Indians; but luckily five other boats hove in sight, and the Indians turned on them, one of which they were compelled to abandon to save the rest. One man was killed on board the boat first attacked, and several horses wounded.

On the 23d of July, Capt. M'Curdie, with twenty men, on his passage in a boat from Fort Washington to Limestone, were attacked by about the same number of Indians, who had concealed themselves among the willows on the margin of the river near which the boat passed without discovering them until fired on, which was returned with so much promptitude, that the enemy were forced to retreat. One man was killed and four wounded on board the boat.

On the 26th of August, four men who had been up the Kentucky river above the settlements were attacked by about 30 Indians as they approached the settlement; three of them were killed, and the other wounded, who made his escape.

In the year 1790, a treaty was appointed to be held with the Northern

Indians by Gen. St. Clair on the Wabash; but on experiment, it was found that no terms which could be acceded to, could be obtained from the Indians. It was therefore determined to carry hostilities into the Indian country. An expedition was accordingly planned under the command of Gen. Josiah Harmer, against the Miami village, situated where Fort Wayne now stands. The army rendezvoused at Fort Washington early in October, consisting of one company of artillery, two hundred and fifty infantry regular troops, and twelve hundred militia from Kentucky and the back part of Pennsylvania. At the same time this army marched, a detachment under the command of Major Hamtramock marched for Vincennes, in order to make a diversion in Harmer's favour. When Gen. Harmer had arrived near what is now called St. Marys, an Indian was made prisoner; from some information received from him, the General was induced to detach Col. Hardin with six hundred men to the village, where he arrived the next day (October 15) and found the village nearly in ashes, there being only two Indians seen, who were both fired on and probably wounded, as both their horses came into camp that night with bloody saddles, and an Indian was found dead a few days after, supposed to be one of them. The whole of the army came up on the 17th. On the 18th of October, Col. Trotter was detached with three hundred men in pursuit of a trail which had been discovered the day before—he had not marched far before an Indian was discovered on horseback, on his right front. He was pursued by the cavalry, overtaken and killed. A second Indian was also discovered, who was pursued by the field officers and by them driven on the cavalry, who dispatched him, but not before he had given sergeant Johnson a mortal wound. Col. Trotter then continued his march; but he had advanced but a short distance before he was informed by one of his videts, that there was a large body of mounted Indians pursuing in their rear. The wounded men having been sent back with a small escort, it was apprehended they would be cut off; the cavalry were therefore ordered immediately back to overtake them, and halt until the main body of the detachment should come up. The whole then returned towards the camp so far as to secure the safety of the wounded man and his escort. They then resumed their march, and late in the evening a signal of three cannon was fired at the camp, which was for them to return, which they did. The next morning a detachment of about the same number of that out under Col. Trotter, was ordered out under the command of Col. John Hardin, who pursued the same rout which had been taken by Col. Trotter the day before. A short distance beyond where the Colonel had commenced his retrograde movement, an encampment of Indians was discovered, and a push made on it by the advance, but it was found to have been abandoned except by 8 or 10 Indians, who immediately fled and escaped by the aid of the thick bush wood. Capt. Faulconer of the Pennsylvania militia, was ordered to form on the left, which he did, but so far as not to be able to see the rest of the detachment when it moved, and were therefore left behind. The detachment had marched nearly two miles before it was discovered that Faulconer was missing. It being near night, Col. Hardin concluded to move on to the first water and suitable ground, and there encamp, whilst Major Fountain should go in quest of Capt. Faulconer. Shortly after Fountain started, a gun was heard in front, and it was thence concluded that the enemy were close at hand and the detachment discovered. They moved briskly towards where the gun was fired, and within about a mile came in sight of the enemy's encampment, which was flanked on one side by a morass, with one also in front, which was immediately crossed by the detachment, consisting of less that two hundred men, who, before they could form received the fire of seven hundred Indians. The detachment immediately gave way and fled, nor could all the exertions of the officers rally them. Fifty-two men were killed in a very few minutes. The enemy continued the pursuit until they met Maj. Fountain with Capt. Faulconer's party, when they were checked, after which they retreated. The remainder of the detachment arrived in camp that night. The 20th was employed in destroying the corn and other vegetables found at the village. During the day several Indians were killed in the neighborhood. On the 21st the army commenced their march homeward, and proceeded seven miles to the Black Swamp. That night Col. Hardin and Maj. Willis were detached and sent back with five or six hundred men, with the expectation of surprising the enemy, who it was expected would return that evening to their village. The detachment did not arrive at the village until about sunrise the next morning, which prevented the intended surprise. A few Indians were discovered on each flank; those on the left instantly fled, and were pursued in every direction by the militia. Those on the right, about forty in number, endeavoured to gain a copse of wood, which was observed by Major Fountain, who ordered Captain Armstrong with the mounted riflemen to prevent it. As soon as the duty was performed, Fountain ordered a charge with a company of cavalry, and pushed on, expecting his troops were following—but alas! he went alone in the midst of four savages: he did great execution with his sword, but fell at last, covered with wounds. Lieut. M'Coy seeing the Major's situation, rushed up from the rear of the cavalry with four men only (John Bush, Silas Meason and two by the name of Moore) to rescue him; three of them were wounded, and the fourth had his sword knocked out of his hand by a ball from the enemy. Major Willis was advancing to support Major Fountain, when he was attacked by a large party from down the river. The conflict was sharp, but short: Major Willis and Lieut. Frothing fell here. Captain Ashton, with the few men he had, fell back on the St. Joseph. The Captain, Ensign and four or five men were all that escaped. Brigade Major Ormsby had collected 80 to 90 men on the river, ready to meet those who were in pursuit of Ashton. Here the contest was renewed across the river—Ormsby's party checked the enemy until Hardin brought up a reinforcement. The contest continued from nine in the morning until one o'clock in the afternoon, when unfortunately, a party under Maj. James M'Millin was mistaken for a party of the enemy; a retreat was immediately ordered, which created some confusion, thereby giving the enemy a great advantage. A general massacre of the wounded now took place. When Maj. M'Millin arrived on the ground where the contest had been, he saw nothing but the dead on both sides. Col. Hardin lost in the day's action about 132 men. Maj. M'Millin stated that there were a great many dead Indians in the river; so that their loss was very considerable also, a more convincing proof of which need not be assigned, than that the enemy did not pursue or harrass the army on its return to Fort Washington, at which place it arrived by easy marches, on the 4th of November, in good order, bringing in all the artillery, ammunition and baggage.[243]

SECTION 35

The Hubble Expedition
[May 18, 1827]

About the last of January 1791, a large party of Indians attacked Dunlap's Fort on the Big Miami. They continued the siege for 25 hours, without injuring a single person, when they judged it prudent to retire. They left eight of their party dead on the ground, and it was supposed as many more who were killed were taken privately off. The Indians killed or drove off all the stock they could come at, and burnt and destroyed all the corn not within the fort. On their approach towards the fort before the siege, the Indians fell in with four white men, two of whom they killed, the other two made their escape.

About the same time, the Indians took a block house on the Muskingum, and put 15 souls to death.

In the year 1791, Capt. William Hubble, who had previously removed to Kentucky from the state of Vermont, with his family, and after having fixed his family in the neighborhood of Frankfort, then a frontier settlement, had returned to the Eastward on business, and was a second time on his way to Kentucky, by the Ohio River. On the Monongahela, one of the branches of the Ohio, he procured a flat boat, and embarked with Mr. Daniel Light, Mr. Wm. Plascut and his family, consisting of his wife and eight children, destined for Limestone, Kentucky. On their progress down the river Ohio, and soon after passing Pittsburgh, they saw evident traces of Indians along the banks, and there was evident reason that a boat which they overtook, and which, through carelessness, was suffered to run aground on an island, had become a prey to these merciless savages. Though Capt. Hubbell and his party stopped some time for it in the lower part of the river, it did not arrive, and it has never been by them heard of since. Before they reached the mouth of the Great Kenhawa, they had by several successive additions, increased their number to twenty, consisting of nine men, three women and eight children. The men, besides those already named, were John Stoner, an Irishman and a Dutchman (whose names are not recollected) Messrs Ray and Tucker and a Mr. Kilpatrick, who had two daughters also on board. Information received at Galliopolis confirmed the expectation, which appearances had previously raised, of a serious conflict with a large body of Indians; and, as Capt. Hubbell had been regularly appointed by the party, commander of the boat, every possible preparation for a formidable and successful resistance to any expected attack was promptly made. The nine men were divided into three watches for the night, which were alterately to continue awake and be on the look out for two hours at a time. The arms on board, which consisted principally of old muskets much out of order, were collected, loaded and put in the best possible condition for service. At about sunset on the 23d day of March 1791, this party overtook a fleet of six boats in company, and intended to have continued with them, but as their passengers seemed more disposed to dancing than fighting, and soon after dark, notwithstanding the remonstrances of Capt. Hubbell, they commenced fiddling, and dancing and drinking, instead of preparing their arms and taking the necessary rest preparatory to battle—it was deemed more hazardous to be in such company than without them. It was therefore determined, to proceed rapidly forward by aid of the oars, and to leave those thoughtless fellow travellers behind. One of the boats however, belonging to the fleet, commanded by Capt. Greathouse, pursued the same plan for a short time, but at length all the crew fell asleep, and the boat ceased to be propelled by oars fell behind, whilst Capt. Hubbell and his party glided forward steadily alone. Early in the night a canoe was dimly seen floating down the river, in which it was supposed there were Indians reconnoitering; and other indications of the neighbourhood and hostile intentions of a formidable party of savages noticed.

It was now agreed, that should an attack, as was probable, be defered till morning, every man should be up before the dawn of day, in order to make as great a show as possible, of numbers and strength; and, that whenever an action did take place, the women and children should lie down on the cabin floor, and be protected as well as they could by trunks and other baggage placed around them. In this perilous situation they continued during the night, and the Capt. who had not slept more than an hour since he left Pittsburgh, was too deeply impressed with the eminent danger which surrounded them, to obtain any rest at that time.

Just as day light began to appear in the east, and before the men were up and at their posts, agreeably to arrangement, a voice at some distance below them in a plaintive tone, repeatedly solicited them to come on shore, as there were some white persons who wished to obtain a passage in their boat. This the Captain very naturally and correctly concluded to be an Indian artifice, and its only effect was to arouse the men and place every one on his guard. The voice of entreaty was soon changed into the language of indignation and insult, and the sound of distant paddles announced the approach of the savage foe. At length three Indian canoes were seen through the mist of the morning rapidly advancing. With the utmost coolness the Capt. and his companions prepared to receive them. The chairs, tables and other incumbrances, were thrown into the river, in order to clear the deck for action. Every man took his position, and was ordered not to fire until the savages had approached so near, that (to use the words of Captain Hubbell) "the flash from the guns might singe their eye-brows," and a special caution was given, that the men should fire successively, so as there might be no interval. On the arrival of the canoes, they were found to contain about twenty-five or thirty Indians each. As soon as they had approached within the reach of musket shot, a general fire was given from one of them, which wounded Mr. Tucker in the hip so severely that his leg hung quite loose, and Mr. Light received a ball just below the ribs. The three canoes placed themselves at the bow, stern and right side of the boat, so that they had an opportunity, of raking in every direction. The fire now commenced from the boat, and had a powerful effect in checking the confidence and fury of the Indians. The Capt. after firing his own gun, took up that of one of the wounded men, raised it to his shoulder and was about to discharge it, when a ball from the enemy took away the cock; he coolly turned round, seized a brand of fire from the kettle, which served as a caboose, and applying it to the pan, discharged his piece. A very regular and constant fire was kept up. The Captain was just in the act of raising his gun a third time, when a ball passed through his right arm, and for a moment disabled it. Scarcely had he recovered from the shock and recovered the use of his hand, which had been paralized by the wound, when he discovered the Indians in one of the canoes about to board the boat in the bow, where the horses were placed, and which covered them in some measure from the sight of the boat's crew. They had approached so near, that some of them had actually seized the sides of the boat with their hands. Severely wounded as the Captain was, he caught up a pair of horsemen's pistols and rushed forward; on his approach the Indians fell back when he discharged one of the pistols at the foremost with effect. After firing the second pistol, he found himself without arms and was compelled to retreat, in doing which he stepped on a pile of small wood which had been prepared for burning in the kettle, when the thought struck him that he could use it to advantage in beating off the enemy, which thought he put into practice, and for some time used so actively and forcibly, that they were prevented from entering the boat, and ultimately wounded one of them so severely, that with a yell they suddenly drew off. All the canoes immediately discontinued the contest with Hubbell, and went in pursuit of Greathouse's boat which had appeared in sight. Here a striking contract was exhibited to the firmness and intrepidity which had just been displayed. Instead of resisting the attack, the people on board of this boat retired to the cabin in dismay. The Indians entered it without opposition, and rowed it to shore, where they instantly killed the Captain and a lad about 14 years of age. The women they placed in the centre of their canoes, and manning them with fresh hands, determined on again attempting to take Capt. Hubbell's boat, and without loss of time pursued it. A melancholy alternative now presented itself to these brave but almost desponding heroes, either to fall prey to their enemies, or run the hazard of killing these unfortunate women, who the Indians had placed in the canoes with themselves, with the hope of deriving protection by keeping as much as possible behind the women, and hereby expose them to the fire of Hubbell and his party. But self preservation is the first law of nature, and the Captain very justly remarked, there would not be much humanity in preserving their lives at such a sacrifice, merely that they might become victims of savage cruelty, at some subsequent period.

There were now only four men left on board Capt. Hubbell's boat, capable of making any defence, and the Captain himself severely wounded in two places. The second attack was however, resisted with incredible firmness and vigour. Whenever the Indians would rise to fire, their opponents generally gave the first shot, which in most instances proved fatal. Notwithstanding the disperity of numbers, and the exhausted condition of Hubbell's party, the Indians in a short time shewed evident signs of despair in success, and the canoes successively drew off to the shore. Just as the last one was departing Capt. Hubbell called to the Indian who was standing in the stern of his canoe and on his turning round, discharged his piece at him. When the smoke which for a moment obstructed the vision was dissipated, he was seen lying on his back, and appeared to be severely, perhaps mortally wounded.

Unfortunately the boat now drifted near to the shore where the

Indians were collected, and a large concourse of apparently between four and five hundred were seen running down on the bank. Ray and Plascut, the only men remaining unhurt, were placed at the oars, and as the boat was not more than twenty yards from shore, it was deemed prudent for all to be down in as safe a position as possible, and attempt to push forward with the utmost practicable rapidity. While in this situation, nine balls were shot into one oar and ten in the other, without touching the rowers, who were hidden from view, and protected, by the side of the boat and blankets in the stern. During this frightful exposure to the fire of the savages, which continued about twenty minutes, Mr. Kilpatrick observed a particular Indian, whom he thought a favourable mark for his rifle, and, notwithstanding the solemn warning of Capt. Hubbell, rose to shoot him. He immediately received a ball in his mouth which passed out at the back part of his head, and at the same instant another through his heart, and fell dead. This presented to his afflicted daughters and fellow travellers who were spectators to the awful occurrence, a spectacle which we need not attempt to describe.

The boat was now suddenly carried out into the middle of the current, and soon taken beyond the reach of the enemy's balls. Our little band reduced as they were in numbers, wounded, afflicted and almost exhausted by fatigue, were still unsubdued in spirit; and being assembled in all their strength, men, women and children, with an appearance of triumph, gave three hearty cheers, calling on the Indians to come on again if they were fond of the sport.

Thus ended this awful conflict, in which out of nine men, two only escaped unhurt. Tucker and Kilpatrick were killed on the spot,—Stoner was mortally wounded and died on his arrival at Limestone, and all the rest except Ray and Plascut, were severely wounded. The women and children were all uninjured excepting a little son of Mr. Plascut, who after the battle was over, came to the Captain, and with great coolness, requested him to take a ball out of his head. On examination it appeared that a ball that had passed through the side of the boat, had penetrated the forehead of this little hero and remained under the skin. The Captain took it out, when the lad observed *"that is not all,"* raised his arm and exhibited a piece of bone at the point of his elbow, which had been shot off and hung by the skin. His mother exclaimed, "why did you not tell me of this?" "Because," he cooly replied, "the Captain directed us to be silent during the action, and I thought you would be likely to make a noise if I told you."

The party made the best of their way down the river—the object was to reach Limestone that night. The Captain's arm had bled profusely; he was compelled to close the sleeve of his coat in order to retain the blood and check its effusion. In this situation he was under the necessity for want of hands, to steer the boat with his left hand, until about 10 o'clock at night, when he was relieved by Mr. William Brooks, who resided on the bank of the river and who was induced by the calls of the suffering party to come out to their assistance. By Mr. Brook's aid and that of some others who were in the same manner brought to their relief, they were enabled to land at Limestone that night about 12 o'clock.

Immediately on the arrival of Mr. Brooks, Captain Hubbell, relieved from labour and responsibility, sunk under the weight of pain and fatigue, and for a while became entirely insensible. When the boat reached Limestone he was unable to walk and was obliged to be carried up to the tavern. Here he had his wounds dressed, where he continued until he acquired sufficient strength to proceed homeward.

On their arrival at Limestone, they found a considerable armed force, about to march against the same Indians, from whose attacks they had so miraculously escaped, and so severely suffered. They now learned that on the preceding Sunday, the same party of Indians, had cutt off a detachment of men ascending the Ohio from Fort Washington at the mouth of Licking river, and had killed with their tomahawks, without firing a gun, twenty one out of twenty two men of which the detachment consisted.

Crowds of people as might be expected, came to examine the boat which had been the scene of so much heroism and such horrid carnage, and to visit the resolute little band, by whom it had been so gallantly and persevereingly defended. On examination it was found that the sides of the boat were literally filled with bullit holes. There was scarcely a space of two feet square in the part above the water, which had not either a ball remaining in it, or a hole, through which a ball had passed. Some persons who had the curiosity to count the number of poles [holes] in the blankets hung up as blinds in the stern of the boat, affirmed that in the space of five feet square, there were one hundred and twenty two. Four horses out of five were killed, and the escape of the fifth amidst such a shower of balls appeared almost miraculous.

The day after the arrival of Capt. Hubbell and his companions, the five remaining boats which they had passed on the night preceding the attack, reached Limestone. Those on board remarked, that during the action they distinctly saw the flashes, but could not hear the reports of the guns. The Indians it appears had met with too formidable a resistance from a single boat to attack a fleet, and suffered them to pass unmolested: and since that time it is believed that no boat has been assailed on the Ohio.

The force which marched out to disperse this formidable body of savages, discovered several dead Indians on the shore, near the place of action. They also found the bodies of Capt. Greathouse and of several others, men women and children, who were on board his boat. Most of them appeared to have been *whipped to death!* as they were stripped, tied to trees, and marked with the appearance of lashes, and large rods which were evidently worn with use lying near them.[244]

Setting the Date for Statehood

[May 25, 1827]

The application of the Convention held at Danville on the 26th of July 1790, to Congress to become an independent state, met the approbation of Congress, and on the 4th of Febr. 1791 they passed the following act:

"AN ACT declaring the consent of Congress, that a new state be formed within the jurisdiction of the commonwealth of Virginia, and admitted into this union, by the name of the state of Kentucky; passed and approved February 4th 1791.

"Sec. 2. *Be it further enacted and declared,* That upon the aforesaid first day of June, one thousand seven hundred and ninety two, the said new state by the name and style of Kentucky, shall be received and admitted into this union, as a new and entire member of the United States of America." (See laws of U.S. vol. 1, p. 282, Oswald's edition.) [245]

It has been already noticed, that the embarrassment and procrastination which Kentucky met with on her first application to Congress, was the result of Eastern policy and jealousy. The presumption was *then strong;* but the fact was now fully verified. Vermont was brought forward with Kentucky, admitted at the same session, and *was entitled to a representation in Congress one year sooner than Kentucky.* The following is a copy of an act for the admission of the state of Vermont into this Union. (Approved February 18th 1827.)

"The state of Vermont having petitioned the Congress to be admitted as a member of the United States, *Be it enacted by the Senate and House of Representatives of the United States of America in Congress assembled, and it is hereby enacted and declared,* That on the 4th of March 1791, the said state by the name and style of "the state of Vermont" shall be received and admitted into this union as a new and entire member of the United States of America." [246]

This superior advantage acquired by the state of Vermont, was not the reward of any patience or resignation displayed by her. She had not acquired her independence by submission, petition and compact. She had not obtained the consent of the state to which she originally appertained, even once, much less four or five times. She had not procured the previous approbation of Congress. Her separation was arbitrary, violent and insolent. She had seized on all the public lands in the district, and even on such as by the disposition of her parent state, had become private property. But there was in the case of Vermont a practicability of immediate admission, which did not exist in the case of Kentucky. She had organized herself—Kentucky had not. Vermont could be admitted as a state *in esse*—Kentucky only as a state *in futuro*. But had Kentucky in the year 1788, organized herself under the consent of Virginia, then twice obtained, she might at this time have come forward with the same advantages which Vermont possessed, and probably have obtained the same prompt and complete admission.[247]

On the 9th of March 1791, the President of the U. States authorised Charles Scott, John Brown, Harry Innis, Benjamin Logan and Isaac Shelby, or a majority of them, to call into service, a corps of volunteers from the district of Kentucky, to march on an expedition against the Indians North West of the Ohio, to be commanded by Brigadier General Charles Scott; and also to provide measures for the defence of the frontiers of the district. In pursuance of these powers, an expedition was undertaken in the May following, by Gen. Scott against the Wabash Indians, in which thirty two warriors were slain, fifty eight prisoners taken, and all their corn destroyed.

The following detail of facts relative to the above expedition, is from the pen of Gen. Scott himself:

"The army marched four miles from the bank of the Ohio on the 23d of May. They resumed their march on the 24th and pushed forward with the utmost industry, directing their route to Ouioctanon in the best manner their guides and information enabled them, though greatly deficient in both.

"By the 31st they had marched 135 miles, over a country cut by four large branches of White river, and many smaller streams, with steep muddy banks;—during this march, they traversed a country alternately interspersed with the most luxuriant soil and deep clayey bogs, from one to five miles in width, rendered almost impervious, by brush and briars. Rain fell in torrents every day, with frequent blasts of wind and thunder storms. These obstacles impeded their progress, wore down the horses and destroyed the provisions.

"On the morning of the 1st of June, as the army entered an ocean of prairie, they discovered a man on horseback, a few miles to the right; a detachment was sent to intercept him, but he escaped. Finding themselves discovered, the army determined to advance with all the rapidity their circumstances would permit, rather with the hope than the expectation, of reaching the object sought that day; for the guides were strangers to the country which they then occupied. At 1 o'clock P.M. having marched by computation 155 miles from the Ohio, as they penetrated a grove, which bordered an extensive prairie, they discovered two small villages to the left, at two and four miles distance.

"The guides now recognized the ground, and informed them that the main town was four or five miles in front, behind a copse of wood, which jutted into the prairie—Col. John Hardin was immediately detached, with sixty mounted infantry, and a troop of light horse Capt. McCoy, to attack the village to the left, while the main body moved on briskly in order of battle, towards the town, the smoke from which was then discernible; the guides were mistaken with respect to the situation of the town; for instead of standing at the edge of the plain, it was found in the bottom bordering on the Wabash river. On turning the point of the copse of wood, one house only presented itself to view in front. Capt. William Price was ordered to assail that with forty men, which order he executed with great gallantry; killing two warriors. When they gained the margin of the eminence, which overlooks the villages on the bank of the Wabash, they discovered the enemy in great confusion, endeavouring to escape in canoes over the river. Lieut. Col. Commandant Wilkinson, was instantly ordered to rush forward with the first battallion; the order was executed with promptitude, and the detachment gained the bank just as the rear of the enemy had embarked; and regardless of a brisk fire kept up from a Kicapoo town on the opposite bank, they in two minutes unloaded five canoes crowded with Indians—The Wabash was many feet above fording at this place—Col. Wilkinson was therefore detached to a ford two miles above, which the guides informed them was more practicable. The enemy still kept possession of the Kickapoo town; King's and Logsdon's companies were ordered to march down the river below the town, and cross under the direction of Maj. Barbee, in order to dislodge them: several of the men swam the river, and others crossed in a small canoe. This movement was unobserved, and the men had taken post on the bank, before they were discovered by the enemy, who immediately abandoned the village. About this time word was brought that Col. Hardin was incumbered with prisoners, and had discovered a stronger village farther to the left, which he was preparing to attack. Capt. Brown was immediately detached with his company, to support the colonel, but the distance being six miles, before the captain arrived, the business was done, and Col. Hardin joined the army a little before sun set, having killed six warriors and taken fifty two prisoners.—Capt. Bull the warrior who discovered the army in the morning, had gained the main town and given the alarm, about one hour before the arrival of the army; but the villagers on the left were uninformed, and had no place to retreat.—The next morning it was determined, to detach the Lieut. Commandant Wilkinson with five hundred men, to destroy the important town of Kethtepe-conunk, at the mouth of Eel river, eighteen miles from the camp, on the west side of the Wabash; but on examination it was discovered that the men and horses, were too much crippled and worn down by a long and laborious march, and the active exertions of the preceding day, that three hundred and sixty men only could be found in a capacity to undertake the enterprize; and they preferred to march on foot. Col. Wilkinson marched with his detachment, at half after five in the evening, and returned to camp next day at one o'clock, having marched thirty six miles in twelve hours and destroyed the most important settlement of the enemy in that quarter of the federal territory. The inhabitants of the village were principally French, and lived in a state of civilization. By the books, letters and other documents found there, it is evident, that, that place was in close connexion with and dependant on Detroit; a large quantity of corn, variety of household goods, peltry and other articles, were burned with this village, which consisted of about seventy houses, many of them well finished.

"Misunderstanding a white flag which appeared on an opposite eminence on the afternoon of the 1st inst an aged squaw was liberated with a message to the savages, that if they would come in and surrender, their town should be spared, and that they should receive good treatment.—On the 4th sixteen of the weakest and most infirm of the prisoners were discharged, with a talk to the Wabash tribes. On the same day after having burned the towns and adjacent villages, and destroyed the growing pulse, the army began their march for the rapids of the Ohio, where they arrived on the 14th without the loss of a single man by the enemy, and five only wounded; having killed thirty two warriors and taken fifty eight prisoners. It is with much pride and pleasure, we mention, that no acts of inhumanity, have marked the conduct of the Kentucky volunteers on this occasion; even the inveterate habit of scalping the dead, ceased to influence. Forty one prisoners were delivered to Capt. Ashton of the United States Regiment at Fort Steuben.

"The excessive wetness of the weather, and the consequences thereby produced, rendered it impossible to carry terror and desolation to the head of the Wabash.

"The corps were equal to the object, but the condition of the horses, and state of the provisions, were insuperable obstacles."[248]

SECTION 37

The Western Defense Council
[June 1, 1827]

By virtue of the authority from the President of the United States vested in Charles Scott, John Brown, Harry Innis, Benjamin Logan, and Isaac Shelby, they held a meeting in Danville on the 8th day of April 1791, at which the following proceedings were had:

"Whereas the President of the United States by instruction, bearing date the 9th day of March 1791, hath authorised Chas. Scott, John Brown, Harry Innis, Benjamin Logan and Isaac Shelby, or a majority of them, to call into service a corps of volunteers from the District of Kentucky, to march on an expedition against the Indians Northwest of the Ohio, and to be commanded by Brig. Gen. Charles Scott.[249]

"The board all meet, and having taken into consideration the business to them referred, came to the following resolutions, viz:—

"*Resolved*, That the plan of the proposed expedition be communicated to the people inhabiting the District of Kentucky, and that it be earnestly recommended to the officers of the militia and other influential characters in the several counties, to engage and enlist such number of volunteers as may be necessary to serve on the said expedition, and to make report of their success to the board at their next meeting.

"*Resolved*, That a meeting of the board be held at this place on the 2d day of May next, in order to receive returns of the men recruited for the said service, and to make final arrangements for putting the said expedition in motion.

"The board having taken into consideration the exposed situation of the frontiers of the District, and the necessity of establishing guards for the protection of the defenceless inhabitants.

"*Resolved*, That pursuant to the authority for that purpose in us vested by the President of the U. States, by letter bearing date the 10th day of March, Brig. Gen. Scott be empowered and required to call into service, any number of militia of the several counties within the District not exceeding 326 privates, as he may think necessary, for a term not exceeding sixty days, and to station them on the frontiers in such manner as he may think most conducive to the public safety, paying due regard in calling out the said militia, to the apportionment heretofore observed in the several counties, and in providing for their support, to confine him-self to the instructions received from the Secretary of War.

"The board then adjourned to met again at Danville on the 2d day of May.[250]

"*Charles Scott, Harry Innis, John Brown, Benjamin Logan, Isaac Shelby.*"

On the 25th day of June, the same gentlemen were commissioned by Arthur St. Clair, then commander in chief of the armies of the United States, to set on foot and carry into execution another expedition against the town of Kekiah on the Ouabashe. The following is an extract from this commission:

"Whereas the President of the United States did further authorise a second expedition of the same nature, provided the general or command-ing officer of the troops upon the Ohio should judge the public interest should require the measure, and direct the same under his hand, and seal; and the said expedition having been carried into effect, and now judging that a second expedition of a like nature with the former, would be highly conducive to the public interest, I Arthur St. Clair, Maj. Gen. commanding the troops of the United States upon the Ohio, do hereby direct that another expedition be set on foot in the District of Kentucky, and carried into execution upon the same principles and stipulations, and under the same regulations and restrictions as that lately commanded by Brig. Gen. Scott, excepting only, that the number of men to be employed on the said expedition, do not exceed the number of 500, officers included; that they rendezvous at Fort Washington on the 15th of next month, or as soon afterwards and not exceeding the 20th as possible; and that their operations be directed against the town of Kekiah on the Ouabashe, and any other towns of the hostile Indians, to which their force may be adequate.

"In witness whereof I have hereunto set my hand and seal at Fort Washington, June 25th 1791.[251]   "A. ST. CLAIR"

"*Extract of a letter from Governor St. Clair to Brig. Gen. Scott, dated Fort Washington, June 25: 1791.*

"SIR—I was yesterday favoured with your communications by your son, of the 20th inst. which gave me great pleasure, and I beg you to accept my cordial congratulations upon the success that has attended your opera-tions, which have been conducted to a happy issue under very unfavoura-ble and embarrassing circumstances, with a prudence and vigor that reflects the highest honour upon you sir, and the officers and men under your command. I shall immediately send forward the account to the War Office, to be laid before the President of the United States, to whom it cannot fail to be very acceptable."

Crooked legs, the chief of the Ouiactenon tribe, together with 13 warriors, arrived at that post, under pretence of treating, the same day that Gen. Scott arrived at their towns; a runner was immediately dispatched after them upon the discovery of the approach of our army; but they did not get back to the towns until the army had been several days on their march homeward. Crooked legs and his party returned again to Vincennes, and were the first who gave notice of what had happened to their towns from the attack made by General Scott. They expressed great satisfaction with the treatment of Gen. Scott to the prisoners, but were lost in astonishment at his not scalping the dead.[252]

In the month of August 1791, agreeably to the arrangement by the board of officers appointed by the President of the United States, and also by Gen. St. Clair, an expedition was carried on against Kikiah under the command of Gen. James Wilkinson, in which ten warriors were killed, and thirty five prisoners taken—two towns were burnt, and five hundred acres of corn destroyed.[253]

On the 11th day of April, six scouts from Fort Scott fell in with seven Indians on the Ohio, six miles below the fort, when a skirmish ensued—the Indians were routed, and four horses and some colts retaken, which had been stolen from Loudon's Station on Drennon's Lick waters. Seven blankets with some kettles and deerskins were also taken, and two of the Indians badly wounded.

On the 25th day of May, the Indians killed a family about 12 miles from Danville, consisting of a man and his wife and five children.

A party returning from New Orleans, were on the 11th, attacked on the Tennessee river at the mouth of Duck creek, by 25 Indians, and three of the party killed and one wounded. About the last of June, three men were killed by the Indians, on the road from Bullitt's Lick to Nashville. An officer and two privates, on their way from St. Vincennes to Louisville, were attacked by a party of Indians on the bank of a creek; the two privates were killed, but the officer saved himself by jumping into the creek and secreting himself under water among the roots of a tree.

On the 23rd of June, nine men who were travelling the new road from Strode's Station, through the wilderness by the way of Sandy, were defeated and driven back from the East Fork of Sandy, by a party of Indians: happily no lives were lost, notwithstanding the enemy were within about 15 paces when they fired.[254]

On the 2d of July a treaty was entered into by Wm. Blount, Governor of the Territory Southwest of the Ohio (now Tennessee) on the part of the United States, and the Cherokee tribe of Indians, near the mouth of French Broad, on the Holstein river.

The following is a copy of a letter from Wm. Blount, Esq. to the honorable Harry Innis, George Muter, Samuel M'Dowell, Caleb Wallace, George Nicholas, Christopher Greenup and Benjamin Logan, Esqs.

dated, Treaty Ground near the mouth of French Broad, on the bank of
Holstein, July 2d, 1791:

"GENTLEMEN—I have had the pleasure to receive your letter, which you
did me the honour to write to me on the 5th of June, by Cols. Shelby and
Kennedy. —After much difficulty, on this day a treaty has been made and
signed, between myself on the part of the U. States, and the Cherokees
(which I have great hope will be kept by both parties) upon the principles
of the treaty with the Creeks. For the bounday I agreed on, I refer you to
Cols. Shelby and Kennedy.

"It would have afforded me great pleasure to have better served the
interest of your country, but it was not in my power—and I assure you,
that while I have the administration of Indian affairs in my hands, that I
shall be equally attentive to the true interests of Kentucky, as to that part of
the Territory over which I have the honour to preside as governor. I am,
gentlemen, with great respect your most obedient humble servant,[255]
                                                    WM. BLOUNT."

The following is an extract of a letter from the Governor of Virginia, to
Brig. Gen. Scott, dated Council Chamber, Richmond, Aug. 4th 1791:

"SIR—I have lately received a letter from the Secretary of War, informing
me, that in case a more extensive combination of Indian nations should be
formed than is at present calculated on, the commanding general of the
troops to the westward is authorised to call for such numbers and species
of militia, as the nature of the case may require. Should such a demand be
made, you will consider it as peculiarly your duty to use every exertion in
your power, to insure the most compleat compliance with it.

"I am much disappointed at not having been able as yet to procure a
compleat return of the strength of your district. Let me intreat your
attention to this business. If it can be obtained by the next session of the
General Assembly, it will be very satisfactory.

"I am sir respectfilly your obedient servant, [256]
                                                    "BEVERLY RANDOLPH.
"Brig. Gen. Scott."

About the 1st of October, twelve men were attacked and defeated by
Indians on Richland creek, on their way to Kentucky—two of whom
were killed and one wounded. About the same time they stole 16 horses
on Brashears' creek.[257]

SECTION 38

Wilkinson's Drive against the "Oubache"

[June 23, 1827]

In the month of July 1791, another successful expedition marched against the Ouabache Indians, commanded by Brig. Gen. Wilkinson, the particulars of which have been mislaid.* The following copy of a letter from the Secretary at War, respecting that expedition, will give some idea of the result:

"WAR DEPARTMENT, 29th Sept. 1791
"SIR—I have the honor to acknowledge the receipt of the copy of your report of the 29th ult. to Maj. Gen. St. Clair, which I have submitted to the President of the United States:

"I have by this day's post instructed Maj. Gen. St. Clair, if he had not already performed that pleasing duty, to thank you in the name of the President, for the zeal perseverance and good conduct, manifested by you in the command of the expedition—and for the humanity observed towards the prisoners whom you captured—and also to thank the officers and privates of the volunteers, for the activity and bravery, while under your command, and to express his hope, that you and they may enjoy in future entire peace, as a reward for your services.

"Mr. Belli was waiting the muster rolls of your corps. He has settled the accounts, and returned with the money for the amount.

"I have the honor to be with great respect, sir your most obedient humble servt. [258]   H. KNOX.
"Brigadier Gen. James Wilkinson."

On the 8th of October 1791, the North Western army, under the command of Maj. Gen. A. St. Clair, moved from their first station about 12 miles from Fort Washington, on their march for the Maumee village. This army consisted of about 1400 men, who on the 4th day of November, were

*The editor will thank any gentleman who will furnish him with an account of the particulars of this expedition.

defeated by the combined Indian forces, near the Maumee village. Out of the whole army, 733 men only escaped, 233 of whom were wounded.

Among the killed, were Gen. Butler; Col. Oldham; Majors Clark, Hart and Ferguson, Captains Bradford, Tipton, Smith, Purdie, Newman, Kirkwood, Piatt, Price, Swearingen, Cribbs and Guthrie. Lieutenants Warren, Speer, Lukins, M'Nickle, M'Math, Hopper, Rood, Kelso, Boyd and two others. Ensigns Beatty, Cobbs, Balsh, Brooks, Chase, Turner, Purdie and two others. Quarter Masters Ward, Reynolds, and Sample. Adjutants Anderson and Burgess; besides militia officers, Doctor Grayson.

Wounded—Colonels Gibson and Dark. Major Butler. Captains Ford, Doyle, Dark, Buchanon, Madison, Trueman, Slough and three others. Lieutenants Duberts, Price, Greathouse, Crawford, M'Rea and two others. Ensigns Morgan, Bines and four others. Dr. Gano. —Total 44 officers killed—26 wounded.[259]

PIOMINGO or the Mountain Leader, the principal Chief of the Chickasaw Indians, with 22 of his warriors who had joined Gen. St. Clair at Fort Washington, left the army the day before the action, fell in with a party of the enemy and killed eight without the loss of one of his party, and but one wounded. He had reconnoitred their camp, and was of opinion that their force was between two and three thousand.[260]

On the 11th day of November, Gen. Scott wrote a circular letter to the different county Lieutenants, of which the following is a copy:

"SIR—We have now received certain intelligence that the army have been defeated. The loss is very great. The garrison at Fort Jefferson intercepted, and many, many brave wounded gallant men are now left on the road, unable to travel, and without any provision but the flesh of the packhorses. This case requires immediate exertion. I have appointed a rendezvous of *volunteers* at Craig's mills the 15th instant, completely equiped, with arms and ammunition, and twenty day's provisions. I trust that no exertions on your part will be wanting when the safety of our country and the lives of brave men are in danger. The circumstances require the greatest despatch, and no friend to his country can now be idle.

"Believe me with respect, yours,[261]   CH: SCOTT.
"P.S. The volunteers who are not ready by the 15th inst. are to follow as soon as possible."

Copy of a letter from Gen. St. Clair to Gen. Wilkinson, dated Camp 81 miles advanced of Fort Washington, Nov. 1st 1791.
"SIR—I have the honour to enclose to you a letter from the War Office which came to my hand last night as did that also for Gen. Scott, Harry Innis, and John Brown Esqs. which I request you to take the trouble to transmit to them. By the same conveyance I am directed to present to you, the thanks of the public in the name of the President of the U. States, for

the zeal, perseverance and good conduct manifested by you, in the command of the expedition against L'Anguille, and for the humanity observed towards the prisoners whom you captured; and also to thank the officers and privates of the volunteers, for their activity and bravery while under your command. This sir is a very pleasing task to me, and what I should have taken upon myself to do immediately on receiving your report, had I not conceived it more honorable to you, that it should be preceded by the orders of the President, and more proper in me to wait those orders, than to undertake to guide the public mind. It is now sir, that with the greatest pleasure to myself, I thank you in the name of the President of the United States, for the zeal, perseverance and good conduct manifested by you, in the command of the expedition against L'Anguille, and for the humanity observed toward the prisoners. And I do in the same manner thank the officers and privates of the volunteers, for their activity, and bravery while under your command; and it is the ardent wish and hope of the President, that those expeditions, calculated chiefly to procure relief from a savage enemy, and tranquility to Kentucky, may be followed by their full effect; and that you and they may enjoy future peace as a reward for your services.

"With very great regard, I have the honor to be, sir your most obedient servant,[262]   A. ST. CLAIR,
                              "Commanding the troops of the United States.
"GEN. WILKINSON."

The following is the copy of a letter from Maj. Gen. St. Clair, to Maj. Brown upon the dismission of the militia who had served in the army under his command.

"SIR: I request the favour that you will make known to the militia, the regret I feel for the loss they have sustained in their late gallant commander, Liut. Col. Oldham, and other brave officers and soldiers. It is with pleasure I acknowledge the satisfaction received from the general orderly behaviour and the harmony and good understanding that prevailed between them and the other classes of troops which composed the army during the campaign. If some of them did desert the service of their country at a critical moment, it reflects a lustre upon those who were not to be influenced by the base example; but as that very desertion occasioned the absence of a considerable body of the troops at the time of the action, and may thereby have been the cause of the misfortunate that befel us, it will be the duty of every officer to use his utmost endeavours that they be brought to condign punishment agreeably to the laws of the country. While I wish the militia individually a safe return to their families and to their country and happiness, I cannot resist the giving them the further proof of my good will, by observing that in no case where I have seen militia employed, has there been that subordination and prompt obedience of orders, which are necessary to the success of military operations; and I recommend it to them, should they be again called into their country's service, to endeavour to acquire the habits and to practise them with alacrity, as the only means under God, by which either personal honour, or public advantage can be obtained.

"With much respect, I am sir, your very humble servt.

(Signed) A. ST. CLAIR[263]

"Maj. Brown, commanding the militia from Kentucky."

SECTION 39

St. Clair's Dreary March to Defeat

[June 29, 1827]

The official account of the expedition carried against the Indians, by Gen. St. Clair, in his letters to the Secretary at war.

"FORT WASHINGTON, Oct. 6, 1791.

"SIR—I have now the satisfaction to inform you, that the army moved from Fort Hamilton, the name I have given the fort on the Miami, on the 4th at eight in the morning, under the command of Gen. Butler.

"The order of march and encampment I had regulated before, and on the third returned to this place, to get the militia. They marched yesterday, and consist of about 300 men, as you will see by the enclosed abstract of the muster. I have reason to believe, however, that at least an equal number will be up here by the 10th—and I have left orders for their following us. The monthly return should have accompanied this letter, but it was not ready when I left camp, and has not been forwarded since. I have hitherto found it impossible to reduce the officers commanding, to punctuality with respect to their returns, but they are mending. Our number, after deducting the garrisons of this place and Fort Hamilton, are about 2,000, exclusive of the militia. I trust I shall find them sufficient, and should the rest of the militia come on, it will make the matter pretty certain; but the season is so far advanced, that I fear the intermediate posts, which would indeed have been highly necessary, it will be impossible to establish. In that, however, I must be governed by circumstances, of which I will take care that you shall be apprized in due time. Should the enemy come to meet us, which seems to be expected, there will be no difficulties; but if they expect us at the Miami villages, the business will wear another face, and the intermediate posts become more essential.

"Since the quarter master has been here, and got into his geers, which it took him a little time to do, I am very well satisfied with him, and do believe he will answer the description which you were pleased to give of him. His business seems now to be well arranged.

"In order to communicate with some degree of certainty with your office, I have directed Captain Buel when he arrives, to send a sergeant and twelve men, to a house that has been newly erected, half way between this place and Lexington, to each of which two men are to be sent off, on every Monday morning, to carry dispatches. Those for the War Office, or any other public letters, to be put into the hands of Mr. Charles Wilkins, merchant of Lexington, who has engaged to forward all I have occasion to send, regularly once a fortnight; and should you, sir, think proper to use the same route for any of yours, if they are sent to his care, he will forward them to me. I have been led to refer this channel of communication to that of the river, because it appears to be rather the more certain of the two, though it may be a little more tedious; and because desertion continues to prevail among the troops, and the sending small parties to such a distance, gives great opportunities to effect it. Gen. Butler informs me, that no less than twenty-one went off the night before the army moved from Fort Hamilton. I am this moment setting out for the army, which I hope to overtake tomorrow evening, and will write you again as soon after as may be.

"With great respect &c.   ARTHUR ST. CLAIR[264]
"The Hon: Maj. Gen. Knox, Secretary at War."

Copy of a letter from Gen. St. Clair, dated Camp 8 miles advanced of Fort Washington, November 1, 1791.
"SIR—Since I had the honour to write to you on the 21st ult. nothing very material has happened, and indeed I am at present so unwell, and have been so for some time past, that I could ill detail it, if it had happened; not that that space of time has been entirely barren of incidents; but as few of them have been of the agreeable kind. I beg you to accept a sort of journal account of them, which will be the easiest for me.

"On the 22d the indisposition that hung about me for some time, sometimes appearing as a billious cholic, and sometimes as a rheumatic asthma, to my great satisfaction, changed to a gout in the left arm and hand, leaving the breast and stomach perfectly relieved, and the cough which had been excessive, entirely gone. This day Mr. Ellis, with sixty militia from Kentucky, joined the army, and brought up a quantity of flour and beef.

"23—Two men taken in the act of deserting to the enemy, and one for shooting another soldier, and threatening to kill an officer, were hanged on the grand parade, the whole army being drawn out. Since the army has halted, the country around this and ahead for 15 miles has been well examined. It is a country, which had we arrived a month sooner in it, and with three times the number of animals, they would all have been fat now.

"24—Named the Fort Jefferson (it lies in lat. 40, 4, 22 N) and marched the same Indian path serving to conduct us about six miles, and encamped on good ground, and an excellent position—a rivulet in front, and a very large prairie, which would, at the proper season, afford forage for a thousand horses, on the left. So ill this day, that I had much difficulty in keeping with the army.

"25—Very hard rain last night; obliged to halt to-day on account of provisions, for although soldiers may be kept pretty easy in camp under the expectation of provisions arriving, yet they cannot begin to march in advance, and take none along with them. Received a letter from Mr. Hodgson by express—13,000 lbs. flour will arrive the 27th.

"26—A party of militia sent to reconnoitre, fell in with five Indians, and suffered them to slip through their fingers. In their camp, articles to the value of twenty dollars were found and divided. The Virginia battalion is melting down very fast, notwithstanding the promises of the men to their officers. Thirteen have been discharged by Col. Darke to-day.

"27—Gave orders for enlisting the levies with the condition of serving but their time in their present corps. Piomingo arrived in camp with his warriors. I was so unwell I could only see him and bid him welcome; but entered no business. Considerable dissatisfaction among the levies about their enlistment.

"28—Some clothing sent for to Fort Washington for the recruits arrived, was begun to be distributed, and will have a good effect; but enlisting the levies does not meet with that encouragement that might have been expected. It is not openly complained of by the officers, but is certainly privately by some of high rank, and the measure of tempting them with warm clothing condemned. Mr. Hodgson writes me that he is sending forward a quantity of woolen overalls and socks, by Gen. Butler's orders. I have ordered them to be deposited at Fort Jefferson. Some few Indians about us; probably those which the militia fell in with a few days ago. Two of the levies were fired upon about three miles off; one killed, two of the militia likewise. One of them got in, and the other missing, supposed to be taken.

"29—Piomingo and his party, accompanied by Capt. Sparks and four good riflemen, going on a scout. They do not propose to return under ten days, unless they sooner succeed in taking prisoners.

"30—The army moved about 9 o'clock, and with much difficulty made seven miles, having left a considerable part of the tents by the way, the provision made by the quarter master for that purpose was not adequate—three days flour issued to the men, to add the horses that carried it to his arrangements—the Indian road still with us.

"31—This morning about sixty of the militia deserted. It was at first reported that one-half of them had gone off, and that it was their design to plunder the convoys which were upon the road. I detached the first regiment in pursuit of them, with orders to Maj. Hamtramck, to send a sufficient guard back with Benham (a commissary) whenever he met with him, and follow them about 25 miles below Fort Jefferson, or until he met a second convoy, and then return and join the army. Benham arrived last night and to-day (November 1) the army is halted to give the road cutters an opportunity of getting some distance ahead, and that I might write to you. I am this day considerably recovered, and hope that it will turn out what I first expected it to be, a friendly fit of the gout, come to relieve me from every other complaint.

"Yesterday I was favoured with yours of the 28th and 29th September. I have enclosed my communications and their answers. My orders for the post to them are not yet definitive, but they will be very soon, in the mean time I expect they are both at work.

"With great respect, I have the honour to be sir,
your most obedient servant,   ARTHUR ST. CLAIR.[265]
"The Hon: Maj. Gen. Knox, Secretary at War."

Copy of a letter from major general St. Clair, to the Secretary of War, dated Fort Washington, Nov. 9, 1791.

"SIR—Yesterday afternoon the remains of the army under my command got back to this place, and have now the painful task to give you an account of as warm and as unfortunate an action as almost any that has been fought, in which every corps was engaged and worsted, except the first regiment that had been despatched upon a service I had the honour to inform you of in my last dispatch, and had not joined me.

"On the third inst the army had reached a creek about twelve yards wide, running to the South-west, which I believed to have been the river St. Marys, that empties into the Miami of the Lake; arrived at this place about 4 o'clock in the afternoon, having marched nearly nine miles, and were immediately encamped upon a very commanding piece of ground in two lines, having the above mentioned creek in front; the right wing composed of Butler's, Clark's and Patterson's battalions, commanded by

Maj. Gen. Butler, formed the first line: and the left wing, consisting of Bedinger's and Gaither's battalions, and the second regiment, commanded by Col. Darke, formed the second line, with an interval between them of about seventy yards, which was all the ground would allow.

"The right flank was pretty well secured by the creek, a steep bank and Faulkner's corps—some of the cavalry and their pieces covered the left flank. The militia were thrown over the creek, and advanced about one quarter of a mile, and encamped in the same order. There were a few Indians who appeared on the opposite side of the creek, but fled with the utmost precipitation on the advance of the militia. At this place, which I adjudged to be about fifteen miles from the Miami village, I had determined to throw up a slight work, the plan of which was concerted that evening with Major Ferguson, wherein to have deposited the men's knapsacks and every thing else that was not of absolute necessity, and to have moved to attack the enemy as soon as the first regiment was come up; but they did not permit me to execute either, for on the 4th, about half an hour before sunrise, and when the men had been just dismissed from the parade (for it was a constant practice to have them all under arms a considerable time before daylight) an attack was made upon the militia; those gave way in a very little time, and rushed into camp through Maj. Butler's battalion, which together with Clark's, they threw into considerable disorder; and which, notwithstanding the exertions of both those officers, was never altogether remedied the Indians following close at their heels. The first however of the front line, checked them, but almost instantaneously a very heavy attack began upon the line, and in a few minutes it was extended to the second likewise. The great weight of it was directed against the center of each, where the artillery was placed, and from which the men were repeatedly driven with great slaughter. Finding no great effect from our fire, and confusion beginning to spread from the great number of men who were falling in all quarters, it became necessary to try what could be done by the bayonet.

"Lieut. Col. Darke was accordingly ordered to make a charge with part of the second line, and to turn the left flank of the enemy. This was executed with great spirit. The Indians instantly gave way, and were driven back three or four hundred yards; but for want of a sufficient number of riflemen to pursue this advantage, they soon returned and the troops were obliged to give back in their turn. At this moment they had entered our camp by the left flank, having forced back the troops that were posted there.

"Another charge was made here by the second regiment, Butler's and Clark's battalions, with equal effect, and it was repeated several times, and always with success; but in all of them many men were lost, and particularly the officers, with some raw troops, was a loss altogether irremediable. In that I just spoke of, made by the second regiment and

Butler's battalion, Major Butler was dangerously wounded, and every officer in the second regiment fell except three, one of which, Mr. Graton, was shot through the body.

"The artillery being now silenced, and all the officers killed except Capt. Ford, who was badly wounded, more than half the army fallen, being cut off from the road, it became necessary to attempt the regaining of it, and commence a retreat if possible. To this purpose the remains of the army was formed as well as circumstances would admit, towards the right of the encampment; from which, by way of the second line, another charge was made upon the enemy, as if with the design to turn their right flank, but in fact to gain the road. This was effected—and as soon as it was open, the militia took along it, followed by the troops, Major Clark with his battalion covering the rear.

"The retreat under those circumstances, was, you may be sure, a very precipitate one—it was in fact a flight. The camp and artillery were abandoned, but that was unavoidable, for not a horse was left alive to have drawn it off, had it otherwise been practicable. But the most disgraceful part of the business is, that the greater part of the men threw away their arms and accoutrements even after the pursuit (which continued about four miles) had ceased.

"I found the road strewed with them for many miles but I was not able to remedy it—having had all my horses killed, and being mounted on one that could not be pricked out of a walk, I could not get forward myself, but sent forward an order either to halt the front, or to prevent the men from parting with their arms, were unattended to.

"The route continued quite to Fort Jefferson, twenty-nine miles, which was reached a lettle after sun setting.

"The action began about half an hour before sunrise, and the retreat was attempted at half an hour after nine o'clock.

"I have not yet been able to get returns of the killed and wounded; but Maj. Gen. Butler, Lieut. Colonel Oldham of the militia, Majors Ferguson, Hart, and Clark are among the former; Col. Sargent, my adjutant general, Lieut. Col. Darke, Lieut. Col. Gibson; Major Butler and the Viscount Malertie, (who served me as an aid-de-camp) are among the latter, and a great number of Captains and subalterns in both.

"I have now sir, finished my melancholy tale—a tale that will be felt, sensibly felt by every one that has sympathy for private distress or for public misfortune. I have nothing, sir, to lay to the charge of the troops, but their want of discipline, which from the short time they had been in service it was impossible they should have acquired, and which rendered it very difficult when they were thrown into confusion, to reduce them again to order, and is one reason why the loss has fallen so heavily upon the officers, who did every thing in their power to effect it. Neither were my own exertions wanting; but worn down with illness, and suffering under a painful disease, unable either to mount or dismount a horse without assistance, they were not so great as they otherwise would, and perhaps ought to have been.

"We were overpowered by numbers; but it is no more than justice to observe, that though composed of many species of troops, the utmost harmony prevailed through the whole army during the campaign.

"At Fort Jefferson I found the first regiment, which had returned from the service they had been sent upon without either overtaking the deserters or meeting the convoy of provisions. I am not certain, sir, whether I ought to consider the absence of this regiment from the field of action, as fortunate or otherwise. I incline to think it was fortunate; for I very much doubt whether, had it been in the action the fortune of the day would have been turned; and if it had not, the triumph of the enemy would have been more compleat, and the country destitute of every means of defence.

"Taking a view of the situation of our broken troops at Fort Jefferson, and that there were no provisions in the fort, I called on the field officers, viz: Lieut. Col. Darke, Majors Hamtramck, Zeigler and Gaither, together with the adjutant general, for their advice what would be proper further to be done; and it was their unanimous opinion that the addition of the first regiment as it was, did not put the army on as reputable a footing as it was in the morning, because a great part of it was now unarmed—that it had been then found unequal to the enemy, and should they come on, which was probable, would be found so again; that the troops could not be thrown into the fort, both because it was too small, and that there was no provision in it; that the provisions were known to be upon the road at the distance of one or at most two marches; that, therefore, it would be proper to remove without loss of time, to meet the provisions, when the men might have the sooner an opportunity of some refreshment; and that a proper detachment might be sent back with it, to have it deposited in the fort.

"This advice was accepted, and the army was put in motion again at ten o'clock, and marched all night, and the succeeding day met with a quantity of flour; part of it was distributed immediately, part taken back to supply the army on its march to Fort Hamilton, and the remainder, about fifty horse loads, sent forward to Fort Jefferson. The next day a drove of cattle was met for the same place, and I have information that both got in. The wounded who had been left at that place, were ordered to be brought here by the return of the horses.

"I have said, sir, in a former part of this letter, that we were overpowered by numbers; of that however, I have no other evidence, but the weight of the fire, which was almost a deadly one, and generally delivered from the ground, few of the enemy shewing themselves afoot, except when they were charged, and that in a few minutes our whole camp, which extended above three hundred and fifty yards in length, was entirely surrounded and attacked on all quarters.

"The loss, sir, the public has suffered by the fall of so many officers, particularly Gen. Butler and Maj. Ferguson, cannot be too much regretted, but it is a circumstance that will alleviate the misfortune in some measure, that all fell most gallantly doing their duty. I have had very particular obligations to many of them, as well as to the survivors, but to none more than to Col. Sargeant—he has discharged the various duties of his office, with zeal, with exactness and with intelligence; and on all occasions, afforded me every assistance in his power, which I have also experienced from my aid-de-camp, Lieut. Denny, and the Viscount Malertie, who served with me in the action as a volunteer.

"With every sentiment of respect and regard, I have the honour to be, sir, your most obedient servant.   ARTHUR ST. CLAIR[266]
"The Hon: major general Knox, Secretary at War."

"P.S. Some orders that had been given to Col. Oldham over night, and which were of much consequence, were not executed, and some very material intelligence was communicated by Capt. Slough to General Butler in the course of the night, before the action, which was never imparted to me, nor did I hear of it, until after my arrival here."

SECTION 40

A New State, a New Governor, a New Beginning
[October 12, 1827]

[The letter that follows continues St. Clair's report to Knox (Section 39)]
"PHILADELPHIA, JANUARY 29, 1792.
"Sir:—To the letter of the 9th of November, which I had the honor to address to you from Fort Washington, a postscript was added, relating to information communicated by Capt. Slough to Gen. Butler, and not imparted by him to me, and that did not come to my knowledge till after the army got back to that fort. As the nature of the information was not mentioned the postscript must have appeared mysterious and it is proper that I should explain it.

"Captain Slough, Sir, was intended to have been the bearer of the letter, and so it was endorsed upon the cover, and therefore I thought it needless to insert the particulars; and had he presented it, you no doubt would have enquired into it fully, and all ambiguity would have ceased; but at the moment he should have set off, some account of the situation of Colonel Gibson (who is his uncle) induced him to delay his journey; and the packet was put into the hands of another person, then going to Lexington.

"You will be pleased, sir, to recollect it was stated in the letter, that in the night preceding the 4th of November, the militia were in advance of the rest of the army. For greater security, and to intercept any small parties of Indians that might be approaching with predatory views, it was thought fitting that a party of regular troops should be advanced from a quarter to half a mile, in front of the militia. The party was taken from the right wing which formed the front line, then under the immediate command of General Butler; and Capt. Slough was the officer ordered out by him for those purposes. In the night, it seems, he discovered the Indians approaching in such numbers, that he thought it necessary to draw in his party, and immediately made report of what he had discovered to General Butler, from whom he had received his orders—He proposed to the General to make the same report to me; but the General replied to him, that as he must be fatigued he had better lay down to sleep and he himself would give the information.

"This is, as nearly as I can recollect, the account Capt. Slough gave me at Fort Washington.

"The orders given to Col. Oldham, mentioned also in the postscript as not executed, were, that he should send out, from his command, an hour at least before day, and as much earlier as possible, four or five parties of twenty men, with an officer to each, in different directions, for the purpose of making discoveries. I was very anxious on this point and not without some doubt that it might be punctually attended to. The adjutant general was therefore, about the dawn of the day, but rather before it, sent to Col. Oldham, that I might be certain of that precaution having been taken. Col. Oldham was met by him at some distance from his encampment, and informed him the parties were not then gone out but would be despatched the moment he returned. Unhappily he never returned.

"I have the honor to be, sir, your most obedient servant.

A. ST. CLAIR.[267]

"The Hon. Maj. Gen. Knox, Secretary of War."

PIOMINGO, or the MOUNTAIN LEADER, This principal chief of the Chickasaw Indians, with a small party of his nation who had joined the American army under Gen. St. Clair, left it the day before the action (4th

Nov) and fell in with and killed eight of the enemy without any loss, and but one of his party wounded. From the extent of the ground covered by the enemy in their encampment, which he carefully examined, Piomingo was of opinion, that the number of Indians who fought Gen. St. Clair, was more than 2,000.

On the 15th of February 1792, the Indians killed a man at the Slate Creek Ironworks.[268]

On the 5th of March they stole 10 or 12 horses from near Grant's Station on North Elkhorn, and the following night burnt two dwelling houses with all the furniture, the owners having left them late in the evening.

About the same time, the Indians stole a number of horses near Limestone; they were pursued by a party of 26 men under captains Kenton & M'Intire and overtaken about 40 miles up the Little Miami, and attacked in the night at their camp. The Indians repelled the attack with so much vigour, that the whites were obliged to retreat and make their escape; one of them was killed and another wounded.

On the 15th of April the Indians killed a man between Georgetown and Cincinnati; and after other acts of barbarity, they drove a stake through his body into the earth, leaving by his side a war club.

On the 27th of April they killed three white men and three negroes, on Elkhorn, and took several prisoners. The wife of one of the men that was killed, together with another woman, prevented nine Indians from entering their cabins, which they attempted, as also to burn it; and by discharging a loaded musket at them, killed one on the spot when the others thought prudent to retreat. They burnt several houses on that day. On the following day they killed one man and took another prisoner. A party of Indians who had taken some negroes prisoners, were persued, overtaken and the prisoners retaken and one of the Indians killed; one white man was also killed. On the day after, two men were killed by the Indians at the upper Bluelicks in Mason county.

On the 28th April, the Indians took a boy near the Falls of Ohio, together with a number of horses. They were pursued and overtaken, upon which they tomahawked and scalped the boy, and made their escape, leaving the horses and all their baggage.

A man who had been taken prisoner about this time made his escape and came home.

He said he was taken prisoner by fifteen Indians, and kept several days within the inhabitants; during which time the Indians obliged him to call people out of their houses, while the Indians lay in ambush to murder them whenever they should appear; happily it had not the intended effect—part of the Indians were Delawares and part Shawanese—they told him they did not intend taking prisoners except negroes, which they could sell at Detroit for two kegs of taffy a piece. They therefore wished him to conduct them to where they could get negroes; but he told them he knew of no place where there were negroes, that was not also strong with white men. They informed him that a number of their people were encamped near the Ohio on the other side. When they approached the Ohio, they exhibited signs of fear least the Kentuckians had gone forward to the Ohio in order to intercept them, they therefore stopped a few miles on this side to wait until it was night, and cross the river before day. During the night the prisoner unloosed his cords whilst the Indians were asleep, and made his escape.[269]

About the last of May 1792, the Indians (seven in number) attacked a house on the Rolling fork of Salt river, in which they killed a man and wounded a woman.[270]

Agreeably to the provisions of the constitution, the first General Assembly for the State of Kentucky, convened in Lexington on Monday the 4th day of June 1792.[271]

On the third day of June, Isaac Shelby Esq. who had been chosen the first Governor, arrived in Danville on his way to Lexington, to enter on the duties of his office, where the inhabitants of that town, by a committee, presented to him the following address:

"TO ISAAC SHELBY ESQ.

"*Sir*—The inhabitants of the town of Danville beg leave in the warmest manner, to congratulate your excellency on your appointment to the Chief Magistracy of this State.

"Unacquainted as to flattery or studied panegyrics they only wish in the plain language of truth, to express the great satisfaction they feel on the appointment, and of your acceptance of the office.

"Although they may not be the first to address you on this occasion, yet they will give place to no other part of the State in attachment to your person, and that they will at all times give every aid and support in their power (which may be required) to assist you in the execution of the great trust comitted to your charge.

"And they beg leave to add their sincere wishes for your personal happiness, and to implore the Great Governor of the Universe to have you and the people over whom you preside in his holy keeping.

"By direction of the inhabitants,

"CHRISTOPHER GREENUP, THOMAS BARBEE,
GREENBURY DORSEY."[272]

"June 3d, 1792."

To which his Excellency returned the following answer:
"Gentlemen—I feel myself sensibly impressed with the duties of the office to which I am called by the voice of my country—I hope with the

assistance of the Divine Ruler of the Universe, to discharge the trust reposed in me, in such a manner as may give general satisfaction to the good people of our infant State.

"This being the first address which hath been presented to me since the existence of the State of Kentucky, I beg leave through you, gentlemen, to return to the inhabitants of Danville my sincere thanks for this mark of their approbation and personal attachment, and the readiness they have expressed to aid and support me in the execution of my office.

"Should any circumstance occur which may require my aid to promote the happiness of the good people of this town, they may rely on my exertions to forward such measures as far as may be consistent with my situation. I feel, from long residence in the neighborhood, a particular attachment to them, not only for the present mark of their esteem, but for the civilities which I have uniformly received from them.

"I have the honor to be with esteem and regard, gentlemen, your most obedient and humble servant.　　　　　ISAAC SHELBY."[273]
CHRISTOPHER GREENUP, ESQ.　THOMAS BARBEE, ESQ.
GREENBURY DORSEY, ESQ.
"June 3d, 1792"

On the 4th day of June 1792, the day appointed by the Constitution for the first meeting of the first Legislature elected for the State of Kentucky, Isaac Shelby Esq. the Governor elect, arrived in Lexington from his seat in Lincoln county, to enter on the duties of his office. He was escorted from Danville, by a detachment of the Lexington troop of horse, and was met a few miles from town by the county Lieutenant, the troop of horse commanded by Capt. Todhunter and the Trustees of the town. The Light Infantry commanded by Capt. James Hughes, received him at the corner of Main and Cross streets with military honors. After attending the Governor to his lodgings, the Horse and Infantry paraded on the public square, and fifteen rounds alternately, and then gave a general discharge in favor of his excellency.

The following address was presented to Governor Shelby, by the Chairman of the board of Trustees of the Town of Lexington.

"SIR—The inhabitants of the town of Lexington beg leave through us, to present to your excellency their sincere congratulations on your appointment to the office of Chief Magistrate of the State of Kentucky.

"Truly sensible that no other motive than a sincere desire to promote the happiness and welfare of your country, could have induced you to accept an appointment, that must draw you from those scenes of domestic ease and private tranquility, which you enjoy in so eminent a degree.

"Having the fullest confidence in your wisdom, virtue and integrity, we rest satisfied, that under your administration, the constitution will be kept inviolate, and the laws so calculated, as to promote happiness and good order in the state.

"In the name of the inhabitants of Lexington we bid you welcome; and assure you that we, and those we represent, have the warmest attachment to your person and character.

"May your administration insure blessings to your country; honour and happiness to yourself.

"By order of the Trustees of Lexington.   JOHN BRADFORD, Ch.
"*His Excellency, ISAAC SHELBY, Esq.*
Governor of the State of Kentucky."

THE GOVERNOR'S REPLY.

"LEXINGTON, JUNE 4, 1792.[274]

"*Sir*—I receive with the warmest sentiments of gratitude and respect, your very polite and genteel address; which, added to the friendly treatment exhibited by you this day in conducting me to this place, commands my most cordial respect and esteem—and although I am thoroughly sensible of my want of experience, and abilities, to discharge the very important duties committed to me; the warm congratulations only of my country induces me to come forward with some hopes, that, by a strict attention to the duties of my office, and a firm adherence to public justice (both of which I trust are in my power) I may in some degree merit a part of that confidence which they have placed in me.

"Unacquainted with flattery I only use the plain language of truth, to express my warm attachment to the inhabitants of this place, and assure them through you, Sir, that I shall be happy to render them any services in my power, which may not be incompatible with the interest of our common country.

"I have the honour to be with great regard and esteem, Sir, your most obedient servant.   ISAAC SHELBY.[275]
Mr. JOHN BRADFORD, *Chairman of the Board of Trustees of Lexington*"

SECTION 41

To "Gentlemen of the Senate and House"

[October 19, 1827]

STATE OF KENTUCKY

House of Representatives, Thursday, June 7, 1792.

The Speaker laid before the house a copy of the address delivered by the Governor yesterday to both houses of the Legislature in the Senate Chamber, which is in the following words:

"Gentlemen of the Senate and House of Representatives.

"As the prosperity of our country will depend greatly on the manner in which its government shall be put in motion, it will be particularly incumbent on you, to adopt such measures as will be most likely to produce that desirable end.

"Amongst the means which ought to be used for that purpose, none will be found more efficacious, than the establishing public and private credit on the most solid basis. The first will be obtained by a scrupulous adherence to all public engagements, the last by a speedy and uniform administration of justice.

"The happiness and welfare of this country, depends so much on the speedy settlement of our land disputes; that I cannot forbear expressing my hope, that you will adopt every necessary measure to give full operation to the mode pointed out by the constitution for that purpose.

"It will be essentially necessary that you should pass laws regulating the future elections of members to the state Legislature. The having those elections made without any kind of undue influence, is an object highly worthy of Legislative attention.

"It is also incumbent on you, and the interest of the state requires that you should as soon as possible, appoint two Senators to represent this State in the National Senate; and pass the necessary laws to prescribe the time and manner of electing this states' proportion of members to the House of Representatives.

"A law obliging sheriffs and other public officers, to give security for the due performance of the duties of their respective offices, will be essentially necessary.

"Your humanity as well as your duty, will induce you to pass laws to compel the proper treatment of slaves, agreeable to the direction of the constitution.

"*Gentlemen of the House of Representatives.*

"It will be your peculiar duty to point out the manner by which the public supplies shall be raised. Small as our money resources are I flatter myself you will find them fully equal to the necessary expenditures of the government; I conceive that both the honor and interest of the state require, whatever may be the amount of those expenditures, that the funds for their payment should be adequate and certain.

"The constitution has made it your duty, at the present session, to cause to be chosen commissioners, for the purpose of fixing the place for the permanent seat of Government.

"*Gentlemen of the Senate and House of Representatives.*

"You may be assured of my hearty co-operation in all your measures, which shall have a tendency to promote the public good.

"The unorganized state of our government, and the season of the year render every proper dispatch of the business that will come before you, so much your duty and interest, that I shall forbear any thing on that head.

ISAAC SHELBY."[276]

Answer of the House of Representatives to the Governor's Address.
"Sir—The Representatives of the people of the State of Kentucky, have considered the address made by you to both houses of the Legislature on the 6th instant.

"We congratulate you on the arrival of this period, when we see our wishes for years past, consummated by the formation of a constitution and government organized.

"It affords us pleasure that the voice of our country, (almost unanimous) has called to the office of Chief Magistrate, one who from an early period, has experienced the inconveniences and danger we have in common been subject to, by our far removal from the assistance of government, & our adjacent situation to hostile savages.

"The communications made, will be early and particularly attended to; we feel sensibly the force they ought to have on those whose only object will be the prosperity of the state, and are happy in the reflection, that every measure that will lead to its advancement, will not only receive your cheerful concurrence, but derive from your cooperation, sufficient efficacy to ensure happiness to our fellow-citizens, and beg leave to assure you, sir, that we will leave nothing in our power undone, which will tend to perpetuate the liberty and happiness of this Commonwealth.

"We feel anxious that you may be happy in the enjoyment of uninterrupted health; that your administration may be truly advantageous to the

first republic in the Western Territory, and leave the sensations of gratitude imprinted, and not to be obliterated by time."

SIGNED ROBERT BRECKINRIDGE, Speaker."[277]

[Secretary Knox's report in full:]

*"The causes of the existing hostilities between the United States and certain Tribes
of Indians North West of the Ohio, stated and explained from official and authentic
documents, and published in obedience to the orders of the President of the United
States, on the 26th January 1792.*

"A recurrence to the journals of the United States in Congress assembled,
of the early stages of the late war, will evince the public solicitude to
preserve peace with the Indian tribes, and to prevent their engaging in a
contest in which they are in no wise interested.

"But although partial treaties or conventions were formed with some
of the Northern and Western tribes, in the years 1775 and 1776, yet those
treaties were too feeble to resist the powerful impulses of a contrary
nature, arising from a combination of circumstances at that time; and
accordingly all the various Indian nations, (the Oneidas, Tuscaroras and a
few individuals of the Delawares excepted,) lying on our frontiers, from
Georgia to Canada, armed against us.

"It is yet too recent to have been forgotten, that great numbers of
inoffensive men, women and children, fell sacrifice to the barbarous
warfare practised by the Indians, and that many others were dragged
into a deplorable captivity.

"Notwithstanding that these aggressions were entirely unprovoked,
yet as soon as the war ceased with Great Britain, the United States, instead
of indulging any resentment against the Indian nations, sought only how
to establish a liberal peace with all the tribes throughout their limits.

"Early measures were accordingly taken for this purpose. A treaty
was held, and a peace concluded in the year 1784, with the hostile part of
the Northern Indians, or six nations at Fort Stanwix.[278]

"In January 1785, another treaty was formed with part of the Western
tribes, at Fort M'Intosh on the Ohio; to wit, with the Wyandots, Delawares, Ottawas and Chippewas.[279]

"During the same year, treaties were formed at Hopewell on the
Keowee, with all the powerful tribes of the South, excepting the Cherokees, the Chocktaws and Chickasaws.[280]

"In January 1786, a treaty was formed with the Shawanees, at the
confluence of the Great Miami with the Ohio.[281]

"It was not long before certain turbulent and malignant characters,
residing among some of the Northern and Western tribes, which had
formed the treaties of Stanwix and Fort M'Intosh, excited uneasiness and
complaints against those treaties. In consequence of representations upon
this subject, on the 5th of Oct. 1787, Congress directed, "That a general

treaty should be held with the tribes of Indians within the limits of the United States, inhabiting the country North West of the Ohio and about Lake Erie, as soon after the first of April next, as conveniently might be, and at such place, and at such particular time as the Governor of the Western Territory should appoint, for the purpose of knowing the causes of uneasiness among the said tribes, and hearing their complaints; of regulating trade, and amicably settling all affairs concerning lands and boundaries between them and the United States.

"On the 2d day of July 1788, Congress appropriated the sum of twenty thousand dollars, in addition to fourteen thousand dollars before appropriated, for defraying the expenses of the treaties which had been ordered or might be ordered to be held in the present year, with the several Indian tribes in the northern departments, and for extinguishing the Indian claims; the whole of the said twenty thousand dollars, together with six thousand dollars of the said fourteen thousand dollars, to be applied solely to the purpose of extinguishing Indian claims to the lands they had already ceded to the United States, by obtaining regular conveyances for the same, and for extending a purchase beyond the limits theretofore fixed by treaty; but that no part of the said sums, should be applied for any purpose other than those above mentioned.

"Accordingly, new treaties were held at Fort Harmar, the latter part of the year 1788, and concluded on the 9th day of January 1789, with a representation of all the six or northern nations, the Mohawks excepted— and with a representation of the following tribes, to wit: The Wyandots, Delawares, Ottawas, Chippewas, Pottiwattamies and Sacs. By these treaties, nearly the same boundaries were recognized and established by a *principle of purchase,* as had been stipulated by the former treaties of Fort Stanwix and Fort M'Intosh.

"Thus careful and attentive was the government of the United States, to settle a boundary with the Indians on the basis of fair treaty, to obviate the dissatisfactions which had been excited, and to establish its claim to the lands relinquished on the principle of equitable purchase.

"It does not appear that the right of the Northern and Western Indians, who formed the several before mentioned treaties to the lands thereby relinquished to the United States, has been questioned by any other tribes; nor does it appear that the present war has been occasioned by any dispute relatively to the boundaries established by the said treaties.

"But on the contrary, it appears that the unprovoked aggressions of Miami and Wabash Indians upon Kentucky and other parts of the frontiers, together with their associates, a banditti, formed of Shawanese and out cast Cherokees, amounting in all to about one thousand two hundred men, are solely the causes of the war. Hence, it is proper that their conduct should be more particularly adverted to.

"In the year 1784, when messages were sent to the Wyandots and Delawares, inviting them to meet the commissioners, first at Cayahoga, and afterwards at Fort M'Intosh, their neighbors, the *Miami Indians* were also included in the said invitation; but they did not attend.

"In the year 1785, these *invitations were repeated;* but the messengers upon their arrival at the Miami village, had their horses stolen, were otherwise treated with insolence, and *prevented fulfilling their mission.*

"At a second council of the tribes, convened in 1788, at the Miami river, the Miami and Wabash Indians were pressed to repair to the treaty with great earnestness, by the Chiefs of Wyandots and Delawares; the Wyandot Chiefs particularly, presented them with a large belt of wampum, holding one end of it themselves, and offering the other to the hostile Indians, which was refused. The Wyandots then laid it on the shoulders of a principal Chief, recommending him to be at peace with the Americans; but without making any answer, he leaned himself and let it fall to the ground; this so displeased the Wyandots, that they immediately left the council house.

"In the mean time, the frontier settlements were disputed by frequent depredations and murders, and the complaints of their inhabitants, (as might be expected,) of the pacific forbearance of the government, were loud, repeated and distressing—their calls for protection, incessant—till at length they appeared determined by their own efforts to endeavor to retaliate the injuries they were continually receiving, and which had become intolerable.

"In this state of things, it was indispensable for the government to make some decisive exertion for the peace and security of the frontier.

"But notwithstanding the ill success of the former experiments; and the invincible spirit of animosity which had appeared in certain tribes, and which was of a nature to justify a persuasion that no impression could be made upon them by pacific expedients, it was still deemed advisable to make one more essay.

"Accordingly, in April 1790, Anthony Gamelin, an inhabitant of Post Vincennes, and a man of good character, was dispatched to all the tribes and villages of the Wabash river, and to the Indians of the Miami village, with a message, purporting that the United States were desirous of establishing a general peace with all the neighboring tribes of Indians, and of treating them in all respects, with perfect humanity and kindness and at the same time, warning them to abstain from further depredations.

"The Indians in some of the villages on the lower part of the Wabash, appeared to listen to him, others manifested their inability to restrain their young warriors, and all referred the messenger to the Indians at the Miami village. At that village some appeared well disposed, but the Chiefs of the Shawanese returned the messages and belts, informing the messenger, however, that they would, after consultation, within thirty nights, send an answer to Post Vincennes. The promised answer was never received. While the messenger was at the Miami village, two negroes were brought in from our settlements, prisoners, and upon his return to L'Anguille, a Chief informed him that a party of seventy warriors, from the more distant Indians, had arrived, and were gone against the settlements.

"In three days after his departure from the Miami village, a prisoner was there burnt to death. Similar cruelties were exercised at the Ouiactinon towns, about the same time, and in the course of three months, immediately after the last invitation, upwards of one hundred persons were killed, wounded and taken prisoners upon the Ohio, and in the District of Kentucky.

"It is to be remarked, that previously to the last invitation, the people of Kentucky, who, in consequence of their injuries, were meditating a blow against the hostile Indians (as before intimated,) were restrained by the President of the United States, from crossing the Ohio, until the effort of the friendly overture intended to be made should be known.

"It is also to be observed, that the Wyandots and Delawares, after having frequently and fruitlessly endeavored to influence the MIAMI and WABASH Indians to peace, upon mature conviction, finally declared, that force only could effect the object.

"As an evidence that the conduct of the hostile Indians, has occasioned by other motives than a claim relative to boundaries; it is to be observed, that their depredations have been principally upon the district of Kentucky, and the counties of Virginia, lying along the south side of the Ohio, a country to which they have no claim.

"It appears by respectable evidence, that from the year 1783, until the month of October 1790, the time the United States commenced offensive operations against the said Indians, that on the Ohio and frontiers on the south side thereof, they killed, wounded and took prisoners, about one thousand five hundred men, women and children; besides carrying off upwards of two thousand horses, and other property to the amount of fifty thousand dollars.

"The particulars of the barbarities exercised upon many of their prisoners, of different ages and sexes, although supported by indisputable evidence, are of too shocking a nature to be presented to the public. It is sufficient upon this head, to observe, that the tomahawk and scalping knife, have been the mildest instrument of death. That in some cases, torture by fire, and other execrable means have been used.

"But the outrages which were committed upon the frontier inhabitants, were not the only injuries that were sustained; repeated attacks upon detachments of the troops of the United States, were, at different times made. The following from its peculiar enormity, deserves recital. In April 1790, Major Dougherty was ordered to the friendly Chickasaw on public business. He performed this duty in a boat, having with him

Ensign Sedam, and a party of fifteen men. While ascending the Tennessee river, he was met by a party of forty Indians, in four canoes, consisting principally of the aforesaid banditti, of Shawanese and outcast Cherokees. They approached under a white flag, the well known emblem of peace. They came on board the Major's boat, received his presents, continued with him nearly one hour, and then departed in the most friendly manner. But they had scarce cleared his oars, before they poured in a fire upon his crew, which was returned as soon as circumstances would permit, and a most unequal combat was sustained for several hours, when they abandoned their design, but not until they had killed and wounded eleven out of fifteen of the boat's crew. This perfidious conduct in any age, would have demanded exemplary punishment.[282]

"All overtures of peace failing, and the depredations still continuing, an attempt at coercion became indispensable. Accordingly, the expedition under Brigadier General Harmar, in the month of October 1790, was directed. The event is known.

"After this expedition, the Governor of the Western Territory, in order that nothing might be omitted, to effect a peace without further conflict, did, on his arrival at Fort Harrison, in December 1790, send through the Wyandots and Delawares, conciliatory messages to the Miamies, but still without effect.

"The Cornplanter, a war Chief of the Senecas and other Indians of the same tribe, being in Philadelphia in the month of February 1791, were engaged to undertake to impress the hostile Indians, with the consequence of their persisting in hostilities, and also of the justice and moderation of the United States.

"In pursuance of this design, Col. Proctor, on the 14th of March, was sent to the Cornplanter to hasten his departure, and to accompany him to the Miami village, and messengers were sent to the Indians, declaratory of the pacific sentiments of the United States towards them. But Colonel Proctor and the Cornplanter, although zealously desirous of executing their mission, encountered difficulties of a particular nature, which were insurmountable, and prevented the execution of their orders.

"Major General St. Clair, in the month of April, sent messages from Fort Harmer to the Delawares, expressive of the pacific designs of the United States, to all the Indian tribes.

"A treaty was held at the Pointed Post, by Col. Pickering, in June 1791, with a part of the Six Nations, at which the humane intentions of the General Government towards them particularly, and the Indian tribes generally, were fully explained.[283]

"Capt. Hendricks, a respectable Indian, residing with the Oneidas, appearing zealously disposed to attempt convincing the hostile Indians of their mistaken conduct, was accordingly sent for that purpose, but was frustrated by unforeseen obstacles, in his laudable attempts.

"The different measures which have been recited, must evince, that notwithstanding the highly culpable conduct of the Indians in question, the government of the United States, uninfluenced by resentment, or any false principles which might arise from a consciousness of superiority, adopted every proper expedient to terminate the Indian hostilities, without having recourse to the last extremity; and, after being compelled to resort to it, has still kept steadily in view the re-establishment of peace, as its primary and sole object.

"Were it necessary to add proofs to the pacific and humane dispositions of the General Government towards the Indian tribes, the treaties with the Creeks and Cherokees, might be cited as demonstrative of its moderation and liberality.

"The present partial Indian war, is a remnant of the late general war, continued by a number of separate banditti, who, by the incessant practice of fifteen years, seem to have formed inveterate and incurable habits of enmity against the frontier inhabitants of the United States.

"To obtain protection against lawless violence, was a main object for which the present government was instituted. It is indeed a main object of all governments. A frontier citizen possesses as strong claims to protection as any other citizen. The frontiers are the vulnerable parts of every country; and the obligation of the government of the United States, to afford the requisite protection, cannot be less sacred in reference to the inhabitants of their Western, than to those of their Atlantic frontiers.

"It will appear from a candid review of this subject, that the General Government could no longer abstain from attempting to punish the hostile Indians.

"The ill success of the attempts for this purpose, is entirely unconnected with the justice or policy of the measure. A perseverance in exertions to make the refactory Indians at least sensible, that they cannot continue their enormous outrages with impunity, appears to be as indispensable, in the existing posture of things, as it will be advisable whenever they shall manifest symptoms of a more amiable disposition, to convince them, by decisive proofs, that nothing is so much desired by the United States, as to be at liberty to treat them with kindness and benificence.

"H. KNOX, Secretary of War. WAR DEPARTMENT, January 26, 1792." [284]

H.H. Brackenridge on the Indian Problem

[October 26, 1827]

"Thoughts on the present Indian War,
by H. H. BRACKENRIDGE, *of Pittsburg."*

"Being occasionally in this city, I feel myself impelled to give my sentiments on this subject, and I give my name, in order to obtain confidence: because it is to be presumed, that a man will not lightly avow what he has not weighed, and in which he has not confidence himself.

"I am struck, seeing in the Gazettes, extracts of letters that were never written, and paragraphs penned from ignorance or mistake of facts. Having resided some years in the western country, and being interested, I have thought much on the subject—and though I may not know more than the most ignorant man there, yet I am persuaded that I know more than the wisest man that has never been there.

"The writers of extracts, and the paragraphists in the first place, endeavor to affect the public mind, by holding up *the original right of the aborigines to the soil.* It is a right of which I have never thought with much respect. It is like the claim of the children: it is mine, for I first saw it—or what that of the Buffaloe might be—it is mine, for I have first run over it. I consider the earth as given to man in common, and each should use his share, so as not to exclude others, and should be restricted to that mode of using it, which is most favorable to the support of the greatest numbers, and consequently productive of the greatest happiness, that is, the cultivation of the soil. I pay little regard, therefore, to any right which is not founded in *agricultural occupancy.*

"But supposing these natives to have had an absolute and exclusive right, it is not destroyed by a supervenient right on our part, in consequence of our treaty with great Britain? During the war with that power, were not those natives the subsidiaries of the King of England? Were they not in his hand, as the tomahawk and scalping knife was in theirs? Was not the territory in question, ceced [ceded] by the superior power? Shall we treat with the principal, and make concessions in lieu of this concession—and shall we again treat with, the subordinate, and purchase a treaty and concede to them also? Be it so; there is nothing to be said, *for it has been done.* What has appeared in the paper of the other day, from the Secretary at War, has superceded me, in stating and illustrating this.

"But, as to treaties with these Indians, under present circumstances, I can have no confidence in them—Why? Do not savages observe treaties?—no longer than the principle of fear operates; being indolent, and more disposed to acquire by *seizing* than by *earning.* But under *present circumstances,* all treaties with them must be nugatory. While Canada was in the possession of the French, were not these Indians hostile to us, and regardless of all treaties, because it was not the interest of that nation that they should be at peace with us, when it was in their power to instigate them to war? Are we not at this time in the same situation with respect to the Indians, and the British in possession of Canada? Hence it is, that it was expedient and has been found practicable, to establish treaties with the Creeks, or other nations remote from the British province. But with these Indians, treaties cannot be established, or if established, would not be observed.

"Whether the British government, has an eye to the territory ceded, I shall not say, I rather think not; but certainly it has an eye to the Indian trade, and on this account supports the savages. I shall not say that this is done directly by the Government of Canada, or the commandant at Detroit; but certainly through the medium of the Indian agents, and with the knowledge and approbation of the ministry at home. Why else are the posts on the lakes not surrendered, when all pretence of the treaty not being fulfilled on our part, is taken away? How have the Indians north of the lakes been excited and brought to the Miami village to engage in war? Certainly not by the Shawanese or Wabash Indians, but by the voice of the British agents who had stores at Detroit to supply them; two stores called the *Kings,* with ammunition, cloathing and provisions. How have *so large a body of Indians as met our army in the late engagement, been supported but by provisions from the King's store?* They have been supplied from a *King's store,* at what are called the rapids, about sixty miles from the Miami towns. Would Canadian volunteers or militia march to aid these Indians, and not the government solicit or enjoin it? That volunteers did turn out, as our phrase is, I know, though not to what amount they may have been in battle.

"It is not a war, therefore, with Indians merely; it is a war with the British King. Under cover, have we felt the paw of the Lion, and shall we be still lashed with his tail?

"With respect to the *mode* of war still to be pursued; What? Precisely that which was adopted and pursued the last campaign, but the means different. More men and higher pay; because this will procure better men.

"A greater proportion of light infantry, or rifle corps, would be advisable. But the system already adopted, and in part executed, I approve. The establishment of forts in the country, and planting ourselves in the face of the British province, and convincing the Indians that a greater force than the British whom they venerate, are now here.

"It is suggested by paragraphists, that an incursive war of small parties, with a premium for scalps, fighting the Indians in their own way, would be best. It might indeed harrass them, but from the circumstances stated, could produce no substantial and lasting effect. It is also contended that an incursive war of larger bodies, in the manner of the Kentucky volunteers last year, would avail. I say not. I never considered the Kentucky expeditions under Wilkinson or Scott as more than a flourish; honorable to those who went, but little serviceable to those at home. Indians are seldom surprized, or if in part, the whole object is the killing a warrior or two, and the carrying off women and children; an incumbrance more than a spoil.

"There are those who advocate what is called a defensive war, by posts on the frontiers, and ranging companies. I say the best defence, is *offence*. Instead of warding off blows, give one. If you could surround the frontier with a rank and file of men, like the wall of China, and take care that these should never sleep, you might expect some thing. But posts and ranging companies, are but a help, and no effectual defence. It is but watching beasts of prey, who come against our folds instead of penetrating the forests where they haunt, and exterminating the race.

"With respect to the mode of war, I am confident the establishing ourselves in the face of Canada, will alone be effectual; but, with respect to the route, would suggest, whether by the way of Lake Erie would not have been advisable: That is, by establishing a garrison at Presq' Isle, and building armed vessels on the Lakes, to transport troops and convey provisions; again a post on the west of the lake, and from thence the progress to the Miami towns. At least, whether, as things now stand, that route ought not to be embraced? I have not the smallest doubt, but that unless effective arrangements are made for the ensuing summer, and *that*, in the face of the Six Nations, and so as to speedily strike them, they will avow themselves; for I aver, that except a few Chiefs, they are in disposition, hostile, and nothing but the principle of fear restrains them at this moment.

"A garrison at Presq' Isle, would secure their neutrality, or perhaps engage them to act in our favor. It is thrown out by the paragraphists, few of whom I take to be out of this city, that the possession and security of the Western Territory ought not to be an object with these states; *we have*, it seems, soil enough. Be it so.—I enquire what are the best means of protecting the settlements on this side of the rivers? I say the only means are by reaching the source of hostility, and taking the commanding ground of posts to the westward.

"But is not the government bound to give *peaceable possession* of the western soil, to those to whom they have sold, and to their officers and soldiers to whom they have made grants? Shall every things be done to support credit in making a liberal provision for the public debt; even though this has brought a great evil, fortunes rising, like exhalations from the earth, by other means than common industry; and shall the public disregard their faith, pledged in the cases above mentioned? All who wish the preservation of our confederacy, ought to feel an alarm at all ideas of direlection of the claims and rights of any part of the community. The consequences may be fatal to all who have any hopes from government, or any interest in it.

"It may be said, that taking the way of the lakes, building armed vessels, and occupying posts in the neighborhood of Niagara and Detroit, may involve us in a war with Britain.

"Of that, there is no doubt. If our merchantmen are in the power of the British navy, theirs are in the power of our privateers; and they get more by our imports from them in peace, than by the captures they could make in war; and the province of Canada and the fur trade on the west, is a stake which they have to lose.

"If the world has been astonished at our rising, if they have seen the meridian beams of our splendor, in establishing *public credit*, let them not regret our meanness and want of spirit in suffering the out guards of the country, the frontier settlements to be cut to pieces by the axe of the savage, when the probability is, I think, *certainty*, that it is put into their hands by our late inveterate, but discomfited enemy.

"I beg the public to excuse these things written hastily: and let them have their weight with every humane and good man, which the reason of them may support. I say humane, because I am persuaded humanity is not on the side of the savages, but on our side. *They* have been the aggressors. *They* are not to be appeased. They refuse all treaty, or respect none. They cannot, for it is not the will of those by whom they are impelled.

"It is said the British government cannot possibly countenance these people for the commandant and officers at Detroit are humane to our prisoners, and actually purchase them at a great price from the savages. No doubt, it is but a little matter to redeem a captive, but a great matter to have our armies defeated and excluded from the country.

"In looking over what I have written, there is no sentiment that I would retrench, but I add one more viz: Why dread the expence of an effective and lasting armament for the purposes suggested? The moment we take command of the savages, instead of leaving them to Britain, the fur trade of the immense world on the west will amply repay us, creating a trade to the sea coast parts, of which at present, they have no idea. I say *take command* of the Indians; the only way to which, is to place ourselves upon equal ground with our rivals, and impress the savages with an opinion, that we are at least an equal power. All treaty with them until they are humbled and reduced, is absurd; and even then to be considered as of duration, no longer than while the external pressure of a pretended force keep them down.

"After some time, the interests of trade may conciliate and bind them, and we may have it in our power to make a proper use of these people.
"Philidelphia, January 31, 1792." [285]

[Continued in following section, No. 43.—*Ed.*]

SECTION 43

Defense of the Western Attitude
[November 2, 1827]

Thoughts on the present Indian War, concluded.
"I can easily excuse those, who, from motives of humanity, call in question the justness of our cause in the war against the Indians. But should I make my observations theirs, with respect to the ruthful disposition of a savage, that is not soothed continually by good offices, or kept down by fear; could I give my knowledge, recollection and impression of the accumulated instances of homicide, committed by the tribes with whom we are at war; the humane would be more humane, for their feelings would be more awake, not in favor of these people, but of the persons butchered by them in cold blood, or dragged to that pole seen by the soldiers under General HARMER, by the Miami village, where the ground was beat like a pavement by the miserable victims moving round the stake to avoid the still pursuing tortures, which the circle of black coals, at a distance from the piles burned, shewed where they brought their brands or heated gun barrels to afflict the object. All this, though there have been but three instances since the conclusion of the war with Britain, where an Indian has been hurt on our part; one on the Susquehanna and two on the Ohio; with respect to one of which instances, that of M'Guire and Brady, it is a doubt whether they were hostile or peaceable.

"I consider men who are unacquainted with the savages, like young women who have read romances, and have as improper an idea of the Indian's character in the one case, as the female mind has of real life in the other. The philosopher, weary of the vices of refined life, thinks to find perfect virtue in simplicity of the unimproved state. He sees green fields and meadows in the customs and virtues of the savages. It is experience only that can relieve from the calenture of the intellect. All that is good and great in man results from education; and an uncivilized Indian, is but a little way removed from a beast; who, when incensed, can only tear and devour; but the savage applies the ingenuity of man to torture and inflict anguish.

"Some years ago, two French gentlemen, a Botanist and Mineralist, Monsieur Sograin and M. Pike, the Botanist a very learned man and truly a philosopher, but his brain turned with Jean Jacques Rousseau's and other rhapsodies—the man of nature was his darling favorite. He had the Indians with him at his chamber every day. Fitting out a small boat on the Ohio, with only three other persons, and without arms he descended. It was in vain to explain the danger, and dissuade him. He was conscious to himself of loving Indians, and doubtless they could wish him no harm. But approaching the Sciota river, a party came out in a canoe, as he thought, to pay their respects to him; but the first circumstance of ceremony when they came on board, was, to impress the tomahawk and take off the scalp of the philosopher.*

"A great dependence seems to be placed in *Cornplanter* and his party. I know *Cornplanter* and *Big Tree* and *Half Town;* they are good, as Indians, and are well disposed to us, because they can be of little or no account on the other side. Brandt treats them with contempt, and adheres to the British. Instead of bringing them down at a great expence, and presenting them in Philadelphia, and appropriating 800 dollars for their maintenance and vestment, were things but on a right footing, and Presq' Isle garrisoned, we should have no more occasion for Cornplanter, or Big Tree, or Half Town, than they would have for us; and if we gave them goods, they would give us furs.

"As to Cornplanter's speech, I have known my self, a speech made for him, that he never heard. I know a little of the mystery of agent craft, and the mummery of Indian speechifying. An Indian, in the hands of a good interpreter and agent, is a more profitable property than a tame bear or lion presented for a show. I have seen Indian princes in Pittsburgh, as plenty as in the time of Adonibezek, who had three score and ten kings under his table. Many a chief have I seen driven out of a kitchen by a maid with a broom stick, lest he should steal a tin cup or a table spoon. I have seen a certain blind Sam, so called, because blind of an eye, taken down to

*Sougrain was not killed but wounded, he jumped overboard and made his escape. This transaction will be seen in section 30 of these notes—Ed.

this city, passed for a warrior, dining with clubs, and have heard of him presented at a ball on his way down; the favored ladies looking upon themselves as beautified in receiving the salute of a King. When he returned with a laced waistcoat, the vulgar Indians, who before thought him one of them, laughed immoderately at the farce.

"I say, the business with the Indians is war and reduction, and after that, away with the system of agents and interpreters, and leading Indians down to your capitals like pet beasts! Let them stay in their woods and negociate an equal trade. This trade may certainly be a very great object. When the line of savages, that are at present hostile, is removed, our way is open to peaceable and remote nations. I have conversed with those, who, in behalf of great trading companies, had been four years on discovery for the purpose of trade, had penetrated many thousand miles, traversed the country beyond the source of the Missouri, but were delicate in their communications of the route and advantages of trade with the myriads of the natives of those woods; they, however, gave me to understand, that most of the trading companies of Britain, were turning their attention to it.

"Of the vast nations of Indians that are ready to trade with us, were the Miami and Wabash Indians peaceable, there is no conception. It will cost but one effective armament to accomplish this object, and why employ years in doing that which may be done at once? No longer any starved campaign! But I am disposed to believe that Presq' Isle is the route. Let others calculate and explain the saving of expence by this route, I only touch the advantage of beginning with the Six Nations in our rear. It is said that the persons interested in our funds, are against an effective armament, as it may turn away the revenue from the payment of their interest. I could give them a small hint on this head. Be careful not to check the spirit of the people. It is electrical, and if confined may burst— let it have an egress in acquisitions to the west, and you may rest safe.

"It is considered as a great sacrifice to public credit, to have provided for the discharge of the public debt, without discrimination; and it is a prevailing opinion, that the monied interests thus constituted, are a dead weight; (by their extracts of letters and paragraphs in the papers) on the wheels of government, and all this to secure the payment of their interest. But the maxim is, *ne quid nimis*; nothing too much. They may overshoot themselves, and cause the people to revolt, and call in question the original justice of their claims.

"As these are desultory observations, I remark and conclude that some think rather rash in presuming that the King of Britain has given any countenance, directly or indirectly, to the Indian depredations or armaments. I should be sorry to do injustice to any power, and it was with great difficulty that I admitted the idea; but I have been convinced of it, and can have no doubt, because that government could not but have heard of the hostilities, and by one simple word of the commandant of Detroit, to M'Kee and Brandt, we should have had a perfect peace. But M'Kee and Brandt, when messengers, were sent to call the Indians to the treaties at Muskingum and at the Miami, advised them not to go. Witness—I shall suppress my authorities. It may perhaps injure these men in their future trade with the Indians or connexion at Detroit. Good God! that an island where I drew my first breath, where a Milton and a Hume have lived, where a Howard has been sacrificed to humanity—there can be those who can aid, at least not disarm what may be in their power, the savage of his axe, battered on the sculls of their species, in the cottage or the field of the settlements adjoining their province! They could do this by the surrender of the posts; for at that moment I proclaim peace to the westward and ensure safety.

"But the posts are not surrendered, and the Indians are supported. Nay, more. I would not wonder if the British gold has found its way into our states; and some of these sentiments against effectual measures that are thrown out, may come from that source. We are thus between two fires, seduction at home and invasion from abroad.

"The chiefs of the western nations elated with victory, are at this moment at the mouth of Buffaloe creek, which empties into Lake Erie, at no great distance from the post of Niagara, under the auspices of the government of Canada, soliciting and convening the Chiefs of the Six Nations to a council. The chiefs are actually convening, and the populace are clamorous for a war. They talk with irony and sarcasm of the attachment of Cornplanter, Half Town and Big Tree to these states. They exult in the victory obtained: For Indian loves Indian, and, like a bone out of joint, they wish to find their proper place, and coalesce with a like people. It is true, the northern and western Indians have been formerly hostile to each other; but it is well known that the Six Nations were reduced by the campaign under General Sullivan, and ever since submitted. It is in spite of nature; and could they have at least chance of success in revolt, they would join their brethren and the long confined indignancy of their resentment would burst forth. I think this is the occasion, and I am disposed to believe they will think so. A force in their front, a garrison at Presq' Isle, is the talismanic charm in this case. It will intercept the communication of the Indians who are at present open and avowed enemies; and we shall hear no more of council fires at Buffaloe creek, or talks sent to Cornplanter and his people, of shaking him by the hand, and the like, unless he joins them in their warfare. Presq' Isle is the object, and ought to be seized instantly and made the foothold from whence, as with the mechanism of an Archimides, the whole system of the western affairs may be moved and directed.

"It may be thought that I am inhumane to no man or men; but in order to be humane, let me have it in my power. Let myself first be safe, and then I can show what humanity dictates. The question is, whether we shall submit ourselves to the savages, or they to us? I say, let us conquer because we cannot depend upon them; for the weaker ever distrusts the mightier, and the unenlightened man, the sensible, but when we shall have it in our power, let us dispense treaties on principles of reciprocity, (to use the term of the diplomatists) and let them know that we are not about to purchase a treaty, but to make one and preserve it. These principles, founded in nature and truth, will strike the mind of the savage, and we ask no more than he ought to give, or that he has a right to ask. By the immortal Gods! (a Roman oath, but sworn with christian devotion,) if this principle could be made the basis of our negociations, we should govern not only these people, but all the world with whom we have to do. When I say *govern*, I mean *command* of them all that is our right on principles of the laws of nations or of nature. But in our affairs with the western Indians, we have for a series of years, pursued a sickly tampering system of half peace, half war, from which nothing could result but half success. A bold and decisive act of effective hostility at the conclusion of the war with Britain, would have composed these Indians, and preserve in existence, the countless numbers that have fallen victims to torture or death on the bourne of the wilderness. It was, therefore, inhumane not to have adopted this system, which would have been effectual. But I saw and lamented the circumstance of the Congress besieged with candidates for agencies and commissionships and runners, to negociate with these tribes.

"There was not a thing that had ever seen a squaw, or a half king, or a chief, or had heard the guttural sound of a Kickapoo or a Delaware, but would have it that he understood fifty Indian languages, and could interpret, and could draw all the tribes after him, just as a boy would whistle pigeons. Hence, treaty and not war. It is not to be supposed that men at the helm know every thing; they are just as ignorant with respect to affairs beyond their reach, as other people. It is the man on the extremity of any government as I have been, who sees the most absurdities. I shall say no more at present, for I wish all things conducted well, and would rather help forward what ought to be done, than blame what has been transacted.

"Philadelphia, February 4, 1792."[286]

A Sounding Horn
and Hallooing Indians
[November 9, 1827]

About the 16th of June 1792, the Indians killed a man near the Slate Creek Iron Works. On the 28th they tomahawked three women who were pulling flax at Long Lick, Nelson county. On the preceding day, 19 men who were cutting grass at Fort Jefferson, were fired on by the Indians, 4 of whom were killed and 8 taken prisoners; 4 of the prisoners were burnt shortly after they were taken.

About the 1st July, two Perogues with several men and a family on board, were descending the Kentucky river, and near Drennon's Lick, discovered an Indian ahead on the bank of the river, and as they approached, he rattled a small bell, upon which the vessels went to the opposite shore; immediately a horn was sounded by the Indians, which was answered by the halooing of a number of Indians on the same side they had landed, which occasioned them to leave their property and make their escape to the settlement of Elkhorn, where they all arrived safe. They left 6 or 7 hundred dollars worth of property in the Perogues, consisting of bacon, flour and whiskey, intended for the Mississippi market.* [287]

On the 8th of July 1792, information was received at Fort Washington, by some prisoners who had escaped from the Indians of the murder of Major Trueman on the Auglaice river by the Indians, after having been a prisoner with them four days. Mr. Freeman, Debachi and Jarrett, accompanied Major Trueman with a flag, sent by General Wilkinson to the Indians, as was also Col. John Hardin but in a different direction. Colonel Hardin was also killed after being some time a prisoner. About this time, two men were killed, and a boy taken in a canoe on the Ohio, about two miles above Fort Washington.

On the 11th of August 1792, seven Indians approached the house of a

---

*One of the owners of the Perogues, together with the spies, went down the next day to see if the Indians had taken off the vessels, and to their great surprize, found them safe and untouched, except about $20 cash, which they suspected was taken by one of the crew. At the place where the Indians were supposed to be seen, were wolf tracks, near which place was an old mare with a small bell on.

Mr. Stevenson in Madison county, very early in the morning, and before the family were out of bed; six entered the house, and firing into the bed where Mr. and Mrs. Stevenson were lying, broke the arm and thigh of Mrs. Stevenson; they also killed a young man who was in the house. Mr. Stevenson jumped out of bed and was instantly attacked by an Indian with his knife, who stabbed him in several places. A young man in the house seized a rifle, and shot the Indian who was in contact with Mr. Stevenson, upon which the rest ran off.

On the 21st of August, a party of twelve Indians were discovered approaching the Rolling Fork of Salt river, Nelson county. They were pursued by Major Brown, overtaken, and four of them killed and two badly wounded. Major Brown had one man killed and two slightly wounded—his party consisted of thirty. About the same time two negroes were taken prisoners at Mann's Lick.[288]

"Copy of a letter written July 17th 1792.
"I send you the latest accounts from Fort Washington, which place I left on the 15th inst. Intelligence came to Fort Jefferson on the 8th, by two prisoners who made their escape from the Indians in the evening of the 4th, from labouring in a cornfield. One of them was taken prisoner at the time General Harmer was defeated, and belonged to Capt. Zeigler's company, the other is William Duer of Captain Buchanan's company of levies. They bring certain accounts of the death of Maj. Trueman, Mr. Freeman, Debachi and Jarrett, who were with him; but bring no account of Colonel Hardin, as they came from a different part of the country from that to which he was destined. The Indians informed them, that on the 25th of June, they had been at Fort Jefferson, and had taken eight men prisoners, that were out making hay, (which account does not admit of a doubt, as I saw an officer who was an eye witness to that transaction,) that as soon as they had moved the prisoners a small distance, they divided them, 4 were given to the Shawanese, and 4 to the Chippewas. The Shawanese burnt theirs shortly after the division, but the Chippewas took theirs home with the intention of making labourers of them. The Indians are determined on war, and will not treat, but kill every white man who attempts to go to them, either with or without flag; they are fully possessed with the idea of the practicability of cutting off the escort with provisions to the out posts, and by that means, starve them to a surrender, which they mean shortly to attempt, and for that express purpose, keep out two spies constantly, to give information when the next escort of provision will pass. The prisoners further inform that four pieces of the cannon that was taken from General St. Clair, are now lying near the battle ground."

Official accounts from Fort Washington, dated 15th July, states:
"That notwithstanding the pacific overtures of the United States, the

Indians are for war. Maj. Trueman, and those with the first flag are murdered at Auglaice river—that Colonel Hardin's fate is doubtful, but there is hopes that he has escaped by going to Sandusky."

About the 8th of July, the Indians killed a man and took a boy prisoner about two miles above Fort Washington in a canoe on the Ohio river. About the 20th, a party of Indians, some on foot and some on horse back, drove off from Fort Washington, 20 beeves. On the 21st they killed one and wounded two men on Brashears' creek.

About the first of August, four men from Madison county, fell in with three Indians on the Kentucky river above Boonsborough. When the Indians were discovered they were on horseback, but they instantly dismounted and the horses ran off; the white men followed and caught the horses. Upon their return to where they first discovered the Indians, they were fired on by them, and one of the party wounded in three places.[289]

In the latter part of the month of September, General Wilkinson, whose head-quarters were at Fort Washington, made an extensive excursion to the battle ground of General St. Clair, and about the head waters of the Miami. He discovered two pieces of brass cannon, which were left on the field of battle on the previous 4th of November. Notwithstanding every hostile appearance evinced by the Indians, it was understood the General considered himself restrained from offensive operations.

On the 9th of September, a party of Indians fired on two wagoners on the road between Lynn's Station and Brashears' creek, and wounded them both, one of whom they scalped, the other ran off, having only a slight wound; the wounds of the one who was scalped did not prove mortal. The Indians took seven horses from the two waggons.[290]

The following is the copy of a letter from his excellency Governor William Blount of Tennessee, to the Governor of Kentucky, dated September 11th 1792.

"I have this morning received undoubted information, that the five lower towns of the Cherokees are for war, and the other part of the nation for peace. That a party would set out from these towns, under the command of John Watts, on the 7th or 8th instant, (not certain which, as my information differs on this head,) consisting of from three to five hundred warriors, of whom one hundred are said to be Creeks; their destination is only conjectural, but believed to be Cumberland† or the frontiers of Knox county.

"This information is given, that you may be prepared, in case they should think proper to visit the frontiers of your state.

†The settlements in West Tennessee were at that time known by the name of Cumberland.
—ED.

"You will no doubt, from having seen John Watts at the treaty of Holston, be a little surprised that he heads the party.

"I must then inform you, that a Mr. Panton, a British trader of Pensacola, paid the Cherokee nation a visit in May last, and invited Watts to accompany him to Pensacola; Watts has lately returned with arms and ammunition, and war is the result."[291]

On the 23rd of September, the Indians killed two men at the Iron works on Slate Creek.

On the morning of the 20th September, two hundred Creek Indians attacked a station in the Cumberland settlements, and continued the siege for 24 hours, during which time, they made several attempts to set the houses on fire, but failed; they left eight of their party on the ground; the whites lost two killed. These are supposed to be a part of those mentioned by Governor Blount in his letter to the Governor of Kentucky.

Thus it will be seen, that the infant state of Kentucky, was not only surrounded by savage enemies on every side, but forbidden by the general government, from taking the most effectual method of securing themselves against invasion, by adopting the means recommended by Mr. Breckinridge, viz. to carry the war into their own country.

On the 6th of Oct. a company of six men who were travelling through the wilderness, were fired on by fifteen Indians on Richland creek, and one of them killed and another wounded.

November the 1st the Indians took three prisoners at Fort Jefferson.

The following account of the attack on Buchanan's Station, is copied from a Knoxville paper of the 20th October 1792.[292]

"The party who attacked the Station, consisted of 197 Cherokees, 83 Creeks, and the Shawanese warrior, with his party, consisting of 30, the whole commanded by John Watts. The Shawanese warrior, a Creek chief, and several others were killed, and a number wounded, among whom are JOHN WATTS, who, it is highly probable, cannot recover. He was shot in both thighs, the ball passed through the upper part of one, and lodged in the other.

"John Watts is a half breed; a stout, bold and enterprising man, about 40 years of age, the life and spirit of the junior part of the Cherokee nation.[293]

"The Shawanese warrior was a half breed; he resided at the Running Water for upwards of three years past with his party. At the last council at Will's town, when it was ascertained that the five lower towns, should go to war against the United States, he rose, and stretching out his hands, he said, 'with these hands have I killed three hundred men; I will kill three hundred more, drink my fill of blood, and set down and be happy.'

"The middle Striker and Otter Lifter, two other signers of the treaty of

Holston, were also leaders in this attack. The latter as late as the month of July, gave the most unequivocal proofs of his attachment to the United States in going on board the boats, in which were the goods for the Chickasaw and Chocktaw conference, continued with them until they had passed the lower towns, and conducted himself in such a manner as left no reason but that he would boldly have defended them, in case they had been attacked by hostile parties of his own or any other nation.

"It is not presumable, this sudden change of conduct is justly to be charged upon the Spanish government."[294]

On Saturday the 6th instant. a company of travellers, on their way from Kentucky through this territory, were fired on in the wilderness; two men were killed and said to be mortally wounded. The party who attacked this company, consisted of fifty warriors, and were headed by the noted Cherokee chief, Talhoteski, a signer of the treaty of Holston, and one who accompanied John Watts in his visit to Governor O'Neal, in July and August last. Inspired with a spirit of war by the inflammatory persuasion of Governor O'Neal, he painted himself black before he left Pensacola, declaring himself for war, and with that appearance and spirit he passed through the Creek nation.[295]

While he was at Pensacola, Governor O'Neal shewed him five Magazines. "This, said he, is for the Cherokees, that for the Creeks, those two for the Chickasaws and Chocktaws, and this for ourselves, to assist you if necessary."[296]

SECTION 45

Horse Thieves, Raiders, and the Infernal Excise Duty

[November 16, 1827]

About the 5th of January 1793, a party of Indians stole horses from Logan county; they were pursued across Cumberland river, overtaken, all the horses recovered, one of the Indians killed and one of the pursuers wounded.

On the 17th of January, three men were killed at the Bear Wallow, on the road from Kentucky to Tennessee.

February 25th, the Indians stole a number of horses from Bear Grass.

March 8th, the Indians fired on two men on Brashear's creek, wounded both their horses, and took one of the men prisoner.

About the same time, a company on their way through the wilderness, were defeated by Indians near the Hazle Patch; two of whom were killed and two badly wounded, and a child taken prisoner.[297]

The following is copied from the Knoxville Gazette of the 12th January 1793.

"On the 7th of December, a party of the Cavalry in service for the protection of Mero district, about eight miles from Nashville, were fired on by about twenty Indians, who put them to flight, killed *John Hankins*, who was scalped and his body much mangled.

"On the 29th of the same month, *John Haggard* was killed and scalped, about six miles from Nashville. Twelve balls were shot into him. His wife was killed last summer by the Indians, and he has left five small children in poverty and wretchedness.

"The Indians carry on horse stealing according to custom in that district, without cessation.

"On Monday the 31st of December, the Indians drove off eighteen head of very valuable horses from Big Pigeon, Jefferson county, near where Richardson's family were murdered, and wantonly killed several cattle and hogs.

"Lately arrived at Willstown, nine Shawnese, who have passed on to Creeks and Choctaws, for the purpose of exciting them to go to war with the United States. They are to return through the Cherokee towns, with the expectation of meeting that nation in full council at Estanaula. They informed the Cherokees, that the Shawanese were determined to fall on the Chickasaws and cut them off, for joining the army of Gen. St. Clair."[298]

The following is the notice published in the Kentucky Gazette on the 15th of February 1793, of a supper given in honor of the French Revolution, and the success of her arms.

"As the events of the French Revolution must be interesting to every lover of liberty; so the success of their patriotic arms must be proportionately pleasing. The citizens of this country, however distant, think nothing uninteresting, which affects the cause of freedom. They have received intelligence of the victories gained by the patriotic French. To rejoice with brethren and freemen, and to celebrate their victorious arms, was the object of a ball and supper, given in Lexington, by subscription, at Messrs. Love and Brent's, on Friday evening the 8th inst.

"The company was numerous and brilliant, their dresses were decorated with the national colors, and the ball was conducted with the greatest ease and regularity. At 11 o'clock the company retired to the supper room. The decorations displayed an elegant execution, with a taste which could acommodate the occasion. At the head of the table, was displayed the National flag of France in the field of which were these words. 'Le Convention Nationale.* Sep'bre. 21st, 1792.' In the middle of the table, was fixed a staff supporting the cap of liberty; on the right and left of which appeared the National and American Flags, the staffs of which, were connected with each other, and with that of the cap of liberty, by a blue ribbon, on the wave of which, in gold letters was this motto, 'By freedom joined.' At the foot of the table was the American Flag on which was inscribed, 'Independence declared, July 4th 1776.' On top of the sphere was the American Eagle. The supper was plentious and handsome. The occasion inspired pleasure, and the patriotic satisfaction which beamed from the eyes of the fair, added lustre to their beauty. After supper, the company returned to the ball room, where the Cap of Liberty and the flags were then displayed.

"A gentleman who is on a visit to this country, was so obliging as to favor the company, by singing the following lines written for the occasion, to the tune of 'With harmony and flowing wine.'

> "Join every voice to raise the song,
> To *Freedom* festive strains belong,
> Hail! every voice, with loud applause,
> Successful *Freedom's* glorious cause,
> Behold fair *Freedom's* flame arise,
> And spreading wide to distant skies,
> Make tyrants struck with terror, fly
> The glorious flame shall never die!
> For *Freedom* shall, through every clime,
> Extend her rights—their source divine,
> Proclaim to all, the great decree—
> That MAN was made by *nature* free.
> Thy *patriots*, FRANCE, shall still be sung,
> A great reward, by beauties tongue,
> And *Freemen* too, shall join to pay
> The honors of the free born lay.
> With them let every heart rejoice,
> To them we give the applauding voice—
> Adorning history's brightest page,
> Their name shall live from age to age."

*The memorable day in which royalty was by a decree, of the National Convention, forever abolished in France.

"The ladies shortly afterward retired, and the following toasts were drank, viz.

"1. *The Patriots of France*—May success ever attend their glorious struggle in the cause of Liberty.

"2. The Republican interest of the United States.

"3. *The good people of Ireland.*—May their exertions never remit, till they possess *freedom*, the right of all, the just reward of the brave.

"4. May the flame of Liberty be immortal, and extend to the utmost limits of the earth.

"5. May wisdom, counsel, and conduct execute the measures of the French Republic.

"6. *The Patriotic Fair*—Who have honored the evening with their presence.

"7. May savage barbarity be transformed into patriotic civility.

"8. Freedom to every nation in every age.

"The company then dispersed. No individual, however great his merits, was toasted. The great and general cause of liberty, claimed their wishes; to it they drained the festive glass.

"The company was numerous, and what has been improperly called mixed, no disagreeable circumstance occurred to disturb the harmony or interrupt the pleasures of the evening. All was a joyous happy meeting of the Fair and Free. To the glorious occasion of the meeting no less than to the great exertions of the Managers is this to be attributed."[299]

March the 21st 1793, a party of Indians fired on the post-rider and two others on Laurel river in the wilderness, on their way from the east; the post-rider was killed, and the other two wounded.[300]

On the 26th of March, nine men, two women and eight children, who were on their way through the wilderness to Kentucky, were attacked by a party of Indians between the Hazle Patch and Laurel river, about an hour before sunset. The nine men dismounted and defended the women and children for about fifteen minutes, during which time they fired four or five rounds; but being overpowered, and the Indians closing in on all sides, (there being about thirty,) the whole were killed and taken except four, who escaped, one of which was wounded badly.

Names of the killed and missing, Joel Carder and his family, James Anthony and family, Flournoy Spilman and Thomas Penniston,† James Jones wounded. Robt Hill, James McFarland and Wm. Anthony escaped unhurt.[301]

On the 1st of April, Morgan's station on Slate creek was taken and burnt by a party of thirty-five Indians; two of the inhabitants were killed and nineteen taken prisoners. The Indians were immediately pursued by

†Penniston and one of the children who was missing, came in a few days after they were defeated.

a strong party, who after following about thirty miles, found the whole of the prisoners tomahawked and scalped, one of whom was not dead, notwithstanding the skull, for at least three inches in diameter, was broke and very much depressed. She was taken to Lexington and placed under Doctor Richard Downing, where she entirely recovered.

On the same evening (April 1, 1793) the Indians stole about 30 horses from Mann's Lick. Also fired on a boat descending the Ohio river at the 18 mile Island.

On the 2d April, the Indians took a boy prisoner at Eastin's Mill in Jefferson County, took him to the Ohio river, and there set him at liberty, and gave him a knife and tomahawk; they also took a man the same day on his way from the Salt Works at Bullett's Lick, to Steel's Ferry on the Kentucky river.[302]

Maj. (afterwards Colonel) Wheatley, a few days after the defeat of the party on the 26th of March, went with a party of men to the place where the defeat happened. He there found most of their horses and baggage and three children; (one of which had been taken from another party about the 1st of March.) It is supposed some sudden alarm caused the Indians to leave the ground immediately, by means of which the children were preserved. The child that had been taken from the company which was defeated the first of March, had straggled off from the camp, whilst the Indians were engaged in the attack made on the 26th, and was therefore left. The children had all suffered very much for want of food.[303]

On the 5th of April, a large party of Indians fired on six boats descending the Ohio river, but did no other injury than the killing of one horse.

On the same day, a body of Indians, supposed to be fifty, attacked a station on Russell's Creek, and continued the seige near 24 hours without effecting any thing. The inhabitants had been apprized of their approach, in time to make preparations to receive them. They killed a man near the station on their approach, into whose body they shot 19 balls.[304]

A letter from a gentleman at Nashville to his friend in Lexington, dated April 8th observes; "To see the country all in forts, breaking up, leaving their farms, their houses and corn burnt up, is truly deplorable. At this time, nearly half the country are in forts."

Capt. Kenton with about 34 men, went up the Ohio river the day after Morgan's Station was destroyed, with a view, if possible, to intercept the Indians. They fell on a trail of a party of Indians on Point Creek, coming into the settlement; he followed the trail, and at night finding he was near them, sent forward spies to discover their fires. Unfortunately the spies got into the camp before they discovered it. The Indians were alarmed by a dog who flew out at the spies, and instantly fired on them. The spies returned the fire, upon the hearing of which Kenton's whole party advanced to the place, when the Indians retreated, leaving their baggage, amongst which was a quantity of powder, lead and blankets. Kenton had one man killed. It is supposed two Indians were killed and carried off, from some discoveries that were made next morning.[305]

On the 13th April 1793, the Indians killed two men on the Rolling Fork of Salt River, and tomahawked and scalped another. Same day a man was killed in Hardin's settlement.

About the same time the Indians took a boat between Louisville and the mouth of Salt River, bound to Nashville; there were three men on board, who made their escape by abandoning the boat and running ashore in their canoe.

April 30th 1793, the Indians took two men prisoners on Brashears creek, previous to which, one of them was slightly wounded in the thigh. After taking them some distance, they tomahawked and scalped the wounded man; he was found and carried home alive, but died shortly after.

About the 1st May, the Indians stole several horses from Morgan's Station on the waters of Licking; they also fired on two men near Fort Hamilton, and wounded one dangerously.

On the 15th of May the Indians took two boys near the mouth of Goose creek in Jefferson county, and after taking them some distance, tomahawked and scalped one of them, after which the body was cut and mangled in a most savage manner.

May 20th, a boat destined to Illinois, from Kentucky, was taken by the Indians near the mouth of Ohio, and every man on board (sixteen in number) killed; their heads and hands cut off, and their bodies ripped open. The boat was loaded principally with merchandize.

June 5th, a party of seven men were attacked by the Indians near Big Barren river, on the road to Nashville, three of whom were killed and two wounded.[306]

About the last of June, information was received from Nashville, that a son of General Robinson had just arrived at that place from the Chickasaw nation, with information, that great offers had been made by the Spaniards to that nation, to induce them to break with the United States, which offers were treated with contempt by the Chief of the nation, and especially the *Mountain Leader*.

Mr. Robinson gave the farther information, that about 400 creeks and Cherokees had lately passed by the Chickasaw nation towards the Mississippi, and that they might shortly be expected, either to visit Cumberland or Kentucky.[307]

The law imposing a duty on distilled spirits, and stills employed in distilling spirits within the United States, began to be enforced in Kentucky about this time, and was very much opposed by the people generally. The following preamble and address, will give a tolerable idea of the disposition of the people on that subject, with the reasons of their dissatisfaction.

"At a meeting of sundry inhabitants of the State of Kentucky in Lexington, the 8th of July 1793.

"Richard Steele, Robert Sanders, John Hambleton, Daniel Barbee, William Trotter, Joseph Rogers, Thomas A. Thompson and Peter Barnett, having taken into consideration the excise law, and the circumstances of our country, are of opinion, that collecting taxes under the excise law, in specie only, will be oppressive to the people of this country, in our present situation, as we can not carry our produce to market through the Mississippi. Therefore, we are of the opinion that it is not improper to address, first the people of Kentucky, second the Legislature of the state, and thirdly the Congress of the United States.

"Friends and Countrymen,

"We have taken into consideration the Excise law passed by Congress, and are of opinion it is unjust, because our navigation is stopt (by the Spaniards) which is our natural and Constitutional right, while the other states in the Union have their ports open, and can sell their produce for specie; and as allegiance and protection are reciprocal the United States ought to see that we are equally protected in our trade, before we are to be expected to pay equal taxes under the excise law, in specie only. If we pay seven cents per gallon in Kentucky, when our navigation is stopped, it will be much more burthensome to us, than it would be if our navigation was open. If this be true, then it will follow of course, that the excise law, is much more oppressive to the people of Kentucky, than to those of the other states. It is the business of the Legislature, to find out ways and means to have justice done to all parts of the community. If we were allowed to pay our taxes under the excise law in produce, at a reasonable price, it would be more just; though not fully so; and if this was fully made known to the distillers, before they were required to pay, they might make choice, either to pursue or quit the business. We hope you will join us in our petitions to the Legislature of this State, and also to Congress; and although we are informed, our former petition, †† or memorial to Congress, concerning this business, was laid on the table and neglected, yet we think it is probable they may hear and redress our grievances, if we could bring them to see our situation as it really is. That we are as a barrier to part of the other states against the savages, sustaining such damages as we do, by their murdering and plundering our people, to a very great amount in every year. Our trade being stopped—our country but very little improved, and of course we cannot have cider and beer, as substitutes for spirits distilled, as the people have in the old country. It is to be hoped they will hear and redress our grievances.

RICHARD STEELE, Ch'm."[308]

††The petition here referred to is not in our possession.—*Editor.*

The Democratic Society
[November 23, 1827]

On the 22d day of August 1793, a meeting of a number of citizens of the town of Lexington, was held at the house of Robert M'Gowan, for the purpose of taking under consideration, the propriety of establishing a Democratic society, when the following proceedings were had.

"On motion, *Resolved*, that the citizens here present, form themselves into a *Democratic Society*, embracing the laudable objects of the Philadelphia Democratic Society.

"*Resolved*, That citizens William Murray, John Bradford, James Brown, Thomas Irwin, Robert M'Gowan and Thomas Todd, or any three of them be a committee for the purpose of drawing articles and rules for the government of this society, and that they make report at the State House on Wednesday the 28th inst. at which time and place, the citizens of the county of Fayette are requested to attend, to assist in carrying those laudable principles into execution.

"*Resolved*, That citizen John Bradford, be requested to publish the proceedings of the Philadelphia Democratic Society, in his next Gazette, and those proceedings."

"By order of the meeting, August 22d, 1793.

PRINCIPLES, ARTICLES and REGULATIONS. *Agreed upon by the* MEMBERS of the DEMOCRATIC SOCIETY *in Philadelphia, May* 30, 1793, *and which were adopted by the Democratic Society of Kentucky.*

PRINCIPLES, ARTICLES and REGULATIONS.

"The Rights of Man, the genuine objects of Society, and the legitimate principles of government, have been already developed by the successive revolutions of America and France. These events have withdrawn the veil, which concealed the dignity and the happiness of the human race, and have taught us, no longer dazzled with adventitious splendor, or awed by antiquated usurpation, to erect the temple of Liberty on the ruins of Palaces and Thrones.

At this propitious period, when the nature of Freedom and equality is thus practically displayed, and when their value (best understood by those who have paid the price of acquiring them) is universally acknowledged, the patriotic mind will naturally be solicitous, by every proper precaution, to preserve and perpetuate the blessings which Providence hath bestowed upon our country; for, in reviewing the history of nations, we find occasion to lament, that the vigilance of the people has been too easily absorbed in victory; and that the prize, which has been achieved by the wisdom and valor of one generation, has too often been lost by the ignorance and supineness of another.

"With a view, therefore, to cultivate a just knowledge of rational liberty, to facilitate the enjoyments and exercise of our civil rights, and to transmit, unimpaired to posterity, the glorious inheritance of a *free Republican Government*, the *Democratic Society of Pennsylvania*, is constituted and established. Unfettered by *religious* or *natural* distinctions, unbiassed by party and unmoved by ambition, this institution embraces the interest, and invites the support of every virtuous citizen. The public good is, indeed, its sole object; and we think, that the best means are pursued for obtaining it, when we recognize the following, as the fundamental principles of our association.

"I. That the people have the inherent and exclusive right and power of making and altering forms of government; and that for regulating and protecting our social interests, a *republican government* is the most natural and beneficial form, which the wisdom of men have devised.

"II. That the republican institutions of the United States, and the state of Pennsylvania, being framed and established by the people, it is our duty as good citizens, to support them. And in order effectually to do so, it is likewise the duty of every freeman to regard with attention, and to discuss without fear, the conduct of the public servants, in every department of government.

"III. That, in considering the administration of public affairs, men and measures should be estimated according to their intrinsic merits; and, therefore, regardless of party spirit or political connection, it is the duty of every citizen, by making the general welfare the rule of his conduct, to aid and approve those men and measures, which have an influence in promoting the prosperity of the commonwealth.

"IV. That in the choice of persons to fill the offices of government, it is essential to the existence of a free republic, that every citizen should act according to his own judgment, and, therefore, any attempt to corrupt or delude the people in exercising the rights of suffrage, either by promising the favor of one candidate, or traducing the character of another, is an offence equally injurious to moral rectitude and civil liberty.

"V. That the *people of Pennsylvania*, form but one indivisible community, whose political rights and interests, whose national honor and prosperity, must, in degree and duration, be forever the same; and, therefore, it is the duty of every freeman, and shall be the endeavor of the Democratic Society, to remove the prejudices, to conciliate the affections, to enlighten the understanding, and to promote the happiness of all our fellow citizens.

"Having united under these principles, we adopt the following rules and regulations, for transacting the business of the institution:

"*Article I.* The society shall be co-extensive with the state; but for the convenience of the members, there shall be a separate meeting in the city of Philadelphia, and one in each county which shall choose to adopt this constitution, a member admitted in the city, or in any county, shall of course be a member of the society at large; and may attend any of the meetings wherever held.

"*Article II.* A meeting of the society shall be held in the City of Philadelphia, on the first Thursday in every month, and in the respective counties, as often, and at such times as they shall by their own rules determine. But the president of each respective meeting, may convene the members of any special occasion.

"*Article III.* The election of new members and of the officers of the society, shall be by ballot, and by a majority of votes of the members present at each respective meeting. But no new member shall be voted for at the same meeting at which he is proposed. The names of the members proposing any candidates for admission, shall be entered in a book kept for that purpose. Every member on his admission, shall subscribe to this constitution, and pay the sum of half a dollar to the treasurer for the use of the society.

"*Article IV.* The officers of the meeting in the city of Philadelphia, shall consist of a President, two Vice Presidents, two Secretaries, one Treasurer, and a corresponding committee of five members; and the meeting of the respective counties, shall choose a President and such other officers as they may think proper. The officers of the meeting held in the city of Philadelphia, shall be chosen on the first Thursday in January in every year.

"*Article V.* It shall be the duty of the corresponding committee, to correspond with the various meetings of the society, and with all other societies, that may be established on similar principles, in any other of the United States, and to lay all communication which they shall make and receive, together with such other business as they shall from time to time deem proper, before the society, at a meeting held within their respective counties.

"*Article VI.* It shall be the duty of the secretaries to keep minutes of the proceedings of the several meetings; and of the treasurer, to receive and account for all monies to them respectfully paid." [309]

The foregoing constitution was unanimously adopted by the democratic society of Kentucky, with the name of *Kentucky* in place of *Pennsylvania*, *Lexington* in place of *Philadelphia* &c. &c.

The following are the proceedings of the Democratic Society of Kentucky at their first meeting.

"At a meeting of the Democratic Society, at the State House in Lexington, on Wednesday the 28th day of August, 1793:
"The society proceeded to the election of officers, when a majority of votes were in favor of *John Breckinridge,* Chairman; *John Bradford* and *Robert Todd,* Vice Chairmen; *Thomas Todd* and *Thomas Bodley,* Clerks; *Alexander M'Gregor,* Treasurer; *William Murray, James Hughes, James Brown, James Moore* and *Robert Todd,* a committee of correspondence.

"*Ordered,* That the corresponding committee, be directed to write a circular letter to the citizens of this state, explanatory of the principles and objects of this society.

"Extract from the minutes,
Test   THOMAS TODD, THOMAS BODLEY, C.D.S."[310]

CIRCULAR
To the Citizens of Kentucky.

"The *Democratic Society of Kentucky,* are now organized, and have committed to us the charge of developing to you their principles and objects.

"They are impressed with the sentiment, that a democracy by representation, is the best mode of government, which the wisdom of man hath devised, and that all just power can be derived only from the people; of consequence the people have the exclusive right of framing and altering their form of government. That in order to preserve the inestimable blessing of liberty, from the open attacks of avowed tyranny, or the more insidious, though much more destructive machinations of ambitious or intriguing men, it becomes the people to watch over the conduct of their officers in every department of government.

"Experience has shown, that the hope of impunity, has tended to the encouragement of crimes, in public even more than in private life. The man who virtue may not restrain from the breach of an important public trust, may be awed by the vigilant and piercing eye of his fellow citizens. This power would be insufficient to preserve, pure and uncontaminated, the best of all possible governments. We ought to be extremely cautious in the choice of men, who are to represent us in the exercise of the powers of government. Their public characters ought to be examined with strictness and attention free from party or religious prejudices, and unaffected by their occupation, fortune or connections. The attempt to influence the vote of a free man, either by the wily arts of promised favor, or by base calumniation, ought to be spurned at with contempt and abhorrence.

"These are in the abstract, the principles of the society. Their objects are to disseminate those principles, and to conciliate affectionate sentiments towards each other, among their democratic fellow citizens. That those objects may be effected, they propose not only to discuss the proceedings of government, but to examine into the conduct of its officers in every department. They will discuss and examine with candor, but with the firmness and freedom becoming citizens, zealous for the liberties of their country.

"The blotted page of history has recorded the fatal effects which the neglect of similar precautions have occasioned. Had the citizens of Athens been attentive to the conduct of their public men the pitiful stratagem of Pisistratus would not have imposed upon his country an odious tyranny. To recite every similar event with similar consequences, would extend our letter beyond the bounds which we propose. Too numerous indeed are the instances, which, in former times, a like inattention presents for our instruction. What were then called revolutions, were only a change of tyrants; or if a moment of freedom intervened, it was as the transient beams of the sun between two storms. To the present age has it been reserved to witness revolutions. In America, we sought not shelter from the oppression of one tyrant, under the talons of another. The rights of man, the principles of a government formed to protect those rights, and insure to our fellow citizens and our latest posterity the blessings of freedom and equality, were the objects of our political deliberations. France has since caught the glorious flame! Long had her people been deprived of the rights bestowed by their benificent creator. At length they have arisen in their strength, and like an inundation, have, at once, swept away their tyrants and their Gothic structures. May success and freedom reward their merits.

"Fellow Citizens: we invite you to form meetings in your several counties, to join and to correspond with the *Democratic society of Kentucky*. To this society, the members of meetings in any county of the state, formed on similar principles, will have admission. They declare the society co-extensive with the state.

"These principles and regulations, we have been directed to announce to you; we doubt not, that impressed with the justice and importance of those principles, you will give them your support.

"Thus will you preserve the blessings of freedom and merit the gratitude of posterity.

"WILLIAM MURRAY, JAMES HUGHES, JAMES BROWN, JAMES MOORE, ROBERT TODD, Committees of Correspondence for the Kentucky Democratic Society."[311]

A treaty appointed to be held at Sandusky about the 1st of August, failed. The Indians declined attending. Information of the failure, was received by Gen. Wayne at Hobson's Choice, (the headquarters of the North Western Army, near Cincinnatti,) from Niagara in 18 days. This was appalling information to the kentuckians, who had calculated largely on the blessings consequent on a state of peace.

The following is the copy of a despatch from the commissioners to General Wayne, on the subject of the treaty.[312]

"FORT ERIE, Aug. 23d, 1793.
"Sir,—We are on our return home from the mouth of Detroit River, where we lay four weeks waiting for the Indians to close their private councils at the rapids of the Miami's, that we might all remove to Sandusky and open the treaty. But, after sending repeated deputations to us, to obtain answers to particular questions, they finally determined not to treat at all. This final answer we received on the 16th inst. when we immediately began to embark to re-cross Lake Erie.

"Although we did not effect peace, yet we hope that good may hereafter arise from the mission. The tranquility of the country north west of the Ohio, during the supposed continuance of the treaty, evinced your care of our safety; and we could not leave this quarter, without returning you our unfeigned thanks.

"We are, sir, with due respect,
"Your most obedient humble servants,
        Signed "B. LINCOLN, BEVERLY RANDOLPH, TIMOTHY PICKERING,
                            Commissioners of the U. States.[313]
"Maj. Gen. *Anthony Wayne*, Fort Washington."

SECTION 47

The Last Stand
of the Ohio Tribes
[November 30, 1827]

About the first of September 1793, the Indians fired on 4 men, a woman and three children in a canoe on the Ohio river, near the mouth of Guiandot; two of the men were killed, and one wounded through the fleshy part of the thigh. The Indians attempted to board the canoe, but were kept off with poles and paddles, until the canoe floated beyond their reach, by which means, those on board escaped falling into their enemy's hands.

On the 7th, the Indians took two young men prisoners at Clarksville, opposite the Falls of Ohio.[314]

After the failure of the contemplated treaty at Sandusky, the President of the United States, seems to have been awakened to a sense of his duty to protect the western country; not because of the sufferings of the settlers, but from the contempt offered to the general government, in the refusal of the Indians to treat. The following is copied from two letters of the same date, from Maj. General Anthony Wayne to Maj. Gen. Charles Scott.

"Head Quarters, Hobson's Choice, Sept. 18, 1793.
"(morning)
"DEAR SIR.—I received an express the night before last from the Secretary at War, dated the 3d instant, with positive orders from the President of the United States, to make those audacious savages feel our superiority in arms, and to prevent the murder of helpless women and children. He is confident that I shall be well and powerfully supported in this arduous task, by the brave and virtuous mounted volunteers of Kentucky. Advance then my dear sir, participate of the glory, and produce a conviction both to him and the world, that that confidence has been well founded.

"Present my best and kindest wishes to our brothers in arms, and assure them that there shall be ample justice done to their bravery and conduct in my communications to the President of the United States.

"Head Quarters, Hobson's Choice, Sept. 18, 1793.
"(evening)
"DEAR SIR.—Since writing you this morning, an express arrived from Col. Hamtramck, announcing that that fort was attacked yesterday morning. There was but thirty Indians seen, who had disappeared; but after the express had proceeded some miles on his way, he heard a firing of artillery.

"Yours friendly,   ANT. WAYNE.[315]
"MAJ. GENERAL SCOTT."

From the following letter from General Scott to General Wayne, it appears the former had written three letters, on the 18th, 22d and 24th of Sept. 1793, of which we do not possess copies; but their general contents may be inferred from the letter of General Wayne of the 26th, in these words:

"Head Quarters, Hobson's Choice, Sept. 26, 1793.
"DEAR SIR.—I have to acknowledge the receipt of your letters of the

18th, 22d and 24th instant, and am truly astonished at the reluctance discovered by too many of the mounted volunteers to meet the common enemy, in order to save the effusion of much innocent blood, as well as difficulty and danger in future.

"This is not a common or little predatory war, made by a few tribes of Indians; it is a confederated war, forming a chain of circumvallation round the frontiers of America, from Canada to Cape Florida—and unless the fire kindled at the Miami of the lake* is extinguished by the blood of the Hydra, (now a little way in our front,) it will inevitably spread along the frontiers of Pennsylvania, Virginia, Kentucky, the Territory South West of the Ohio, South Carolina and Georgia inclusive.

"One united and gallant effort of the Legion and Mounted Volunteers, will save the lives of many, very many thousands of helpless women and children.

"You will, therefore, immediately advance with every man you may have collected, or that you can collect by the 1st of October, leaving a sufficient number of officers to bring forward the drafts that are to be made agreeable to the enclosed copy of a letter to his excellency Governor† Shelby, for that purpose.

"Wishing you life and happiness, I am with sincere esteem.

"Your most ob't humble serv't.   ANTHONY WAYNE.[316]
"Maj. General Scott."

"Georgetown, September 28, 1794

"Sir—I have just now received despatches from Maj. General Wayne, containing a requisition of me, for such a number of the militia of this state to be drafted, and marched forward to him, as will make up the deficiency of the mounted volunteers that were called for by him before.

"You will, therefore, immediately proceed to draft from your regiment of militia under your command, sixty five men, and to march them to this place on the 10th day of next month. Notwithstanding the men may be drafted, I am authorized by General Wayne to say, that all such men as come forward properly mounted and equipped, shall be considered as mounted volunteers, and paid accordingly, on condition they join the legion and the Kentucky volunteers, at the head of the line at Fort Jefferson, on or before the 15th day of October next.

"You are sensible that the honor and the interest of the state will so much depend on the success of the present expedition, that I need say

*The place where the different hostile nations held their councils, preparatory to the late contemplated treaty.—ED.
†The letter from Gen. Wayne to Governor Shelby here referred to, is not in our possession; but its contents may be inferred from the letter from Governor Shelby to Lieut. Col. Levi Todd, which follows Gen. Wayne's letter.

little to urge you, to make every exertion to send your quota of men into the field.

"I am with great respect, Your most obedient servant,

"ISAAC SHELBY.[317]

"LIEUT. COL. LEVI TODD, Fayette County."

The Democratic Society met in Lexington on Monday the 7th of October 1793, when the following resolution was read and ordered to lie on the table until the next meeting, and to be then taken up and discussed:

"The citizens of this Commonwealth, having for a series of years been anxiously hoping, that the free use of an all important right; which they received from NATURE, and which is now wantonly and cruelly controlled and abused, would have been long since secured to them; and finding so far as they have been able to gain intelligence, that this want so inseparably connected with their happiness as a civilized and free people, instead of approaching, is perhaps receding:

"*Resolved*, That the free and undisturbed use and navigation of the river Mississippi, is the NATURAL RIGHT of the citizens of this commonwealth; and is unalienable, except with the SOIL; and that neither time, tyranny nor proscription on the one side, or non user on the other, can ever sanctify the abuse of this right."[318]

The above resolution was taken up by the Society on the 16th November.

About the 10th of October 1793, two Indians fired on a lone man near Green River, on horseback, one of the balls wounded the man slightly across the breast, the other passed through his horses neck. As soon as they fired, both the Indians run up to the man, who as they approached, dismounted on the opposite side, and endeavored to make his escape on foot. He was pursued by the two Indians, so closely by one of them, as to convince him he could not escape by running; he therefore turned suddenly on him, and fired his rifle, wounded the Indian through the lower part of the abdomen, which stopped his pursuit. By this time the other Indian approached, when the white man again attempted to escape by flight, but found it impossible; he then clubbed his rifle, and with it, striking his pursuer, so checked his pursuit, that he retreated in turn, and the white man pursued, when the Indian stumbling, fell and lost both his knife and tomahawk, which the white man instantly seized and put the Indian to death. The white man then went in pursuit of the wounded Indian, but when he got within sight of him, discovered him on his feet with his gun in his hand, he therefore deemed it imprudent to approach him, but went to the nearest settlement, where he obtained a sufficient force and returned; and found the Indian had shot and stabbed himself, and was dead.[319]

On the same day, the Indians attacked White's Station, about ten miles from Fort Washington, killed a man and two children.[320]

A meeting of the democratic society was held in Lexington on the 15th of November, when the resolution laid on the table on the 7th of October was taken up, and the following proceedings had thereon.

"The Society resolved itself into a committee of the whole, upon the subject of the free navigation of the Mississippi river; and after some time spent in the discussion, came to several resolutions, which were reported to the society, and unanimously agreed to as follows:

"The citizens of this commonwealth, having for a series of years been anxiously hoping, that the free use of an all important right, which they received from NATURE, and which is now wantonly and cruelly controled and abused, would have been long since secured to them.

"*Resolved*, That the free and undisturbed use of the navigation of the river Mississippi, is the NATURAL RIGHT of the inhabitants of the countries bordering on the waters communicating with that river; and is unalienable except with the SOIL; and that neither time, tyranny nor proscription on the one side, nor acquiesence, weakness, or non user on the other, can ever sanctify the abuse of this right.

"*Resolved*, That the inhabitants of the western country, had a right to expect, that the present federal government would before this time, have taken effectual measures to obtain from the King of Spain, an acknowledgment of their undoubted right to the free navigation of the river Mississippi; that they ought as freemen, highly interested in the event of that business, to have received information of the causes which have hitherto delayed the negociation: and that it was the duty of the representatives of the people to have called upon the executive, the Federal Government, for an account of what has been done respecting it.

"*Resolved*, That the inhabitants of the western country, have good cause to suspect, that the applications for the acknowledgment of this their just and invaluable right, have been feeble, and that the attainment of it is not wished for by a part of the United States.

"*Resolved*, That under these circumstances, it is a duty which the inhabitants of the western country owe to themselves and their posterity, to demand of the Federal Government, that they take such stepts, as will immediately put them into the free enjoyment of this their just right; that to make this demand effectual, they should unite in an application for that purpose, and that to bring about concert in this application, a proper communication ought to be opened between the different settlements in the western country.

"*Resolved*, That there be a committee appointed, to prepare an address to the inhabitants of the western country, inviting them to a correspondence on this subject, calling on them to unite in their efforts on this occasion, exhorting them to sacrifice all smaller considerations to the attainment of this great object; and recommending it to them to be prepared to surmount all difficulties which may be thrown into its way, either by pusillanimity and an improper regard to local interests at home; or by the arm of power and tyranny abroad.

"*Resolved,* That they also prepare in the name of the inhabitants of the western waters, a remonstrance to the President and Congress of the United States, on this subject, stating (in the bold, decent and determined language, proper to be used by injured freemen, when they address the servants of the people,) that we consider the feeble attempts which have been made by the executive, under the present government, and the total silence of Congress on this important subject, as strong proofs that most of our brethren in the eastern parts of America, are totally regardless whether this, our just right, is kept from us or not.

"That we expect and demand from the government, that they take immediate and effectual stepts to procure and secure to us the enjoyment of that right; that we apply to them and wish to be put into the enjoyment of this right through their intervention. Although we feel a conviction that we are strong enough to obtain that right by force, yet an attachment to the American Union, love to our brethren, respect to the government, and a sincere desire of preserving peace and harmony, have determined us to pursue this mode of application, through which we hope speedily and effectually to procure it on the application of government; and that we shall not be driven to use those means to effect it, with which we have been furnished by the God of nature.

"*Resolved,* That it will be proper to make an attempt in a peaceable manner, to go with an American bottom properly registered and cleared into the sea, through the channel of the Mississippi; that we may either procure an immediate acknowledgment of our right from the Spaniards; or if they obstruct us in the enjoyment of that right, that we may be able to lay before the Federal Government, such unequivocal proofs of their having done so, that they will be compelled to say whether they will abandon or protect the inhabitants of the western country.

"Whereas the laws now in force in this commonwealth, are in their operation sanguinary, cruel and unjust, from the multitude of inferior crimes which are capitally punished, whereby many offenders are liable to be destroyed, who might be reformed and restored good members of society; and whereas the experience of all ages hath shewn that cruel and sanguinary laws, defeat their own purpose, by engaging the benevolence of mankind to withhold prosecution, to smother testimony, or to listen to it with bias; and by producing in many instances a total dispensation and impunity, under the names of pardon and privileges of clergy; when, if the punishments were only proportioned to the injury, men would feel it their inclination, as well as their duty, to see the laws observed, and the power of dispensation, so dangerous and mischievous, which produces crimes, by holding up a hope of impunity, might be totally abolished; so that men, while contemplating to perpetuate crime, would see their punishment ensuing as necessarily as effects follow their causes.

"*Resolved*, That a committee be appointed to draft a memorial to the General Assembly, requesting that a radical change may be made in our criminal code; by creating a system 'where by punishments may be proportioned to crimes, and that such punishments be made as analagous as possible to the nature of the offences,' and that the said memorial when drafted, may be laid before the society for their approbation." [321]

SECTION 48

Harassed Kentuckians

[December 14, 1827]

In the address of the Democratic Society to the western people, it was stated, that a vile and disgraceful attempt had been made under the former confederation to barter away to the Spaniards, our right to the navigation of the Mississippi. It cannot be strange that a people harrassed as the Kentuckians were, by the Indians, and not only no relief afforded them, but forbidden by the general government to cross the Ohio river in a hostile manner, except in the immediate pursuit of Indians, who had made depredations on the inhabitants, by killing, taking prisoners or stealing horses, should be highly excited, when they received the information contained [in] a speech of Mr. Monroe, delivered in the convention of Virginia in 1788, which had not been known in Kentucky generally, until about this time. The following extract from that speech, will not only give the outlines of that business, but discover the local narrow policy by which a part of Congress and their agent were influenced; but also show what reliance could be placed on the efforts pretended to be making by the General Government, in securing to the people of the west, the enjoyment of that inestimable right.

Extract of a speech delivered by Mr. Monroe, in the Virginia Convention.
"After the peace, it became the business of Congress to investigate the relation of these states, to the different powers of the earth, in a more extensive view than they had hitherto done, and particularly in the commercial line; and to make arrangements for entering into treaties with them on such terms as might be mutually beneficial to each party. As the result of the deliberations of the day, it was ordered, 'that commercial treaties be formed; if possible, with said powers, those of Europe in particular, Spain included, upon similar principles, and these commissioners, Mr. Adams, Mr. Franklin and Mr. Jefferson, be appointed for that purpose.' So that an arrangement for a treaty of commerce with Spain had already been taken. Whilst these powers were in force, a representative from Spain arrived, authorized to treat with the United States, on the interfering claims of the two nations, respecting the Mississippi, and the boundaries and other concerns, wherein they were respectively interested. A similar commission was given to the Honorable the Secretary of Foreign Affairs, (Mr. Jay,) on the part of the United States, with these ultimata; 'That he enter into no treaty, compact or convention whatever, with the said representative of Spain, which did not stipulate our right to the navigation of the Mississippi, and the boundaries as established in our treaty with Great Britain.' And thus the late negociation commenced, and under auspices as I supposed, very favorable to the wishes of the United States: For Spain had become sensible of the propriety of cultivating the friendship of these states. Knowing our claim to the navigation of this river, she had sent a minister hither, principally to treat on that point— and the time would not be remote, when, under the increasing population of that country, the inhabitants would be able to open it, without our assistence or their consent. These circumstances being considered, was it not presumable she intended to make a merit of her concession to our wishes, and to agree to an accommodation upon that subject, that would not only be satisfactory, but highly pleasing to the United States? But what was the issue of this negociation? How was it terminated? Has it forwarded the particular object in view, or otherwise promoted the interests and harmony of the States, or any of them? Eight or ten months elapsed without any communications of its progress to Congress: At length a letter was received from the secretary, stating that difficulties had arisen in his negociation with the representative of Spain, which, in his opinion, should be so managed, as that even their existence should remain a secret for the present, and proposing that a committee be appointed with full power to direct and instruct him in every case relative to the proposed treaty. As the only ultimata in his instructions respecting the Mississippi and the boundaries, it readily occurred, that these occasioned the difficulties alluded to, and were those he wished to remove. And for many reasons this appeared, at least to me, an extraordinary proposition. By the

articles of confederation, nine states are necessary to enter into treaties. The instruction is the foundation of the treaty; for if it is formed agreeable thereto, good faith requires that it be ratified. The practice of Congress hath also been, always, I believe, in conformity to this idea. The instructions under which our commercial treaties have been made, were carried by nine states. These, under which the Secretary now acted, were passed by nine states. The proposition then would be, that the powers which, under the constitution, nine states only were competent to, should be transferred to a committee, and the object thereby to disengage himself from the ultimata already mentioned in his existing instructions. In this light the subject was taken up, and on these principles discussed. The Secretary, (Mr. Jay,) being at length called before Congress to explain the difficulties mentioned in his letter, presented to their view the project of a treaty of commerce, containing, as *he* supposed, advantageous stipulations in our favor in that line, in consideration for which, we were to contract to forbear the use of the navigation of the river Mississippi, for the term of twenty-five or thirty years, and earnestly advised our adopting it. The subject now took its decided form—there was no further ambiguity in it, and we were surprized for reasons which have been already given, that he had taken up the subject of commerce at all. We were greatly surprised it should form the principle object of the project, and that a partial or temporary sacrifice of that interest, for the advancement of which, the negociation was set on foot, should be the consideration proposed to be given for it. But the honorable Secretary, urged that it was necessary to stand well with Spain; that the commercial project was a beneficial one, and should not be neglected; that a stipulation to forbear the use contained an acknowledgment, on her part, of the right in the United States; that we were in no condition to take the river, and therefore gave nothing for it; with other reasons which perhaps I have forgotten, for the subject in detail, has nearly escaped my memory. We differed with the honorable Secretary almost in every respect. We admitted indeed the propriety of standing well with Spain; but supposed we might accomplish that end at least on equal terms. We considered the stipulation to forbear the use, as a species of barter, that should never be countenanced in the American states, since it might tend to the destruction of the society itself; for a forbearance of the use of one river, might lead into more extensive consequences, to that of the Chesepeake, the Potomac, or any other of the rivers that emptied into it. In short, that the councils of the confederacy, should be conducted with more magnanimity and candor, should contemplate the benefit of all parts upon common principles, and not the sacrifice of one part for that of another. There appeared to us a material difference between stipulating by treaty to forbear the use, and not being able to open the river. The former would be considered by the inhabitants of the western country as an act of hostility, the latter might be justified by our inability. And with respect to the commercial part of the project, we really thought it an ill advised one on its own merits.

"Thus was this project brought before Congress, and so far as I recollect, in this form, and upon these principles. It was the subject of tedious and lengthy discussion in that honorable body. Every distinct measure that was taken, I do not now remember, nor do I suppose it of consequence. I have shown the outlines of the transaction, which is, if I apprehend rightly, all that the committee wish to possess. The communications of the Secretary, were referred to a committee of the whole house. The delegates of the seven easternmost states, voted that the ultimata in the Secretary's instructions, be repealed; which was reported to the house and entered on the journal by the Secretary of Congress, that the question was carried. Upon this entry, a constitutional question arose to this effect: "Nine states being necessary by the Federal Constitution, to give an instruction, and seven having repealed a part of an instruction so given, for the formation of a treaty with a foreign power so as to alter its import, and authorize under the remaining part thereof, the formation of a treaty, on principles altogether different from what the said instruction originally contemplated—can such remaining part be considered as in force, and constitutionally obligatory?" We pressed on Congress for a decision on this point often, but without effect. Notwithstanding this, I understood it was the intention of the Secretary to proceed and conclude a treaty, in conformity to his project, with the minister of Spain. In this situation I left Congress."

It was at that time, the opinion of Mr. Monroe, that a majority of the Senators present, with the President, were disposed to relinquish the navigation of the Mississippi to Spain, on the terms proposed by Mr. Jay. The northern states were inclined to give it up, because it was their interest to prevent the growing southern and western power and influence; and as mankind in general, and states in particular, are governed by interest, the northern states would not fail of availing themselves of every opportunity of checking the growth of the western country, and thereby prevent the southern interest, which was identified with the west from preponderating. Is it then strange, that with a knowledge of these facts, the Democratic Society, whose avowed object was to promote the interest of the state, should have used the language contained in their address.[322]

The result of the campaign under Gen. Wayne will be seen in the following "Extract of a letter, dated Head Quarters S. W. Branch of Miami, 14, October 1793."
"The commander in chief takes this opportunity of returning his most grateful thanks to General Posey, and to the officers of the legion in general, for the ready cheerfulness with which they have executed every

order, and for the worthy example which they have uniformly shown upon every occasion, during the rapid advance of the army to this place, which affords a pleasing presage to future success.

"On the 16th inst. two Sergents of Capt. Lee's troop of Cavalry was killed by the Indians; and on the 17th, one of our escorts of 90 men under the command of Lieutenant Lowry and Ensign Boyd, charged with 28 wagons loaded with corn, contractor's stores, and two with goods, the property of Mr. Hunt, was attacked by a party of Indians, supposed to be about 60, a little after day light at the 23 mile tree, a few miles advanced of Fort St. Clair; after the exchange of a few shot, Lieutenant Lowry and Ensign Boyd fell, this damped the spirits of the men, in such a manner as to occasion a route; the Indians seizing the opportunity of keeping it up, took possession of the wagons, but were in so great a hurry to get off, that they only took time to cut out the horses, stave all the liquor except what they carried off, and plundered Mr. Hunt's wagons, leaving the wagons and corn in the road. The escort lost 15 killed, including the two officers, who died bravely, and nine missing. Lieut. Colonel Adair of the mounted volunteers, who lay in advance of the escort about six miles, with forty or fifty of his men, upon hearing of the disaster, immediately repaired to the ground of the defeat, took the trail of the Indians, and followed them between thirty and forty miles, but not being able to come up with them, and being out of provisions, returned.

"General Scott, with one thousand mounted volunteers including officers, is now encamped at a prairie, two miles advanced of Fort Jefferson. One of the volunteers was killed upon their march.

"The commander in chief waits the arrival of about seven hundred, that were sent off yesterday to Fort Hamilton for flour and corn, under an escort commanded by Lieutenant Colonel Hamtramk; at which arrival he will march from this place to within a few miles of General St. Clair's late battle ground, and there take a strong position for future operations; unless the season and a sufficient supply of provision will justify his farther advance.

"It is expected the Indians will attack the army before they separate, being informed through sundry channels, that they have pledged themselves to each other—to their respective nations and to the British, that they will defeat the army. It is apprehended that, as there were British officers with the Indians at the defeat of Gen. St. Clair, some may think proper to be with the Indians upon the present occasion. Our army are strong, feel themselves in high spirits, and are ready for a meeting with the enemy."[323]

Thus ended the campaign of 1793, without effecting a single object tending to promote the safety of Kentucky against the depredations of the Indians; and the publication of Mr. Monroe's speech in the Virginia

Convention, served but to increase the jealousies of the western people against the eastern states, that they would consent to no measures that would render safety to the settling of the western country. The prejudices of the Kentuckians against Mr. Jay, who had consented to barter away the navigation of the Mississippi river to Spain, for twenty-five or thirty years, were fully expressed on receiving information that he was appointed Envoy Extraordinary to Great Britain.[324]

SECTION 49

"To the Inhabitants of Western America"
[December 21 and 28, 1827]

On the 15th November 1793, two men were killed by the Indians near Massie's Station on the Ohio.

On the same day, two Indians fired on a man within a mile of Frankfort, on his way to George Town; he received no other injury but the loss of his hat.

About the same time, twenty-five volunteers fell in with a party of Indians about 14 miles from Nashville; and an engagement instantly ensued, in which the volunteers had three men killed and four wounded; they killed four Indians, took two prisoners with the whole of their baggage.[325]

The following address to the inhabitants of Western America, was submitted to a meeting of the Democratic Society, held on the 15th November 1793, by one of its members, approved and directed by the Society to be published in the Kentucky Gazette.

"To the Inhabitants of Western America.
"In the history of America, few more remarkable events have occurred, than are exhibited at the present moment. The inhabitants of Western

America, are deeply interested in the important transactions of the present day; ages may revolve before a crisis of equal magnitude to them may arrive. A vast variety of circumstances combine to render this period, as affecting their future happiness, too important to be neglected. As it is the right, so is it the duty of freemen, to examine into, approve or condemn the conduct of those who assume the reins of government. When the happiness of a people is at stake, forms must yield to substance; no inquiry is improper—no decent language too strong, to mark with precision the dangers that may attend supineness or inattention. Interest with its dissembling cant and train of specious virtues, prudence, caution and affection for peace, is not more injurious to society, than the fatal apathy to which man is subjected. How long, fellow citizens, shall we indulge our visionary expectations of national importance? How long shall we fondly hope, that our all important rights, are held sacred by the government of the Union? Can the most sanguine, the most interested or partial federalist, mark a period at which our visions are to be realized? If silence is a virtue, may ye its votaries, alone feel its benefits—there are some of the sons of America, who yet dare to think and speak; and when occasion may require, to act in support of those rights which nature has been pleased to bestow on them. Few of those gifts are so important to us as the free use of the western waters. Is there an individual who resides west of the Allegany mountains, that has not from his migration, considered this as an essential to his property.

"The result of the negociations to obtain this right, is too well known and felt, to require much comment. I claim as my right, and consider it as my duty to attempt to trace to their source, the causes of this unhappy event. In the course of this enquiry, it is to be lamented, that the two grand impediments to our prosperity, will appear to be:

"First, an unwarrantable attachment to the local interest of the Atlantic States, (and more particularly the Eastern) on the part of their inhabitants.

"Second, that undue influence which British commerce and other subordinate and efficacious means have on the minds of certain classes of citizens. To place this subject in a proper point of view, and to establish these two melancholy facts, let us turn our attention to the military arrangements adopted by our executive, and the great political phenomenon discovered by the Atlantic States, in their conduct to the cause of liberty espoused by the French nation—we will begin with the latter, as being of the most general importance.

"The neutrality of America on this occasion, must strike us the distant observers, with the most serious astonishment, when we behold her free born sons, who have so lately escaped the chains of British despotism, and who, by her noble exertions, have kindled the flame of liberty, through regions absorbed in wretchedness, and devoured by their rapacious and venal governments.

"We flatter ourselves, that uniformity of conduct, will mark the steps of those on whom heaven has pleased to affix the sacred stamp of freedom, and first to employ as the advocates of the birth right of man. But when we behold the freemen of America, so far lose sight of the dignified station assigned them by Heaven, as to desert the standard of liberty, and prefer to the Godlike employment of advancing the happiness of man, a cold and interested neutrality, unworthy the guardians of freedom, must not every virtuous American, blush for his country, and lament the inglorious part he has taken in the great work of redeeming man from slavery? She, to whom the unhappy victims of tyranny, looked up for relief in time of need, has proved herself, instead of their friend, the enemy to liberty.

"Bound by the ties of gratitude, sound policy and affections to the cause of freedom as strongly as we ought to be, what can justify the shameful defection of which we are guilty, towards our allies, our friends and enslaved millions? But independent of every social, generous consideration, the western inhabitants cannot but consider this affected neutrality, not only as injurious to the real interest of their Atlantic brethren, but as replete with every evil to themselves, because we are in danger thereby, in losing the advantages, which the ever memorable occasion has offered of fixing our right to the navigation of the Mississippi, upon a firm and honorable footing; and because we might have wrested from the British, the power of massacreing our innocent fellow citizens. That these two grand and important objects might have been, and that they may yet be obtained, there can exist no doubt, if there is truth in human calculations, all that is required to accomplish this event, is, that the partial interests of the Union should yield to the general good—and that our eastern brethren should not view us as their rivals, but as their friends, as long as they are entitled to the name, if there exists more than the name of federal association, we have a right to their assistance. Now is the important crisis, when the enfeebled arm of despotism is ready to sink, when the infernal association against France and liberty, is on the brink of dissolution—let the man whose soul is formed, devoid of those affections that gave dignity to human nature, whose God is gold, torture his brain for palliatives for this neutrality, they must all center in the narrow point of commercial interest. From this partial view of the interested source must spring the affected fondness for peace. The commercial interest of the Atlantic shore, in opposition to the voice of America, has induced our executive to affix a stain on our political character, which nothing but the most speedy and decisive conduct can efface. It is in vain we boast our invaluable privileges, while we lend an assisting hand to enslave our friends, our allies and mankind. If we persist in our neutrality, we demonstrate to the world, that our immediate case and interest are more important in our view than the rights of man, the obligations of gratitude, and the powerful dictates of the voice of liberty. A fondness for war, is certainly a mark of corruption, either in a nation or individual, but there can exist no doubt, that in the present depraved state of man, occasions occur that justify that resort, independent of the tinsel glory of conquest; with views infinitely superior to the common incentives to war, might the United States seize the present moment with honor and to effect. The inhabitants of W. America, must feel the strongest indignation, when they reflect on the neglect of this important period. It is not the murmuring of a restless or inquiet mind, but it is a truth too evident, that thus far the great interests of the whole, is sacrificed to the partial and local interests of a few commercial cities by our neutrality. Let us for a moment direct our attention to the consequences, that thus far have resulted from the pacific determination of the United States. It is true, that a few men have derived considerable advantages from the influx of the common plunder of the contending powers. But listen to the complaints of our injured flag, the sea is no longer safe to our ships, they are plundered and insulted in the most wanton and aggravating manner, and the name of a people, possessing the means of doing themselves complete and adequate justice, has become contemptible. In addition to the injuries done us at sea, the distress of the frontiers of America, afford the most convincing proofs of the folly and injustice of our pretended neutrality. Under this veil, the innocent and defenceless, fall victims to British policy; for it is a fact, established, that the blood of our citizens is daily shed, by means the most perfidious and inhuman that ever disgraced a civilized nation. The miserable instruments the savages, are the weapons which that corrupt and fallen nation employs to the destruction of thousands, and this in the times of neutrality and peace. Without British incentives and more efficacious supplies, the Indians must and would yield to the arms or more conciliatory measures of America; if they flowed from pure motives. The history of the present war, displays such striking marks of imbecility, that those who have the least knowledge of the strength of America, cannot hesitate to determine that their hand and heart are not engaged in union in this business. The most rational solution that offers itself to this political mystery, is, that the present military arrangements are the effect of eastern policy, to silence the dying groans of our slaughtered citizens, and that the authors of the plan, feel not a desire that the war should terminate to the interest of the western country. They are not so destitute of information, as to be ignorant where their operations might be directed to accomplish the greatest general good. The mighty vengeance of America, has been in vain directed against the defenceless inhabitants of the woods. The voice of humanity and the voice of reason and justice require, that the arms of the injured country, should be levelled against those with whom the contest really exists.

"To confirm the melancholy fact, that the armaments of the United States are merely ostensible, and calculated only to fill the purses of a few men, let the most dispassionate enquirer, call to his recollection, the infinite variety of follies (to say the least) committed both in the cabinet and field. The immense sums of money that have been dissipated at different times, to organize and supply the Legions of America, have thus far been productive of no one good consequence to the Union. To the most puerile theory, they have added the most ridiculous practice. In opposition to the dear bought experience of those who have contended with savages; the farce of military parade is obstinately adhered to, at the expence of a sea of blood. To pass in silence over the two disgraceful campaigns of 1790 and 1791, we cannot but stop a moment, and compare the probable consequences, that must have followed from an adherence to the plan of employing the volunteers of Kentucky, with the issue of the ever memorable campaign of 1793.

"The successful expeditions carried on from Kentucky, in addition to the unanswerable arguments in favor of a desultory war with savages, as far exceeds the present school taught theory, as the different issues of the campaigns. But our Secretary at war is of a different opinion, the mechanism of the manuel exercise, and the evolutions of Steuben, are so essential in his view as not to be dispensed with. Perhaps a consideration of equal importance operates with him. It is the great difficulty there would be, so to modify his accounts, as to render a million of dollars necessary to defray the expenses of an army of ragged militia. No private baggage, no packsaddles, no boats, nothing but a simple dollar a day for 1000 men for 40 or 50 days. Why there is no room to display a knowledge of finance, and hardly any use for a Secretary at War.

"But let us resume the history of the American warfare, and for the present leave the follies of masters and servants; they would engross a volume, and would only serve to divert our attention from objects more important than the petty larcenies of ministerial instruments. The specious mark of humanity to the savages, is assumed, to divert the attention of those who anxiously wish for the termination of the Indian war. How lost to their interest! How insensible to their dignity, have the United States been in their mock parade of treaty at Sandusky.

"The commissioners of the Union, with 100,000 dollars in their purse, are submitted to the safe conduct of those with whom the war really exists. They are compelled to run a gauntlet from place to place, and under all the horrors of an uplifted tomahawk, to ask a question, the result of which they knew, before they left Philadelphia. Behold then the mighty vengeance of America, prepared to burst on the devoted heads of the defenceless savages. The din of arms resounds through the continent. And behold her united efforts produce the formidable legion in dread array. Vast are the preparations; immense are the expenditures, they are greatly exceeded by the boasted and imaginary havoc made by the great legionary chief—the horrid carnage which the irresistable dragoon must have made, could not have been more efficacious than the prudence and alertness displayed in creating fortifications, in addition to the great tactical accuracy of motion, with a rich effusion of military ardour, that might have ensured immortal honors to the arms of America. Let us follow this formidable phalanx, through the difficulties and dangers to which it was exposed, in the vast extent of savage wild, over which its victorious banners were displayed. From the banks of Ohio, until its arrival at its *destined* station, its progress was irresistable. To inspire with confidence the federal troops, and to silence the clamors of a jealous people, the wisdom of the cabinet again annexed the yeomanry of Kentucky. Happy presage of unanimity and success. A coalition replete with victory. Behold then the great legionary chief prepared for the dreadful onset. The peaceful citizen waits with impatience the news of victory, and marks on his family map the imaginary route from Jefferson to the Miami village; from thence to the plains of Sandusky or the banks of Lake Erie. He dreams of Indians charged and routed, and is transported with the consternation of Detroit. But, alas! the baseless fabric vanishes, and to his astonishment, he finds the immense armament, with the expenditures and arrangements of a year, terminate in the insecure possession of a few acres of ground, six miles in the advance of a post, purchased before with the lives of a thousand men. Is this the fair result of the united efforts of America, or is it the foul effects following from an impure and defective course? Can the rankest sycophant that infests the Federal Court, attribute the issue of this dishonorable campaign to accidental circumstances! No, the fact must be evident to the most careless observer, that the present warfare is a specious mask, calculated only to amuse the nation and promote the interest of a few. No man can hesitate to acknowledge, that if the United States had determined to act with that spirit which became them, they must have long been in possession of their northern posts, and thereby been enabled to afford protection to their frontiers, either by conciliating the affections of the savages, or by the force of arms. This desirable object was evidently more properly to be obtained by contending with the British nation itself, (particularly since the European convulsions) than by a fruitless & dishonorable warfare with its instruments, the savages. But the wily politician of the east, anticipates a variety of evils to his country, by removing the barriers to emigration: he foresees that a vigorous & decided conduct on the part of the Union, would terminate to the advantage and prosperity of the western country, & this is sufficient to induce him to throw every possible difficulty in the way, either by giving an improper direction to affairs, or retarding them by vain and fruitless negociations.

"Thus far his eastern policy suceeded to admiration. The glory of America is tarnished by a shameful defection from the cause of freedom. Her arms are disgraced, her commerce insulted and abused, and her western country sacrificed to local policy and British influence.

"This melancholy picture is incomplete, without we review the conduct of the United States, respecting the navigation of the Mississippi, and trace their ill judged policy in the south. Much has been said on this important subject; and too much cannot be said to convince, if possible, our Atlantic brethren of the injustice done us, by withholding this our all important right. But we will reserve the detail of unfriendly proceedings in this business for another occasion—and lament that they all conspire to render us an unimportant people.

"The period has arrived, when the inhabitants of western America, ought to awake from their lethargy, and pursue this interesting subject through all its attendant difficulties. In addition to our numerous petitions to Congress, let us with one voice, again lay before that body our real state, and warn them of the consequences that may follow from an inattention to our just demand.

"It would be unnecessary at this time to anticipate the consequences that may result from this unhappy event. It is difficult to determine to what extent the exertions of an injured people may reach. Our cause is good, our interest is one. As we value our own and the prosperity of future generations, let us, with a conduct marked with coolness and determination, exert every nerve to obtain this invaluable right. Let us carefully watch over circumstances as they occur, and be always ready to seize a favorable moment to accomplish our desired object. We require not the veil of secrecy. Let us act in open day—the magnitude of the object will justify our anxiety. Time and unanimity will determine the event, and may God grant us a happy issue."

The last week in January 1784, the copy of a message from the President of the United States to Congress, delivered December 5th, 1793, arrived in Kentucky, and appeared in the Kentucky Gazette on the 12th day of February, the last clause of which is in these words:

"On the subjects of mutual interests between this country & Spain, negociations & conference are now pending. The public good requiring that the present state of these, should be made known to the Legislature in confidence only, they shall be the subject of a separate and subsequent communication."

No people had ever been more degraded and insulted, or borne degradation and insult with a more submissive patience, than the people of Kentucky. To search for an example in the governments of despots, would be fruitless; for, although partiality and oppression could then be found, they are divested of duplicity, and the oppressors and oppressed, understand each other; the latter expect what they receive, and although they may be mortified, are not disappointed. To freemen, both the mortification and disappointment are exquisite, because having no right to calculate on partiality or oppression, the actual experience of either is intolerable.

The people had been lately informed, that an attempt had been made in a negociation with Spain, to cede the navigation of the Mississippi river to that nation, for twenty-five or thirty years, [by] the American Minister, it was therefore natural for them to conclude, that some project equally inimical to their interests, was embraced in the President's communication; and more especially, as at that time, several French officers had just arrived in Kentucky, with the avowed purpose of raising a sufficient force, to take from the Spaniards the possession of Louisiana, if not willingly surrendered, and granting to the people of Kentucky, the free use of that river. This fact was known to the President at that time, and shortly after a proclamation was issued, forbidding all citizens to attach themselves to the enterprize.[326]

SECTION 50

Resolving the Western Problems
[January 4, 1828]

The distresses experienced from the depredations of the Indians, added to those occasioned from the want of money to discharge the excise on the distillation of whisky, which was now pressed on them, without the possibility of disposing of the product of the soil, added to the neglect shown to every application made to the general government to procure for them the navigation of the Mississippi river, or the delivery of the posts occupied by the British within the limits of the United States, from which the Indians received supplies that enable them to continue their hostilities, presented a gloomy prospect to the people of Kentucky.[327]

About this time, John Jay was appointed Minister Plenipotentiary to the court of Great Britain. Let it therefore be recollected, that shortly after the treaty of peace with that nation, Spain, who pretended that some difficulties existed between her and the United States with respect to our boundaries, as well as the navigation of the Mississippi, and to adjust those difficulties, sent over a minister with full power to treat with Congress on both subjects. Congress deeming the claims set up by Spain untenable, yet out of mere complaisance to that nation, appointed John Jay to negociate the business; and that nothing should be hazarded on so momentous a subject, Congress left nothing to the discretion of Mr. Jay, but expressly instructed him, "that he should enter into no treaty with the Minister, which did not recognize and preserve inviolate, our right to the navigation of the river Mississippi, as stipulated in our treaty with Great Britain." Thus commenced our first negociations on this subject—negociations which were set on foot at the *instance* of Spain, and which were opened by an American Commissioner, bearing with him positive instructions. This precaution on the part of Congress, was worthy of that (then in part) patriot body. Like true fathers of their country, they would not submit the rights of any part of their sons, to the discretion of any *one* man; they would not submit even to discussion, the grand territorial rights of any branch of the republic. The event showed their precaution was well judged; though it was not within the reach of human foresight to have scanned, that an event so extraordinary could have followed. This John Jay, thus instructed to open his negociations with the Spanish Minister, which he continued for nearly a year, without communicating one syllable to Congress respecting its progress. He at length wrote to Congress, stating that *great difficulties* had arisen between him and the Spanish Minister, but it was necessary those difficulties should be kept a *secret*; and at the same time proposed to Congress to appoint a *special committee* to receive his communications, and to instruct him from time to time. Congress not comprehending the extent of this project, calls this Mr. Jay before them to know what were the *great difficulties* that could have arisen under the pointed instructions, which required both *secrecy* and an *extraordinary committee*. He is brought forward, and a secret truly it was; not however, growing out of his commission, nor one that a meditation to eternity on the powers he possessed, could ever have fairly suggested. It was that he thought it beneficial to the *commercial* interest of America, that he should yield the navigation of the Mississippi for twenty-five or thirty years. That Gardoque (the Spanish Minister,) had offered some *commercial* advantages in exchange for it, and that as the Spaniards had some pretensions to the exclusive occupancy of the mouth of that river, their offer to swap with us, contained an *acknowledgment* (this Mr. Jay was a lawyer) of our right to the navigation. These liberal, honest and irresistable arguments, had their influence on the members of no less than *seven* states; but fortunately for Kentucky, 9 states were necessary to meddlle with treaties, the swap was therefore not made. The patriots in Congress growing alarmed at the attempt to barter away the territorial rights of one part of the Union, for some commercial advantages to another, and as the conduct of their commissioner, who, when sent to *assert* a right, had well nigh *chaffered* it away, in consideration perhaps too, of some regulations on the subject of Codfish or Molasses, were glad to let the subject rest; and in this state did it sleep, until the adoption of the new government.

From this government we were taught to expect every thing. The western country populating with rapidity, and Spain still desirous that we should understand each other, again *makes overtures* for an eclaircissement of this right. An American Ambassador is sent forward, our right is asserted, and (as we were told) real negociations opened. Under the auspices of this strong nerved government, had this right been discussing for at least four years. And what had these discussions produced? Another *secret!!!*

Hoodwinked as were the people of Kentucky, they could no longer suffer such naked shifts to amuse them. Who, after contemplating the history of this business, could any longer have any faith in the friendly intentions of Congress? If there was one, he was certainly capable of being the firmest of believers. What in the name of common sense could attach itself to this subject, that should require secrecy? A negociation was opened on an *unalienable* right, a right on which the importance of half America depended. A right which even Jay himself acknowledged was ours, and which, as notoriously as it was wrongfully withheld by the Spaniards. What secret then could be hatched out of such a negociation unless one derogatory of this right? That there was such an one we have the strongest reason to conjecture.

Jay, with positive instructions, and with the patriot part of Congress as sentinels over him, had well nigh yielded it. As the negociations still assumed the same veil of secrecy, what conjecture could the people of Kentucky have formed upon reading the President's message to Congress, in which he says, ("on the subjects of mutual interests between this country and Spain, negociations and conferences are now depending. The public good requiring that the present state of these, should be made known to the legislature in *confidence* only,") but that this secret is a full brother to that recommended by Mr. Jay. If every other executive communication is adverted to, no secrets will be found. Even the communication respecting the posts withheld by the British, though quite similar, is made no secret of; although it had been long conjectured that there must have been a secret in that business.

If the magnitude of the object—if the patience of the injured, and the duration of the injury had any claims to the notice of Congress, this right ought to have held the first place in their deliberations. If want of attachment to this injured country had prevented any real efforts on the subject, insult to the government of America, ought to have had some influence. That government would resent insults, and insults too, very highly refined, it was only necessary to advert to the recent official philipics against the French minister. If intemperance towards, or even insult to a *public character* by the representative of our dearest ally, deserved national reprehension, how ought insult and depredation committed by a contemptible and hostile nation upon another, to have been treated? In the first case, although the insult was at best, but extremely refined, and even equivocal as to its very existence; yet so jealous was the government of America, of the honor and dignity of even a public servant, that the alarm after having been resounded through the United States, by judges, by senators, by governors and by secretaries, both officially and exofficially, by their subscribed publications and anonymous squibs in the newspapers, crossed the Atlantic, endangered our alliance with the most magnanimous and powerful nation upon earth, and was then occupied (not in whispers) all the legislative, executive and judicial wisdom of America. If America thus suddenly recoiled at even the shadow of an insult on its honor, through the sides of a public servant, what ought its feelings and conduct to have been, when for ten years the nation had been insulted, and its citizens plundered, by a nation hostile in its policy, alien in its principles, and between whom there never existed, either sympathy or gratitude? Was the *insult* of a republican Frenchman to an American *servant* of the people, more heinous in the sight of Government, than the depredations of the haughty vassal of a Spanish despot, on a whole American *colony*? Should a Frenchman not be suffered even to shrug himself at the dictum of a public *officer*, and charge it with partiality, while a whole American *colony* is compelled to bend the knee to the creatures of Spanish despotism, for the privilege of their best and fairest rights? Could, in short, that government intend what is just and right towards the Western country, who pursued with ardour, all other object but those, without the attainment of which, the west must be forever contemptible.

Could the most glimmering hope have been entertained, that government would procure this right, although at a period somewhat distant, the people would have endeavored to sit down with patience and await the event. But they could not flatter themselves with the most distant prospects.

Ten years negociation had produced *two secrets*. The issue of the first had been seen; but the issue of the second was in the womb of time, where for aught could be known, might remain as long as the secret of Free Masonry has. This then was the close of the ill fated negociations on this most important right. It is true, they had been communicated in whispers to a body, whose very whispers, were not to be entrusted to plebian ears.

From these premises, the conclusion was evident. From government the people of the west had nothing to hope. It was never intended to invest them with the right of freely navigating the Mississippi. Its procurement evidently depended on the people alone; and that appeared to be the most critical moment. Such a conjuncture of favorable circumstances as then presented themselves, seemed to have been designed by providence for the completion of this event.[328]

Overtures were making to the people in the valley of the Mississippi by the government of France, to aid in taking possession of Louisiana; and French officers were sent among them to raise men for this purpose. What the conduct of the people were on this subject, may be very easily guessed. This was truly a crisis, and a rational conclusion with many, that if the present favorable opportunity was neglected, such another might never again present itself, and no doubt these considerations prompted many to join the French standard.[329]

SECTION 51

The Grand French Design

[January 11, 1828]

The dissatisfaction so strongly evinced by the citizens of Kentucky, at the detention of the military posts by the British, within the limits of the United States, as well as at the withholding from them the free navigation of the river Mississippi by Spain, encouraged the French government to plan an expedition against Louisiana, and attempt to raise forces in Kentucky to accomplish that project. The following gentlemen, viz. *Augustus La Chaise, Charles Delpeau,* —— *Mathurin* and —— *Ligneux,* were authorized to engage officers and men, and were furnished with commissions in blank, to be filled with such names as they could depend on, to prosecute the enterprise. General George Rogers Clarke, accepted the commission of Major General, and on the 25th of January 1794 published the following proposals in the Centinel of the Northwestern Territory, printed in Cincinnati.[330]

Cincinnati, January 25th 1794
"GEORGE R. CLARKE Esq. Major General in the armies of FRANCE, and commander in chief of the FRENCH REVOLUTIONARY LEGIONS on the Mississippi river.

PROPOSALS,
For raising volunteers for the reduction of the Spanish posts, on the Mississippi, for opening the trade of the said river, and giving freedom to its inhabitants, &c.

"All persons serving the expedition, to be entitled to one thousand acres of land—those that engage for one year, will be entitled to two thousand acres—if they serve two years or during the present war with France, they will have three thousand acres of any unappropriated lands that may be conquered. The officers in proportion pay, &c. as other French troops. All lawful *plunder* to be equally divided agreeably to the custom of *war*. All necessaries will be provided for the enterprize, and every precaution taken to cause the return of those who wish to quit the service, as comfortable as possible, and a reasonable number of days allowed them to return, at the expiration of which time their pay will cease. All persons will be commissioned agreeably to the number of men they bring into the field. Those that serve the expedition, will have their choice of receiving their lands or one dollar per day.

A Copy   G.R. CLARK" [331]

Previous to the appearance of Gen. Clark's proposals, Governor St. Clair had issued the following Proclamation.

"Territory of the United States, North West of the Ohio.
"By ARTHUR ST. CLAIR, Governor of the Territory of the United States North West of the Ohio.
"A PROCLAMATION.
"Whereas, a war at present exists in Europe, between France on the one part, and certain other powers on the other parts; and although the United States are allied to France, yet they are not parties in the war, but are at peace with the other powers, and particularly with Spain, from which political situation results by the laws of nations, the duties of an exact neutrality, and a conduct perfectly equal and impartial towards all the belligerent powers, the observation of which neutrality, has been enjoined upon the citizens of the United States, by the President in his proclamation of the 22d day of April 1793. And it having been communicated through the Secretary at War, that the representations of Spain have made representations to him, of the designs of certain French men by the names of *La Chaise, Charles Delpeau, Mathurin* and *Signieux* to *excite* and *engage* as many as they could, whether of our citizens or others, to undertake an expedition against the Spanish settlements within our neighborhood. I have thought fit to issue this proclamation, requiring all the inhabitants of the Territory of the United States North West of the Ohio, and they are hereby required and commanded, to observe a strict neutrality towards Spain, to abstain from every hostility against the subjects or settlements of that crown, and forbidding all and every of the said inhabitants, to join themselves to the said *La Chaise, Charles Delpeau, Mathurin* and *Signeux*, or either of them, in any attempt they may meditate against the Spanish settlements on the Mississippi, or to aid or abet them

in the same, in any manner whatever; and all persons who may offend, may depend upon being prosecuted and punished with the utmost rigor of the law. And I do hereby require and command, all officers civil and Military, to use their utmost endeavors, to prevent the said *La Chaise, Delpeau, Mathurin* and *Signeux,* or either, from making any levies of men, or other preparations within the Territory, and to imprison them should they have the audacity to attempt it, and to restrain all and every of the inhabitants from joining themselves to them, or either of them.

"In testimony whereof, I have caused the seal of the Territory to be affixed to these presents, and signed the same with my hand. Done at the City of Marietta, in the county of Washington, the seventh day of December, one thousand seven hundred and ninety-three, and of the Independence of the United States, the eighteenth year.

ARTHUR ST. CLAIR.[332]

"By the Governor's command,   A.M. DUNN,
"For WINTHROP SARGEANT, Sec'y."

The Indians continued their depredations on the people of Kentucky, as well as those coming to or going from it.

On the 1st December 1783 [1793], five men coming through the wilderness were fired on, one of whom was killed and two wounded.

On the 13, February 1794, the Indians wounded a man at his sugar camp on M'Connell's run in Scott county, who survived but a short time.

On the 10th, [February, 1794] they killed a man on Brashear's creek and took another prisoner.

About the 1st of March 1794, Capt. William Hardin, in pursuit of a party of Indians who had stolen horses from Hardin's settlement, was wounded through the body; the wound did not prove mortal. All the horses were recovered. About the same time two men were killed in Mero district; also two others near the Red Banks on the Ohio.

On the 5th of March 1794, the Indians fell in with three wagons loaded with goods, on their way from Cincinnati to Fort Hamilton, killed the wagoners, destroyed the wagons and all the goods which they could not carry away.

On the 11th of March 1794, the indians attacked a company (travelling through the wilderness) on Richland creek, four of whom were killed and one wounded, who died shortly after. About the same time they killed four in one family on the Rolling Ford of Salt River. They also killed a man near Nashville, and were immediately pursued by a strong party as far as the Tennessee river, where they were overtaken at their encampment, and eleven of them killed and two (squaws) taken prisoners, being the whole of the party.

March 19th 1794, thirteen men who had gone out as a scout on the waters of Red River, were attacked in their camp about day break; they had two of their party killed and lost eight rifles, and all their baggage.

About the 20th of April, the Indians fired on a boat in the Ohio river, near the mouth of Scioto, and killed a man on board. About the same time three men were killed in the wilderness, on Yellow creek, on their way to Kentucky.

May 6th 1794, the Indians killed two men who were digging ore for the Bourbon furnace.[333]

On the 2nd May 1794, the following proclamation of the President of the United States was published in the Kentucky Gazette.
      "By the President of the U. States of America.
            "A PROCLAMATION.

"WHEREAS, I have received information that certain persons, in violation of the laws, have presumed, under a color of a foreign authority, to enlist citizens of the United States and others, within the state of Kentucky, and have there assembled an armed force for the purpose of invading and plundering the territories of a nation at peace with the United States: And, whereas, such unwarrantable measure, being contrary to the laws of nations, and to the duties incumbent on every citizen of the United States, tend to disturb the tranquility of the same, and to involve them in the calamities of war. And whereas it is the duty of the executive to take care that such criminal proceedings should be suppressed, the offenders brought to justice, and all good citizens cautioned against measures likely to prove so pernicious to their country and themselves, should they be seduced into similar infractions of laws.

"I have, therefore, thought proper to issue this proclamation, hereby solemnly warning every person not authorized by the laws, against enlisting any citizen or citizens of the United States, or levying troops or assembling any persons within the United States for the purposes aforesaid, or proceeding in any manner to the execution thereof, as they will answer the same at their peril; and I do also admonish and require all citizens to refrain from enlisting, enrolling or assembling themselves for such unlawful purposes, and from being in any wise concerned, aiding or abetting therein, as they tender their own welfare, in as much as all lawful means will be strictly put in execution for securing obedience to the laws, and for punishing such dangerous and daring violations thereof.

"And I do moreover charge and require all courts, magistrates and other officers, whom it may concern, according to their respective duties, to exert the powers in them severally vested, to prevent and suppress all such unlawful assemblages and proceedings, and to bring to condign punishment, those who may have been guilty thereof, as they regard the due authority of government, and the peace and welfare of the United States.

"In testimony whereof, I have caused the seal of the United States of America, to be affixed to these presents, and signed the same with my hand. Done at the city of Philadelphia the 24th day of March, one thousand seven hundred and ninety four, and of the Independence of the United States of America, the eigheenth.

"GEO. WASHINGTON,

"By the President,   EDMUND RANDOLPH."[334]

At a numerous meeting of respectable inhabitants of the state of Kentucky, at the State-house in Lexington, on Friday the 13th of May 1794.

They proceeded to take under consideration, their right to the navigation of the Mississippi; and being impressed with the importance of the subject, declined coming to any resolution thereon, until the sense of the people was more generally known: Whereupon, a committee was appointed to give public notice to the good people of Kentucky, that a general meeting will be held in the State House in Lexington, on Saturday the 24th inst to begin at 10 o'clock in the morning, for that purpose. We therefore request the good people of Kentucky in general, to attend said meeting, in order to have this important subject fully investigated.

ROBERT BRECKINRIDGE, GEORGE NICHOLAS, ROBERT JOHN-
SON, Members of committee[335]

Reply of Lord Dorchester, to the Indians of the seven villages of lower Canada, as deputies from all the nations who were at the general council held at the Miami, in the year 1793; except the Shawanous, Miamis and Loups.

"*Children*—I have well considered your words, and now am prepared to reply.

"*Children*—You have informed me that you are defeated by the seven villages of lower Canada, and by all the nations of the upper country, which sent deputies to the general council held at the Miami, except the Chiwanous, Miamis' and Loups.

"*Children*—You remind me of what passed at the council fire held at Quebec, just before my last departure for England, when I promised to represent their situation and wishes to the King their father, and expressed my hope, that all the grievances they complained of, on the part of the United States, would soon be done away, by a just and lasting peace.

"*Children*—I remember all very well; I remember that they pointed out to me the line of separation which they wished for, between them and the United States, and with which they would be satisfied and make peace.

"*Children*—I was in expectation of hearing from the people of the

United States, what was required by them. I hoped I should have been able to bring you together, and make you friends.

"*Children*—I have waited long and listened with great attention; but I have not heard one word from them.

"*Children*—I flattered myself with the hope that the line proposed in the year 1783, to separate us from the United States, which was immediately broken by themselves as soon as the peace was signed, would have been mended, or a new one drawn in an amicable manner; here also I have been disappointed.

"*Children*—Since my return, I find no appearance of a line remains; and from the manner which the people of the states push on, and act and talk on this side, and from what I learn of their conduct towards the sea, I shall not be surprised if we are at war with them in the course of the present year; and if we are, a line must be drawn by the warriors.

"*Children*—You ask for a passport to go to New York; a passport is useless in peace; it appears, therefore, that you expect we shall be at war with the states before you return, you shall have a passport, that whether peace or war, you shall be well received by the King's warriors.

"*Children*—They have destroyed their right of preemption; therefore, all their approaches towards us since that time, and all the purchases made by them, I consider as an infringemt on the King's rights, and when a line is drawn between us, be it peace or war, they must lose all their improvements and houses on our side of it; the people must all be gone, who do not obtain leave to become the King's subjects, what belongs to the Indians, will of course be confirmed and secured to them.

"*Children*—What further can I say to you—you are our witnesses, that on our part we have acted in the most peaceable manner, and borne the language of the United States with patience; and I believe our patience is almost exhausted.

"Given under my hand at the castle of St. Lewis, in the City of Quebec, on the 10th day of February, in the year of our Lord, 1794.

Signed,   "DORCHESTER.

"*By his Excellency's command,* Signed HIMAN WITSIUS RYLAND, Sec'y."[336]

SECTION 52

The Founding of
Transylvania University

[January 18, 1828]

At the May session of the Virginia Legislature 1780, a law passed entitled "An act to vest certain escheated lands in the county of Kentucky, in Trustees for a public school." In which law it was "enacted, that eight thousand acres of the land within the said county of Kentucky late the property of Robert M'Kenzie, Henry Collins and Alexander M'Kee, be, and the same are hereby vested in William Fleming, William Christian, John Todd, Stephen Trigg, Benjamin Logan, John Floyd, John May, Levi Todd, John Cowan, George Meriwether, John Cobb, George Thompson and Edmund Taylor. Trustees, as a free donation from this Commonwealth, for the purpose of a public school or Seminary, &c."[337]

On the 5th day of May 1783, the Legislature of Virginia passed another law entitled "An act to vest certain escheated lands in the county of Kentucky, in Trustees for a public school."[338]

In this act the same lands mentioned in the former act are again vested in William Fleming, William Christian, Benjamin Logan, John May, Levi Todd, John Cowan, Edmund Taylor, Thomas Marshall, Samuel M'Dowell, John Bowman, George Rogers Clarke, John Campbell, Isaac Shelby, David Rice, John Edwards, Caleb Wallace, Walker Daniel, Isaac Cox, Robert Johnson, John Craig, John Mosby, James Speed, Christopher Greenup, John Crittenden and Willis Green, who were constituted a body corporate and politic, to be known by the name of the "Trustees of Transylvania Seminary" with all the powers usually given to corporate bodies.

The fifth section of the last recited act provides, that "all lands within the said district,* the whole amount of which does not exceed twelve thousand acres that now are, or hereafter may become escheated to the Commonwealth, shall when escheated, be vested in the said Trustees and their successors &c," in addition to the eight thousand acres before specifically designated, making the whole grant twenty thousand acres, and which were declared to be "forever exempted from all public taxes."

---

*Now State of Kentucky.

This act further provided, that the first meeting of the Trustees should be held at Crow's station† on the second Monday in November 1783, and that thereafter they should hold two stated sessions in every year, in the months of April and October, at any convenient place within the district.

On the second Monday in November, (tenth) 1783, the Trustees met at Crow's station in pursuance of the act of Assembly, and unanimously appointed the Rev. David Rice chairman, and Doct. Ebenezer Brooks clerk.

Upon motion it was "Resolved, As the prosperity and happiness of States depend in a great measure on the liberal education of the inhabitants; as this end cannot be obtained without proper funds to support the public institutions of learning; and as the funds appropriated in this country by act of Assembly for this laudable purpose are at present incompetent thereto, that therefore subscriptions be opened in order to receive donations from those whose public spirit and generosity would induce them to encourage the promotion of useful knowledge; and that David Rice, Samuel M'Dowell, Caleb Wallace, Walker Daniel, James Speed, Christopher Greenup and Willis Green be appointed to draw up, and circulate such subscriptions; but that separate subscriptions shall be taken for real and personal property."

Meetings of the board were held on the 11th December 1783, and on the third of March 1784, at which last meeting, the board was informed by one of its members, that he had passed a receipt to the Rev. John Todd of Louisia county in Virginia, for a Library & Philosophical apparatus, presented as an encouragement to science, to the Transylvania Seminary. The board "on motion, Resolved, That money shall immediately be procured by subscription, (and if not attainable that way), by loan, for the purpose of transporting the library & apparatus belonging to the Transylvania Seminary, payable by the several collectors to Mr. James Thompson, out of which a liberal sum not exceeding £50 shall be delivered by him to Mr. John Mosby, for the purpose aforesaid, and that the surplus, if any, remain in Mr. Thompson's hands, subject to a future order of the board."

Meetings of the Trustees were held on the 11th of October 1784 and on the third and fourth of November; at the latter of which, it was resolved, that a Grammar School be established in Lincoln county, near the dwelling of the Rev. Mr. Rice.[339]

Sundry meetings of the Trustees, took place until the 26th of May, 1775 [1785], at which time the Committee appointed to engage a teacher, reported that they had employed the Rev. James Mitchel, upon which the board engaged Mr. Mitchel for one year from that date, at a salary of one hundred and twenty pounds per annum, to be paid quarterly. Dr. Brooks was allowed the sum of £50 for his services as clerk.[340]

†Now Danville.—Ed.

On the 18th of July, 1787, a second committee was appointed to draw up a petition to the Legislature of Virginia, to appropriate one sixth of the surveyors fees in the District of Kentucky, to the use of Transylvania Seminary. On the 17th of April, 1788, the Board changed their place of meeting from Danville (Crow's Station) to Lexington, where their meetings have been held ever since.[341]

Every attempt to raise money by subscription failed, and on the 14th of October 1788, a committee was appointed to lease out the lands in the neighbourhood of Lexington, at not less than £3 per 100 acres, per annum, two thirds in cash and one third in beef, pork, flour or grain, for the term of three lives. On the 15th of April 1789 a committee was appointed with powers to appoint an Usher or Ushers, in case the number of students should exceed fifteen, at a salary of not more than £50 per annum; at which time Mr. Isaac Wilson was appointed Grammar master, at a salary of £100 per annum. The books and philosophical apparatus having arrived, were deposited at the house of Levi Todd, Esq. for the use of the Grammar school, the Grammar master having been authorised to teach such of the sciences as should be required, and he capable of teaching. At this meeting the Rev. D. Rice resigned his seat as Chairman and Harry Innis was appointed in his place.[342]

On the 15th of March 1790, the first settlement with the treasurer was made by the board of Trustees that appears on record, when it appeared, that the whole amount which had been received was £99 16s 6d, which had been paid over the Grammar master, and for other expences; and there remained a balance of £4 17s due Robert Johnson and of £6 14s 9d due James Garrard; to meet which, was a debt due from Peter January & Son, of £17 12s 6d in merchandize.[343]

On the 20th of December 1790 the Legislature passed a law vesting in the Trustees of Transylvania Seminary one sixth of the fees that shall become due to "the principal Surveyors in the several counties within the District of Kentucky, then in office, from and after the first day of January 1791."[344]

On the 12th of April 1791, the number of students had in the course of the year, been reduced from 13 to 5.[345]

On the 11th of October 1791, the Rev. James Moore was appointed Grammar master, with a salary of £25 per annum in addition to the tuition money; and to take charge of the Library and philosophical apparatus for the use of the school provided the number of students is not less than fifteen.[346]

On the 10th of April 1792, John Hawkins, Esq. was appointed Chairman, in the room of Harry Innis, resigned.[347]

On the 8th of April 1793, John Hawkins resigned as chairman, and John Bradford was appointed in his place.[348]

Every effort was made by the Trustees to raise money to enable them to carry on the school; subscriptions, loans, and finally a lottery was resorted to, but without effect. To aid the Trustees in their efforts, a number of gentlemen in Lexington and its vicinity, formed themselves into a company by the name and style of the Transylvania Company, and in the year 1790 or '91, purchased the lot of ground on which Transylvania University now stands, and erected thereon a two story brick building. The building having been completed, Thomas January, Samuel M'Millin and John Moylan gentlemen, were appointed a committee by the Transylvania company, to make a tender thereof to Transylvania Seminary, upon the condition that the trustees should establish it, the permanent seat of the Seminary.

James Crawford, Levi Todd and John Coburn, were appointed a committee on the part of the Trustees of Transylvania Seminary, to confer with the committee from the Transylvania committee, upon whose report, on the 8th of April 1793, the following resolutions passed the Board of Trustees.[349]

"Resolved, That this board doth accept the offer made by the committee of the company called the Transylvania company, and that they tender their sincere thanks to that company for their generous offer."

"Resolved, That the permanent seat of the Seminary, be established on the lot of ground in the town of Lexington, adjoining Messrs. January's, and which is the same mentioned in the offer made by the company of gentlemen who call themselves the Transylvania company, and accepted by this board in the resolution immediately preceding this."[350]

On the 19th of October 1794 [1793], the Rev. James Moore, was unanimously elected President for the ensuing year. Mr. Moore failed to accept the appointment previous to the 5th day of February 1794, on which day the board proceeded to elect a President, whose services were to commence on the 9th day of the following October. On counting the ballots, a majority appeared in favor of the Rev. Harry Toulmin.

The election of Mr. Toulmin occasioned considerable excitement in the board, and especially among the friends of Mr. Moore, and finally the yeas and nays on the question of his appointment, were taken, and were as follows: Ayes, Breckinridge, Coburn, Dudley, Johnson, Lewis, A. Parker, J. Parker, Trotter and Wilson—Noes, Hawkins, Morton, Campbell, Crawford, L. Todd, R. Todd and M'Dowell—Ayes 9, Noes 7.[351]

As soon as the vote was taken, Mr. Crawford resigned his seat, and with great warmth, predicted the downfall of the institution, and charged the board with committing the management of it into the hands of an infidel.

The election of Mr. Toulmin President, (who was an Unitarian,) was the ostensible cause of the setting up a sectarian institution, avowedly in opposition to the Transylvania University, which was ultimately effected in the establishment of the Kentucky Academy.

On the 26th of October 1795, John Bradford resigned his seat as Chairman of the Board, and Colonel John Campbell was elected in his stead.[352]

The Rev. Harry Toulmin continued President until the 4th of April 1796, when he resigned, and on the 23d of the September succeeding, the Rev. James Moore was unanimously elected to fill the vacancy occasioned by this resignation.[353]

On the 3d of October 1796, the Board of Trustees received information from the Kentucky Academy, "that they were desirous to communicate on the subject of an union of the two Seminaries." Upon which, William Morton, John Breckinridge and Thomas Lewis, were appointed a committee "to receive any proposition that may be made by the said Kentucky Academy on the subject—and to communicate freely with them or with a committee appointed by them, and make report." This committee met one appointed by the Kentucky Academy, with whom they agreed on the terms of an union, which was reported to their respective boards.

A few of the Trustees of the Transylvania Seminary, were opposed to an union on any principle; believing it a scheme to bring the whole under the control and management of a particular religious sect; and whether this opinion was well or ill founded, it prevented a comsummation of the Union, until November 2d 1798, when a majority of each board united in a petition to the legislature to pass a law to unite together the Transylvania Seminary and Kentucky Academy, to be thereafter known by the name and style of TRANSYLVANIA UNIVERSITY.

At this time the union of these institutions took place, the pecuniary resources of the Transylvania Seminary, were extremely low; and the only motive of some of its Trustees to consent to the union, was the hope of acquiring in cash £600; a sum reported to be in the treasury in the Kentucky Academy; but after the union, when the treasury came to be examined, it was found to be empty of cash, and the only fund was notes and bonds, to an amount less than £500, with some subscriptions, no part of which could be collected. So that the only advantage obtained by the union, was the addition of ten of the trustees of the Kentucky Academy, to the same number of those of Transylvania Seminary, to manage the concerns of Transylvania University.[354]

SECTION 53A

The Seeds of Controversy
[January 25, 1828]

On the 22d December 1798, "an act for the union of the Transylvania Seminary and the Kentucky Academy," passed, to take effect from and after the 1st day of June following; and James Garrard, *Samuel M'Dowell*,* Cornelius Beatty, Frederick Ridgely, *Robert Marshall*, George Nicholas, *James Crawford, Joseph Crockett, Bartlett Collins, Andrew M'Calla*, William Morton, *Robert Steele, John M'Dowell*, Alexander Parker, *Caleb Wallace*, James Trotter, Levi Todd, *James Blythe*, Thomas Lewis, John Bradford and Buckner Thruston, were appointed trustees, to hold their first session at the seat of Transylvania Seminary in the town of Lexington, on the second Tuesday in January 1799.

January 8th 1799, (the second Tuesday in the month) the day appointed by law for the first meeting of Trustees for Transylvania University, a meeting was held at the seat of Transylvania Seminary, where the whole of the Trustees except James Garrard, Samuel M'Dowell, Robt. Marshall, Joseph Crockett and James Crawford, attended, qualified and took their seats, when John Bradford was elected chairman. The late President, Assistant Treasurer and Clerk of the Board of Trustees of the Transylvania Seminary, were continued at their former salaries; and a professorship of Medicine, and one of law and politics was established. The two stated sessions of the board in each year, were fixed to be held on the first Mondays in April and October.[355]

Doctors F. Ridgley and Samuel Brown were elected professors of Medicine, and George Nicholas Esq. professor of law and politics.

On the 18th of October 1799, James Brown, Esq. was appointed professor of law, vice George Nicholas, Esq. deceased, and the Rev. James Moore, whose time of service had expired, was unanimously elected President, until the second Monday in October 1802.[356]

On the 20th of October 1799, the Rev. James Blythe was unanimously elected professor of science; and on the same day the Reverend James Welsh was duly elected professor of languages.[357]

In forming the union between the Transylvania Seminary & the Ky. Academy, it was agreed between the two boards, that ten Trustees from

*Those names in Italic, were Trustees in the Kentucky Academy.

each institution, to form a board of Trustees for the University, Together with the Governor of the state, (Colonel James Garrard). By this means half the new board, (exclusive of the Governor) were attached to those sectarian principles, which was the cause of setting up the Kentucky Academy in opposition to the Transylvania Seminary, viz: Samuel M'Dowell, Robert Marshall, James Crawford, Joseph Crockett, Andrew M'Calla, Robert Steele, John M'Dowell, Caleb Wallace, James Blythe and Bartlett Collins. It was therefore the policy of the old trustees of Transylvania Seminary, to reduce the number of their opponents, and add as many to their own side: Whether that policy influenced them in the election of Mr. Blythe and Mr. Welsh, as professors or not, the effect was the same, and of which they appear to have availed themselves. For from that time forward, the sectarians remained in the minority generally, on every question affecting party principles.

In consequence of the law requiring 11 members to constitute a board, and the great difficulty of convening that number on any ordinary business, the Trustees at their first meeting, appointed a standing committee of nine of their body, any five to constitute a board, with full power to transact any business which could be legally confided to a committee.[358]

On the 15th day of June 1801, a petition signed by nine of the students of Transylvania University, was presented by one of them in behalf of the whole, to the Chairman of the Board of Trustees; in this petition a number of charges were set forth against Mr. James Welsh, professor of languages in the University. The Chairman transmitted the petition to the Chairman of the standing committee; with directions that they call the professor and petitioning students, before them, and if possible settle the matter, and not suffer it to be made public. On the 17th of June, the standing committee took up the charges against the professor Welsh, and made some progress until the 22d, when it was decided that the business could only be settled by the Board of Trustees, and therefore requested the Chairman to convene them at the University of the succeeding day, which was accordingly done.[359]

On the 23d of June the Trustees met, when the parties appeared, and as the investigation was with open doors, the house was very much crowded. Before the business commenced, it was decided by the board, that no student who had subscribed the charges, should be admitted as a witness to prove any of them. The investigation closed on the 1st of July 1801, having continued before the board from the 23d June, during the whole time the house continued to be crowded with spectators. The following question was asked by Mr. Welsh, of one of the witnesses, viz: "Have you not heard arguments made use of in this University, against christianity in general, and prayer in particular." This question was deemed by the board improper and was not answered. After the evidence was closed, Mr. Welsh addressed the board and was followed by one of the complaining students. The subject was closed by the Trustees entering up the following resolutions, on each of which the yeas and nays were taken, viz:

"1. Resolved, As the opinion of this board, that in the course of this enquiry, the petitioning students have behaved with decency and propriety.

"YEAS—Bearty, R. Todd, L. Todd, M'Pheters, Collins, Russell, Lewis, Trotter, Overton—9.

"NAYS—Morton, Patterson, M'Calla, Crawford, M'Dowell, Steel, Parker—7.

"2. Resolved, In the opinion of this board, that nothing has appeared in evidence in the course of this enquiry, that can affect the moral character of Mr. James Welsh.

"YEAS—Morton, Patterson, M'Calla, Maccoun, Crawford, M'Pheters, M'Dowell, Parker and Steel—9.

"NAYS—Beatty, R. Todd, Trotter, Collins, Lewis, Russell and Overton—8 [7?].

Resolved, As the opinion of this board, that from the general dissatisfaction of the students, with Mr. James Welsh as professor, he can no longer be useful in the institution in that capacity.

"YEAS—Bradford, R. Todd, L. Todd, Trotter, Collins, Russell, Lewis, Overton and C. Beatty—9.

"NAYS—Patterson, M'Calla, M'Coun, Marshall, Crawford, M'Pheters, M'Dowell and Parker—8.

"Resolved, As the opinion of this board, that nothing has appeared in the course of this enquiry, that has materially affected the character of Mr. James Welsh as a professor.

"YEAS—Morton, Patterson, M'Calla, Crawford, M'Pheters, M'Dowell, Parker and Steel—9 [8?].

"NAYS—Beatty, R. Todd, L. Todd, Trotter, Collins, Russell, Lewis and Overton—8.

"Resolved, That Mr. James Welsh resume the duties of his office as professor of the languages in the Transylvania Seminary, and that the students return to their duty, as soon as the faculty shall have delt with them as they think proper, and their suspension is taken off.

"YEAS—Morton, Patterson, M'Calla, M'Coun, Crawford, M'Pheters, M'Dowell, Parker and Steel—9.

"NAYS—Beatty, R. Todd, L. Todd, Trotter, Collins, Russell, Lewis and Overton—8.

"Resolved, That as no method had been prescribed to the students, by which they might attempt to procure a redress of their grievances, they ought not to meet with censure, because they have petitioned the board for that purpose. Passed unanimously."

In the whole of the proceedings on the petition of the students, the trustees on almost every question, divided in such manner, as that those who belonged to the Kentucky Academy voted on one side, and those who belonged to the Transylvania Seminary on the other.

The day after the proceedings closed, fifteen students left the University; in consequence of which, the board of trustees met on the 10th of July, and after calling on the president and professors, to lay before them in writing, the state of the University, shewing the number of students that are at present in the University, and the number that had left in one account of dissatisfaction, and from what class.

In consequence of the information obtained from the president and professors, the board came to the following resolution.

"Whereas, it appears to the Board of Trustees, that the cause why the greater part of the students who have left the University, is owing entirely to a dissatisfaction with Mr. James Welsh the professor of languages. Therefore,

"Resolved, As the opinion of this board, that Mr. James Welsh can no longer be serviceable to this University as a professor. The yeas and nays were as follows:

"YEAS—Bradford, R. Todd, L. Todd, Trotter, Collins, Russell, Lewis, Overton and Beatty—9.

"NAYS—Patterson, M'Coun, M'Calla, Crawford, M'Pheters, Marshall, M'Dowell and Parker—8.

In consequence of this resolution, Mr. Welsh resigned his professorship, and on the 23d day of July, Mr. Alexander M'Kechan was elected in his place.

Cornelius Beatty, Esq. was elected Chairman in the place of John Bradford who resigned.[360]

A report having been circulated that meetings of the students were held in the University buildings after night, for the purpose of discussing religious controverted or deistical questions, on the 5th of April a petition of the students was presented to the board, praying that a committee be appointed to enquire into the report. Upon which John Bradford, James Crawford, Andrew M'Calla and Levi Todd, were appointed for that purpose, who reported, "that there is not any society in the University for discussing deistical sentiments, nor even for examining or debating on controverted points of religion. And that the laws of the University on this subject, are carefully attended to by professors and students. That the report had originated, either from mistaken ideas, or with those who are unfriendly to the institution."[361]

On the 6th of October 1802, General Robert Todd was elected Chairman in the place of Cornelius Beatty, who resigned.[362]

On the 7th, the Rev. James Moore was elected President for two years, and the Rev. James Blythe professor of science, and Andrew Steele professor of languages.[363]

On the 2d day of April 1803, Col. JAMES MORRISON, who was elected a trustee at the last stated meeting of the board in the room of Felix Grundy, was qualified and took his seat.[364]

On the 18th of October 1803, Colonel James Trotter was appointed Chairman in the room of Robert Todd resigned.[365]

October 1st 1804, the board of trustees resolved that a professor of Natural Philosophy, Geography and the Mathematics, be appointed for six years, and the Rev. James Blythe was unanimously elected. Also that a professor of the dead languages be appointed for the same length of time, and Mr. Ebenezer Sharp was unanimously elected. Likewise a professor of Moral Philosophy, Logic, Criticism and Belles Letters, for the term of one year. As the term for which a President of the University had expired, the Rev. James Blythe was appointed President protem for one year, if a President should not be elected within that time.[366]

On the 1st of November 1804, the Rev. Rob't. H. Bishop was unanimously elected professor of Moral Philosophy, Logic, Criticism and the Belles Letters, until the first Monday in October 1810.[367]

On the 10th of October 1804, Henry Clay, Esq. was unanimously elected professor of Law and Politics, in the room of James Brown, Esq. removed, and Doct. James Fishback professor of Medicine by an unanimous vote.[368]

On the 16th of October 1807, John Monroe, Esq. was elected professor of law and politics, in the room of Henry Clay, Esq. who resigned.[369]

On the 16th of November 1808, Mr. T. Le Duc, was appointed an assistant to the professor of languages, part of whose duties were to teach the French language. His salary three hundred dollars per annum. Mr. Le Duc resigned in April 1809.[370]

On the 8th of April 1809, Doctor Benjamin W. Dudley, was appointed professor of Anatomy and Physiology, Doctor James Buchanan professor of Institutes of Medicine, Doct. James Overton, professor Materia Medica and Botany, and Doctor Elisha Warfield professor of Surgery and Midwifery.

On the 29th of December 1809, Mr. Bertrand Guerin was appointed a teacher of the French language in Transylvania University.

From the year 1804 until 1810, nothing remarkable in the transactions respecting Transylvania University occurred. All the lands belonging to the institution, except those south of Green river were sold, and the money laid out in bank stock, which produced a much better revenue than that produced from the rents of the land; and as the land had been let on rent for three lives, most of whom were still living, the tenants became the purchasers at a very reduced price, as no other person would give as much as the tenant.[371]

Transylvania Tends to Business

[February 1, 1828]

On the 15th of June 1815, the board of Trustees acceded to a proposition made them by Richard Higgins and Co. which was a gratuity of four acres of ground and the sale of four acres more.

On the 6th of October 1815, the following preamble and resolutions were unanimously adopted by the board of Trustees of Transylvania University, viz:

"Feeling gratified at the return of the Hon. Henry Clay to his country, and desirous of giving a testimony of their regard, and expressing the opinion they entertain of his conduct whilst acting as one of our Ministers in the late negociations at Ghent, the Trustees of Transylvania University have adopted the following resolutions.

"Resolved, That in negociating the late treaty, our ministers have shewn a zeal, firmness and talents, highly honorable to themselves and to the government of the United States; that for their eminent services, is ably vindicating and supporting our national rights and character, they are entitled to receive the reward due to distinguished patriotism, the warm approbation and united applause of their countrymen.

"Resolved, That Edmund Bullock, Dr. Frederick Ridgley, James Prentiss, and William T. Barry, be a committee to wait on the Hon. Henry Clay and present him with the foregoing resolution."

On the 11th Nov. 1815, Dr. Thos. Cooper was elected Professor of Chemistry, Mineralogy and Natural History; who declined accepting, and on the same day Dr. H. Holley was elected President.[372]

On the same day Dr. Benj. W. Dudley was appointed Professor of Surgery; Dr. Coleman Rogers, Professor of Anatomy; Dr. Samuel Brown, Professor of the Theory and Practice of Medicine; Dr. William H. Richardson Professor of Midwifery and Diseases of Women and Children, and Charles W. Short Professor of Materia Medica and Botany.[373]

On the 12th March 1816, the Rev. James Blythe resigned his Professorship.[374]

On the 18th March 1816, the Rev. Luther Rice was elected President, but declined accepting.[375]

On the 28th Feb. 1817, Dr. Blythe was unanimously elected Professor of Chemistry, and Dr. James Overton Jr., was elected Professor of the Theory and Practice of Medicine in the room of Dr. Samuel Brown, who declined his appointment.[376]

In the month of February 1818, an act passed "further to regulate Transylvania University," in which it is enacted, "That the power and authority of the present Trustees of Transylvania University, over and concerning the said institution, the funds, estate, property, rights and demands thereof, shall forever cease and determine; that thirteen shall be the number of the trustees, that shall hereafter manage the said institution and the concerns thereof, and Henry Clay, Edmund Bullock, Robert Trimble, John T. Mason, Robert Wickliffe, James Prentiss, Hubbard Taylor, John Pope, Lewis Sanders, Samuel H. Woodson, John Brown, Charles Humphreys, and Thomas Bodley," were appointed Trustees, in whom all the funds, estate, property, rights, demands, privileges, and immunities of what kind or nature soever, belonging or in any wise appertaining to the said University, shall, be invested in the Trustees of said institution (appointed by said act) and their successors in office, for the uses and purposes only, of said institution &c. who were to hold their first session at the University on the first Tuesday of March following.[377]

On the 2nd day of March 1818, agreeably to law, a majority of the Trustees met in the University and were qualified, when a committee was appointed to attend to the completion of the building on the University lot.[378]

A resolution had been entered into by the former board, to remove the seat of the University to a lot procured from Richard Higgins & Co. and to enable the board to erect the necessary buildings. A committee had been appointed to sell the lot on which the University now stands, to which the members of the Transylvania Company objected, stating that the express terms on which the lot was transferred to the University, were that the permanent seat thereof should be established on that lot; urging, that if it was removed without their permission, the right to the lot would revert back to the company; the board therefore rescinded the resolution for removing, and contracted for the building on the Seminary lot, the house that was afterwards finished by the new board, to effect which the committee above named were appointed.[379]

On the 14th of March, Robert Wickliffe Esq. was appointed Chairman, who continued in office until the 6th of August 1821, when he resigned, and Col. James Morrison was appointed in his place.[380]

On the 7th April 1818, Dr. Horace Holley was elected President with a salary of $3000 per annum, Robert H. Bishop and Ebenezer Sharp Professors in the Transylvania University, each unanimously. On the same day the resignation of Dr. Daniel Drake Professor in the Medical department was received, and Dr. Overton was elected Professor of the Theory and Practice of Medicine, Dr. Dudley Professor of Anatomy and Surgery, Dr. Richardson, Professor of Midwifery and the Diseases of Women and Children, Dr. Short Professor of Materia Medica and Botany, and Dr. Blythe Professor of Chemistry, (all of them unanimously,) for an indefinite period.[381]

On the 8th of August 1818, the Rev. C. Henry was unanimously elected Professor of Languages. On the same day Dr. Blythe resigned his professorship in the Medical department, and Mr. John Roche was appointed a Tutor, to assist the professor of Languages, at a Salary of $450 per annum.[382]

On the 19th of Dec. 1818, the oath of office was administered to Dr. Holley and to the Professors and Teachers.[383]

On the 14th July 1819, Dr. J. W. Webster of Boston was unanimously elected Professor of Chemistry and Mineralogy, Dr. Samuel Brown Professor of the Theory and Practice of Physic, and Dr. Charles Caldwell Professor of the Institutes of Medicine; all unanimously.[384]

On the 25th of Sept. 1819, Dr. James Blythe was unanimously elected Professor of Chemistry in the room of Dr. J. W. Webster, who declined accepting his appointment. On the same day Dr. Granville Sharp Patterson was elected Professor of Anatomy, who declined accepting.[385]

On the 18th Nov. 1819, Daniel N. Bradford was appointed Tutor, and C. S. Rafinesque as Professor of Natural History and Botany, and took the oath of office; and ———— Nalte was appointed a Tutor in the Mathematical department on a salary of $600 per annum, together with his board and a room.[386]

February 26th 1820, Thos. L. Caldwell was elected unanimously a Tutor in the place of John Everett resigned.[387]

In March 1820, Dr. C. Caldwell was commissioned by the Board of Trustees to go to Europe for the purpose of procuring books and suitable apparatus for the use of Transylvania University.[388]

In conformity to an act of the General Assembly passed the 18th December 1821, entitled "An act to establish a Literary Fund and for other purposes," Sec. 6 provides, that prior to the 1st day of February 1822 the board of Trustees shall file with the Cashier of the Bank of the Commonwealth of Kentucky, a correct and detailed statement of all the debts due by said institution contracted prior to the 1st day of December 1821, which order was complied with, and the aggregate amount of the debt was $26,073.75½ cents.[389]

On the 5th of May 1823, the board passed the following resolutions:

"Resolved, That the Trustees of Transylvania University, as a testimony of their deep sense of the loss sustained by this institution in the death of their late highly respected Chairman, Col. James Morrison, who departed this life on the 23rd of April, 1823, at the City of Washington, will wear black Crape on the left arm for one month.

"Resolved, That the Trustees, Faculties, and Students of Transylvania University, will unite with the Citizens of Lexington, and such others as may choose to join in a funeral procession on Monday the 19th day of May 1823, in honor of the memory of Col. James Morrison, late Chairman of the board of Trustees.

"Resolved, that Mr. Holley, President of this institution, be requested to deliver a suitable oration on the above occasion.

"Resolved, That a committee of five viz:—Thomas Bodley, Geo. T. Chapman, Elisha Warfield, John W. Hunt and James Trotter be appointed to superintend and make the necessary arrangements incident to the Funeral procession in honor of the memory of the late Chairman of the board of Trustees, Col. James Morrison." [390]

On Monday the 19th of May 1823, the Trustees, to wit: John Bradford Chairman, P.T., John W. Hunt, James Trotter, James Fishback, Edmund Bullock, John Tilford, Charles Wilkins, Elisha Warfield, Elisha I. Winter, Benj. Gratz, Charles Humphreys, William Leavy, Henry Clay, and George T. Chapman, with a large concourse of the citizens assembled in the College green, where they formed and moved in regular procession to the Episcopal Church, when an appropriate oration was delivered by President Holley; after which the Trustees returned to the University, when they passed the following resolutions.

"Resolved, That the thanks of the board be presented to Mr. Holley, for the funeral oration which at the request of the board, be this day delivered on the occasion of the death of the late Col. James Morrison, Chairman of this board; and that he be requested to furnish a copy of it for publication, and for preservation, among the archives of this institution." [391]

Col. Morrison bequeathed to Transylvania University in perpetuity the interest on $20,000, to be applied to the payment of a professor in that institution, to be denominated the MORRISON PROFESSOR, as also the residue of his estate, after satisfying and paying all the enumerated bequests. The Trustees considering the manificent provisions made for Transylvania University by Col. Morrison in his last will testament, and that it might conduce to a speedy settlement of the affairs of his estate, in which the University as a residuary legatee, is materially interested, and that it would at the same time be a testimony of grateful respect to his memory, and that it would be a manifestation of regard, and might contribute to the comfort of his widow and relict: therefore,

"Resolved, That the assent of the Trustees of Transylvania University, as the residuary legatee, be, and it is hereby declared and given to any arrangement the acting executor of the said James Morrison, may make for the surrender forthwith to Mrs. Morrison of any portion of his real estate, not exceeding $15,000 in lieu and full satisfaction of the $15,000 in land, which by the will of the said Jas. Morrison, she has in her power by the last will and testament to dispose of."[392]

On the 10th of July 1826, a committee was appointed by the Board of Trustees, to confer with the executor of Col. James Morrison, deceased, in respect to the residuary legacy bequeathed by the said Morrison to Transylvania University, and to consider and report to the board when and where in the town of Lexington, it may be expedient to erect an edifice to be denominated the Morrison College, according to the directions of the will of the deceased.[393]

This committee reported, "That the Executor met them and furnished a full and clear exhibit of the affairs of the estate, evincing every disposition to meet the wishes of the board, and to enable your committee to understand the situation of the estate, and the prospects as respects the University, furnished a schedule of the lands yet owned by the estate as well as a conjectural estimate of the result of the estate, both of which papers we herewith submit. From all the information, we are of opinion, that we are not to expect any cash payments at present, and have been informed by the Executor, that if in the power of the trustees to use, for the purpose of carrying into effect the objects of the will, any part of the unappropriated real estate, not necessary to the complete execution of the will, that he will convey it."

Accompanying this report of the committee was a schedule of the whole estate of Col. Morrison including cash on hand, together with a conjectural estimate of the residuary estate comprehended in the devise to the University.

On the 20th of Sept. 1824, Thomas J. Matthews was elected Morrison Professor in Transylvania University, and to fill the Chair lately occupied by President Bishop, who had resigned.[394]

The Holley Years at Transylvania

[February 22, 1828]

The flourishing state to which Transylvania had risen in 1824, excited both envy and jealousy in the breasts of some who had formerly participated in its management, whilst in a languid state. It was evident to all, that the change was principally to be attributed to the judicious choice of a President. It was therefore natural that some who were in office at the time when the last election was made, and who were not re-elected, should feel dissatisfied, and more especially at the flattering prospects of success under the management of a new Board of Trustees.

The brilliant talents of the President, had filled the empty seats of the University with students, consequently the only means of checking its growing greatness was, to destroy the popularity of the presiding officer; to accomplish which, the most probable measure was to attack his religious character. A Pamphlet edited by a Mr. M'Farland in Paris, was therefore selected for this purpose, and filled, in addition to the editorial productions, with anonymous publications, charging Mr. Holley with infidelity, and the Trustees with a violation of the duties imposed on them by their election, as well as by their oath of office.

This attack was considered as an attack on the institution itself, and was noticed by a writer in the Lexington Public Advertiser of April 3rd 1824, in these words, "As a silent spectator, I have noticed the origin and progress of this presbyterian war against the administration of the University, and have long since made up my mind that for the benefit of morals, genuine religion, and the peace of society, the leading individuals in the noisy and distracting outcry, ought to be pointed out by name, and held up to public view."[395]

Mr. M'Farland was the Pastor of a Presbyterian congregation in Paris, and there is no doubt, obtained most of his information from citizens of that denomination in and near Lexington, who were in the habit of charging Mr. Holley with inculcating into the minds of the youth under his care, Anti-Christian principles. The Trustees, conscious of the injurious tendency to the interests and standing of the institution which a belief of those charges would have, and feeling it their duty to use every means in their power to counteract those injurious reports, recommended to the President and Academical Faculty, (viz: Horace Holley, L.L.D President; Robert Hamilton Bishop, A.M. Professor of Natural Philosophy and History; John Roche A M Professor of the Greek and Latin Languages; Mann Butler A M Professor of Mathematics,) to devise and report a plan of Religious instruction in the University, who, on the 5th of April 1824, made the following report, which was unanimously adopted by the board.

At a meeting of the Academical Faculty of Transylvania University, April 5th 1824, the President submitted for consideration, the following preamble and resolutions, which in substance he had twice brought before the Faculty several months since; but had consented to the postponement of a final determination upon them, in consequence of the doubts of their utility, which were expressed by the Rev. Professor of Natural Philosophy and History. It being understood that these doubts were removed, and that there was a prospect of a unanimous adoption of the measure, the President again called the attention of the Faculty to this interesting and important subject.

The by laws of the University, (page 8,) contains an article in regard to religious instruction and worship of the institution, in these words.— "It shall be the duty of the President, or in his absence, of one of the Professors, to perform divine service on every Sabbath, at least once in the chapel of the University, to such officers and students as may chose to attend. And it is particularly enjoined upon the students to attend public worship somewhere on the Sabbath." This duty was discharged for a considerable time by the President, when at his own request, he was permitted in consequence of his numerous duties, in the superintendence of the establishment, and in its general improvement, as well as in various departments of instruction, to omit this public weekly labour. The principle religious sects having churches in town, the students had an opportunity to attend such as they, or their parents, prefered. It is believed that in this way they have generally received religious instruction, and participated in public worship during the whole of the present administration of the affairs of the University. The Faculty however knowing it to be the earnest desire of the Trustees, as well as their own, to have as far as possible, the best advantages of religious instruction, & worship secured to the youth of the institution; and finding from experience that an improvement can be made in the existing regulation upon this subject, recommend to the Trustees the adoption of the measure, which provides, as it is believed, in a safe and effectual manner, for the accomplishment of the several purposes involved in this object of general solicitude, while it guards against dangers and abuses.

The members of the Faculty are aware, that sectarian peculiarities ought not to be introduced into a State University, when there is no established Church with legal privileges, and where young men are collected within its walls, from families of all religious denominations and to receive instruction in literature and science. At the same time it appears to be the general desire and expectation, in accordance with some of the best and strongest principles of our nature, that the great doctrines of our common religion, those in which the good and pious of all denominations agree, should be taught with the other branches of education, if a mode of doing this can be adopted, without opening the door for political & sectarian divinity to enter, and disturb and pervert the minds of the students, and thus give just occasion for offence to the parents and friends.

The principles of religion, in which the enlightened and benevolent of all denominations harmonize, are happily the most important, and are such as all patriots and devout men would wish to see inculcated in a State University, leaving the particular tenets of different sects to be taught in families, parishes and theological schools. The plan now offered, embraces as many points as the nature of the case appears to admit with propriety, and provides the same kind and degree of safety for the University in this respect, which are provided for the community at large under our free government, namely, the equal distribution of the proper means and opportunities among the ministers of the various religious denominations. All the sects are included in this catholic measure. None have a right to complain while all have the privilege of appearing before the youth of the University to recommend and enforce their common religion. The exclusion of any would be a departure from the principles which have governed, and still govern the instructors and the Board of Trustees. Although respectable Clergymen from all religious denominations are thus allowed to contribute their aid to the interests of the University in promoting the great doctrines of our holy religion, and in illustrating and enforcing the pure morals, which it requires; yet, from the actual circumstances of the town and its immediate vicinity, there are four or five denominations whose Ministers will have the opportunity to officiate chiefly in the regular course. These are the Roman Catholics, the Episcopalians, the Presbyterians, the Baptists, and the Methodists. Provision is made to give to others a suitable opportunity to be heard.

With these views, the Faculty respectfully offer the following resolutions to the consideration of the Trustees, as the result of their deliberations.

"Resolved, by the Trustees of Transylvania University, that as they have heretofore considered it their duty, and have made provision in their laws to discharge it; though the execution of this design, in the manner presented, has been interrupted by the force of circumstances, so they still consider it their duty to cause the great doctrines and virtues of our common religion, as they are gathered from the word of God in the Old and New Testament, to be taught in this institution, as far as it is practicable, free from all sectarian peculiarities, and from all the bitterness of religious controversy.

"Resolved, by the Trustees of Transylvania University, that the imperative form of the existing article in our by laws upon this subject, since the President has been allowed at his own request to omit the performance of the labour assigned to him, and which was virtually modified at the time of granting this indulgence, be now, and it is, exchanged for the permissive.

"Resolved, that in order to carry into effect for the future, what has always been the desire of this Board, as well as the President and the Professors, and what is believed to be accordant with the wishes of the Legislature and the People, and to secure the impartial instruction of the Students in the most useful and important principles of our belief, the Ministers of the religious denominations in Lexington be invited to preach in turn, during the Academical session, in the Chapel of the University, at 9 o'clock in the morning of each Sabbath; and that the Students who live in town, be required to attend, unless excused by the Faculty upon satisfactory evidence of conscientious objections on their own part, or on that of their parents or guardians.[396]

"Resolved, that each Clergyman have the liberty to invite, with consent of the Chairman or President, any Minister in good standing of his own or any other denomination, to officiate in his turn; and in order to enjoy the benefit of the talents, learning and piety of distinguished and useful Preachers in good standing from abroad, when they may be travelling through our part of the country, it is resolved that the Chairman of the Board, or the President of the University, be authorised to invite such persons to officiate in the Chapel, either at 9 o'clock in the morning, or at a suitable time in the day or evening. Should the hour of 9 in the morning be selected, in this case notice must be given, on the preceding day to the gentleman whose turn it may be to preach at that time, and his consent must be obtained.

"Resolved, that for the present, the Ministers of the following Churches in Lexington, the Roman, the Episcopalian, the Presbyterian, the Baptist and Methodist Episcopal, be requested by the Chairman, to preach in turn in the Chapel, according to the foregoing arrangement, and that the third Sunday of the present month be the period to begin this duty, it being understood that where there are Ministers of the same denomination, they be requested to take the turn alternately. Should any of the Ministers decline to preach under this arrangement, the others are requested to take their turn in order.

"Resolved, that as the community may desire to know what is the character of every kind of instruction given in the University, and as it is in all respects useful to gratify this desire, it is proper to announce in this connexion, what has been heretofore known to be the practice of the institution, that the examinations are as they always have been, public; and that decorous and reasonable questions may be put to the students under examination, by any respectable person, present, not only as it regards literature and science in general, but also the principles which are taught in Moral Philosophy and Religion, so far as the latter is included in the course, principles which it is the avowed purpose of the instructer in this department, as well as his duty and his inclination, to illustrate and enforce, agreeably to the known wishes of the Trustees and the Public, in perfect conformity with the word and will of God as expressed in the Sacred Scriptures; it being understood as the simple object of this annunciation, that nothing be taught in opposition to the divine revelation of truth contained in the Old and New Testament the oracles of the religion of the country. The Trustees, as well as the several Faculties, have always been desirous, and still are, of rendering the examinations as extensively useful as possible, and of making them a satisfactory test of the real character of the education given in the University.[397]

"HORACE HOLLEY, D D President, Robert Hamilton Bishop, A.M. Professor of Natural Philosophy and History, John Roche, A M, Professor of the Greek and Latin Languages, Mann Butler, A M, Professor of Mathematics. Adopted unanimously by JOHN BRADFORD, esq. Ch'm Thomas Bradley, esq, Charles Humphreys, esq, John Westley Hunt, esq, Elisha Warfield, esq, Rev. James Fishback, D D, Elisha J. Winter, esq, Rev. Geo. Thomas Chapman, A M, James Trotter, esq, William Leavy, esq, Charles Wilkins, esq, Benjamin Gratz, A M, Rev. George Christopher Light."

Religious Instruction and Worship in Transylvania University—"On Monday last the following plan of Religious Instruction and Worship in the University was, by unanimous vote of the Academical Faculty, laid before the Board of Trustees, and was by them unanimously adopted, 13 of the 17 members being present. By a resolution in which all concurred, their names are subscribed to the measure. It was also resolved that the Editors of Newspapers in the town be requested to insert in their columns a copy of this result of the Faculty and Board. It is believed that this is a measure eminently calculated to unite public sentiment, to secure general confidence, to advance the interests of truth, to extend Catholicism and to excite a spirit of emulation in the cause of religious liberty. It would have been gratifying to every patriot and philanthropist, to witness the unanimity and excellent tone of feeling with which a measure having so many relations to personal and sectarian partialities and antipathies, was received and adopted by an unusually full meeting of our large Board of Trustees, embracing a representation of the ancient Church of God under the Old Covenant, and of the most respectable and popular denominations under the New. The truly religious and liberal will rejoice to find that an experiment is now to be made in earnest, and under circumstances which warrant no small degree of confidence in its success to ascertain how far the professed believers of the Bible and worshipers of God, though they are known by different names and associations, can harmonize in the management of the great interests of education as connected with the most important and practical truth and duties of religion. Our situation is as novel as it is interesting, and is well fitted to attract the attention and enlist the hopes of all the friends of human improvement and happiness. The candid and reflecting will see in this measure the reality of a religious influence, in its prompt, and cordial adoption for the most valuable ends. In the list of names here presented to the public, may be found the representatives of seven religious denominations, namely, the ancient People of God, the Roman Catholics, the Episcopalians, the Presbyterians, the Congregationalists, the Baptists, and the Methodists; and among these several Clergymen, who though sincerely devoted to the principles of their respective communions, are heartily engaged in this auspicious enterprize in favour of our common religion. A strong persuasion is cherished, and an earnest prayer is offered, that our UNIVERSAL FATHER AND FRIEND will in his gracious Providence bless and prosper this united effort to do more than ordinary good in removing prejudice, allaying jealousy, in awakening confidence, in reviving charity, enlivening hope and in extending the benevolent dominion of religion and virtue.   HORACE HOLLEY.[398]

SECTION 55A

The Age of the Bigots
[March 7, 1828]

Agreeably to the direction of the Board of Trustees of Transylvania, their Chairman addressed the Ministers of the several congregations in Lexington, in the following words.

"LEXINGTON, April 13, 1824.

"Reverend Sir.—

"I have the honor to transmit to you a copy of the preamble and resolutions which have been recently adopted by the Trustees of Transylvania University, on the subject of Religious instruction and Worship in the Chapel. Agreeably to the authority thus vested in me, I respectfully invite you to take your turn, with the pastors of the other churches in town, in performing this valuable service for the University and the cause of Religion. The Ministers are expected to preach in the order in which the churches are named in the Resolutions. The favour of an answer is requested as soon as convenient, that details for the execution of the measure may be completed

"Respectfully yours,   "JOHN BRADFORD, Chairman." [399]

This invitation was promptly accepted by all the Ministers residing in Lexington except two. They united in a joint letter to the Chairman of which the following is a copy.

"LEXINGTON, April 16.

"To the Chairman of the Board of Trustees of T University.

"Dear Sir.—Your polite communication of the 13th inst. inclosing 'a copy of the preamble and resolutions which have been recently adopted by the Trustees of Transylvania University, on the subject of religious instruction and worship in the Chapel,' has been duly received. And we heartily beg leave to present to the Board through you, our thanks for the honor done us by the accompanying invitation to take our part in the proposed arrangement.

"As Ministers of the Gospel of Jesus Christ our Lord, we are not at liberty to decline the use of any suitable occasion for offering in his name, salvation from sin and eternal death to our fellow men. And we add, that we feel the deepest solicitude for the future usefulness and eternal welfare of the youth of our University.

"But there are several preliminary enquiries which we feel it our duty respectfully to make of the Board, before we shall be prepared to give a final answer to the proposition which has been submitted to us, and

"1st. Shall we be permitted freely and fully to preach the doctrines of the word of God, as they appear to us, and as we announce them to our stated hearers?

"We are induced to make this inquiry, from noticing in the preamble of the resolutions inclosed to us, the following clause. 'The principles of religion in which the enlightened and benevolent of all denominations harmonize, are happily the most important, and are such as all patriots and devoted men would wish to see inculcated in a State University, leaving the particular tenets of different sects to be taught in families, parishes, and theological schools. The plan now offered embraces as many points as the nature of the case appears to admit with propriety.'— And again, 'all the sects are included in this Catholic measure,' and while the sects having an established connection with the town, 'will have the opportunity of officiating chiefly in regular course, provision is made to give to others a suitable opportunity to be heard.'

"Now it is known sir, there are sects who reject what all those specified in the arrangement for regular service, along with ourselves, consider fundamental and vital doctrines of the Bible. These are for example, the doctrines of the Trinity, of Christs' atonement for sin, of the total depravity of man &c. &c. At least three or four sects which have all some followers in our state, and some of them powerful for numbers in other states, consider these doctrines which lay at the foundation of all we say, and mingle necessarily and leadingly with every religious service we perform, as unscriptural, irrational and in Part even idolatrous. Now in preaching a common religion, in which from the very terms of the resolutions, such views seem to be necessarily excluded, we must either violate our own consciences by omitting all these vital principles or else violate our honor, by preaching what the preamble and resolutions appear so obviously to forbid. Such at least has been the impression made upon our minds, by an examination of the subject, and we now await your explanation.

"2nd. Is it meant by the resolutions of the honorable body of which you are the organ, that the only reason for making this arrangement to supply the stated religious services of the Chapel, was the want of time on the part of the President to attend to their performance?

"It is required as stated by the board, by the laws of the University, that the President, or in his absence one of the Professors, perform divine service on every Sabbath at least once, in the Chapel of the University &c. &c. This duty it is said in the preamble, was discharged for a considerable time by the President, when at his own request he was permitted in consequence of his numerous duties in the superintendence of the establishment, and in its general improvement, as well as in various departments of instruction, to omit this public weekly labour. Yet the community, and even individuals connected with the government and inspection of the institution, have been in the habit of saying and thinking, that Mr. Holley could not preach with safety to the University, as he did not preach the religion of the State. This arrangement also goes to exclude Mr. Holley from any share in the public religious instruction of the youth, though in the rotation, such a service could not be oppressive.—And it is said that an improvement can be made in the former arrangement—that it is an object of general solicitude and of general desire and expectation &c. &c. Now the former seems to rest his exclusion entirely on the ground of other employments preventing his discharge of this duty;—while the latter would seem to import that the interests of the establishment called for that exclusion. In the former case we should by the very first step we take, bring ourselves to a ministerial level with the President as his substitutes. And in this view we must say that however inferior to him as men, we cannot as Ministers of Jesus Christ, assume any attitude which would recognize his Ministerial character, or rank ourselves with him, as religious instructers.

"We beg therefore to be informed as to the understanding of the Board on this point. And lastly.

"Is it expected that our appearance before the youth of the University in this way, will involve any compromise with the President on the points now at issue before the public?

"It is known to your honorable body that we disapprove many of the President's leading religious opinions, and habits of life, as disqualifying him to be the sound and safe religious instructer in Christian precept or Christian example. With these views, while we feel the deepest desire for the best instruction of our youth, we shall feel most unwilling to take any step which may involve or be considered to involve our approbation or compromise, or withdrawal of our objections on these defective and dangerous features of his public character.

"We respectfully therefore present to the Board through you, sir, these enquiries, on which we solicit information. On their reply to these, our decision or the invitation with which they have honored us, will entirely depend.

"With sentiments of high consideration, your obedient servants."[400]

———

The publicity given in the public prints to the preamble and resolutions of the Board of Trustees, in which the Ministers of all the Churches in Lexington, were invited to participate in the religious duties in the Chapel of the University, naturally excited an enquiry, whether any would decline accepting that invitation, and if they did, the reason. In all the proceedings, of the Trustees in relation to this new project, every act that could have evinced personal feeling towards those who were considered hostile to Mr. Holley, appears to have been studiously avoided; and how to act on the receipt of the above answer to the letter of their Chairman, presented some difficulty. The writers of this letter were Clergy men of high respectability, and therefore an answer to their letter could not be prudently neglected; and to enter into a defence of Mr. Holley's religious principles, which engrossed the greater part of the interrogatories contained in the reply, was deemed improper. The Trustees after some reflection on the subject, desired their Chairman to return the following response.

"LEXINGTON, May, 1824.

"Gentlemen.—You reply to the letter of invitation, which I wrote to you, requesting you to participate in conducting the religious exercises in the Chapel of Transylvania University, I laid before the board of Trustees, who, for answer, have directed me to say to you, that the method for religious instruction adopted, was not designed to involve an investigation of the orthodoxy of any sect or denomination of persons, or to institute an enquiry into the religious tenets of any individual. The principles of each denomination are known by their confessions of faith and books of discipline, and it is expected by the Board that each preacher, who may occupy the Chapel, will preach religious truth, as he understands it, in sincerity.

"In relation to the religious interests of the institution, the Board desire to pursue as impartial a course of conduct towards the different denominations as will comport with the divine truth of the Scriptures.

"They deem it important in a State University, that the President, as well as all the teachers and officers, be secured, as far as possible against the sectarian jealousies attendant on religious instruction, and have thought it expedient, in accordance with the plan submitted to the Board by the President and the Professors of the Academical Faculty, and which has been printed and transmitted to you, in common with others, to give opportunity to the members of the several denominations to serve the University and the cause of divine truth by taking their turns in conducting the religious exercises of the Chapel.

"The Board are not indifferent about the religion to be taught. They design, as they have expressed it, that the pure religion of the Bible be included, Several members of the Board of different denominations are preachers of the Gospel, and are as zealous, and as much in earnest, as you can be, for the success of the fundamental principle of divine truth, which you in common with ourselves profess. We do not expect you to be answerable for the orthodoxy of any other person or persons, in the part which you are invited to take; nor is it understood that a compromise of the religious sentiments of any individual, who may fill the desk, in which he may differ from any other person will be made in his appearance before the youth of the University; but it is expected that each Clergyman will heartily cooperate with the Board of Trustees in endeavouring to advance the best interests of the institution by preaching the everlasting truths of the Bible, and that the desk will not be prostituted to the unhallowed purpose of religious controversy or personal abuse.

"The Board refer you to the preamble and resolutions transmitted to you with my former communication as the only answer, which they deem it necessary to make, considering as not compatible, either with their duty or dignity, to take notice in this case of any interrogatories or statements, which may be improper in their nature or spirit, The Board are the more satisfied with the propriety and utility of the course, which they have pursued, as they have the pleasure to find, that all the other denominations, with which they have had correspondence, the Roman Catholic, the Episcopalian, the Baptist, and the Methodist Episcopal, have approved the plan adopted, and promptly accepted of the invitation to aid the University in performing this interesting service.

    "Yours respectfully,   JOHN BRADFORD, Chairman."[401]

A response was given to the above letter of the Chairman, in which a final refusal to accept the invitation to preach in the Chapel, was announced.

    Those Ministers of the Gospel, who promptly accepted the invitation to preach in the Chapel of the University, continued their services but a very short time; so that the benefits so confidently expected, by the Trustees, to result from the measure, entirely failed; therefore Mr. Holley came to the determination to resign his appointment as President, at the close of the next session, of which determination he notified the Trustees on the ——— day of ———.

    In consequence of the resignation of the President, it became the duty of the Trustees to make use of every measure they could devise to fill the vacancy, by the time the Chair should become empty, but without effect. Mr. Holley was therefore invited to continue another session, to enable the Trustees to supply his place, to which he assented; but having made arrangements to go to Europe by the way of New Orleans, at which place he would be necessarily detained some time, he applied to the Board of Trustees to permit him to withdraw from the University before the end of the session, to enable him to leave New Orleans before the approach of the sickly season, to which the Trustees assented, and on the 24th day of March 1827, received his final resignation, accompanied with the follow ing very interesting address.

                      (To be continued in our next)

The Holley Legacy
[March 14, 1828]

At a meeting of the board of Trustees of Transylvania University, on the 24th of March, 1827, Mr. Holley read a report of the present situation of the University, which was received, and entered of record.

"To the Honourable Board of Trustees of Transylvania University.

"Gentlemen—My term of office as President of Transylvania University being ended, by your acceptance of my resignation, and a committee of your respectable body, having examined the condition of the institution, I beg leave to offer to you my final report, and in form, to surrender into your hands, the highly important trust, with which you were pleased, nearly nine years since, to invest me, under circumstances that lose none of their interest by their connexion with the present. The state of the institution, may be considered in the following order: The number of students for the present session; the condition of the grounds and buildings; the Libraries, apparatus and cabinets; the course of studies; the number of graduates from the beginning; some of the events of the University.

"I. The number of students for the present session. This number is 286, constituted in the following manner: Medical class 190, Seniors 22, Juniors 12, Sophomores 11, Freshmen 10, Preparatory Department 39, Private pupils in the building 2. A catalogue of the names of this number would, according to custom, have been printed in January, had not the session been divided into two for the year. It was my design to have one printed in the course of May next, had I continued in the University. As the Trustees have, by a deliberate vote, returned to the old plan of one session for the year, it remains with them to determine whether a catalogue shall now be published. I have prepared one in manuscript, which is complete, and which accompanies this report.—How many may be found in the classes, under present circumstances, will be reported to you by the Academical Faculty, or by my successor.

"Had there not been a resignation of the Presidency in January 1826, an early period of the session, the news of which spread of course, among the community, and especially in the South, whence we have been accustomed to receive many pupils; and had the gentlemen accepted the offices, to which they were appointed in the law department, upon the excellent plan of multiplying the professorships for the division of labour, and the greater perfection of the instruction; we have abundant reason in testimony of the best character from various quarters, to believe that, notwithstanding the increase of schools and colleges, and pecuniary pressure of the times, our whole number would be very little, if at all less, during the present session, than at any former period.

"II. The condition of the grounds and buildings. Without having seen the report of the committee, I trust I may safely refer to it for evidence, that these are in good order. In the whole establishment, there is not a pane of glass out; the rooms are all clean and inhabitable; the grounds are smooth and have been recently well raked, the gates and fences are as perfect as their age will permit; the pavements are in excellent preservation, and the refectory, with its appurtenances, is fit for immediate occupancy, and is one of the most convenient and agreeable residences in town. The North and West corners, are indeed, sometimes penetrated with rain, and require a little attention from the house wright, to remedy the evil.

"III. The Libraries, Apparatus and Cabinet. In regard to the Libraries, I here present an extract from the report of the last joint committee of both houses of our legislature, appointed to examine the University in all its departments: Law 430 volumes, Medical 2500, Academical 2400, total 5430 [*sic*, actually 5330]. In addition to these, there are about 1000 in the libraries of the two College societies, and about 6000 in the town Library, thus making between 12,000 and 13,000 volumes, to which students can have access, independently of the book stores, and private collections. Of the books belonging to the University, FIVE SIXTHS have been obtained under the present administration of the affairs of the institution, or since the year 1818, when the legislature took it into their more immediate protection. Besides donations which have been numerous, books to the amount of $14775, in the currency of the state, have been placed upon our shelves. Nearly every one of our valuable works in science and criticism, is included in this number. Some additions have been made to each of these libraries, since the report to the legislative Committee. The Medical library now contains between 3000 and 4000 volumes.

"The aparatus in the department of Mathematics and Natural Philosophy, has been greatly enriched, within the present year, by the importation of many valuable and important instruments from France. The Morrison Professor is preparing a complete catalogue of these, and of instruments which we before possessed, and will soon lay it upon your table. The aparatus in the care of the Chemical Professor, and the Anatomical Museum, are in the same condition as mentioned in my last report.

"The cabinet of Minerals, with various specimens of Indian antiquities, which was deposited in the University, by the heirs of John D. Clifford, has been sold, and removed; but nearly two hundred interesting specimens of domestic Minerals have just been received, as a present from Doctor Fowler, of New Jersey, and are now in our cases.

"IV. The course of study. This appears in extenso, at the end of the printed catalogue, which accompanies my report. It is full, and is found, on experiment, to be well arranged, and well adapted to the state of the institution. It has been increased from time to time, until it is equal, as it is believed, to that of our oldest and best seminaries.—The best books are generally such as are likely to continue a long time in favour. The deficiency in regard to the course of study in one particular, will be mentioned in another place.

"V. The number of graduates from the beginning are 580: Bachelors of Arts 182, Masters of Arts 76, those who have received honorary degrees 40, Medical graduates 327, Law graduates 41—Living about 550.

"The first degree conferred by the institution, was in 1802, sixteen years before the regeneration of the University in 1818. In all that time, only 22 persons, as far as the records show, received the honours of Transylvania. Since that date, within a period of less than nine years, and although the course of study has been greatly extended, and the examinations rendered much more severe and exact, 558 alumni have sought and received Academical honours at our hands, and have carried with them, the testimony of our signatures into every part of the community. I should be justly charged with responsibility, if I did not state the fact with pride, and remember it with delight, while I reflect with gratitude upon your constant co-operation, and that of my able and faithful colleagues, in the responsible task of instruction. This alone is, and will be considered by the candid public, as a full and unanswerable refutation of the calumnies, which our enemies have invented, and industriously circulated. We are satisfied with the contrast.—Are they?

"VI. Some of the wants of the University—These may be briefly enumerated.—The revival of the Law school, with increased Professorships, a Professorship of Modern languages, especially of the French and Spanish, a Gymnassium, with a suitable extent of ground for the requisite variety of exercises, both useful and ornamental, a provision for the continued increase of the Academical and law Libraries, and the Cabinet of Minerals and the foundation of a gallery, as soon as practicable, for the reception of the productions of genius, in the arts of sculpture, painting and engraving.

"In regard to the first of these wants, the revival of the law school with increased Professorships, my opinion remains the same, as when the subject was discussed at large before the board. Your deliberations then resulted in the determination to establish four Professorships; to have a short law session at the University for public lectures, with the understanding that the interval would be spent by the student in a law office, or in legal study with some competent jurist; to have one of the Professors from Louisiana, where the civil law is adopted; & to have particular attention paid to the science of political economy and legislation. This plan has met with very general, if not with universal approbation, and has drawn forth in letters, now in my possession, the most explicit praise from a distinguished lawyer and statesman of Louisiana, and from an able and successful lecturer on the science of jurisprudence in Maryland.

"I have unquestionable evidence, that very many young men are ready to enrol their names as members of the law school of Transylvania, were it revived on this plan, and put into immediate operation.

"The importance of a Professorship of Modern languages, especially of the French and Spanish, has long been felt and often mentioned among yourselves. Our position with regard to Spanish America, our increasing intercourse with its States and Governments, and their importance to our commercial and political advancement, together with the bearing which their efforts must have upon the common cause of civil and religious liberty, all point to the propriety of attending immediately and fully to their language, while we offer suitable inducements to lead them to attend, in the same way, to ours, that we may extensively benefit each other, and both do our duty, in relation to the great interests of mankind.

"The French is called for, not only as in an eminent degree, the language of polite life, diplomacy, Mathematics, Physics, and modern Tactics, but because it contains as valuable and various literature, as any language in the world, not excepting even our own.

"It is acknowledged by all, to be indispensible to a successful and agreeable intercourse with different countries. A knowledge of it is now demanded by public opinion, for an accomplished scholar.

"Gymnastics have already begun to occupy a space in the eyes of the friends and patrons of education in our country, that their course to popular favour cannot be arrested; and no institution can expect to maintain a successful competition before the community, without a provision for this department of the physical formation of character. Indeed and happily, Physical education has advanced in importance, just in proportion to the progress of sound philosophy. It is astonishing, that more attention has not been paid to it, in the systems of instruction, both in England and America. Workshops, the labour of the garden and the field, the exercises of the Circus, the tennis court the dancing hall and fencing room, with an area for Military drilling and accomplishments, besides many other modes of exertion, are naturally suggested under this head. We have always suffered for want of an extensive play ground, and of adequate motives to call out our students regularly and effectually to these vigorous and manly exercises. A suitable establishment of this kind is as favourable to good morals, and to intellectual advancement, as it is to the health and strength of the body. The lawn in front of the University hall, where these exercises have been forbidden, remains in my opinion still unsuited to them, and ought to be appropriated, as it has been, to walking, conversation, reflection and other purposes, not calculated to annoy the occupants of the public or private rooms of the building.

"In reference to the libraries, we want a much greater supply of works in modern civil law and politics; in general history, and especially the histories of our own states, in criticism, poetry and the arts, in Mathematics and in general Literature.—Although we have many good dictionaries, there are still more and better, of which we are in want. This supply is not so much for our under graduates, as for the graduated classes, and the Professors.

"A gallery for the productions of genius, in sculpture, painting, and engraving, is of course not suggested as an article of necessity, or of equal importance with those which have been already enumerated; but as a department highly interesting and desirable, in the contemplation of the ultimate perfection, to which we hope Transylvania will attain.

"It is not to be supposed that much would be done in this way, even if a depository were established, and yet were there such an apartment, and were but moderate exertions to be made, by the friends of the institution, donations, as I have had occasion to know on other subjects, would multiply beyond the first conception of any of you; and a collection of works, would be insensibly formed, that would be of the greatest service in the cultivation of taste, and the promotion of a legitimate enjoyment.

"It is with great respect and deference, that I make these suggestions, and leave them with your better judgment, and your united wisdom. They have occupied my mind often, for years, and I have continually looked forward to a period when our means would allow us to put them into execution.—Our personal and local jealousies, our political contentions and our sectarian divisions, have thus far prevented a result which all enlightened men must acknowledge to be eminently desirable.

"If you gentlemen Trustees, now ask me, 'must we, or the town, or the county provide the pecuniary means adequate to these effects,' I frankly and decidedly answer, no. You cannot do all that is required, nor the half, nor quarter, nor sixteenth. The town can do something, the county more, but no one section of the community ought to have this burden cast upon it, and most unquestionably no one section will assume or consent to it. This is a state institution, declared so repeatedly and solemnly by the state itself, assembled in its representatives; and they will doubtless refuse to let it pass out of their hands. What then is the result?—Plainly this, the state must endow it amply; and endow it speedily or bear the disgrace of its decline, and perhaps of its fall. Individual efforts has heretofore chiefly maintained it, and large subscriptions have been collected from among yourselves and your neighbours. This resource is exhausted, or nearly so; and especially the motives are wanting which are to rekindle private exertions; unless the commonwealth, shall see its true interests in this particular, and act correspondingly. Useful and successful as Transylvania has been, and to a certain extent may continue to be, it can never maintain its eminence, and continue to reflect lustre on the state, while it levies and collects contributions among its sister states.

"Gentlemen—I rejoice to be able to state with truth and sincerity, that we have lived, met, and acted, in harmony, and in mutual confidence, for the whole time of our administration of the affairs of the University, since my connexion with it.—You have generously and promptly sustained me in all the trials incident to my office & have given to me, in private life, the hand of sympathy and friendship. My days have been happy among you and I part from you with the sincerest eviction and regret, a regret softened indeed, but not prevented, by the various and exhilerating prospects before me. Allow me to assure you of my unalterable attachments, and my continued regard for the interests of Transylvania University.

"May God bless you, myself and the institution, and its friends and alumni, whereever in his providence he may cast them.

"HORACE HOLLEY.[402]

"Lexington Ky. March 24, 1827."

John Bradford, Richard H. Chinn and Thomas Bodley were appointed by the Board of Trustees, for the purpose of expressing to Dr. Holley, their approbation of his administration of Transylvania; who drafted the following address to Mr. Holley, which was unanimously concurred in.[403]

"March 24th, 1827

"Dear Sir—The Trustees of Transylvania University, being deeply impressed with a sense of the value and importance of your faithful and distinguished services in presiding over the institution for nearly nine years past, have appointed the undersigned, a committee to express to you their decided approbation of the course you have pursued, in the discharge of the arduous duties which devolved upon you.

"When they recollect that during the sixteen years which preceded your coming among us, that only twenty two persons received the collegiate honours of this institution, and that during your comparatively short stay, five hundred and fifty eight young men have graduated and gone forth into the world, learned, enlightened and adorned, and who are now the pride and ornaments of our common country, they cannot but deeply regret the causes which have induced you to separate yourself from the institution.

"Within the walls of Transylvania, the fond recollections of the polite, kind, generous, learned accomplished and much loved President will never perish.

"The patronage of the Commonwealth may be withdrawn, the institution may decline, the walls themselves may be crumbled; but so long as the name remains, there will be associated with it, those remembrances that flow from mutual attachments; or have a habitation in the hearts of those who are susceptible of the emotions of gratitude.

"To whatever clime your destiny may direct you, you will be pursued by the esteem and confidence of those, who have been so long and so intimately associated with you, and whom we, on this occasion, represent. Farewell.

"JOHN BRADFORD, R.H. CHINN, THOS. BODLEY, Committee,[404]
"To Horace Holley, D.D. & L.L.D."

SECTION 56

"A Numerous Meeting of Respectable People"

[November 7, 1828]

The feelings and disposition of the people of Kentucky in the month of May 1794, respecting the navigation of the Mississippi and the occupying of military posts by the British, within the boundary of the United States, from which the Indians were furnished with arms and ammunition to enable them to murder our citizens, are plainly developed in the following proceedings.

"On Saturday the 24th May 1794, a numerous meeting of respectable citizens from different parts of this state assembled in Lexington; and after taking into consideration the degraded and deserted situation of this country, both as to its commerce and protection; and coolly deliberating thereon—the following resolutions were adopted:—

"I. Resolved, That the inhabitants West of the Apalachian mountains, are entitled by nature and by stipulation, to the free and undisturbed navigation of the river Mississippi.

"II. That from the year 1783 until this time, the enjoyment of this right has been uniformly prevented by the Spaniards.

"III. That the General Government whose duty it was to have put us in possession of this right, have, either through design or mistaken policy, adopted no effectual measures for its attainment.

"IV. That even the measures they have adopted, have been uniformly concealed from us, and veiled in mysterious secrecy.

"V. That civil liberty is prostituted, when the servants of the people are suffered to tell their masters, that communications which they may judge important, ought not to be intrusted to them.

"VI. That we have a right to expect and demand, that Spain should be compelled immediately to acknowledge our right, or that an end be put to all negotiations on that subject.

"VII. That the injuries and insults done and offered by Great Britain to America, call loudly for redress; and that we will, to the utmost of our abilities, support the General Government in any attemt to obtain redress.

"VIII. That as the voice of all Eastern America has now called on the President of the United States to demand that redress of Great Britain; Western America has a right to expect and demand, that nothing shall be considered as a satisfaction, that does not completely remove their grievances; which have a stronger claim to satisfaction, both from their atrocity and continuance.

"IX. That the recent appointment of the *enemy* of the Western country, to negotiate with that nation, and the tame submission of the General Government, when *we* alone were injured by Great Britain, make it highly necessary, that we should at the time, state our just demands to the president and Congress.

"X. That the inhabitants of the Western Country have a right to demand, that their frontiers be protected by the General Government, and that the total want of that protection which they now experience, is a grievance of the greatest magnitude.

"XI. That the attainment and security of these our rights, is the common cause of the Western people, and that we will unite with them in any measures that may be most expedient for that purpose.

"XII. Resolved, as our opinion, that measures ought to be taken, to obtain the sense of the inhabitants of this state at large, that no doubt may be entertained of their opinions and determinations on these important subjects; that we may be able, when it shall be necessary, to communicate as a state, with the other inhabitants of the Western Country.

"XIII. Resolved; That it be recommended to each county in the state, to appoint a committee, to give and receive communications on these subjects; to call meetings of their counties, and when it may be judged expedient to call upon the people to elect proper persons to represent them in convention, for the purpose of deliberating on the steps which will be most expedient for the attainment and security of our just rights.

"By direction and in behalf of the meeting of the citizens of the state of Kentucky.

Attest   "GEORGE MEETER [Müter], Ch'mn."[405]
                                              JOHN BRADFORD, Clerk.

Lexington, May 28, 1794."

The following remonstrance was drawn up and published for the purpose of obtaining signatures:

"To the PRESIDENT and CONGRESS of the
UNITED STATES OF AMERICA.

"The REMONSTRANCE of the subscribers, citizens of the Commonwealth of KENTUCKY, sheweth:

"That your remonstrants have observed with concern and indignation, the injuries and insults offered to the United States by the King of Great Britain. He has violated in important parts, the treaty of peace, the observance of which might have obliterated the remembrance of former injuries. He has, by means of his agents, supplied arms, ammunition, clothing and provisions to those merciless savages, who have so long ravaged the Western frontier of these States.—He has interposed, unsolicited, and negotiated truces for Portugal and Holland, with the piratical states, in order to turn the rapine of those African barbarians solely on the American commerce. His vessels of war, and the piratical vessels of his subjects, by his orders, in violation of the law of nations, have despoiled the commerce and insulted the neutral flag of America. He has made no compensation for the property of citizens of these states, carried away by his troops contrary to treaty. And, that we might escape no species of injury which could be heaped on the weakest and most despicable of nations, he holds within the territory of the United States, in defiance of treaty and of right, posts fortified and garrisoned by his armies.

"That these injuries and insults call loudly for redress, and that we will, to the utmost of our abilities and in any mode that can be devised, support the General Government, in the firmest and most effectual measures, to obtain full satisfaction for all our wrongs.

"That your remonstrants and the other inhabitants of the United States west of the Alleghany and Appalachian mountains, are entitled by nature and stipulation, to the free and undisturbed navigation of the river Mississippi; and that from the year 1783 to this day, they have been uniformly prevented by the Spanish King, from exercising that right. Your remonstrants have observed with concern that the General Government, whose duty it was to have preserved that right, have used no effectual measures for its attainment. That even their tardy and ineffectual negotiations have been veiled with the most mysterious secrecy. That that secrecy is a violation of the political rights of the citizen, as it declares, that the people are unfit to be entrusted with important facts relative to their rights, and that their servants may retain from them the knowledge of those facts. Eight years are fully sufficient for the discussion of the most doubtful and disputable claim; the right to the navigation of the Mississippi, admits of neither doubt or dispute. Your remonstrants, therefore, conceive that the negotiations on that subject have been unnecessarily lengthy and they expect, that it be demanded, categorically of the Spanish King, whether he will acknowledge the right of the citizens of the United States to the free and uninterrupted navigation of the river Mississippi, and cause all obstructions, interruptions and hindrance to the exercise of that right in future to be withdrawn and avoided; that immediate answer thereto be required; and that such answer be the final period of all negotiations upon this subject.

"Your remonstrants further represent, that the encroachment of the Spaniards on the territory of the United States, is a striking and melancholy proof of the situation to which our country will be reduced, if a tame policy should still continue to direct our councils.

"Your remonstrants join their voice to that of their fellow citizens in the Atlantic states, calling for satisfaction for the injuries and insults offered to America, and they expect that such satisfaction will extend to every injury and insult, done or offered, to any part of America by Great Britain and Spain, and as the detention of the posts and the interruption of the navigation of the Mississippi, are injuries and insults of the greatest atrocity, and of the longest duration, they require the most particular attention to those subjects.

"Your remonstrants declare that it is the duty of the General Government to protect the frontiers, and that the total want of protection which is now experienced by every part of the Western frontier, is a grievance of the greatest magnitude and demands immediate redress.

"*Si vultus tibi, monstrata radice vel Herba non ficret levius, fugeres radice vel Herba Proficiente nihil curiarier—*

Hor Ep. 2 v. 149.

"Suppose you had a wound, and one had show'd
An herb, which you applyed but found no good,
Would you grow fond of this, increase your pain,
And use the poisonous medicine again?"

The late appointment of John Jay as envoy extraordinary to the Court of London, brought so strongly to the recollection of the people of this country, his former iniquitous attempt to barter away their most valuable right, that they could not refrain from testifying their abhorrence of the man, whose appointment at this critical period of their affairs, they consider as tragically ominous. Although they had not forgotten, nor even faintly remembered his former act of treason against them; yet they hoped, from the office he filled, he was in as harmless a situation as he could be placed; and that no effort of power or policy, could drag him forward, so long as he held his office, and set him once more to chaffering with our rights. With these impressions, a number of respectable citizens of Lexington and its vicinity, on May 31st 1794, ordered a likeness of this evil genius of Western America to be made, which was soon well executed. At the appointed hour he was ushered forth from a barber's shop, amidst the shouts of the people, dressed in a *courtly* manner and placed erect on a platform of the pillory. In his right hand, he held uplifted a rod of iron; in his left he held extended, Swift's late speech in Congress on the subject of British depredations. On one side of which was written,

Nemo repente fecit turpissimus.—Juv. Lat. 2 v. 33.

No man e'er reached the heights of vice at first.

—*Non deficit alter*. Virg. AEo. 6.

A *second* is not wanting.

About his neck was suspended by a *hempen* string, "Adams' defence of the American constitution;" on the cover of which was written—

Scribere jussit Aurum. OV. Ep.

Gold bade me write.

After exhibiting him in this condition for some time, he was ordered to be guilotined, which was soon dexterously executed, and a flame instantly applied to him, which finding its way to a quantity of powder, which was lodged in his body produced such an explosion, that after it, there was scarcely to be found a particle of the *disjecta membra Plenipo*.[406]

On the 15th of May 1794, the Indians defeated a company on their way from the Crab Orchard through the Wilderness, a small distance beyond Rock Castle, four of whom were killed and two wounded.

On the 23rd, they killed a family, about 12 miles from Shelbyville.[407]

SECTION 57

British Encroachment
in the Northwest
[November 14, 1828]

On the 6th June, 1794, the Indians killed a man at Mann's lick—On the 7th, they killed another within 4 miles of the same place.—On the 8th, they stole eight horses from the force of Salt River; and about the same time, killed two men and wounded another on Brashear's creek.[408]

The following is the notice taken by the President and Congress of the United States, of the speech delivered to the Indian deputies from the Miami's, at the Castle of St. Lewis in the city of Quebec, and which was published in these notes, Section 51.

"United States, May 21st 1794.
"Gentlemen of the Senate and of the House of Representatives.

"I lay before you certain information, whereby it would appear, that some encroachment was about to be made on our territory by an officer and party of British troops. Proceeding upon a supposition of the authenticity of this information, although of a private nature, I have caused the representation to be made to the British Minister, a copy of which accompanies this message.

"It cannot be necessary to comment upon the very serious nature of such an encroachment, nor to urge that this new state of things suggests the propriety of placing the United States in a posture of effectual preparation for an event, which, notwithstanding the endeavours making to avert it, may by circumstances beyond our control, be forced upon us.
GEO. WASHINGTON."[409]

"In the SENATE, May 28th, 1794.
"ORDERED, that the Message of the President of the United States of this day, with the communications referred to therein, together with the communications referred to in the message of the President of the United States of the 21st inst. be printed for the use of the Senate.
"Attest,   SAM. A. OTIS, Sec'y."

"*UNITED STATES, May 23, 1794.*

"Gentlemen of the Senate, and of the House of Representatives.

"I lay before you the copy of a letter from the Minister Plenipotentiary of his Britanic Majesty, in answer to a letter from the Secretary of State, communicated to Congress yesterday; and also the copy of a letter from the Secretary, which is referred to in the above mentioned letter of the Minister.   GEO. WASHINGTON."[410]

Copy of a letter from the Secretary of State of the United States:

"PHILADELPHIA, May 20th, 1794.

"SIR—It cannot be unknown to you that a speech, said to be addressed on the 10th day of February 1794, to several Indian nations, and ascribed to the governor-general of his Britanic majesty at Quebec, has appeared in most of the public prints in the United States. With so many circumstances of authenticity, after remaining so long without contradiction, it might have justified us in inquiring of you, whether it was really delivered under the British authority.—Our forbearance thus to inquire, is conformable with the moderation which has directed the conduct of our government towards Great Britain; and dictates, at the same time, our hope, from the dictation of yours that its views would prove ultimately pacific, and that it would discountenance every measure of its officers having a contrary tendency.

"Even now, sir, while I entertain a firm persuasion, that in assuming this speech to be genuine, I cannot well err, I shall be ready to retract the comments which I am about to make, if you shall think proper to deny its authenticity.

"At the very moment when the British ministry were forwarding assurances of goodwill, does Lord Dorchester foster and encourage in the Indians, hostile dispositions toward the United States. If it was a part of the American character to indulge suspicion, what might not be conjectured *as to the influence* by which our treaty was defeated in the last year, from the assembling of deputies from almost all the nations who were at the late general council on the Miami, and whose enmity against us cannot be doubtful? How nearly would that suspicion approach to proof, were we to recollect, that so high an officer as himself, would not calmly hazzard this expression: 'I should not be surprised, if we are at war with the United States in the course of the present year; and if we are a line must then be drawn by the warriors.'

"But this speech only forbodes hostility; the intelligence which has been received this morning, is, if true, *hostility itself*. The President of the United States, has understood, through channels of real confidence, that governor Simcoe, has gone to the foot of the Rapids of the Miami, followed by three companies of a British regiment; in order to build a fort there.

"Permit me then to ask, whether these things be so? It has been usual, for each party to a negotiation, to pay such a deference to the pretensions of the other, as to keep their affairs in the same posture, until the negotiation was concluded. On this principle, you complained, in your letter of the 5th July, 1792, of the jurisdiction attempted to be exercised, under the State of Vermont, within the district occupied by the troops of your king; and demanded that our government should suppress it, from respect to the discussion which was pending. On this principle, you were assured, that proper measures should be adopted. On the same principle, you renew on the 10th of March, 1794, a similar application; and are answered, that the measures of the government should correspond with its assurances. Accordingly, although the forts, garrisons and districts, to which your letters relate, are confessedly within the limits of the United States, yet have our citizens been forbidden to interrupt you in the occupancy of them. What return then, have we a right to expect?

"But you will not suppose that I put the impropriety of the present aggression upon the pendency of the negotiation. I quote this only to show the contrast between the conduct observed on your part towards us, and on our part towards you. This possession of our acknowledged territory, has no pretext of *statu quo* on its side; it has no pretext at all. It is an act, the *hostility of which cannot be palliated* by any connexion with that negotiation. It is calculated to support any enemy whom we are seeking to bring to peace.

"A late mission of the United States to Great Britain, is an unequivocal proof, after all that has happened, of the sincere wish of our government to preserve peace, and a good understanding with your nation. But our honour and safety require that *an invasion shall be repelled*.

"Let me therefore, inform you, sir, that I have it in charge from the President of the United States, to request and urge you to take immediate and effectual measures, as far as in you lie to suppress these hostile movements; to call to mind, that the army of the United States, in their march against the enemy, will not be able to distinguish between *them and any other* people associated in the war; to compare these encroachments with the candour of our conduct, and the doctrines which you have maintained; and to admonish those who shall throw obstacles in the way of negotiation, and tranquility, that they will be responsible for all the unhappy consequences.

"I have the honour to be, with respect, sir, your obedient servant;
(signed)   "EDM. RANDOLPH."[411]
"Mr. HAMMOND, *Minister Plenipotentiary of his Britannic Majesty.*"

HAMMOND'S ANSWER.

"PHILADELPHIA, 22d May, 1794.

"SIR—In answer to your letter of the 20th current, which I did not receive until late in the afternoon of yesterday, it is necessary for me to premise, that whatever may be my personal opinion, with respect to the style and manner in which you have thought proper to address me, upon the present occasion, it is not my intention to offer any animadversion upon them; but to proceed with temper and candour to the examination of the subjects of your letter.

"Though I never can acknowledge the right of this government to require from me so categorically, as you have required it, an explanation of any measure emanating from the governor of Canada, over whose actions I have no control, and for whose conduct I am not responsible; I am willing to admit the authenticity of the speech to certain Indian nations, to which you have alluded, and which you have ascribed to the Governor-General of his majesty's possessions in North America. But in order to ascertain the precise sense of the only passage of that speech, to which you have reference, and of which you have given merely a partial citation, I shall quote the passage at length.

" 'CHILDREN—Since my return, I find no appearance of a line remains, and from the manner in which the people of the States push on and act, and talk on this side, and from what I learn of their conduct towards the sea, I shall not be surprised, if we are at war with them in the course of the present year; and if so, a line must then be drawn by the warriors.'

"From the context of this whole passage, it is manifest that Lord Dorchester was persuaded, that the aggression which might eventually lead to a state of hostility, had proceeded from the United States; and so far as the state of Vermont, to which I presume his lordship principally alluded, was implicated, I am convinced that that persuasion was not ill founded. For notwithstanding the positive assurances, which I received from your predecessor on the 9th of July 1791, in answer to my letter of the 5th of the same month, of the determination of the general government, to discourage and repress the encroachments, which the state and individuals of Vermont had committed on the territory occupied by his Majesty's garrisons, I assert with confidence, that not only those encroachments have never been in any manner repressed, but that recent infringments in that quarter, and on the territory in its vicinity, have been committed. Indeed, if this assertion of mine could require any corroboration, I would remark, that through the space of fifty days between my letter of the 10th of March, 1794, upon this subject, and your answer of the 29th of April 1794, you did not attempt to deny facts which I then stated, and which I now explicitly repeat.

"In regard to your declaration that 'Governor Simcoe has gone to the foot of the rapids of the Miami, followed by three companies of a British regiment, in order to build a fort there,' I have no intelligence that such an event had actually occurred. But even admitting your information to be accurate, much will depend on the place, in which you assert, that the fort is intended to be erected, and whether it be for the purpose of protecting subjects of his majesty residing in the districts dependent on the fort of Detroit, or of preventing that fortress from being straitened by the approach of the American army; to either of which cases I imagine that the principle of the *statu quo,* until the final arrangement of the points in discussion, between the two countries shall be concluded, will strictly apply. In order however, to correct any inaccurate information you may have received, or to avoid any ambiguity relative to this circumstance, I shall immediately transmit copies of your letter and of this answer, as well to the governor general of his Majesty's possessions in North America, and the Governor of Upper Canada, as to his Majesty's Mininters in England, for their respective information.

"Before I conclude this letter, I must be permitted to observe, that I have confined it to the unrepressed and continued aggressions of the State of Vermont, alone, the persuasion of Lord Dorchester, that they were indicative of an existing hostile disposition in the United States, against Great Britain, and might ultimately produce an actual state of war on their part. If I had been desirous of recurring to other sources of disquietude, I might, from the allusion of his Lordship to the conduct of this government towards 'the sea,' have deduced other motives or apprehension, on which from the solicitude you evince to establish a "contrast between the temper observed on your part towards us, and on our part towards you," I might have conceived myself justified in dilating. I might have adverted to the privateers originally fitted out at Charleston, at the commencement of the present hostilities, and which were allowed to depart from the port, not only with consent, but under the express permission of the governor of South Carolina.

"I might have adverted to the prizes made by these privateers, of which the legality was in some measure admitted, by the refusal of this government to restore such as were made antecedently to the 5th of June 1793. I might have adverted to the permission granted by this government to the commanders of the French ships of war, and of privateers, to dispose of their prizes by sale, in ports of the United States. I might have adverted to the two privateers, le Petit Democrat (now la Cornelia,) and the Carmagnot, both which were illegally fitted out in the river Delaware, and which in consequence of my remonstrances and of the assurances I received, I concluded would have been dismantled; but which have remained during the whole winter, in the port of New York armed, and now are, as I am informed, in a condition to proceed immediately to sea. I might have adverted to the conduct which this government has observed towards the powers combined against France in the enforcement of the embargo. For, while the vessels of the former are subjected to the restrictions of that measure, the latter have been permitted to depart from Hampton Roads though three weeks had elapsed subsequently to the imposition of the embargo, though they were chiefly laden with articles 'calculated to support an enemy whom we are seeking to bring to peace.' I might have adverted to the uniformly unfriendly treatment which his majesty's ships of war, and officers in his majesty's service, have, since the commencement of the present hostilities, experienced in the American ports. And lastly—I might have adverted to the unparalleled insult, which has been recently offered at New Port, Rhode Island, (not by a lawless collection of people,) but by the Governor and counsel of that state, to the British flag, in the violent measures pursued towards his Majesty's sloop of war Nautilus, and in the forcible detention of the officers by whom she was commanded. I have however, forborne to expatiate upon these points, because I am not disposed to consider them, as I have before stated, as necessary elucidations, of the immediate object of your letter, and much less to urge them in their present form, as general topicks of recrimination.

"I have the honor to be with great respect, sir, your most obedient humble servant.

(Signed)   "GEORGE HAMMOND."[412]

                         "PHILADELPHIA, April 29, 1794.
"SIR—Very soon after the receipt of your letter of the 10th ultimo, I took more than one opportunity of mentioning to you verbally, that the government of the United States was sincere and constant in its determination to fulfil its assurances, concerning the districts occupied by the British troops, and the acts of violence said to be committed under the authority of the State of Vermont, on the persons and property of British subjects, residing under the protection of your garrisons.

"I indeed promised to give you an answer in writing, at an earlier day than this. But being anxious to obtain particular information from a gentleman who was in town, well acquainted with the places to which you refer, and from some accident, not being able as yet, to lay my hands upon the letter of Mr. Jefferson to you, on the 9th July 1792, I was hopeful, that my personal declarations to you, would continue to receive such full confidence, as to afford sufficient opportunity for the most particular enquiry. But being disappointed in seeing that gentleman, I think it best to answer your letter, without further delay.

"I have it in charge from the President of the United States, again to assure you that his purpose to cultivate harmony with your nation, and to prevent the measures of which you complain in the above letters, continue unchanged. Orders will be therefore immediately repeated upon this point, to repress the violences which you state, and they shall be accompanied with an injunction to use against the refractors every coercion which the laws will permit. We have received no intelligence of the particular facts, to which you refer. But to prevent all unnecessary circuity in first inquiring into them and next transmitting to the city the result, the proper instructions will be given to act, without waiting for further directions.

"In these measures, sir, you will see a real disposition in us to friendship and good neighbourhood; and I shall be justified by your own recollection, when I claim the merit of our having been uniform in the same demonstrations.

"I have the honour to be, sir, with great respect, your most obedient servant,

(Signed)   "EDM. RANDOLPH.[413]

"MR. HAMMOND, Minister Plenipotentiary of Great Britain."

SECTION 58

The French Conspiracy

[November 28, 1828]

On the morning of the 30th of June 1794, an escort under the command of Maj. M'Mahan, were attacked by the Indians under the walls of Fort Recovery; their number were from ten to fifteen hundred; they assailed the fort in every direction, but were repulsed with great slaughter; they renewed the attack, but at a more respectful distance, keeping up a constant and very heavy fire the whole of the day, and at intervals during the night and following morning, but were compelled to retire between the hours of 12 and 2 o'clock, with loss and disgrace, from the very field where they had on a former occasion, been proudly victorious.

Our loss was 21 men killed, and 29 wounded; among the former were the gallant Maj. M'Mahan, the brave Capt. Hartshorne, Lieut. Craig and Cornet Torry; among the latter the intrepid Capt. Taylor of Dragoons, and Lieut. Drake, of the infantry.

In the course of the action, upwards of two hundred horses were killed or taken; but it is certain a considerable number of them were taken away laden with *dead Indians.*

The Indians could have received no information respecting this escort: Their object no doubt was, to attempt to carry the fort by a *coup de main*. Maj. Wells, who examined the ground occupied by the Indians the day and night previous to the attack, was of opinion, the Indians had double the number in this affair, that they had on the 4th of November, 1791.[414]

The following correspondence took place between the Secretary of State of the United States, and the Governor of Kentucky, respecting a contemplated enterprize against the Spanish dominion on the Mississippi, under the authority of the Government of France.

"To his excellency the Governor of Kentuckky:
"PHILADELPHIA, Aug. 29, 1793.
"SIR—The commissionars of Spain, residing here have complained to the President of the United States, that certain persons at this place, are taking measures, to excite the inhabitants of Kentucky to join in an enterprize against the Spanish dominions on the Mississippi; and in evidence of it have produced the printed address now inclosed. I have it therefore in charge from the President, to desire you to be particularly attentive to any attempts of this kind among the citizens of Kentucky; and if you shall have reason to believe any such enterprize meditated, that you put them on their guard against the consequences, as all acts of hostility committed by them on nations at peace with the United States, are forbidden by the laws, and will expose them to punishment: And that in every event, you take those legal measures, which shall be necessary to prevent any such enterprize.

"In addition to considerations respecting the peace of the general union, the special interests of the State of Kentucky, would be particularly committed; as nothing could be more inauspicious to them than such a movement, at the very moment when those interests are under negotiation between Spain and the United States.

"I have the honor to be, with the greatest respect and esteem, sir, &c.
TH: JEFFERSON."[415]

"KENTUCKY, October 5th 1793.
"SIR—I have just now been honoured with your favour of the 29th of August, wherein you observe that the Spanish commissioners have complained to the President of the United States, that certain persons are taking measures to excite the inhabitants of Kentucky to join in an enterprize against the Spanish dominions on the Mississippi. I think it my duty to take this early opportunity to assure you, that I shall be particularly attentive to prevent any attempts of that nature from this country. I am well persuaded, at present, none such is in contemplation in this State. The citizens of Kentucky, possess too just a sense of the obligations

they owe to the general government, to embark in any enterprize that would be so injurious to the United States.

"I have the honor to be, with very great respect and esteem, sir, &c.
"ISAAC SHELBY.
"The Honorable Thomas Jefferson, Esq. Secretary of State."

"To his Excellency the Governor of Kentucky:
"SIR—I have received from the Representatives of Spain here, information of which the following is the substance. That on the second of October, four Frenchmen of the names of La Chaise, Charles Delpeau, Mathurin and Gignoux, set out in the stage from Philadelphia for Kentucky; that they were authorised by the Minister of France here, to excite and engage as many as they could, whether of our citizens, or others on the road, or within your government, or any where else, to undertake an expedition against the Spanish settlements within our neighborhood, and in event to descend the Ohio and Mississippi, and attack New Orleans, where they expect some Naval co-operation: That they were furnished with money for those purposes and with blank commissions to be filled up at their discretion. I enclose you the description of these four persons in the very words in which it has been communicated to me.

"Having laid this information before the President of the United States, I have it in charge from him, to desire your particular attention to these persons, that they may not be permitted to excite within our territories, or carry from thence any hostilities into the territory of Spain. For this purpose it is more desirable that those peaceable means of coersion should be used which have been provided by the laws; such as the binding to good behaviour these, or any other persons exciting or engaged in these unlawful enterprizes, indicting them or resorting to such other legal process as those learned in the laws of your State may advise. When those fail, or are inadequate, suppression by the militia of the State has been ordered and practised in other States, I hope that the citizens of Kentucky, will not be decoyed into any participation in these illegal enterprises against the peace of their own country, by any effect they expect from them on the navigation of the Mississippi. Their good sense will tell them, that it is not to be effected by half measures of this kind, and that their surest dependence is on those regular measures which are pursued and will be pursued by the general government, and which flow from the united authority of all the States.

"I have the honor to be &c.   TH. JEFFERSON."
"Lesignalement du Sicur La Chaise, taille 5 peids 5 pouces, figure alongee, cheve a rond grand favrois, taille bien faite.

"Signalement de Delpeau, taille de 5 pieds 9 pouces, figure alongee, les yeux les once grand cheveaux alongee, un peu blonde, pale da la figure.

"Signale de Gignoux, taille 5 pieds 6 pouces cheveux et sourcils chaten, nes gros, bouche moyenue mentou ronde."[416]

JANUARY 13th, 1794.

"SIR—After the date of my last letter to you, I received information that a commission had been sent to General Clark, with powers to name and commission other officers, and to raise a body of men; no steps having been taken by him (as far as has come to my knowledge) to carry this plan into execution. I did not conceive it was either proper or necessary for me to do any thing in the business.

"Two Frenchmen, La Chaise and Delpeau have lately come into this State: I am told they declare, publicly, they are in daily expectation of receiving a supply of money, and that as soon as they do receive it, they shall raise a body of men and proceed with them down the river. Whether they have any sufficient reason to expect to get such a supply, or any serious intention of applying it in that manner if they do receive it, I can form no opinion.

"I judge it proper, as the President had directed you to write to me on this subject, to give you this information, that he may be apprised as I am of the steps which have been and are now taking here in this matter. If the President should hereafter think it necessary to hold any further communication with the executive of this State on this subject, I wish him to be full and explicit as to the part he wishes and expects me to act. That if what is required of me, should in my opinion, be within my constitutional powers, and in the line of my duty, I may hereafter have it in my power to shew that the steps which I may take were not only within my legal powers, but were also required by him.

"I have great doubts even if they do attempt to carry their plan into execution, (provided they manage their business with prudence) whether there is any legal authority to restrain or punish them, at least before they have actually accomplished it. For if it is lawful for any one citizen of this State, to leave it, it is equally so for any number to do it. It is also lawful for them to carry with them any quantity of provisions, arms and ammunition: and if the act is lawful in itself, there is nothing but the particular intention with which it is done that can possibly make it unlawful; but I know of no law which inflicts a punishment on intention only, or any criterion by which to decide what would be sufficient evidence of that intention, if it was a proper subject of a legal censure.

"I shall upon all occasions, be averse to the exercise of any power which I do not consider myself as being clearly and explicitly invested with; much less would I assume power to exercise it against men who I consider as friends and brethren; in favour of a man whom I view as an enemy and a tyrant. I shall also feel but little inclination to take an active part in punishing or restraing any of my fellow citizens for a supposed intention, only to gratify or remove the fears of the minister of a prince who openly withholds from us an invaluable right, and who secretly instigates against us a most savage and cruel enemy.

"But whatever may be my private opinion as a man, as a friend to liberty, an American citizen and an inhabitant of the Western waters, I shall at all times hold it as my duty to perform whatever may be constitutionally required of me as Governor of Kentucky, by the President of the United States.

"I have the honor to be, with very great respect, your most ob't serv'nt.   ISAAC SHELBY.[417]
"The Hon. Thomas Jefferson, esq. Secretary of State."

"FROM EDM. RANDOLPH.
"PHILADELPHIA, March 29, 1794.
"SIR—The letter which your excellency addressed to my predecessor on the 13th of January,1794, has been laid before the President of the United states, and I have it in charge from him to recal to your view the state of things with which it is connected.

"You were informed, sir, on the 29th of August 1793, that the commissioners of Spain had complained of attempts to excite the inhabitants of Kentucky to an enterprize against the Spanish dominions on the Mississippi; that the President requested you to be attentive to circumstances of this kind; that if such an enterprise was meditated, your citizens ought to be put on their guard against the consequences; and that you should adopt the necessary legal measures for preventing it; as acts of hostility committed by our citizens against nations at peace with the United States, were forbidden by the laws, and would subject the offenders to punishment.

"That every effectual exhortation might be combined with a sense of duty, it was at the same time represented to you, that 'in addition to considerations respecting the peace of the general Union, the special interests of the State of Kentucky, would be particularly committed; as nothing could be more inauspicious to them, than such a movement: the very moment when those interests were under negotiation between Spain and the United States.'

"Your excellency's answer on the 5th of October, 1793, gave a satisfactory assurance of your readiness to counteract any design from Kentucky against the Spanish dominions on the Mississippi; of your persuasion that none such was then in contemplation in your State; and of your citizens possessing too just a sense of the obligations, which they owe to the general government, to embark in any enterprize so injurious to the United States.

"It was, therefore, with full confidence in your zeal, that on the 6th of November, 1793, upon the representation of the commissioners of

Spain, you were farther informed, that on the 2nd of October, 1793, four Frenchmen of the names of La Chaise, Charles Delpeau, Mathurin and Gignoux, had set out in the Stage from Philadelphia to Kentucky, authorised by the then Minister of France here, to engage as many as they could, whether of our citizens, or others, on the road, or within your State, or elsewhere, to undertake an expedition against the Spanish settlements within our neighborhood, and in event to descend the Ohio and Mississippi, and to attack N. Orleans, where naval cooperation was expected; and that they were furnished with money for these purposes, and with blank commissions, to be filled up at their discretion. Your execellency was requested to check their hostilities, and in doing so to prefer those peaceable means of coersion which had been provided by the laws, (such as binding to good behaviour or indicting, or to resort to such other legal process, as those learned in the laws of your State might advise). The letter conveying the foregoing intelligence, proceeds thus: 'when these fail, or are inadequate, a suppression by the Militia of the State has been ordered and practised to other States. I hope the citizens of Kentucky will not be decoyed into any participation in these illegal enterprizes against the peace of the country by any effect which they may expect from them on the navigation of the Mississippi. Their good sense will tell them that it is not to be effected by half measures of this kind: and that their surest dependence is on those regular measures which are pursued, and will be pursued by the general Government, and which flow from the united authority of all the States.'

"After the impression made by your letter of the 5th of October 1793, you will naturally conclude, how difficult it was to reconcile it with your last of the 13th January, 1794.

"As the constitution and laws of the United States, are to govern the conduct of all; so cannot it well be imagined, that the President intended to impose upon your excellency any departure from them. You were asked to prefer peaceable means of coersion; and for the purpose to consult those who were learned in the laws of your State, to designate legal process. I shall not presume upon the imperfect knowledge, which can be obtained here, of the jurisprudence of Kentucky to determine, whether any, or what species of process was admissible. I beg leave to observe, that if in the opinion of the judges, no preventative or other step could be supported, the President required none. My Predecessor, in his letter of November 1793, arguing from what is usual in the United States; and recollecting what prevails in Virginia, many of the laws of which are understood to be incorporated in your code, naturally suggested the propriety of binding to good behaviour and indicting. And indeed what government can be so destitute of the means of self defence, as to suffer with impunity, its peace to be drawn into jeopardy by hostilities levied within its territory, against a foreign nation in order to be prostrated at the will of tumultuous individuals, and scenes of bloodshed and civil war to be introduced.

"You intimate a doubt, sir, whether the two Frenchmen La Chaise and Delpeau, can be restrained or punished, before they have actually accomqlished their plan, and assign as a reason for the doubt, that any number of your citizens may lawfully leave your State, and carry with them any quantity of provisions, arms and ammunition. Hence you conclude that these acts being lawful, a particular intention can not render them unlawful, and that no criterion exists for deciding such an intention. If there be no peculiarity in the laws of Kentucky, and it is allowable to reason from general principles, or an analogy [with] the practice of other States, we might expect from a candid revision of these sentiments that a contrary result would arise in your mind. That foreigners should meddle in the affairs of a government where they happen to be, has scarcely ever been tolerated, and is often severely punished. That foreigners should point the force of a nation against its will to objects of hostility, is an invasion of its dignity, its tranquility and even safety. Upon no principle can the individuals, on whom such guilt can be affixed, bid the government to wait, as your excellency would seem to suppose, until their numbers shall defy the ordinary animadversions of law: and until they are incapable of being subdued but by the force of arms.

"To prevent the extremity of crimes is wise and humane; and steps of precaution have therefore been found in the laws of most societies.

"Nor is this offence of foreigners, expiated or lessened by an appeal to a presumed right of the citizens of Kentucky, to enlist under such banners without the approbation of their country. In a government instituted for the happiness of the whole with a clear delineation of the channels in which the authority derived from them must flow, can a part only of the citizens, wrest the sword from the hands of those magistrates whom the whole had invested with the direction of the Military power? They may it is true, leave their country; they may take arms and provisions with them; but if these acts be done, not on the ground of mere personal liberty, but of being retained in a foreign service for purposes of enmity against another people: satisfaction will be demanded, and the State to which they belong cannot connive at their conduct, without hazzarding a rupture. The evidence of a culpable intention is perhaps not so difficult as your excellency imagines; it is at least a familiar enquiry in penal prosecutions, and ought not to be an objection to your interference on this occasion. But here suffer me to repeat, that the President wishes you to do nothing more than the laws themselves permit. Let them have their free course by such instructions as you think adequate and advisable; and I trust that they will prove competent to rescue the United States from a painful altercation with a foreign sovereign.

"As these unlawful assemblages of military force may assume various forms, Congress have not been unmindful, that the civil aim may some-times be unequal to the task of sustaining civil authority. They have therefore, by an act of May the 2nd 1792, conferred on the Marshals and their deputies, the same power in executing the laws of the United States, as Sheriffs and their deputies in the several States have by law in execut-ing the laws of their respective States; They have rendered it lawful for the President, in case of invasions to call forth the Militia, or to issue his or-ders for that purpose to such officer of the Militia as he shall think proper. They have empowered him to call forth the Militia of one State, for the suppression of an insurrection in another, under certain circumstances; and to subdue by the Militia any combination against the laws which may be too powerful for ordinary judicial proceedings.

"Thus far have I addressed your excellency upon the constitutional right of the government; which perhaps are in strictness the only topics, belonging to the present occasion. But as it may not be known that the navigation of the Mississippi has occupied the earliest labours of the executive, and has been pursued with an unremitted sincerity, I will lay before you a sketch of the pending negociation as may be communicated, consistently with the respect due to the nation in treaty with us, and the rules observed in such cases.

"The primary object in the instructions to Mr. Carmichael, who has resided for a considerable time at Madrid as Charge des Affairs of the United States, has been to throw open to your commerce that river to its mouth. In December 1791, it was *verbally* communicated to the Secretary of State by one of the commissioners of Spain here, that his Catholic Majesty, apprised of our solicitude to have some arrangements made respecting our free navigation of the Mississippi, and the use of a port thereon, was ready to enter into a treaty at Madrid. And great indeed was that solicitude; for although this overture was not as to the peace, what might have been desired, yet was it attended without delay, and accepted.

"As a proof of the interests taken by the government on this subject, I might mention, that not only was Mr. Carmichael, who had acquired an acquaintance, with persons and circumstances in Spain, made a member of the commission, but Mr. Short was added, as being more particularly informed of the navigation to be treated of.

"Instructions, comprehensive, accurate and forcible, were prepared by my predecessor; and if at this stage of the business it were proper to develope them to public view; I should expect, with certainty, that those who are the most ardent for the main object would pronounce that the executive has been deficient neither in vigilence nor in exertion.

"For many months have our commissioners been employed in this important affair at Madrid. At this moment they are probably so em-ployed. The delays which forms may have created; the events of Europe and other considerations which at this season cannot, with propriety, be detailed, dictate a peaceable expectation of the result.

"Let this communication, then, be received, sir, as a warning against the dangers to which these unauthorised schemes of war may expose the United States, and particularly the State of Kentucky. Let not unfounded suspicions of tardiness in government, prompt individuals to rash efforts, in which they cannot be countenanced; which may thwart any favorable advances of their cause; and which by seizing the direction of the military force, must be repulsed by law; or they will terminate in anarchy. Under whatsoever auspices of a foreign agent, commotions were at first raised, the present Minister Plenipotentiary of the French Republic, has publicly disavowed, and recalled the commissions which have been granted.

"I cannot, therefore doubt, that when your excellency shall revise this subject, you will come to this conclusion, that the resentments you profess as a private man, a friend to liberty, an American citizen and an inhabitant of the Western waters, ought not to interfere with your duty as Governor of Kentucky; and that on the other hand, the contemplation of those several characters under which you have considered yourself, ought to produce a compliance with these measures which the President of the United States has consigned to your discretion and execution."

"I have the honour to be, with respect, sir your excellency's most obedient servant,

EDM. RANDOLPH."[418]

SECTION 59

The Wayne-Campbell Exchanges
[December 4, 1828]

The following information was given by a citizen of Western Pennsylvania, who arrived in Lexington on the 14th of June 1794, on his way home from Illinois, which place he left on the 22d May.

"The Delaware and Shawanese Indians living on the other side of the Mississippi, in the Spanish territory, who had been sent last Spring by the Spanish government, under the conduct of a French trader to invade the territory of the United States, and watch on the Ohio and Cumberland rivers; after having committed several violations upon the same territory, they lately retired contrary to the intentions and wishes of the Spanish officers. They being suddenly disappointed, made several attempts to keep them in their service, and for that purpose have held several councils with these Indians who have still offered the most powerful arguments and the most consistent reasons to retire and avoid any hostile measures against either the bad French, or the bad Americans as it was told them alternately. The principal ground they bear upon is this, that they have deserted their country and their own land, even their own friends, who still oppose the American army, and had done so for the sake of peace; therefore, since they had bought peace at so dear a price, it would be inconsistent to give it away for a cause which is a stranger to themselves; they also observed that their misfortunes and the hard fate to which their friends were reduced, was the consequence of their imprudently meddling in the war between the British and the Americans. That henceforth they never would share or partake in anything with wars raised between the white people.—That as for themselves, they would fight their own battles and settle their quarrels, if any, with the red people. They also stated in council, that when the Americans offered presents to their friends among the Indians, they always recommended them to remain still and peaceable; while on the contrary, they (the Spaniards) made them presents to bring them to trouble and disturbance. In consequence of all these reasons so alleged by the Indians, and notwithstanding the repeated attempts made by the Spanish government to set them again at mischievous activity, they all without exception, have left Cape Girardo and the neighboring villages, and did go towards the heads of Warameg river to settle and plant corn there, which is about 150 miles from their old villages. The Spanish government have also met with another disappointment with the Chickasaw Indians. Out of seven Indians which they dispatched to the Chickasaw nation, to excite them against the United States, six have been killed by the Chickasaws at the first hint of their mission; the seventh had a very narrow escape, and returned to New Madrid, being half starved and quite naked, even without a gun, carrying nothing but the news. Nevertheless, whatever may be the ill success of this mission to the Spaniards, they solace themselves and are delighted with the expectation of future injury to be done by the Cherokees they have invited to settle at Cape Girardo, to fill up the vacancy that has taken place by the removal of the other Indians. Those Cherokees, though not so numerous as the Delawares and Shawanese, are infinitely more dreaded. They are at this time the highwaymen and assassins of the lower part of Ohio, and the Spaniards lodge them and board them for that purpose. Several traders who intended to bring peltry from the Illinois up to Pittsburgh, have been prevented from fear of being plundered and massacred with their crews by this banditti. Mr. Turner one of the Supreme Judges of the Western territory, being well aware of the impending danger on the Ohio, is detained at present at Post St. Vincennes, waiting for an answer from the commandant of St. Louis, of whom he solicits his interposition and protection from those Cherokees, in order to be secured from their attacks or insults, during his official journey to Illinois, where he is going for the purpose of holding the general Court. Thus, not only the citizens of the United States are impeded by the Spaniards in carrying on their trade, or travelling on the waters or territory of the Union; but even public officers, Supreme Judges are prevented from holding their court, without the previous consent or interference of a Spanish officer. Such is the debased condition of our country! such the pernicious effects of the neglect of Congress to protect this unfortunate portion of the Union."[419]

This information contributed very much to the ease with which volunteers were raised, to join the regular army commanded by Gen. Anthony Wayne, on an expedition against the Indians, and collected lately at the British fort on Miami of the lakes, an account of which follows:

On the 25th of July 1794, General Scott, with a part of the Kentucky volunteers united at Greenville with sixteen hundred regular troops, under command of Gen. Wayne, and the united force marched on the morning of the 24th against the Indians, leaving Gen. Barbee in the rear, with another brigade, in charge of some heavy cannon.

(On the 1st day of August, a man by the name of Newman, belonging to the Quarter Masters department, deserted and went over to the Indians). The day following, they arrived at the river St. Mary's, and erected two blockhouses to cover the army whilst crossing the river. On the 8th the army reached the Indian villages at the mouth of the river Auglaize, which had been abandoned by the enemy before their arrival; the army remained at this place six days, during which time they were occupied in building a small fort, at which a Major's command was left. In the mean time captain Wells with a party, went to the foot of the rapids, where he took and brought off two prisoners, a man and a woman; on their return they fell in with a party of Indians, and a skirmish ensued, in which captain Wells, and a Mr. M'Clanahan were wounded. Gen. Wayne sent a Mr. Miller and the Indian thus taken, with a letter to the enemy, offering terms of peace; but principally with a view to ascertain their strength & situation, more than with an expectation that the terms offered would be acceded to. The letter contained a threat, that if Miller was not permitted to return immediately, every prisoner in the possession of the Americans would be put to instant death. On the second day's march from Auglaize, Miller (on his return) met the army; he had been escorted by some Indians until they came within hearing of the enemy, and then they retreated.

The army arrived at Roche de Bout on the 18th, and spent the 19th in building a strong work to cover their sick and baggage, and moved on the 20th except about 400 men, who remained at the camp thus fortified.

Maj. Price of the Kentucky volunteers, had moved about 4 miles with the advance party, consisting of two companies of mounted riflemen, when they were suddenly attacked by a large party of Indians, and compelled to retreat. They fell back upon the main body of the regulars, pressed by the savages. The troops were formed in two lines, ready to receive them. The right wing under Gen. Wilkinson, charged, and was instantly followed by the left, which threw the Indians into great confusion; they made a stand of a few minutes, and then fled in every direction. The weather being extremely hot, and the woods very thick, the General checked the pursuit.

Our loss in this action was, one Captain, one Lieutenant and twenty-one men killed, and between seventy and eighty wounded: the loss of the enemy was not known, until after the treaty, where they acknowledged a loss of forty killed, and upwards of an hundred wounded.

After the action, the army moved down to the foot of the Rapids of Miami, about three quarters of a mile from, and in full view of the British fort. A company of young men (principally English and Scotch) from Detroit, had joined the Indians on the day of the battle. They having fallen in with the riflemen of the legion, and some of the Kentucky volunteers, left twenty of their party dead on the field.

The army returned by easy marches to fort Defiance, where it remained some time, making use of the corn left by the Indians, and at the same time strengthening the fort. From fort Defiance the army returned to Greenville after building Fort Wayne, where Maj. Hamtramk was left with five companies to garrison the place.

The day after the battle of the 20th, near the British fort Miami, the following correspondence took place between Major William Campbell, commander of the British forces, and Maj. Gen. Wayne. The correspondence opened on the part of Major Campbell, as follows:

"SIR—

"An army of the United States of America, said to be under your cummand, having taken post on the banks of the Miami, for upwards of the last twenty hours; almost within reach of the guns of this fort, being a post belonging to his majesty the King of Great Britain, occupied by his majesty's troops, and which I have the honor to command, it becomes my duty to inform myself, as speedily as possible, in what light I am to view your making such near approaches to this garrison.

"I have no hesitation on my part to say that I know of no war existing between Great Britain and America.

"I have the honor to be, sir, with great respect, your obedient and very humble servant.   WILLIAM CAMPBELL. *Major*
        24th Regiment commanding a British Post on the banks of the Miami.
"To Maj. Gen. Wayne, &c. &c.
"Miami river, August 21st, 1794." [420]

GEN. WAYNE'S ANSWER.

"SIR,

"I have received your letter of this date, requiring from me the movives which have moved the army under my command, to the position which they at present occupy, far within the acknowledged jurisdiction of the United States of America.

"Without questioning the authority, or the propriety, sir, of your interrogatory, I think I may without breach of decorum, observe to you, that were you entitled to an answer, the most satisfactory one was announced to you from the muzzles of my small arms yesterday morning in the action against the horde of savages in the vicinity of your post, which terminated gloriously to the American arms. But had it continued until the Indians, &c. &c. were drove under the influence of the post and guns, you mention, they would not have much impeded the progress of the victorious army under my command; as no such post was established at the commencement of this present war between the Indians and the United States.

"I have the honor to be, sir, with great respect, your most obedient and very humble servant,
(Signed)   "ANTHONY WAYNE. "Major General, and commander in
                                        chief of the Federal Army.
"Camp on the bank of the Miami, 21st Aug. 1794.
    "To *Maj William Campbell, &c. &c."* [421]

REPLY OF MAJ. CAMPBELL.

"SIR,

"Although your letter of yesterday's date fully authorises me to any act of hostility against the army of the United States of America in this neighbourhood under your command, yet still anxious to prevent that dreadful decision, which perhaps is not intended to be appealed to by either of our countries.

"I have forborne for these two days past, to resent those insults you have offered to the British flag flying at this port, by approaching it within pistol shot of my works, not only single, but by numbers with arms in their hands.

"Neither is it my wish to wage war with individuals; but should you after this, continue to approach my post in the threatning manner you are this moment doing, my indispensable duty to my king and country, and the honour of my profession, will oblige me to have recourse to those measures, which thousands of either nation, may hereafter have cause to regret; and which I solemnly appeal to God, I have used my utmost endeavours to arrest.

"I have the honor to be, sir, with much respect, your obedient, and very humble servant.   WILLIAM CAMPBELL.
                              "Maj. 24th Regt. commanding a fort Miami.[422]
"Fort Miami, Aug. 22d, 1794.
"MAJOR GENERAL WAYNE, &c. &c."

No other notice was taken of this letter than what is expressed in the following one. The fort and works were however reconnoitred in every direction within pistol shot. It was found to be a regular strong built fort, the front covered by a wide river, with four guns mounted on that face. The rear (which was most susceptible of approach,) had two regular Bastions, furnished with eight pieces of artillery; the whole surrounded with a wide deep ditch, with horizontal pickets projecting from the beams of the parapet over the ditch: from the bottom of the ditch to the top of the parapet was about twenty feet perpendicular, the works were also surrounded by an abatis and furnished with a strong garrison.[423]

GENERAL WAYNE'S REPLY

"SIR,
    "In your letter of the 21st inst. you declare, 'I have no hesitation on my part to say that I know of no war existing between Great Britain and America.'
    "Upon my part, I declare the same; and the only cause I have to entertain a contrary idea at present is, the hostile act you are now in commission of; that is, recently taking post, far within the well known and acknowledged limits of the United States, and erecting a fortification in the heart of the settlements of the Indian tribes, now at war with the United States.
    "This, sir, appears to be an act of the highest aggression and destructive to the peace and interest of the Union. Hence, it becomes my duty to desire, and I do hereby desire and demand in the name of the President of the United States, that you immediately desist from any further act of hostility or aggression by forbearing to fortify, and by withdrawing the troops, artillery and stores under your orders and direction forthwith, and removing to the nearest post occupied by his Britanic Majesty's troops at the peace of 1783, and which you will be permitted to do unmolested by the troops under my command.

"I am with very great respect, sir, your most obedient and very humble servant,   ANTHONY WAYNE.
"Major William Campbell, &c. &c." [424]

MAJ. CAMPBELL, IN REPLY.

"SIR,

"I have this moment the honour to acknowledge the receipt of your letter of this date, in answer to which, I have only to say, that being placed here in the command of a British post, and acting in a military capacity only, I cannot enter into any discussion either on the right or impropriety of my occupying my present position; these are matters that I conceive will be best left to the Ambassadors of our different nations.

"Having said this much, permit me to inform you, that I certainly will not abandon this post at the summons of any power whatever, until I receive orders to that purpose from those I have the honour to serve under, or the fortune of war should oblige me.

"I must adhere, sir, to the purport of my letter of this morning, to desire that your army, or individuals belonging to it, will not approach within reach of my cannon, without expecting the consequences attending.

"Although I have said in the former part of my letter, that my situation here is totally military, yet let me add, that I am much deceived if his Majesty the king of Great Britain had not a post on this river, at, and prior to the period you mention.

"I have the honour to be, sir, Your most obedient and very humble servant,
(Signed)   "WILLIAM CAMPBELL,
                            "Major 24th Regt. commanding at Fort Miamis.
Fort Miamis, August 22, 1794.
To MAJ. GEN. WAYNE, &c. &c. &c. [425]

The only notice taken of this was by immediately setting fire to, and destroying everything within view of the fort, and even under the muzzles of the guns.—Had Mr. Campbell carried his threats into execution, it is more than probable he would have experienced a *storm*.

Whitley, Blount,
and the Southern Tribes
[December 12, 1828]

The following is the account given by John E. King who acted as adjutant under Col. William Whitley,* on an expedition carried on by him from Kentucky, with 100 men, joined by Major Orre from Holstien with sixty men, and governor Blount of Tennessee, with 440 against the Southern Indians, in the month of August 1794.

"On the 30th of August, Col. William Whitley, arrived at Nashville with 100 well equiped volunteers from Kentucky. Major Orre from Holstien added to that number sixty men, and the Territory of Cumberland 440, making in the whole six hundred. At the general rendezvous, Col. Whitley was appointed Col. Commandant; but as Major Orre had been mustered into service, and sent on command by Governor Blount; it was thought best to muster the men in his name, but Whitley was honoured as commander in the camp, and in the field.[426]

"On the 8th of September, the army got in motion and advanced ten miles, on the 12th it made a forced march of forty miles through Cumberland Mountain and cane brakes, lighting themselves with fire brands, and reached the banks of the Tennessee at two o'clock in the morning. Whitley directed the men to make their passage across with all expedition possible, the common method was by rafting on logs, poles, bunches of cane &c. at seven o'clock in the morning he mustered two hundred and fifty men including officers, on the South side of Tennessee. This was done with so much care, that the arms were preserved dry and in a condition for action. The troops then marched briskly on the spurs of the mountains up the river, piloted by Mr. Findleston a half breed, in three columns, and aproached the town called Nicka-Jack, previous to which a party had been placed in ambush on the opposite side of the town, to that where they intended to enter, in order to intercept such as should attempt to escape by flight. The troops entered the town precipitately where were

*Col. Whitley was killed at the battle of the Thames in 1813.

about forty warriors, with a considerable number above the town, some of whom were at that time in the act of crossing the river.

"The first hint the Indians had of the approach of Whitley and his party, was the shrieks given at their entry into the town; the wariors made battle with great spirit, but finding themselves overpowered, they betook themselves to the river, (on the margin of which their fort stood) some in canoes, and some escaped by swimming; the water of the river was soon stained with their blood, mingled with brains.—The action continued half an hour. Our damage was two men slightly wounded; the loss of the Indians was fifty-four killed and nineteen taken; amongst the former was the old Chief Breath, he had a commission from the Spaniards. The prisoners said only twelve of their people who were there escaped.

"Col. Whitley left a sufficient number of men to take care of the prisoners and keep possession of the place, and marched the balance up the river to the town called Running Water. The Indians collected in the gap of a mountain through which they had to pass, and on the approach of the army fired on them; Whitley ordered the men to form the line and flank up the mountain, whilst he kept up the fire in the centre, where one Indian was killed and two wounded, when the remainder broke and ran away,—Whitley had one man wounded; he passed on to the town, but found it entirely deserted. This town had been newly built and was in good repair—had a large Town House, Council House, War Post, Maypole and silk colours eight feet square. In this town were ninety houses, well stored with plunder taken from the passengers on the road through the wilderness and frontiers of Kentucky. The squaws and children were well dressed in good striped cloth, cotton, linsey &c. The whole town was laid in ashes and full spoil made of every thing except $1200 worth which was divided among the men. There was sufficient plunder found to prove incontestibly, that these Chickamaugee Indians have been long our enemies. We burned in all, including both towns, 150 houses." [427]

The following letter of the Secretary of State of the United States, to Mr. Hammond, minister plenipotentiary of his Britanic Majesty, together with his answer, are given to show the state of feeling between the two nations relative to the Western section of the United States.

"PHILADELPHIA, Sept. 14, 1794.
SIR:—If after the formation, upon which my letter of the 20th May 1794† is founded, any considerable doubt had remained of Governor Simcoe's invasion; your long silence without a refutation of it, and our more recent intelligence forbid us to question its oath. It is supported by the respectable opinions, which have been since transmitted to the executive, that in

†Notes, Sec. 59.

the late attack on Fort Recovery, British officers and soldiers were, on the very ground, aiding our Indian enemies.

"But Sir, as if the governor of Upper Canada, was resolved to destroy every possibility of disbelieving his hostile views, he has sent to the Great Sodus,—a settlement begun on a bay of the same name on lake Ontario—a command to Capt. Williamson, who derives a title from the state of New York, to desist from his enterprize. This mandate was borne by a lieutenant Sheaffe, under a military escort; and in its town corresponds with the form of its delivery, being unequivocally of a military and hostile nature.

"I am commanded to declare, that during the execution of the treaty of peace between Great Britain and the United States, and until the existing differences respecting it, shall be mutually and finally adjusted, the taking possession of any part of the Indian Territory, either for the purposes of war or sovereignty, is held to be a direct violation of his Britanic Majesty's rights, as they unquestionably existed before the treaty, and has an immediate tendency to corrupt, and in its progress to destroy that good understanding which has hitherto subsisted between his Britanic Majesty and the United States of America. I therefore require you to desist from any such aggression.   "R. H. SHEAFFE.

"Lieut. 5th Reg't & Qr. M. Gen. Dep. of his Britanic Majesty's service.[428]
"GREAT SODUS, 6th August, 1794."

Capt. Williamson being from home, a letter was written to him by Lieut. Sheaffe in the following words:

SODUS, August 16, 1794.
"SIR—Having a special commission and instructions for that purpose from the Lieut. Governor of his Britanic Majesty's province of Upper Canada, I have come here to demand by what authority an establishment has been ordered at this place, and to require that such a design be immediately relinquished, for the reasons stated in the written declaration accompanying this letter; for the receipt of which protest I have taken the acknowledgement of your agent Mr. Little. I regret exceedingly in my private as well as public character, that I have not the satisfaction of seeing you here, but I hope on my return, which will be about a week hence, to be more fortunate.

"I am Sir, your most obedient servant,   R. H. SHEAFFE.
"Lieut. 5th Regt. Q.M.G.D."[429]

[The following letter was written to Britain's Hammond by Randolph.]
"The position of Sodus is represented to be seventy miles within the territorial line of the United States; about twenty from Oswego, and about one hundred from Niagara.

"For the present all causes of discontent, not connected with our Western Territory, shall not be revived the root of our complaints, the detention of the posts. But while peace is sought by us through every channel which honour permits; the governor of Upper Cannada is accumulating irritation upon irritation. He commenced his operations of enmity at the rapids of the Miami. He next associated British with Indian force to assault our fort. He now threatens us, if we fell our own trees and build houses on our own lands. To what length may not governor Simcoe go. Where is the limit of the sentiment which gave birth to these instructions! Where is the limit of the principle, which governor Simcoe avows.

"The treaty and all its appendages, we have submitted to fair discussion, more than two years ago. To the letter of my predecessor on the 29th May 1792, you have not been pleased to make a reply; except that on the 20th June 1793, the 22nd Nov. 1793 and the 12th February 1794, no instructions had arrived from your court. To say the best of this suspension, it certainly cannot warrant any new encroachments, however, it may recommend to us forbearance under the old.

"It is not for the Governors of his Britanic Majesty, to interfere with the measures of the United States towards the Indians within their territory. You cannot, Sir, be insensible, that it has grown into a maxim, that the affairs of the Indians within the boundaries of any nation, exclusively belong to that nation. But Governor Simcoe disregarding this right of the United States, extends the line of usurpation in which he marches, by resorting to the ancient and extinguished rights of his Britanic Majesty. For, if the existing condition of the treaty, keeps them alive on the Southern side of Lake Ontario, the Ohio itself will not stop the career.

"You will pardon me, Sir, if under these excesses of governor Simcoe I am not discouraged by your having formerly disclaimed a controul over, and a responsibility for, the governors of his Britanic Majesty, from resorting to you on this occasion. You are addressed from a hope, that if he will not be restrained by our remonstrances, he may at least be apprised, through you, of the consequences of self defence.

"I have the honour, Sir, to be, with great respect, your most obedient servant,   EDM. RANDOLPH."
"Mr. HAMMOND, Minister Plenipo. of his Britanic Majesty."[430]

THE ANSWER
NEW YORK, Sept. 1794.
"Sir—I this day received your letter of the 1st. current; copies of which I will transmit, by the earliest opportunities that may occur, to Lieutenant Governor Simcoe, and to his Majesty's Ministers in England.

"I have the honour to be, with the greatest respect, Sir, your most obedient humble servant.   GEO. HAMMOND."[431]
"The Secretary of State."

On the 6th of October Mr. Elliot, the contractor and his servant, on their way from Fort Washington to Fort Hamilton, were fired on near the latter place by a party of Indians, Mr. Elliott was killed, but his servant escaped. A party who went out to bring in the body of Mr. Elliott, having got it in the waggon, were attacked by a party of Indians, and defeated; Mr. Elliott's servant, who escaped when he was killed, fell in this attack. The Indians took possession of the waggon and threw out the corps. It was afterwards taken by a party from Cincinnati to that place and interred.[432]

On the 13th day of October 1790, Frederick Bough, in company with a young man of his acquaintance, near Vanmeter's Fort in Nelson county, about twenty-five miles from Bardstown, fell in with a party of five Indians. As the Indians approached he observed to the young man, "I think I see Indians," the young man ridiculed the idea of his seeing Indians, and observed "you are a fool for having such thoughts," and continued on. They soon, however, plainly saw a party of five Indians approaching within a few yards of them; upon which the young man exclaimed, "good God there they are sure enough" and fled precipitately, but in a direction from, (instead of towards,) the Fort, and was soon overtaken by one of the Indians, and instantly killed. Bough took a direction towards the Fort and was fired on by the other four, the balls of three of them took effect; one in the left arm, another in the right thigh and the third through his waistcoat and shirt, and slightly cut the skin on the left side. He was not entirely disabled from running, but attempting to cross a creek, in his way towards the Fort, stuck in the mud, where he was overtaken by the Indians, who pulled him out of the mud, felt of his arm, and finding it was not broken, one of them pulled out of his pouch a strop with a noose at one end, with the evident intention of confining Bough; upon the discovery of which, he suddenly jirked away his hand and gave the Indian a blow on the side of the head which felled him to the ground. By this time two other Indians came up, (the fourth having gone in pursuit of some horses) Bough kicked at the one he had knocked down, but did not hit him. At that moment one of the Indians aimed a blow at Bough's head with his tomahawk, but in his eagerness struck too far, and the handle only struck which nevertheless nearly knocked him down. Bough quickly recovering knocked the tomahawk out of the Indians hand, upon which both exerted themselves to get possession of it, but the Indian succeeded, and entered in to conversation with his companion, who then struck Bough with a stick, and as he advanced to repeat the blow, he stopped suddenly and they all instantly ran off, leaving their blankets and a kettle, which Bough carried with him into the Fort. It was never known why the Indians left Bough in the manner they did; it was supposed they had some cause to suspect they were in great danger, and that flight alone could save them.

On the 29th of November 1794, the Indians killed two men and wounded another near Columbia on the little Miami, and took three prisoners near Cincinnati.[433]

In consequence of the incessant murders committed by the Cherokees, Chickamauga and other Southern Indians, on the people passing to and from Kentucky, the plan of an expedition was matured between Gen. Logan and Col. Whitley, which being communicated to Wm. Blount, Governor of the Territory of the United States South of the Ohio river, the following letters were forwarded from Governor Blount on that subject.

Governor Blount to Colonel Whitley
"Knoxville, Nov. 1, 1794.

"Col. Whitley,

"Sir—I have been informed, first by Housen Kenner, which has been in a greater degree confirmed, since, by the examination of Maj. Orre the bearer, that you passed this place yesterday, with an intention to join General Logan, who is said to have marched from Kentucky in force, to invade the lower Cherokee towns.

"The newspaper you will receive herewith, contains copies of a letter of the 20th ultimo to me, from Double Head, a principal chief of those towns, and my answer to him of the 29th, by which you will understand, these towns, as well as every other part of the Cherokee nation, are considered in the peace of the United States.

"By what authority Gen. Logan has raised an armed force, to invade a nation declared by public authority in peace with the United States I am uninformed. Hence I am compelled to suppose, he has no legal authority for so doing, and command him, you, and all others concerned, to desist from such illegal and unauthorised enterprize.

"Having so recently received from, and given to the Cherokees assurances of peace, as the above mentioned letters will prove, to you, it becomes an official duty in me, to give information to the Cherokees, of the intended invasion of Gen. Logan; and the feelings of humanity equally compel me so to inform you, and if possible the General himself.

"It is my wish to act so that neither party can charge me with improper conduct, and to save the effusion of human blood.

"From the character of Gen. Logan and yourself, I readily believe, that you both wish peace and security, to the frontier inhabitants; but should you preserve in your intended attack upon the lower towns, it is my opinion, that the effect will be, the drawing the lower Cherokees and upper Creeks, highly incensed, upon those exposed people.

"I am your obedient servant,
(Signed) "WILLIAM BLOUNT.
"Col. Wm. Whitley, of Ken. now at West Point."[434]

"Knoxville, Nov. 1, 1794.

"General Logan,

"SIR;—Inclosed is a copy of my letter to Col. Whitley, of this date, forwarded to him express, and one of the newspapers, containing copies

of the letter of Double Head, a principal chief of the Cherokees, of the 20th
ult. to me, and my answer of the 29th as alluded to in my letter to the
Colonel.

"The first (the letter to the Colonel) serving to shew you the information I have received respecting your intended invasion of the lower
Cherokee towns; and the latter the pleasing prospects of a continued
peace between the United States and the Lower Cherokees.

"Upon your receiving this information, I cannot suffer myself to
doubt, but your love of peace and order will induce you immediately to
desist from your intended enterprize. But in this instance, it is my duty
to command as well as inform. Therefore, I command you and the men
with you, or under your command, forthwith to desist from the attempt
of invading the Lower Cherokee towns, who are in the peace of the
United States. And I further command you, not to enter in a hostile
manner the country or lands guaranteed to the Cherokee nation, by the
treaty between the United States and the said Cherokees, commonly
called the treaty of Holston; warning you and them, that in case of a
violation of this order, which is issued by virtue of the authority in me
vested, you and they will answer the same at your peril.

"Having received my appointment from the Federal government, I
am answerable for my acts only to it. Yet it may not be improper to give
you my reasons for my conduct on this occasion. They are contained in
part in my letter to Colonel Whitley, to which I refer you; and an additional one is my great desire to promote the peace and happiness of our
frontier fellow citizens, and our common country at large.

"This letter will be delivered to you by Sergeant M'Clellan, who I
have sent with ten men for that purpose, under instructions to follow
you, to the banks of the Tennessee.

"I am, your ob't servant,
(Signed)   "WILLIAM BLOUNT.[435]
"General Logan, reported to be on his march from Kentucky, with an
army to invade the Lower Cherokee towns."

"WILLIAM BLOUNT, Governor in and over the Territory of the
United States of America South of the river Ohio, and Superintendent of Indian affairs.
"To the Chiefs and Warriors of the Lower Cherokees
"It is only two days since I wrote you in answer to your letter of the
20th October, and informed you, that the citizens of the United States all
wished peace with you, since you are determined to be at peace with
them; and so I then believed. But now I have to tell you, that I am just
informed, that General Logan of Kentucky, has raised, or is about to
raise, a large army of volunteers, unauthorized by government, to invade
and destroy the Lower Cherokee towns.

"The reason given for raising this army to destroy the lower towns is, that the people of the lower towns, have unprovokedly shed a great deal of blood of the frontier citizens, and robbed them of much property, which they yet hold in their hands, consisting of negroes and horses.

"I give you this information, that you may not charge the United States, nor myself of having deceived you, by telling you all wished peace, when a large party are just about to invade your country. I have sent to General Logan, informing him of good talks that have lately passed between you and myself, with orders to desist from his intended invasion of your country, which I hope he will attend to, and return home. But it may be that he will not return, but pursue his first intention, and invade your country—Here I feel myself at a loss in case General Logan does invade your country, how to act for the best: But knowing the Government of the United States wish peace with your nation, and all the world, and believing you have now seen the folly of war, and also wish peace, I advise in case General Logan does enter your country, that you will quit your towns, and remove your stock and other property to the woods, leaving your houses and such of your corn as you cannot remove, to the mercy of General Logan and his party, and forbear to do him or his party the least injury in person or property; relying that government will compensate your losses of horses or corn, in preference to having the blood of their citizens shed in defence of them. Too much blood has been shed already, and if more is shed, it will increase the difficulty of securing the blessings of returning peace. Peace ought to be the wish of both parties; for, in peace consists the true interest and happiness of both parties. War will cost the United States some lives and much money, but it will destroy the existence of your people as a nation forever.

"I would advise you to deliver up at Tellico Block House, to John M'Kee, without delay, all deserters, prisoners, negroes and horses— then the people of Kentucky can have no more cause to invade your country.

(Signed)   WILLIAM BLOUNT.
"*Knoxville, Nov. 1, 1794.*

"The Cherokee Chiefs are requested, after this letter have been explained to them at Wills Town and Look-Out-Mountain town, to forward it to Mr. Dinsmore at the Turkeys Town." [436]

"*Knoxville, Nov. 2, 1794.*
"SERJEANT M'CLELLAN
"The object of your being ordered on duty is, to go express with a letter to Gen. Logan, who, from the information I have received, I have reason to believe is on his march from Kentucky, with an army of volunteers, having an intention to invade the lower Cherokee towns, unauthorised by government. My information respecting the time when the General

would march from Kentucky, is so vague, as not to enable me to form even a conjecture, where or when you will most probably fall in with him; but it is certain if he does not desist from his enterprize, that he will march by way of Mero district, and from thence by way of Ore's trace to the Tennessee, where Ore crossed it.—You will take such course as will intercept him to the greatest certainty, before he arrives at the Tennessee, which will be to turn off the common trace to Nashville, at or near the Crab Orchard, and to proceed by such course, as shall strike Ore's trace from Nashville, to the Tennessee, about half way between the two places, and upon striking it, you will readily discover whether he has passed on towards the Tennessee or not: If he has, you will pursue to the Tennessee; if not, you will turn towards Mero District, and upon finding the General, will deliver him the letter addressed to him.

"It may be you may fall in with a party of the army of Gen. Logan, and not with himself, and to provide against such an event, I herewith deliver to you a copy of my letter to the General, and a copy of my letter to Colonel Whitley, also a newspaper containing copies of Double Heads letter to me, of the 20th ult. and my answer of the 29th, all of which you will read publicly to such party, and make known to them that it is my order and command to them to desist from their attempt to invade the Lower Cherokee towns. And should Gen. Logan, upon your delivering the letter to him addressed, refuse to open it, or after he does open it should neglect to make the contents known, you will in either case inform him, that you have it in command from me, to order him, to desist from his and their intended invasion of the Cherokee country, and in either case, you will read aloud to him, and the men with him or under his command, the letters above mentioned. And to the end that no party may enter the Cherokee towns or country unadvised to their danger, you are commanded to declare to all and every party which appears to have the entering of either for their object, that I have apprized the Indians of their approach, and you may add, that I considered it my official duty so to do, and that a copy of my letter to the Indians on that head, will appear in the next number of the Knoxville Gazette, to the end that the impartial public may judge of the propriety of my conduct in so doing.

"You have herewith a letter addressed 'General Robinson, or Colonel Winchester, Mero District,' with which you will dispatch two of your command from the Crab Orchard, along the old trace, directly to Col. Winchester, and from thence to General Robinson.

"I am your obedient servant.
(signed)   "WILLIAM BLOUNT.[437]

"An after Order.
"MONDAY MORNING, Nov. 3, 1794.
"Serjeant M'Clellan,
"Having received more certain information of the intended movements of General Logan, namely, that he, with his party are to ren-

dezvous at the foot of the Cumberland mountain, on the North side on the 9th inst. I find it proper to order, that you, instead of turning off to the left at the Crab Orchard, push directly with all possible haste, to Mero district, where you will probably arrive before the General leaves that district and deliver the letters to him. But should he have marched from Mero District before your arrival, you will instantly follow him, and pursue to the banks of the Tennessee, if you do not sooner overtake him.

"You are to consider the order of the second instant in full force, except where this order otherwise directs.

"I am your obedient servant,
(signed)   "WILLIAM BLOUNT."[438]

SECTION 61

Choctaw, Creek, Cherokee, and Chickasaw

[December 26, 1828]

An a conference held on the 7th and 8th of November 1794, at Tellico Block House (on the south bank of the Tennessee) between William Blount, Governor in and aver the Territory of the United States of America, south of the river Ohio; and Col. John Watts, of Wat's town (one of the Lower Cherokee towns) and Scolacutta, or Hanging Maw, and other Chiefs of the Cherokee nation, at which were present about four hundred warriors, and several citizens of the United States, namely, Col. Abishai Thomas, Maj. Sevier, Maj. David Craig, Capt. Samuel Henry, commonding at that post, and others.—JAMES CAREY INTER-PRETER.[439]

GOVERNOR BLOUNT.
Addressing himself to Colonel Watts.
"Upon being informed by Mr. M'Kee, that you were here, and wished to see me about the affairs of the nation, I hastened to meet you. I am happy in this interview, because your evidence of the wish of the lower towns

for peace, whose principal chief I have ever considered you, and in Scola-cutta I behold the true head of your whole nation.—Having opened the conference, I shall sit down, and first expect the talk of Col. Watts."

Colonel Watts. "This meeting appears to be ordered by the Great Spirit, and affords me great pleasure. Here is Scolacutta, he is old enough to be my father, and from my infancy he was a great chief of the nation. In the spring of the year, he sent a great talk to the Lower town, telling them he and the upper towns had taken the United States by the hand, with a determination to hold them fast during life, and inviting the Lower towns to do the same. With tears in my eyes, have I thought of this talk, and beheld the folly of the Lower towns, who at first refused to hear it. But just before the destruction of the Running Water and Nickajack by Major Ore, I went to them as well as the Lookout Mountain town, and exerted myself for the restoration of peace; and I verily believe those towns had heard my talk, and were determined to be at peace with the United States. I do not say the Running Water and Nickajack did not deserve the chastisement they received; nevertheless it so exasperated those who escaped from the ruins, that for a time I was compelled to be silent myself; but the Glass went to the Running Water people, and they told the Glass, that notwithstanding the injury they sustained, they had not forgot his (Watt's) good talks, but still hold them fast; and desired him to take measures for the recovery of the prisoners. When this answer was re-ported to me by the Glass, I had my doubts, and would not act upon it, for they had told me so many lies, I was afraid to trust them. I then sent the Bloody Fellow to Running Water, and he returned with the same report, which induced me to come forward to you, knowing you were the man the United States had authorised to transact such business. I deliver this, (presenting a string of white beads) as a true talk and a public talk, from the Lower towns to you. Scolacutta, the head man of the nation, is sitting by me, the Lower towns instructed me to request him not throw them away but to come with me to you to present this talk in their behalf.

"By a prisoner taken by Major Ore, and sent back by Gen. Robertson, I received a letter from him, requiring him to give up a white prisoner and a certain number of negroes, and that the prisoners taken by Major Ore should be restored to their nation. In this letter the General invited me to come to him with a flag; but as the woman was pursued by some bad white people, and obliged to quit her horse and save herself in the cane, although I know Gen. Robertson to be a good man, I thought it important to go to him, besides, I know that an exchange of prisoners could only be negotiated with you. As to prisoners in my town there are none: and when the people of my town once took a man of great worth (Capt. Handly) they restored him without price."

Scolacutta, or *Hanging Maw.* "I too have a talk from the Lower town. They were once my people, but not now. Yet I cannot but think much of the talk I have received by Watts. Before any thing happened to these towns, I had sent them many peace talks, which they would not hear; but now, since the attack made upon them by Major Ore, they send to make peace for them in conjunction with Watts. I am the head man of my nation, as Governor Blount is of the white people. It was not the fault of either that those town were destroyed; but their own conduct brought destruction upon them; the trail of murderers and thieves were followed to these towns. Nevertheless, I cannot neglect the request they have made to me, to make peace for them, as I hope they have seen their folly, and will desist from murdering and robbing the people of the United States, and live in peace. I shall then hope to live much longer; for their bad conduct drew the white people on me, who injured me nearly unto death. This talk I deliver on the part of the Lower towns; and if they do not desist from war and live in peace, I will give them up, to the U. States, to deal with as they shall judge proper.

"All last winter, I was compelled to lie in the woods, by the bad conduct of my own people, drawing war upon me. In the spring of the year a communication was opened with you. You invited me to meet your deputy, John M'Kee, in nine days, which I did. John M'Kee assured me of the peaceful disposition of the United States, and told me and my party to return to their homes and fields; this I also did. I could hear from several parts of the nation, threats against my life, to be effected by killing white people in my neighborhood, and thereby draw them on me and my party. I then solicited that this block house or fort, should be erected, as serving to protect me and my party, as well as the frontier inhabitants, and open a communication between the red people. I still heard murmuring from several parts of my nation, with threats that they would have no intercourse with it, or with John M'Kees but I now see standing around me, many of those very people, who are glad to come to it, and to be in friendship with John M'Kee, and at peace with the U. States. They need not find fault with John M'Kee. I have found him to be an honest man, and never heard any thing from him but the truth." [440]

November 8.

Governor Blount. "It is with pleasure I receive from you the information that Lower Cherokees wish peace with the United States. When you (addressing himself to Watts,) the Bloody Fellow and the Glass, the three greatest chiefs of the Lower towns, come forward with such assurances, I can no longer doubt the sincerity with which they are made. Peace with the whole Cherokee nation has ever been the wish of the United States, and it is yet their wish; so that the Lower towns have only to keep peace on their part, and it will be peace.

"By saying the Lower towns requested you to take measures for the recovery of the prisoners, I understand that they wish an exchange of prisoners; to this I agree, and propose that a general exchange of prisoners shall take place at this post on the eighteenth of December. All negroes in your hands, whether captured or absconded from their masters, are to be delivered up.

"My letter to the Chiefs of the Lower towns of the 1st instant, has informed you of the threatened invasion of those towns by General Logan, with a large party of men from Kentucky, unauthorised by Government.—I have now to add, as my advice to you and your people, that in case Logan should carry his intended invasion of your country into execution; and should he kill many or few of your people, or destroy much of your property, that it shall not prevent the proposed exchange of prisoners, nor prevent the meeting at this place on the 18th of December, when we will endeavour to heal all matters in difference that can at that time exist, between the Lower towns and the United States, and in the mean time let the injuries received by your nation from General Logan be what they may, you will consult the happiness of your nation; and insure the blessing of returning peace by restraining the warriors from turning out and taking satisfaction.—Peace must take place at some time, and the less blood is shed the sooner, and more easily it will be effected. I assure you in case you do not oppose General Logan, nor take satisfaction for such injuries as he may do you, that the United States will pay you for the loss of such houses and corn, as he may destroy, your other property you can move out of the way.*—The United States are very tender of their citizens and love peace; and would prefer paying you for your houses and corn, to having them killed in satisfaction for your injuries, or to being forced into a war with your nation.

"It is essential to the happiness of your nation, that I should speak plainly to you about the Creeks, by whose hands you are sensible the frontier inhabitants of this country have bled at every pore; they are without pretext for such conduct, that these people have not taken their lands; for it is not [is it not] a fact, that in the division of lands among the red people, that the ridge which divides the waters of Mobile and Tennessee, bounds them on the North? Then they pass quite through the Cherokee and Chickasaw lands, to arrive at our frontiers, and there kill our men at their ploughs, or our women and children in their houses.

"If you would secure a continuance of peace with the United States, it will be a duty you owe to yourselves as well as the United States, not to permit the Creeks to pass through your country; or if any should slip through, and your people should discover them on their return with hair or horses, to seize them and bring them to this place, as the Upper towns served one last summer.

"I have now to tell you what I believe to be the general will of the United States with respect to the Creeks, which is, if they do not imme-

*Whether or not Governor Blount's letters to General Logan & Col: Whitley prevented the prosecution of the Campaign is not known; there is no account that it was prosecuted.—ED.

diately desist from murdering the frontier citizens, and also cease to rob them of their property, that next spring or summer, they well see a strong army in their country; and it is will known, that the Chickasaw nation and part of the Choctaws, are friends of the United States, and enemies of the Creeks, and it is recently proved that the upper part of your nations are determined no longer to submit to their insolence and injuries.—You are at liberty to tell to the Creeks what I say, not so much as a threat, but as information to them, to enable them to judge how best to seek their own happiness."

Colonel Watts.—"I wish the time proposed for the exchange of prisoners had been sooner, but as I suppose, you put it off to so distant a day, to afford time to collect them, I agree to it. I fear the damage General Logan will do my nation will be very great, but as you advise, I will instruct all my people, and whatever he may do shall not prevent the proposed meeting and exchange of prisoners.

"What you say about the boundary of the Creek lands is right, but they are a great and powerful nation, and the Cherokees are but few and cannot prevent their passing through their lands when they please to go to war; and on their passage they kill our hogs and cattle, and steal our horses, which we dare not resent. The upper Cherokees were right in seizing one last summer and delivering him up to you, and in killing two others, they live far from the Creek country, and have the white people to support them; but the lower towns are but few, live near the Creeks, and too distant from the white people to be supported by them.—I know the Chickasaws, and five of the Choctaws towns are friends to the United States, and will fight against their enemies."

Scolacutta, or the Hanging Maw.—"I ordered the Creek seized,—I ordered the two Creeks to be killed, and will kill my own people, if they kill white people. Here is some tobacco sent by the Long Warrior, just delivered to me by a runner; you must smoke some of it."—(Here a pipe was handed, and Scolacutta, Col. Watts, the Governor and others smoked)—"He speaks peace for his part of the nation; he has long been a head man, and loves peace."

Governor Blount.—"I have omitted to give you the particulars of General Wayne's victory over the nortern Indians, (addressing himself to Col. Watts) but if you wish to hear them, I will give them."

Colonel Watts.—"I do not. Some of my people were in the action, who have already informed me."

Governor Blount.—"Then I have nothing more to add, except to repeat to you and your nation, that peace is the wish of the United States."[441]

The treaty which was to have taken place on the 18th of December 1794 at Tellico Block House did not succeed, the Cherokees having brought forward two prisoners only; They informed Governor Blount, that they had sent runners to collect prisoners who had not returned—They appeared anxious for peace.[442]

1795, February 17. The Indians attacked a party of men with stores &c. on their way from Cincinnati to Greenville; about seven miles from Fort Hamilton. Three of the party were killed and four wounded—On the same evening the Indians stole 30 horses from Fort Hamilton—A considerable number of Indians had visted Greenville in a friendly manner several days previous to this affair, and left that place about the 14th, and there is strong grounds to suspect that it was by them this mischief was done.[443]

That the inhabitants of Kentucky had good cause to complain of neglect in the general government, respecting their just claim to the free use of the navigation of the Mississippi, must be evident, when a view is taken of the method adopted to give them information, what measures had been taken by the General Government on that subject.—As early as the 29th March 1794, Mr. Randolph addressed a letter to the Governor of Kentucky, informing him that a special messenger had been sent to lay before the succeeding legislature a view of the negotiations with Spain on that subject—This messenger did not arrive in Kentucky until Jan. 1795, after the legislature had adjourned.[444]

SECTION 62

A Young Nation Asserts Its Rights

[January 2 and 9, 1829]

Official correspondence between the special commissioner from the United States, and the Governor of Kentucky, on the subject of the navigation of the Mississippi.

"Frankfort, January 16th, 1795
"SIR,—I have the honour to enclose to you a letter from the Secretary of State, which will fully disclose the object of my mission to this country.

"Of the Presidents intention, to give full effect to the resolution of the

Senate of the United States (herewith enclosed No. 1) by adopting the measure, of sending a special commissioner to detail the faithful history of the negotiations pending between the United States and the court at Madrid, respecting the navigation of the Mississippi, you have some time since been duly apprised, by the department of State (No. 2).

"A series of untoward events, prevented my arrival into Kentucky, at an earlier period.

"As the adjournment of your Legislature prevents the mode of communicating the progress and *real* state of the treaty above alluded to, which was, contemplated by the secretary of State; I shall take the liberty, by your Excellency's permission through the channel of a correspondence with yourself, to give a written narrative of the measures which have been directed, and are now pursuing, under the orders of the President of the United States to obtain and establish, for all time to come, the unimpeded navigation of the Mississippi. Of this information you will be pleased to make such, an use, as may most effectually tend to satisfy the minds of your fellow citizens on the Western waters, by unfolding to them the undisguised state of negotiation, in the issue of which although they, from local considerations, may feel themselves immediately involved, yet in truth, is the whole American republic, materially concerned.

"The genuine and fundamental interests of every part of which being founded on the same great principles of national freedom and prosperity, an injury offered to the remotest point of it, sensibly affects the whole system.

"Should the mode I have suggested of presenting to the public attention, the communications I am charged to make, meet with your approbation after a notification thereof, I shall proceed without delay to adopt the same.

"If any subjects of inquiry occur to your mind, on which you would wish particular information, by specifying them, in the answer with which you will please to favour me, to this address, they shall be particularly noticed, as my inclinations correspond with my instructions, to be candid and explicit, according to the extent of my knowledge, in all the explanations which may be required of me.

"I have the honor to be, with sentiments of proper consideration and respect,

"Your Excellency's most obedient servant,   JAS. INNES.[445]
"His Excellency Isaac Shelby."

"State of Kentucky, Lincoln county,
January 21st, 1795

"SIR,
"I was yesterday honoured with your letter of the 16th inst. by Mr. Lewis.

"The satisfaction I have received from the President's sending a special messenger, to detail a faithful history of the negotiation pending between the United States and the court of Madrid, respecting the navigation of the Mississippi, has been much increased by the choice he has made of a gentleman of your character to fill that office.

"The manner in which you propose to make your communications, is not [only] perfectly agreeable to me, but in my opinion the only proper one. The communications being made to me in my own official capacity, I shall hold it my indispensable duty, immediately to, make them known to my constituents and fellow citizens; for as freemen deeply interested in the event of a negotiation which has for its object, the obtaining and establishing for all time, the unimpeded navigation of the Mississippi, I consider them as entitled to receive every information which can be given them; and that information cannot be given as satisfactorily in any other manner, as it can be done by laying before them the communications which I shall receive on this subject.

"I consider your instructions to lay before the inhabitants of the Western country, the undisguised state of the negotiation, and your own inclinations to be candid and explicit in doing it, strong proofs of the purity of the intentions of the President, and the proper choice he has made of a commissioner to carry his intentions into effect.

"The liberal and truly federal idea which you express 'that an injury offered to the remotest point of the Union, sensibly affects the whole system,' comes fully up to the opinion and wishes of the citizens of this State: All that we ask of the General Government is that we shall be considered as making a part of one people and one government, and the same care should be taken of our just rights, as would be taken of the acknowledged rights of any other part of the United States.

"As I have no doubt your communications on this most important subject, will be considered full and satisfactory, I shall, until I receive them, decline specifying any subjects on which I would wish particular information; but if after I have received those communications, any explanation or further information should appear to me to be necessary to make them perfectly satisfactory, I will do myself the honour, of addressing you on the subject; for I am convinced in a Government founded on the real principles of liberty, and administered with wisdom & integrity, a full and true statement of public measures, will be found to be the only certain way of preserving the affections, and securing the approbation of the virtuous part of the community.

"Permit me to request that our official correspondence may not only not prevent, but be a means of bringing about a personal acquaintance, which from every consideration both public and private, it is my wish to cultivate with you.

"I have the honour to be, with sentiments of the greatest respect, your most obt humble servt.   ISAAC SHELBY.[446]

"The Hon. JAMES INNES."

> "*State of Kentucky, Frankfort,*
> *February* 15, 1795.

"SIR,

"I was duly honoured with your favour of the 21st of January in answer to mine of the 16th of the same month, and in conformity to the plan, I took the liberty to suggest, which you have been pleased to approve, I shall now proceed to make to you the communication, with which I am charged.

"In presenting to public view, the origin and progress of the negociation now pending between the United States of America and the court of Madrid, respecting the navigation of the Mississippi—it may not be irrelevant, to take a retrospective survey of the conduct of the Spanish Government, towards the United States, at that period of their late war with England, when the American revolution began more interestingly to attract the attention of the nations of Europe. By reverting to that juncture of our affairs, it will readily occur to every *recollecting* mind, that the conduct of the Spanish court was more luke-warm, and distant toward the American States, than that of any other European power, who from principles of long established enmity and rivalship, was equally interested in the dismemberment, and consequent debility of the British empire—and although, under the family compact, of the House of Bourbon—that nation in 1778, entered into the war against England, as the ally and associate of France; yet she made no formal recognition of the independence of the United States; and neither in the origin or termination of the war, did she seem to pay the least regard, to the political interests of confederated America. Whether this cold conduct, on the part of Spain, proceeded from the discordancy of the principles of her government, from those which produced our revolution, and the proximity of our chartered boundaries, to her possessions on the continent, it is not material, at this day to enquire; but this, I believe, is a fact, that, although Congress kept an agent with competent powers, at the court of Madrid, from a very early period of the war; yet no pact or treaty of any kind was ever entered into between the two nations.

"This reservedness on the part of the Spanish nation, and their intimate connexion with France, during the existence of a monarchical form of government in that country rendered the polital [political] deportment of the United States, toward the former nation, a matter of delicacy and importance. By the friendship and assistance of France, the establishment of our Independence had been accelerated, and should it have been prematurely jeopardized, by a conflict with a nation in Europe (*and one at least,* we may suppose there was, panting with eager wishes, for such an inauspicious event to us,) on France must we have again relied, for reiterated assistance, such being our real political situation, immediately after our peace with England, 1783—the circumspection, and prudence, with which it behoved the councils of America, to observe with respect to any measure, which might tend in the smallest degree to shake the alliance, and good understanding subsisting between France, and the United States, or even embarras that nation, in the conduct she was to observe towards her new ally, and her old friend, must be strikingly obvious to every person, who bears in mind how much, the safety and happiness of America, at that early epoch of her independence, rested on the political relations, in which certain powers of Europe stood with respect to each other and to herself.

"But we are relieved from this delicate posture of our affairs with respect to Spain, by the arrival at New York, the then seat of Congress of Don Diego de Gardoqui, in quality of Ambassador, from that court, some time in the spring 1785, about two years after the peace at Paris. This Gentleman having had his audience and produced his credentials, by which it appeared that he was invested with authority to treat with the United States, on the subject of commercial arrangements, and Congress without delay, appointed John Jay, Esq. their Secretary for Foreign affairs, to enter into the negotiation with him. Being specially enjoined to make the right of the United States, to the free use of the Mississippi, from its source to the Ocean, the leading feature of any treaty, which should be entered into between the contracting parties.

"This claim of the United States, was brought forward and pressed, at a very early period of the negotiation, and continued to be presented in different shapes, through the whole course of very lengthy and tedious transactions, which took place between the Congressional, and Spanish agents, on the subject of a commercial treaty. Mr. Gardoqui received the assertion of this right, with affected surprise, denied its admissibility as part of the contemplated treaty, and asserted with vehemence, that his court would never assent to its validity, on any principles. He invariably manifested an irritation of temper whenever our rights to the navigation of the Mississippi was urged upon him. This intemperance of the ambassador, was deemed symtomatic of the spirit, which predominated on that subject at this court, with which, from the circumstances before hinted at, good policy dictated to America, the propriety of observing the strictest harmony.

"Thus circumstanced, the American negotiator resorted to the project of ceding to Spain the exclusive navigation of the Mississippi, for twenty five years, which was intended to operate, not as an abandonment of the right of the United States, but as a mean to obtain an end, to wit, the negotiation of that right, on the part of Spain, after the expiration of the above stipulated period. I know well that the proposal of this measure is still sore to the recollection of our fellow citizens on the Western Waters, and that it created great alarms in the minds of the inhabitants of the Atlantic States also. But in narrating the mere history of it, let me not be considered as the defender of its policy, or expediency. It forms a link in the chain of historical facts, which I shall candidly unfold to your view, and in that spirit of candour, I can assert to you, that the proposition, now alluded to as it stands presented, on the records of Congress, was not intended to generate a renunciation, but on the contrary, an acknowledged establishment, of the right of the United States to the free use of the Mississippi—upon this principle: That if Spain accepted this cession from the *United States,* to the exclusive navigation of that river, for a stipulated time, the acknowledgment *of their right to the navigation,* followed as an unavoidable consequence: For the United States must have *possessed the right,* before they could transfer it, and the *acceptance* of the cession was an *acknowledgement of the possession.* The discord which this proposed expedient, produced in the councils of America, is too notorious to require repetition. It occupied not only the attention of congress, for many months, but the subject was also taken up by some of the State legislators, who denounced the measure, as unconstitutional, destructive and dishonourable. In fact, this negotiation, which had exhausted much time, and had progressed so far, as to reduce into shape some specific articles, for future arrangements, between the two nations, was arrested in its course. And it was ultimately deemed proper by the then Congress that the whole business of the Spanish treaty, which from the management of it, had very much agitated the public mind of America should be dismissed from further discussion and turned over as an object of consideration for the present Government of America, which had been adopted, and was then, upon the eve of being put into action. Much about the same period too in July 1789, Mr. Gardoqui, received permission from his court to go back to Spain, on his own private affairs—intending to return and resume the treaty, so soon as the new governmental system should become fully authorized, and begin its functions.—It so happened, however, that after the institution of the General Government, Mr. Gardoqui, the only person empowered by the Spanish court, to treat with the United States, did according to expectations, founded on his own assurances, return to America, and the Secretary of State, who was appointed in September 1789, to whose department this species of executive business appertained—having not arrived from France, the affair of the treaty with Spain could not be immediately acted upon, on account of the respective agents of the two nations, yet, notwithstanding these obstacles, the executive of the United States, did not permit our claim to the navigation of the Mississippi to sleep.

"The nature of the connexions which subsisted at this period, between France and the United States, and between France and Spain, is well known, and has been alluded to. It was perfectly understood by the American government, that although France favoured the pretentions of Spain to the exclusive navigation of the Mississippi within her own boundaries, yet she was well inclined to the prosperity of the United States, and would wish to see an extension of our commerce, of the benefits of which, from existing treaties, she would probably participate. The court of Versailles, therefore, was moved to interpose its mediatoral influence to induce the court of Madrid to acknowledge our right to the navigation of the Mississippi. And this interposition, would probably have produced efficacious consequences, had not the rapid progress of the French revolution, which at first reformed, and afterwards abolished monarchy, cut off all intercourse between the two courts, and placed them in a state of hostility to each other.

"It was expected, that the reassumption of the treaty, would commence under the auspices of the government on this continent, so soon as Mr. Gardoqui should return; an event which never happened; his place in the diplomatic line, being supplied by two gentlemen in the characters of commissioners, from the Spanish court. By them it was proposed, that the executive of the United States should depute some persons to the *Court of Madrid*, to revive the navigation, which Mr. Gardoqui was first authorised to originate in America. Although the transfer of the scene of negotiation, from America to Europe, was an event which was much wished could have been avoided, among other important considerations, on account of the inevitable delay, which it would occasion: yet the proposition was immediately closed with. To give dispatch to this business the agents to execute it, were appointed in Europe. Mr. Short our minister resident at the seven United Provinces, with Mr. Carmichael our Charge des Affaires, at the court of Spain, were appointed commissioners plenipotentiary, to conduct this important negotiation.

"The leading principles by which they were to be governed, in the renewal of this treaty, were amply and forcibly delineated, in the instructions which they received. In which, our right to navigate the Mississippi, from the source to the ocean, and the extension of the southern boundary of the United States to the 31st degree of latitude north of the Equator, resting on two solid and distinct foundations, to wit, the treaties of Paris in 1753 [1763] and 1782-3, and the laws of Nature and of Nations, were directed to be insisted upon, as the indispensible preliminaries, and sine qua nons, to the proposed treaty. It is further enjoined, that any treaty, which may be entered into, shall in every other respect be limited in its duration, but in regard to the above two articles it shall be final and perpetual.

"Our rights to the navigation of the Mississippi from its source, to where our Southern boundary strikes it, cannot be disputed; it is from that point downwards only, that the exclusive navigation is claimed by Spain; that is to say, where she holds the country on both sides, leaving the Mississippi in that statu quo, the Spanish court, it is believed, would without hesitation, enter into commercial regulations with the United States, on terms of reciprocal benefits to both nations, but that it is declined on our part, until our rights to the free use of the Mississippi, shall be most *unquestionably acknowledged and established on principles never hereafter to be drawn into contestation.*

"But as the mere naked right to navigate the Mississippi, would not from the peculiar circumstances attending the Western waters, be completely beneficial, without the use of a port of depot for importations and exportations, somewhere upon the banks of the river, about the mouth of it, contiguous to the sea; the commissioners are instructed to endeavour to purchase, or otherwise obtain, on account of the United States, in a safe and proper position, the right of soil, in as much land as will commodiously answer that purpose.

"The documents, requiring our resident at the Hague, to repair to Madrid, in the capacity of Commissioner Plenipotentiary, for the purpose above stated, having been attended in their transmission, with considerable and very unfortunate delay, he did not arrive at that city as soon as was expected, which consequently retarded the revival of the negotiation. Mr. Short, however, reached the Spanish court in the early part of 1792; from which period, in cooperation with his associate, Mr. Carmichel, the most unceasing efforts have been made by them, to obtain the objects of their mission.

"There was a season since the recommencement of this negotiation, when the Spanish and English nations, seem to be on the verge of hostilities, in which, it was hoped, that the former, from motives of policy and self interest, (that most predominant motive with nations) would have been induced to have done an act of justice, by restoring to the United States an embarrassed participation, in the use of the Mississippi. But this prospect of discord was but of a short duration. A compromise of all disputes, took place between those two courts, and Spain, allied with England, soon became parties, in the confederacy of despots, against the liberties of France.

"The political connexion existing at present, between Spain and England, will not, it may be apprehended, be an advantageous event to our negotiation at the court of the former. For I believe it has rarely happened, that the interests of the United States, have been remarkably patronized, in countries, where Spanish influence has preponderated.

"Notwithstanding the embarrassment, with, it was feared, a combination of political incidents in Europe would produce, our commissioners were, nevertheless, unremittingly assiduous, in pressing the Spanish ministry to enter fully into the leading principles of the negotiation, which they had come to Madrid, for the purpose of reviving. After some ceremonious delays, Mr. Gardoqui was reappointed by the Spanish court to recommence this business.

"The American Commissioners brought forward our claims to the navigation of the Mississippi, and the extent of our Southern boundary; sustained by a memorial, replete with arranged, and irrefragable arguments, drawn from the stipulation of treaties, and the laws of nature and nations. To this memorial, the Spanish agent did not return an answer, and the discussion of the merits of the above memorial, though not positively denied; yet has been cautiously and rather vexatiously avoided, by the Spanish minister, by resorting to every species of evasion, and procrastination, which the pompous parade, and ceremonies of European courts, can readily supply. This unwarrantable, and dilatory conduct of the court of Spain, was soon perceived and considered in its proper light by the Executive of the United States; whose determination it had been, from the first, to pursue our claims to the Mississippi, with *temper* yet *firmness*, and to prevent if possible, an abrupt schism of a negotiation, which had been with so much difficulty reintroduced on the tapis, until every principle of reason and argument appendant to it, should be fairly discussed.

"In order therefore, to cut off all farther retardments, which might originate from ceremonies and formal exceptions, flowing from the alleged incompetency of powers, and the dignity of diplomatic office. It was determined to dispatch an Envoy Extraordinary to the court of Madrid, most unexceptionably and copiously authorised in every particular, to bring this tedious negotiation to an end. To effect this the concurrence of the Senate was necessary, which was at that time not in session; yet the executive, anxious to procure in time a proper character for so important an undertaking, caused an application to be made, first to Mr. Thomas Jefferson and next to Mr. Patrick Henry, (two citizens, equally illustrious for their patriotism and great talents, and well known to be warmly devoted to the prosperity of the Western country,) to enter upon this embassy.

"They having both declined this office, for the sake of expedition, among other weighty considerations, Mr. Pinkney, the American minister at the court of London, has been ordered to hold himself in a state of preparation to repair most expeditiously to the court of Madrid; who, it is probable is at this moment occupied in the arduous affairs of the Spanish treaty, as his powers only waited for the sanction of the Senate, which has been long since convened. His instructions will be similar to those given to commissioners Short and Carmichael, *he will press not only our rights, but will derive all the aid to our interest, which may arise colatterly from the events of the present war in Europe, or any influence which other circumstances may give to the United States.*

"At this distance, and in our present state of information, it will be difficult to assert, what may be the *immediate event* of this negotiation, which seems to be capable of being affected, by a variety of contingencies beyond the control of the American government. We have indisputable right on our side, *which* it is much to be wished for the happiness of mankind, should always form the rule of decission among nations. But perhaps there is much reason to lament, that in the old government of the world, *right* is often *resolved into power*.

"As a young nation, just taking our stand among the empires of the world, before we have arrived at that maturity of strength, and vigor, which a thousand combining events, promise we shall speedily attain—it has been deemed the wiser policy, rather to endeavour to establish our rights, by negotiation, than by a premature resort to the *ultima ratio*. The first being a safer and more certain mode of redress, and such an one, as the present situation of the United States, lays them under an almost paramount necessity, to observe the temporary abstinence from the exercise of a right, which at this period, a combination of political events renders it prudent for us to observe, can never be construed, into a derelection of that right.

"There is no man, who will cast his eyes on the immense and fertile vales which border on the western waters, and mark the rapid progress which population, agriculture, and all the useful arts, are making among them, that can one moment doubt, but that these channels, which beneficent nature has opened for the diffusion of the superabundance of all the necessaries, and comforts of life, yielded by these happy regions, among the poorer nations of the earth, *must* be applied to their great providential end; notwithstanding the obstructions, at present opposed, by an unjust, narrow, and short-sighted policy. It is an event, which the interest of Spain herself desiderates, could she but view that interest, through the proper medium. It is an event, which the happiness of the human species requires. It is an event, in which the United States are interested.

"I am well aware of the jealous apprehensions which are entertained, that some States in the Union, are averse to opening the navigation of the Mississippi. This jealousy as it extends to States, I am confident, embraces too extensive a range. For little minded local, *antifederal politicians*, who infest, in a greater or smaller degree, every State in the Union, I will not be answerable. Yet, I believe, I may fairly affirm, that the interests of the nation at large, coincide in the establishment of this important right, and that to whatever object, their interests point, their government will endeavour to attain. There are two strong political considerations, which will impel the United States, conjointly to struggle without ceasing, until the navigation of the Mississippi is obtained.

"I mean, the principles of national right, and Interest.

"The right of the United States to the navigation of the Mississippi, being established, as it must incontestibly is on the double basis of political compacts, and the title derived from the laws of nature and nations, I know not, on what more substantial grounds rest *their* rights, to navigate the waters flowing through their territories into the Atlantic Ocean. To resign one *right*, to the arm of power would be establishing a precedent by which their others might be claimed and taken. All the motives therefore, flowing from the consideration of political safety, and national pride, aided by paternal incitements would stimulate every State in the Union, to make *one cause, when the last necessity shall demand it*, to reclaim and vindicate this suspended and violated right.

"But the interests of the Atlantic States, are involved in the unimpeded navigation of the Mississippi, on two principles.

"The results of the exports through the western waters, will, with a few exceptions, come into their ports, which will not only greatly augment the national revenue, accruing from the impost and duties on imported articles, but will be beneficial also to merchants, and others, residing at the particular ports of importation.

"Besides, the transportation of the commodities of the country on this side the Apalachian mountains, which will be bulky in their nature, to the market in the American and European sea,—will furnish considerable employment, to the seamen and ships, of the maritime states, which it will be the interest of the western merchants, rather to employ, than to attempt the building of vessels, proper for transmarine voyages, on their own waters, amidst the almost insuperable difficulties, that must attend such an undertaking, which if even practicable, necessary seaman would be wanting, who are always scarce in countries, where lands are fertile and abundant and easily to be acquired.

"In addition to this consideration, the peculiar nature of the inland navigation of the western waters, will never furnish a nursery for sailors. The most expert navigator of the waters of the Ohio, would find himself perfectly helpless, and bewildered, on the deep, and boisterous elements of the ocean.

"The principals of national policy, and interest, thus combining to make the navigation of the Mississippi, as much the common cause of the United States, as any other right they possess, it ought naturally to be presumed, until the revenue shall be shewn, and which, I trust, never can be done, that, that right, has neither ever been, nor ever will be abandoned or neglected.

"To prove that every measure compatible with the situation of the United States, has been adopted to reclaim it, will fully appear by recurring to the joint votes of assentation, on that subject, of the two houses of Congress, which have been forwarded to your Excellency, on a former occasion. The energetic language of the popular branch of that body, I mean the house of representatives, cannot fail to strike the attention of the most cursory observer. If therefore when all the modes of honourable negotiation, shall be pushed to their ne plus ultra, and fruitlessly tried, and the executive shall be found to have essayed in vain, all the pacific measures, belonging to that department of government, and no other alternative remains, but a resort must be made, from the *mode of an amicable adjustment of our claim, to the means constitutionally belonging to the legislature of the Union;* let it not be forgotten, that the united hearts, and arms of the confederate republic of America, which achieved its independence, and can alone vindicate, and establish all the privileges, adhering to it. Precipitation, and partial acts of unauthorised violence, will tend only to weaken our efforts, and instead of accelerating will undoubtedly retard the attainment of our end.

"From this view of the facts (and trust me, sir, it is a just one,) I hope it will appear manifest, that the *wishes of this country* as expressed in your Excellency's letter, have been amply complied with, and that it has ever been considered as making part of the American people, and a component part of the American Government, and that the same care has been taken of the just rights of Kentucky, as has been taken of the acknowledged rights of any other part of the United States, among which, no distinct and appropriate political rights exist; they being made by their government, the common property of them all.

"Yes, sir, the American citizens on the eastern and western waters, form one people, and one government; and he who wishes them separated, is a sinner against the *happiness and prosperity of the present and future generations.* The great author of nature, has founded their union on the broad basis of reciprocity, which will remain as it ought to be, (on the pure principles of representation, engrafted in our government,) eternal, unless dissevered by the wicked machinations of a mad and deluded ambition.

"This retrospective view, of the transactions which I have presented before you, in the train in which they have happened, attended with a few observations, which grew out of those, I trust will shew that the government of the United States, has neither under former, or present organization, abandoned, or been inattentive, to our right of navigating the Mississippi. That right was brought under negotiation, at the very first moment, in which the political circumstances of the United States would permit it to be done. The negotiation respecting it, although attended with some unlucky events, did not expire, with the former Congressional government, but was turned over among the other inchoate, and uncompleted acts of that body to the new governmental system of America, since the operation of which, it has *never been one moment dormant,* when from uncontrolable circumstances, this subject might have rested for a short time, from the absence of the national agents, who were to agitate it, to keep it still in action, the interference of the only foreign court, on whose friendship America could depend, and the only one, the most likely to have weight with the court of Madrid, was solicited to give aid, and effect to the exertions of our own agents, who have been instructed, to treat with Spain, on no other terms, than the previous ratification of the Southern boundary and the right to navigate the Mississippi, from the source to the ocean. A succession of political events, have taken place in Europe, which has retarded the progress of that negotiation, and prevented its being brought as yet, to a favourable issue. To obtain it however, measures correspondent to the importance of the object have been assiduously resorted to and are now in action.

"It must be peculiarly obvious, to a candid, and impartial mind, (and such an one the personage I have now the honour to address, I am sure possesses,) that from the commencement of the administration of the present chief magistrate of America, which happened at a period when our national affairs, were in a perfect state of disorganization, among the number of momentous considerations, which have engrossed his attention, he has without cessation, pursued the navigation of the Mississippi. But on this head, I am sure, it will be necessary for me to say nothing. No apology is required for his conduct. He has too fair a claim to our confidence to be accused of a partial inattention to any of our rights—and will, I trust, be boundlessly confided in, and venerated, until gratitude ceases to be an American virtue.

"Before I conclude this letter, I cannot refrain from returning you my candid thanks, for the flattering and polite manner, in which you have been pleased to express yourself of me personally. The motives which induced the President to depute me hither, were most pure and patriotic, being in conformity to a maxim he has observed in his administration, to satisfy his constituents, by a proper information of his measures, that none of their interests have been unattended to. There may be reason, to lament, that an agent more competent to give proper effect, to such laudable intentions, had not been sent; yet, in zeal, faithfully to execute the trust confided to and in sincere attachment to the happiness and interests of my fellow citizens residing on the Western Waters, as a portion of the great American Republic, I hope I shall be found second to no man.

"For the purpose of cultivating that personal acquaintance between us, which you are pleased to proffer, I mean to do myself the honor of waiting upon you, before I depart from the State; an event from which I anticipate much satisfaction.—Having ever been induced to hold your reputation, both as a soldier and citizen, in perfect esteem.

"With every sentiment of personal respect, and with warm wishes for the continuance and increase of that prosperity which so conspicuously marks this flourishing State over which you have the honour to preside,[447]

"I remain your excellency's Most obedient servant,

JAMES INNES."[448]

"His Excellency Isaac Shelby."

"State of Kentucky, Lincoln County
February 20, 1795

SIR:—Your favor of the 15th of this month, stating the origin and progress of the negotiation now pending/between the United States of America and the court of Madrid, respecting the navigation of the Mississippi, is now before me, and affords me great satisfaction.

"I forbear to make any observations on the transactions which took place in this important business, under the former government of America, because I trust, that schemes so replete with injustice and dishonor as those were which were then agitated, will never be revived, under the present general government.

"The just regard and attention which the President has paid to our rights, and his refusing to enter into any Commercial regulations with the court of Madrid, 'until our right to the free use of the Mississippi shall be most unequivocally acknowledged, and established on principles never hereafter to be drawn into contestation,' deserve our warmest thanks and gratitude. His intentions also, of sending an envoy extraordinary, to bring this *tedious* negotiation to an end, and the choice which he made of those patriots, to whom we would most willingly entrust our dearest interests, to fill that important office, must necessarily add to our sensibility on this occasion.

"We have to lament, that accidents and uncontrollable events, should so long have delayed the completion of this (to us all important) negotiation: This delay, and our being strangers to the real cause of it until this time, will naturally account for the uneasiness and discontent, which prevailed here on the subject; although we have placed as unbounded confidence in the President, as any of the citizens of America; *The proper communications* now made by you sir, on this occasion, and the general satisfaction, which I have no doubt will be the consequence of those communications, will, I hope, sufficiently prove, that a more early communication of the kind, would have prevented all uneasiness and discontent in this country on this subject.

"I anticipate with the utmost confidence, that from the observations which your short stay in this country will enable you to make on the citizens, your candor and judgment will induce, and enable you to report to the President, that there is no reason to apprehend that his efforts, to obtain for us the great object of our wishes, will be weakened, or the attainment itself retarded, by precipitation and partial acts of unauthorised violence, proceeding from the citizens of this country; I flatter myself also, that you will think yourself justified in saying, that the citizens of this country are as warmly attached to the American Union, as the inhabitants of any part of the continent, and that they possess too much understanding and independence to be deceived, 'by the wicked machinations, of mad and deluded ambition.'

"I should do injustice to my own feelings, and violate the trust reposed in me by my fellow citizens, if I did not embrace this opportunity of assuring the President, that the citizens of this country, have but one opinion on this important subject. They consider their right to the free navigation of the Mississippi, as indubitable, and the enjoyment of it as indispensibly necessary to their existence as a people, and they look forward to the attainment of this right, only from the steady, proper and spirited exertions of our government, for they have no expectations of being put into the possession of it, by the voluntary consent of those who now withhold it.

"Allow me, Sir, as the representative of my countrymen, to return you our thanks, for the zealous and able manner in which you have expressed your opinion of our rights, and your wishes for our uninterrupted enjoyment of that right. We shall long remember with pleasure, that so distinguished a citizen of the Eastern part of America, has unequivocally declared his approbation of the great object pursued by the inhabitants of the Western country.

"With every sentiment of respect and esteem I have the honor to be, Sir, Your most obedient servant,   "ISAAC SHELBY.[449]
"HON. JAMES INNIS.

The following are the proceedings referred to in the Correspondence between the Special Commissioner (James Innis, Esq.) from the United States, and the Governor of Kentucky, on the subject of the navigation of the Mississippi:

No. 1
"CONGRESS OF THE UNITED STATES"
"IN SENATE, MAY 15, 1794."

"Mr. Ellsworth, from the committee to whom was referred, certain resolutions moved for the 15th of April last, by the Senator of Kentucky, relating to the navigation of the Mississippi, and the negotiation at the court of Spain, reported.

"That in the negotiation now carrying on at Madrid, between the United States and Spain, the right of the former to the free navigation of the Mississippi, is well asserted and demonstrated, and their claim to its enjoyment is pursued, with all the assiduity and firmness which the magnitude of the subject demands, and will doubtless continue to be so pursued until the object shall be obtained, or adverse circumstances shall render the further progress of navigation impracticable. That in the present state of the business, it would be improper for Congress to interfere. But in order to satisfy the citizens of the United States, more immediately interested in the event of this negotiation, that the United States have uniformly asserted their right to the free use of the navigation of the river Mississippi, and have employed, and will continue to pursue such measures as are best adapted to obtain the enjoyment of this important territorial right, the committee recommend that it be

"*Resolved* by the Senate that the President of the United States be, and he hereby is requested to cause to be communicated, to the executive of the State of Kentucky, such part of the existing negotiation between the United States and Spain, relative to the subject, as he may deem advisable and consistent with the course of negotiations.

"And the report was adopted.

"Ordered, that the Secretary lay a copy of this proceeding before the President of the United States.

"Attest,   *Sam A. Ottis* [Otis,] Secretary."[450]

No. 2

Philadelphia, August 15, 1794.

"SIR—I have not been able to learn, except by an uncertain report, whether the letter which I had the honor of addressing to your excellency on the 29 of March, 1794, has reached you.—If it has, a considerable portion of the task assigned to my department, under the enclosed resolutions of the Senate and House of Representatives, will have been anticipated, and therefore I take the liberty of renewing it by a duplicate.

"When those resolutions passed, little of importance could be added to what had been already communicated. And even now, the subsequent occurrences, have not yet brought the subject to its maturity. But has appeared to the President advisable to send to Kentucky a special Commissioner, who, possessing an accurate and comprehensive knowledge of the whole negociation, and of the views and disposition of the General Government, may frankly and explicitly lay them before the Legislature of your State. Such a character will therefore attend your Excellency as soon as the proper arrangements can be completed; and it is hoped by the President, that you will furnish him with an opportunity of presenting himself and the objects of his mission, to the Legislature.

"In this step, your Excellency will discern a further proof of the anxiety of the President, to remove all grounds of dissatisfaction. And indeed, Sir, I cannot pass by this occasion of asserting my persuasion, that after the most ample disclosure of the public conduct, respecting the Mississippi, you will find that nothing has been left unattempted by him, which his powers, his exertions and the situation of our country would permit.

"I have the honor, to be Sir, With great respect, Your Excellency's Most obedient servant,   EDMUND RANDOLPH."

"True Copy, *George Taylor, Jr.* [451]

"His Excellency the Governor of Kentucky"

SECTION 63

Ending Kentucky's Indian Menace

[January 16, 1829]

Preparatory to the treaty proposed to be held with several tribes of the Indians, at Greenville, on the 15th day of June, General Wayne issued the following Proclamation:

> *"By His Excellency Anthony Wayne, Esquire, Major General and commander in chief of the Legion, and commissioner Plenipotentiary of the United States of America, for establishing a permanent peace with all the Indian tribes and nations North West of the Ohio.*
> L.S.

"A PROCLAMATION.

"Whereas I the said Plenipotentiary, by virtue of the power and authority in me vested, have entered into certain preliminary articles with the following tribes and nations of Indians, viz: The Wyandots, Chippiweas, Potowatomies, Miames, Shawanees and Dilawares, for a cessation of hostilities, and for the mutual exchange and surrender of all prisoners of every description, as well as for holding a general treaty for settling all cases of controversy, and for establishing a permanent peace between the United States and the aforesaid tribes of indians, on or about the 15th day of June next ensuing.

"Wherefore, I do hereby in the name of the President of the United

States, prohibit and forbid all and every person and persons from killing, insulting or injuring any Indian or Indians belonging to the aforesaid tribes or nations, or any of them, (unless in their own defence.) And I do hereby also forbid any party or parties, of citizens of the U. States or either of them; from entering the Indian country, North West of the Ohio, with hostile intentions (without permission from proper authority first obtained) between this period and the end of the pending treaty, as they will answer a contrary conduct at their peril.

"And to the end that the treaty may be carried into complete effect, agreeably to the true intent and meaning of the preliminary articles,* the said Plenipotentiary enjoins all and every person and persons having in his or their possession any Indian prisoners belonging to those or either of those nations, to surrender them and each of them at this place, on or before the said fifteenth day of June next, and for which reasonable expences will be allowed by the public.

"*Given under my hand and seal, at Head Quarters, this 22d day of February,* 1795. ANT'Y WAYNE,
"By order of the Commander in Chief, "W.H. Harrison
"Aid de Camp." [452]

About the 15th of March, 1795, two men who went on shore from a boat descending the Ohio river, to shoot turkeys, were fired on by Indians, and boath wounded; their wounds being slight, they escaped to the boat and saved themselves.

About the same time the Indians killed a man on Goose creek and stole horses.

An express from Piomingo to General Robinson arrived on the 14th March. After giving the General an account of Capt. Colbert (a half blood) with a party of Chickasaws pursuing a party of Creeks, killing ten of them and taking six prisoners, he says to Gen. Robinson, "Do not wait to consult the President, or any other person; count your men and come on."

On the 24th day of March, 1795, the Indians broke into a house in Clarke county, about six miles from Bourbon-furnace, and killed three negroes—a man, a woman and a child.

On the 4th of May, 1795, two men who were hunting horses, in Madison county, were fired on by a party of Indians, and one of them killed.

About the same time the Indians stole horses from Mann's lick. A number of spies who had been on a scout, came across their trail, and pursued them to the Ohio river, where they overtook them and killed three of the Indians, wounded one and retook all the horses.

On the 14th May, 1795, Mr. Nathaniel Massie, with about fifty men,

*These Preliminary articles mislaid or lost.

fell in with a party of about thirty Indians encamped on Paint creek, a branch of the Scioto river, fifteen of whom were warriors, the remainder women and children. An action ensued in which one of the whitemen was killed. The Indians were drawn from their camp, and their horses and baggage consequently fell into the hands of the whites. Massie and his party then steered for Kentucky, and on the next morning about day break they were attacked by the Indians, and after a sharp conflict for a few minutes the Indians retired. One whiteman was wounded in the thigh and two horses killed. The plunder taken sold for $500.

A lad who had been taken prisoner in February, was with the Indians and escaped to the whites during the action on the morning of the 15th. He informed Mr. Massie that this party of Indians had received orders from Gen. Wayne to leave that neighbourhood and come to the treaty, which they positively refused to comply with—They were Shawanese.

On the 25th of May, 1795, the Ohio Packet boat was fired on by the Indians near the three Islands, there were five men on board the boat, four of whom were wounded, two mortally, who died of their wounds. The following day the Indians fired on a family boat, shot twelve balls into the side of the boat, and killed a horse on board.

On the 28th of May, 1795, the Indians took two boys prisoners near the mouth of Kentucky.

On the 29th, a company with whom were a woman and three children, on their way from the Crab-Orchard to the station in the Wilderness, were fired on by a party of Indians, on the waters of Rock Castle—a man and one of the children were killed, and the woman taken prisoner.

From the month of January to the month of June in 1795, 2400 emigrants passed the station on Richland creek, on their way to Kentucky.

Copy of a letter from His Excellency William Blount, Esq. Governor of the South Western Territory, to His Excellency Isaac Shelby Esq. Governor of Kentucky.
"KNOXVILLE, June 11th, 1795.
"SIR:—Having a few days past received a Talk, dated April 3d, from the Chiefs of both the Upper and Lower Creeks, in which they give assurances of peace to the citizens of the United States, including Kentucky and Cumberland, I have believed it necessary to inclose to your Excellency a copy of it. I also inclose a copy of a report of John M'Kee, temporary agent to the Cherokees of the 27th ultimo; Mr. M'Kee, from his long acquaintance with Indians, is not apt to believe them sincere when they give assurance of peace, but now he believes they are much more generally so (young warriors included) than at any time since the war commenced between Great Britain and America. But while I am transcribing to you these papers, which seem to contain the best assurance of peace that I have received from the Creeks and Cherokees, I cannot but lament, that two parties of people have been lately attacked by Indians upon the

road that leads to your country, and if my information be correct, as many as eight killed, wounded & missing. May not these injuries as probably have been done by the Northern as Southern Indians? Both are speaking peace, and are I presume, equally faithless; or perhaps more properly speaking, the chiefs of no Indian nation can govern the whole of their young warriors.

"The conferrence that was to have taken place at Tellico Block-House, with the Cherokees on the 1st instant, is postponed until the annual allowance from the United States in goods shall come forward, and when this will be is uncertain; but prior to its taking place, I shall be under the necessity of again troubling your Excellency about the Cherokee prisoners, yet in the hands of the citizens of Kentucky.

"I have the honor to be, with great respect and esteem, Your most obedient, humble servant,   WILLIAM BLOUNT.
"His Excellency, *Isaac Shelby, Esq.*
Governor of Kentucky."[453]

OAKFUSKEYS, Upper Creek, April 3, 1795.
A TALK from the Chief of the Upper and Lower Creeks assembled, to his Excellency, WILLIAM BLOUNT, Esq. Governor of the Western Territory.
"We the Chiefs of the Upper and Lower Creeks here assembled, inform his Excellency Governor Blount, and all his subjects in the Western Territory, that we are here met and convened with a full resolution to make a firm and lasting peace with the whole of the subjects of the United States, and that we are at this time set about the business of collecting the horses, white prisoners, negroes and all other property in our land belonging to the subjects of the United States, whether from Cumberland,† Kentucky, or any other part of the Western Territory, which according to the present demand of James Seagrove, Esq. Agent of Indian affaires, we the Chiefs of this nation, mean to set off in a few days down to Georgia, at the place appointed to meet our beloved man James Seagrove, Esq. and deliver to him all the said property and white prisoners, at which time, we the Chiefs of this nation have concluded to direct our beloved man James Seagrove, Esq. to forward the property belonging to the Western Territory to that quarter, and at the same time, we the Chiefs intend to request our beloved man James Seagrove, Esq. to write fully our friendly intentions to all the several Governments and officers of the Western Territories.

"We the Chiefs met here, inform Governor Blount and all his officers, that they may put full confidence in what we say, and that we from this time are determined to bury the hatchet, guns and other sharp weapons, and take all white people by the hand like brothers, and never to spill each

†The name by which West Tennessee was then generally known.—ED.

other's blood, any more. We the Chiefs of the Creek nation therefore, inform his Excellency Governor Blount, and all the inhabitants, that they may in future, on receipt of this, work on their farms without the least fear or dread, hunt their stocks, and pass from place to place, without the least apprehension of danger or molestation.

We have to add, that we have this day received a Talk from the Agent of Indian affairs from the United States to the Cherokees, which we take in friendship, and agree one and all to pay attention to. As we had finished all our Talks in favour of peace with the United States this day, therefore hope the Agent of Indian affairs to the Cherokees, will forward these our Talks with despatch to his Excellency Governor Blount and Brigadier General Robertson, and to all other officers and subjects of Western Territory."

"We certify that the above Talk was wrote in our presence, at the request of the Chiefs of the Upper and Lower Creeks.
　(Signed)   "Upper Creeks.
"JOSEPH [his mark] CORNEL, D.A.J.A.
Lower Creek Nation.
TIMOTHY BARNARD, D.A. Indian Affairs, U.S.
"Witness, RICHARD THOMAS, Clerk to the Chiefs of the Upper Creeks." [454]
　"P.S. We have received one prisoner boy named George Brown, son to a Mrs. Brown, formerly a prisoner in this nation."

"TELLICO BLOCKHOUSE,
May 27th, 1795.
"SIR—Annexed you have the proceedings of the council of the Cherokee nation, held at Estanaula on the 20th and 21st instant, I believe sincerely, the Cherokees are in earnest, and determined for peace. The council being put off from the 4th to the 20th, I had an opportunity of being much amongst every description of the nation, and conversing fully. I was several days in company with the Chiefs and warriors of the Lower Towns on the Tennessee, and from every appearance and information I could collect, I think they are now as anxious for peace, as any other part of the Nation, and it is my opinion, that the nation (young warriors included) are generally for peace with the United States. A report had prevailed among them, that they were again to expect a visit from the people of Kentucky and Cumberland, at which they expressed much uneasiness, and asked me if such a thing was anticipated; I assured them of the contrary, and that the people of the two countries were highly desirous of peace, and would not injure them, the Indians had only to keep the peace on their own part, and it would be peace between them and every part of the United States.

"In addition to the assurances of peace on the part of the Creeks given

in council, Chinnebbee, in private conversation, often repeated the same assurances, and told me the people of this Territory might remove the centinels from their doors; but his observations concluded with a hope, that in case any mischief should be done, it would not spoil the good Talks, which seemed to express that he himself had his fears, that some marauding parties of Creeks, may yet do mischief on the frontiers. It is however, due to the three Creek Chiefs to say, that their conduct in and at the Council, appeared open, candid and sincere to such a degree, that they have almost persuaded me, notwithstanding the past conduct of the Creeks, to believe, that that nation wishes and means peace with the United States, this Territory included.

"I have the pleasure to inform your excellency, that the prospects of peace are not confined to the Cherokees and Creeks. All the Cherokees heretofore resident among the hostile Northern tribes, families as well as warriors, have, and are returning to their Nation; and John Taylor, who you know is a well informed Chief of the Cherokees, immediately from Detroit, assures me, that the Northern tribes are sincerely disposed for peace with the United States, and highly displeased with the British.

"I was deprived of the aid of Mr. Dinsmoor's counsil at the Talk, by his detention on business in South Carolina.

"I take this opportunity of offering my opinion, that if Cumberland enjoys peace from the Cherokees (which I think there is good reason to hope) they will owe it to the Chickasaws, and that the frontiers of Washington and Hamilton Districts, may attribute their relief from the scalping knife and hatchet of the Creeks, to the friendly conduct of Scollacutta and his party of the Upper Cherokees last summer, in apprehending the murderer of Ish, and in killing two other Creeks near Maj. Craig's station. They have found the killing and robbing of the people of this country attended with too much danger to themselves.

"Your Excellency will expect from me information respecting the Creek and Chickasaw war. Sometime in April, a deputation was sent by the Cherokees to the Creeks, to urge them to make peace with the Chickasaws, or perhaps more properly to recommend a cessation of hostilities and for other purposes, to which the Creeks readily agreed; but the Cherokee deputies had hardly returned home, before they were followed by Creek runners, with a war club, and an invitation to join them and to go in great force against the Chickasaws. The Turkey to whom the runners first arrived, and delivered the club, desired them to return to their nation, and tell them to forbear to make war upon the Chickasaws, until they made peace with the United States, to which the Cherokees agreed again, so changeable are the Creeks, as the United States have often experienced.

"The Creeks too have received a Talk from the Choctaws, as I was informed, in which they tell the Creeks that they remember the troubles of their former wars, and wish peace; but they cannot account for the conduct of their young warriors, by which the Creeks knowing the disposition of the young Chickasaws not to be friendly, particularly those of the Five Towns, have their fears, that if they prosecute the war against the Chickasaws, that the young Chocktaws, and eventually the whole nation will join the Chickasaws; so that in my opinion, the Creeks will not carry on a war against the Chickasaws, until this breach between them is greater, only by small parties of Creeks, such as the relations of those who have already been killed by the Chickasaws.

"I am with great respect, Your Excellency's most obedient Humble servant,

(Signed)   "JOHN McKEE.
"His Excellency Governor Blount." [455]

Whilst the pleasing prospects of peace with both the Northern and Southern Indians served to amuse the people of Kentucky and Tennessee, the Spaniards were making encroachments on the territory of the United States, by erecting a fort far within the Southern boundary. The first intimation of that event to the people of Kentucky, was from the following article in the Knoxville Gazette of July 3d 1795.

"It is now no longer doubtful, whether the Spanish government have established a fort at the Chickasaw Bluff, in latitude 35 degrees North, upon the East bank of the Mississippi, within the limits of this Territory. The logs, pickets and other materials, were all prepared on the West (Spanish) side of the river, which were brought over with such expedition, that the block house and stockade were erected, and cannon planted in 24 hours. Gayoso, the Governor of the Natches, was himself at the spot, with the Vigilant and two other Gallies: and informed a man who was there at the time he was erecting the block-house that he was determined to establish and maintain at that place, a strong garrison. Certainly the United States, will no longer passively behold the encroachments of the Spanish Government." [456]

The Treaty of Greenville
[January 23, 1829]

"A Treaty of peace between the United States of America, and the Tribes of Indians called the Wyandots, Delawares, Shawanese, Ottoways, Pottowatomies, Miamis, Eelriverwees and Kickapoos, to put an end to a destructive war, to settle all controversies between the said United States and Indian tribes. Concluded August 3d, 1795.
ANTHONY WAYNE, Major General and commander in chief of the army of the United States, and sole commissioner for the good purposes above mentioned, and the said tribes of Indians, by their Sachems, Chiefs and Warriors, met together at Greenville, the head quarters of the said army, have agreed on the following articles; which when ratified by the President, with the advise and consent of the Senate of the United State, shall be binding on them and the said Indian Tribes:

"Art. I. Henceforth all hostilities shall cease; peace is hereby established, and shall be perpetual; and a friendly intercourse shall take place between the said United States and Indian Tribes.

"Art. II. All prisoners shall on each side be restored. The Indian prisoners to the United States shall be immediately set at liberty—The people of the United States still remaining prisoners among the Indians, shall be delivered in ninety days from this date, to the General or Commanding officer at Greenville, Fort Wayne, or Defiance; and ten Chiefs of said Indians shall remain at Greenville, hostages, until the delivery of the prisoners shall be effected.

"Art. III. The general boundary line between the lands of the United States and the lands of the said Indian Tribes, shall begin at the mouth of the Cayahoga river, and run thence up the same to the portage between that and the Tuskarawas branch, to a crossing place above Fort Lawrence. Thence Westwardly to a fork of that branch of the great Miami river, running into the Ohio, at or near which fork, stood Lorrimie's Store, and where commences the portage between the Miami's of the Ohio and Saint Mary's river, which is a branch of the Miami which runs into Lake Erie; thence a Westwardly course to Fort Recovery, which stands on a branch of the Wabash; thence South Westerly in a direct line to the Ohio, so as to intersect that river opposite the mouth of Kentucky or Catawa river. And in consideration of the peace now established, of the goods formerly received from the United States, of those now to be delivered, and of the yearly delivery of goods now stipulated to be made hereafter; and to indemnify the United States for the injuries and expences they have suffered during the war; the said Indian Tribes do hereby cede and relinquish for ever, all their claim to the lands lying Eastward and Southward of the general boundary line now directed and described; and these lands or any part of them, shall never hereafter be made a cause or pretence on the part of the said Tribes, or any of them, of war or injury to the United States, or any of the people thereof, and for the same consideration, and as an evidence of the returning friendship of the said tribes, of their confidence in the United States, and desire to provide for their accommodation, and for that convenient intercourse which will be beneficial to both parties, the said Indian Tribes do also cede to the United States, the following pieces of land, viz: 1st. A piece of land six miles square, at or near Lorrimie's Store, before mentioned. 2nd. One piece of land two miles square, at the head of the navigable water, or landing, on St. Mary's river near Girty's town. 3rd. One piece of land, six miles square, at the head of the navigable water, in Auglaize river. 4th. One piece six miles square, at the confluence of the Auglaize and Miami rivers, where Fort Defiance now stands. 5th. One piece six miles square, at or near the confluence of the river St. Mary's and St. Joseph, where Fort Wayne now stands, or near it. 6th. One piece two miles square, on the Wabash river, at the end of the portage from the Miamis of the Lake, and about eight miles Westward from Fort Wayne. 7th. One piece six miles square at the Aunatannon, or old Weea towns on the Wabash river. 8th. One piece twelve miles square at the British Fort, on the Miami of the Lake, at the foot of the rapids. 9th. One piece six miles square, at the mouth of said river, where it empties into the Lake. 10th. One piece six miles square, upon Sandusky Lake, where a Fort formerly stood. 11th. One piece two miles square, at the lower rapids of the Sandusky river. 12th. The Post of Detroit, and all the lands to the North and West and South of it; of which the Indian title has been extinguished by gifts or grants to French or English Governments, and to so much more land to be annexed to the District of Detroit, as shall be comprehended between the river Raisen on the South, Lake St. Clair on the North end line; the general course of which shall be six miles distant from the West end of Lake Erie and Detroit river. 13th. The Post of Michelamakinac and all the land on the Island on which that Post stands, and the Miami land adjacent, of which the Indian title is extinguished by gifts or grants to the French or English Governments; and a piece of land on the Main to the North of the Island, to measure six miles on Lake Huron, or the strait between Lakes Huron and Michigan, and to extend three miles back from the Lake or Strait. Also the Island De Bois Blarne, being an extra and voluntary gift of the Chippiwees nation. 14th. One piece of land six miles square, at the mouth of Chicago river, emptying into the South West end of Lake Michigan, where a Fort formerly stood. 15th. One piece of twelve miles square, at the mouth of the Illinois river, emptying into the Mississippi. 16th. One piece six miles square at the old Piorias Fort and Village, near the South end of the Illinois Lake, and said Illinois river.

"And whenever the United States may think proper to survey and make the boundaries of the land hereby ceded to them, they shall give timely notice thereof to the said tribes of Indians, that they may appoint some of their wise Chiefs to attend, and see that the lines are run agreeably to the terms of the treaty; & that the said Indian tribes will allow to the people of the United States, a free passage by land or water, as the one and the other may be found necessary throughout their country along the chain of posts herein before mentioned, that is to say, from the commencement of the portage aforesaid, at or near Lorrimie's store, along the said Portage to the St. Mary's, and down the same to Fort Wayne, and then down the Miami to Lake Erie; again, from the commencement of the portage at or near Lorrimie's store, along from thence to the river Auglaize, and down the same to its junction with the Miami at Fort Defiance; again, from the commencement of the portage aforesaid, to Sandusky river, and down the same to Sandusky bay and Lake Erie; and from Sandusky to the post that shall be taken at or near the foot of the rapids of the Miami of the Lake, and from thence to Detroit; again, from the mouth of Chicago to the commencement of the portage between that river and the Illinois, and down the Illinois river to the Mississippi; also from Fort Wayne along the portage aforesaid, which leads to the Wabash, and thence down the Wabash to the Ohio.

"And the said Indian tribes will also allow to the people of the United States, full priviledge of harbours at the mouths of rivers along the Lakes, and joining the Indian lands, for sheltering vessels and boats, and liberty to land their cargoes when necessary for their safety.

"Art IV. In consideration of the peace now established, of the cessions and relinquishments of lands made in the preceding articles by the said Tribes of Indians, and to manifest the liberality of the United States as the great means of rendering this peace stronger and perpetual, the United States relinquish their claim to all other Indian lands Northward of the river Ohio, Eastward of the Mississippi, and Westward and Southward of the great Lakes, and the waters uniting them; according to the boundary line agreed on by the United States and the King of Great Britain, in the treaty of peace made between them in the year 1783, but from this relinquishment by the United States, the following tracts of land are explicitly excepted: 1. The tract of land containing 150,000 acres near the rapids of the Ohio, which has been assigned to Gen. Clark, for the use of himself and his warriors. 2. The Post of St. Vincennes, on the river

Wabash, and the lands adjacent, of which the Indian titles has been extinguished. 3. The lands of all other places in possession of the French and other white people among them, of which the Indian titles has been extinguished, as mentioned in the 3rd article. And 4th, The Post of Massac, towards the mouth of the Ohio; to which several parcels of land so excepted, the said tribes relinquished all title and claim which they, or any of them may have; and for the same consideration, and with the same views as above mentioned, the United States now deliver unto the said Indian tribes, a quantity of goods of the value of 20,000 dollars, the receipt whereof they do hereby acknowledge, and henceforward every year forever, the United States will deliver at some convenient place, Northward of the Ohio, like useful goods, suited to the circumstances of the Indians, of the value of 9,000 dollars, reckoning that value at the first cost of the goods in the city of Philadelphia, or other places of the United States, where they shall be procured.

"The Tribes to which these goods are to be annually delivered, and the proportion in which they are to be delivered are as follows:

"1st.	To the Wyondots, the amount of	$1,000
2d.	To the Delawares, the amount of	1,000
3d.	To the Shawanees, the amount of	1,000
4th.	To the Miamies, the amount of	1,000
5th.	To the Ottowas, the amount of	1,000
6th.	To the Chippiweese, the amount of	1,000
7th.	To the Pottowatomies, the amount of	1,000
8th.	To the Kickapoos, Eelriverwees, and Kaskaskias Tribes, 500 dollars each.	

"Provided always, that if either of the said tribes hereafter, at any annual delivery of their share of the goods aforesaid, desire that a part of their annuity shall be furnished in domestic materials, animals, implements of husbandry and other utensils convenient for them; and in compensation to useful articles who may reside with or near them, and be employed for their benefit, the same shall at the subsequent annual delivery, be furnished accordingly.

"Art. V. To prevent any misunderstanding about the Indian lands relinguished by the United States, in the 4th article, it is explicitly declared that the meaning of that relinquishment is this: The Indian Tribes who have a right to these lands are quietly to enjoy them in hunting, planting and dwelling thereon, so long as they please, without any molestation from the United States. But when those Tribes, or any part of them, shall be disposed to sell their lands or any part of them, they are to be sold only to the United States; and until such sale, the United States will protect all the said Indian Tribes, in the quiet enjoyment of their lands, against all citizens of the United States, and against all other white people who may intrude upon the same. And the said Tribes again acknowledge themselves, and all their tribes, to be under the protection of the United States, and no other power whatever.

"Art. VI. If any citizen of the United States, or any other white person, shall presume to settle upon the lands now relinquished by the United States, such citizens or other person shall be out of the protection of the United States, and the Indian tribes, on whose land the settlement shall be made, may drive off such settler, or punish them in such a manner as they shall see fit; and because such settlement made without the consent of the United States, will be injurious to them, as well as to the Indians, the United States shall be at liberty to break them up, remove and punish the settlers as they shall think proper, and so effect that protection of the Indian's lands herein before stipulated.

"Art. VII. The said tribes of the Indian parties of this treaty, shall be at liberty to hunt within the territory and lands of which they have now ceded to the United States, without hindrance or molestation, so long as they demean themselves peaceably, and offer no injury to the people of the United States.

"Art. VIII. Trade shall be opened with the said Indian tribes, and they do hereby respectfully afford protection to such persons and their property, as shall be duly licenced to reside among them, for the purpose of trade, and to their agents and servants; but no person shall be admitted to reside among them, at any of their towns or hunting camps, as traders, who is not furnished with a licence for the purpose, under the hand and seal of the superintendent of the department N. West of the Ohio, or such other persons as the President of the United States may appoint or authorise to grant licence, to the end that the said Indians may not be imposed upon in their trade: and if any licenced trader shall abuse his privilege by unfair dealing, upon complaint of and proof thereof, his license shall be taken from him, and he shall be further punished according to the laws of the United States. And if any person shall intrude himself as a trader, without such license, the said Indians shall take and bring him before the superintendent, or his deputy, to be dealt with according to law; and to prevent imposition by forged licenses, the said Indians shall once a year, give information to the superintendent of his deputy, of the names of the traders residing among them.

"Art. IX. Least the firm peace and friendship now established, should be interrupted by individuals, the United States and the said tribes agree, that for injuries done by individuals on either side, no private revenge nor retaliation shall take place; but instead thereof, complaints shall be made by the party injured to the other Indian tribes or any of them, to the President of the United States, to the principal Indian chief of the said

Tribes, or of the Tribe to which the offender belongs; and such prudent measures shall then be pursued as shall be necessary to preserve the said peace and friendship, until the legislature or great council of the United States shall make other or equitable provisions in the case, for the satisfaction of both parties. Should any of the Indian Tribes make war against the United States or either of them, and the same shall come to the knowledge of the above mentioned Tribes or either of them, they do hereby engage to give immediate notice thereof to the General, or in his absence, to the officer commanding the troops of the United States at the nearest post. And should any Tribe with hostile intentions against the United States or either of them, attempt to pass through their country, they will endeavour to prevent the same, and in like manner give information of such attempts to the general or commanding officer, as soon as possible, that all cases of mistrust and suspicion may be avoided between them and the United States; and in like manner, the United States shall give notice to the said Indian tribes of any harm that may be meditated against them, or either of them, that shall come to their knowledge, and do all in their power, to hinder and prevent the same, that the friendship between them may be manifestly reciprocated.

"Art. X. All other treaties heretofore made, between the United States and the said Indian Tribes, or any of them, since the treaty of 1783, between the United States and Great Britain, shall henceforth cease and become void."[457]

On the 1st. of August 1795, A letter from STEP. THO. MASON, a Senator from Virginia in Congress, to Benjamin F. Bache, covering a copy of the treaty of *Amity, Commerce* and *Navigation*, Between his Britanic Majesty and the United States of America, &c. appeared in the Kentucky Gazette, accompanied with a copy of the Treaty. In consequence of this publication, public meetings of the people, were held in divers places in the State, with the avowed purpose of investigating the treaty. Whether the inveterate dislike the people of Kentucky had to Mr. Jay, in consequence of his attempt to barter the navigation of the Mississippi to Spain for twenty-five years, or the terms of the treaty with England, had most influence on the people when met, their disapprobation of the treaty, at all those meetings, was expressed in the strongest and most pointed terms. The following are some of the toasts drank at a dinner given to John Brown, Esq. at a public dinner given to him at Brent's tavern, Lexington, on the 8th of Sept. 1795. [Mr. Brown was one of our Senators in Congress, and who voted against ratifying the treaty. Humphrey Marshall, Esq. was the other, and who voted in its favour.]

"The virtuous minority of the Senate of the United States, who voted against the ratification of the infamous treaty, negotiated by the equally infamous JOHN JAY.

"Stephen T. Mason††—May he continue during life, to testify his patriotic independence, to deserve the well acquired approbation of his country, and his memory ever after be embalmed in the hearts of freemen.

"The House of representatives, of the United States—May they remember that the power of impeachment is not a phantom; but the shield of their country's rights."[458]

SECTION 65

Reactions to the Jay and Pinckney Treaties

[February 7, 1829]

It will be seen in the following extract from the speech of Isaac Shelby, Esq. Governor of Kentucky, at the opening of the session of the legislature 1795, as well as from the answer from the House of Representatives, what was the opinion of the people generally in Kentucky, relative to the communication made by James Innis, Esq. respecting the proceedings, had with the court of Spain, relative to the navigation of the Mississippi river, as well as the Treaty made with Great Britain. In relation to the navigation of the Mississippi, the Governor says,

"The communications made by him (the special messenger) to me will be laid before you—I am sorry to be obliged to add, that I have received no subsequent communications from the President, containing any intelligence of the farther progress or accomplishment of the treaty, and that from the late encroachments made by the Spaniards on the

††Whilst the treaty was before the President, and after its ratification had been recommended by the Senate, some member, notwithstanding the injunction of secrecy, had furnished an incomplete copy to a printer, which was published. This circumstance had a tendency to mislead the public mind, and therefore, as the injunction of secrecy had been violated, Mr. Mason considered it proper to furnish a complete copy.

territory of the United States, there is, (I fear) little or no hopes for a successful termination of that negotiation.

"I should not discharge the duty I owe my country, in a manner that would be satisfactory to myself, if I did not call your attention to the treaty lately concluded between America and Great Britain. If this treaty contained stipulations which were only contrary to good policy, although it would be the undoubted right of the State Legislature to express their opinions of those stipulations, it might be a matter of doubt whether it would be expedient for them to do so. But as many of the stipulations contained in this treaty are evidently contrary to the constitution of the general government, I consider it as the indispensible duty of the State Legislature to express their sentiments of such parts of the treaty as are unconstitutional, with the firmness and decency becoming the representatives of freemen. If you view this important question in the same light that I do, I have no doubt but that you will act upon it, in such a manner as will do honour to yourselves and our constitution."

In their response to the Governors speech, the House of Representatives says, "Independent of the general provisions of the treaty lately negociated between America and Great Britain, we think with you sir, that it is the indispensible duty of the State Legislature, to express their sentiments of such parts of the Treaty as are unconstitutional, with the firmness and decency becoming the representatives of freemen."[459]

On the 17th of February, 1796, two Shawanese Indians, one with a long beard came to the plantation of Philip Hammon, who lived about eight miles from Slate Creek Iron Works, in the absence of Hammon, and cut the cloths off a negro woman, killed one hog and stabbed another, and threatened to have Hammon's scalp before the end of summer, for having been the means of the death of 35 of their nation, by sending information to Donnels fork, Green Brier, from Point Pleasant.[460]

In consequence of the Treaty entered into at Greenville, between General Wayne and sundry Tribes of Indians, the Governor of Kentucky issued the following

"PROCLAMATION.

"State of Kentucky, Sct.

"Whereas a treaty of peace between the United States of America and the Tribes of Indians called the Wyandots, Delawares, Shawnees, Ottawas, Chipawas, Pottawatamas, Miamis, Eel River Weas, Kickapoos, Piankishaws and Kaskaskias, was concluded upon at Greenville on the 3d day of August, 1795. And whereas a strict observance of the said treaty, by the inhabitants of Kentucky, may be a means of securing to them, that long wished for, and permanent peace with the said Indian Tribes, so essential to the general welfare of the United States, as well as the particular interest of this State. I have thought proper to issue this my proclamation, hereby recommending a strict observance of the same, and cautioning the citizens of this commonwealth against any infraction of the said treaty.

"Given under my hand as Governor of said Commonwealth, at Frankfort, the twenty-second day of September, 1795, and of the Commonwealth the fourth.   ISAAC SHELBY.
"By the Governor, *James Brown,* Secretary"[461]

Notwithstanding this treaty, between the 27th and 30th of March, the Indians killed a family ascending the Mississippi, between the mouth of Ohio and St. Louis, the family consisted of 12 persons.[462]

The first constitution provided that "All persons qualified to vote for representatives shall elect by ballot (by a majority of votes,) as many persons as they are entitled to have for representatives for their respective counties, to be electors of the Senate.

"The electors of the Senate shall meet &c. and they or a majority of them so met, shall proceed to elect Senators. If on the ballot two or more person shall have an equal number of ballots in their favour, by which the choice shall not be determined by the first ballot, then the electors shall again ballot before they separate, in which they shall be confined to the persons, who on the first ballot shall have had an equal number, and they who shall have the greatest number in their favour on the second ballot, shall be accordingly declared duly elected.

"The Governor shall be chosen by the Electors of the Senate, at the same time, at the same place, and in the same manner that are herein directed to elect Senators."[463]

The foregoing are the provisions of the Constitution for the election of a Governor. In 1796 there were three candidates for the office of Governor, viz: Gen Benjamin Logan, Col. James Garrard and Col. Thomas Todd. On the first ballot by the Electors, Gen. Logan had the greatest number of votes, but not a majority of the whole number of Electors present, upon which the Electors proceeded to a second ballot, when a majority of votes were given to Col. Garrard, who was declared duly elected, and a certificate of his election accordingly given him. General Logan who had the greatest number of votes on the first ballot, contended that he was duly elected, and at the succeeding meeting of the Legislature addressed a letter to the Speaker of the Senate, of which the following is a copy:

"To the Honorable, the Speaker and members of the Senate.
"GENTLEMEN—At the last meeting of the electors held in Frankfort, for the purpose of electing a Governor and Senator, I conceived myself to have been constitutionally chosen Governor of this state, notwithstanding which, the office is at this time exercised by another person.

"As therefore, disputed elections to the office of Governor, are to be determined by you, I have thought it proper to give you the earliest information of my intention of bringing the matter before you, in order that the constitutional question may be investigated, and the dispute determined as soon as a sufficient number of Senators shall be convened for that purpose.

"I am, gentlemen, with the highest respect, your most obedient humble servant,   BENJAMIN LOGAN."[464]

The following petition was filed with the Clerks papers, viz:

"To the Honorable, the Speaker and members of the Senate.

"Your petitioner, Benjamin Logan, represents that the electors having met in Frankfort, agreeably to law, proceeded to ballot for a Governor, when 21 votes were found to be in his favour, being a greater number of votes than were given for either of the other candidates, whereby your petitioner conceives he was duly elected, and ought to have been accordingly declared and returned as governor, by the said electors.

"Your petitioner further states, that the electors afterwards proceeded to a second ballot, which they had no right to do by the constitution of this commonwealth; upon which second ballot James Garrard by one of the committee appointed to examine the ballot boxes, was reported duly elected, and who now does in consequence of that second unconstitutional ballot and report of one of the committee, exercise the office of Governor of this Commonwealth.

"Your petitioner therefore prays, that the said James Garrard may be permitted no longer to exercise the office of Governor of the Commonwealth of Kentucky, and that your petitioner may be admitted into the office of Governor, as if the electors had returned him as such, and as they ought to have done, agreeably to the first and only legal ballot taken by them. And your petitioner as in duty bound will ever pray, &c.

                                                BENJAMIN LOGAN."[465]

The Senate on the 10th of November, in committee of the whole, took up the letter of Gen. Logan, when Col. Bullitt contended that the constitution only provided for a second ballot in a case when the two highest in votes were equal, and that the second ballot by the Electors was not warranted by the constitution, and that consequently General Logan was duly elected and therefore entitled to the office of Governor.

This subject occupied the Senate for many days, during which time great excitement was produced and the lobby of the Senate much crouded.

The debates were warm and in some instances vehement. Messrs. Bullitt and McClung advocated the claim of Logan, and Messrs. Green Clay, Robert Mosby and Hubert Taylor opposed it. The question was finally decided by a vote on the following Resolution moved by Mr.

Mosby: "Resolved, that the Committee has no constitutional authority to take under their consideration the disputed election of the Governor." The votes on the question were for the motion 6, against it 5. The Senate at that time consisted of eleven members only.[466]

No portion of the United States was so effected by the revenue laws as the State of Kentucky, and more especially with the excise law. Debarred the priviledge of exporting the surplus produce of their farms, through the only avenue which it could possibly be done, by the occlusion of the Mississippi by Spain, and perfectly harrassed by a merciless savage enemy, countenanced and encouraged by Great Britain, who regardless of solemn treaty, held possession within the limits of the United States several parts, when the Indians who annoyed the settlements in Kentucky were furnished with arms, ammunition and clothing, to enable them to prosecute their depredations; the people of Kentucky were deprived of the means to procure money sufficient to defray the demands of the excise officer, without great sacrafices. Every mean was resorted to, to evade the payment of the tax, and those whose circumstances would enable them to live comfortably without using their stills, if they could not rent them laid them by, and had the mortification of seeing their grain, if not actually rotting in their cribs or barns, wasted and destroyed by rats, weavel and other vermin or insects. Governor Shelby was not only an extensive farmer but also engaged largely in the distilling business, he therefore was determined not to be incommoded with excise officers whom he despised, as well on account of the despicable characters of many of those who could be induced to accept an office odious to almost every man, woman and children in Kentucky, as well as from his opinion of the impropriety if not the unconstitutionality of the excise law, he therefore rented out his stills. The following letter from Governor Shelby to the Secretary of the Treasury, will show the estimation in which the law as well as the officers who acted under the law were held by them, and the manner in which those officers were treated generally through the country, is evidence that the people in general were of his way of thinking:

Letter to the Secretary of the Treasury from Gov. Shelby on the subject of the Excise.[467]

"To Oliver Wolcot, Secretary of the Treasury
"Sir—I have been informed, that in a letter addressed by you during the last session of Congress to the chairman of a committee of the house of representatives, you stated, "that for want of a District Attorney in Kentucky, no duties could be collected; that the Governor himself refused to pay; and that the people sheltered themselves under his example." For the satisfaction of the public, I shall state a few facts concerning this busines. I rented out my distillery in August 1792, previous to which no application had been made to me by any excise officer to measure my stills

or to take any entry of them: I continued to rent out my stills from that time until the latter end of the year 1793, and the tenants gave me their bonds to keep me indemnified from any demands that might be made on me for the excise during that period: I then took them again into my possession, and commenced working them in January 1794. About the month of April following, I was applied to by an excise officer (for the first time) for the duties of that year. I informed him of the time I had taken my distillery into possession, and that I did not conceive any duties could be due from the time I had commenced working my distillery which he appeared satisfied with. He removed shortly afterwards out of the country, and there was not (to my knowledge) any excise officer in it until the month of January or February 1795. I was then called upon to make an entry of my stills from June 1794, which I did immediately; after I had done this, the officer asked me if I would pay the arrearages, I told him I did not know whether the law required it of me; that I would take counsel on the subject, and that if I found that the law did require it of me, that I would pay them on the first application; otherwise I would not. He said he was not bound to call a second time to demand them: I told him if he did not chose to do so, he might execute his duty immediately and take my property. This he did not do, but went away. I was shortly afterwards advised that the law would not compel me to pay the arrearages; but when the duties from June 1794 to June 1725 [1795] became due, I counted out and laid by itself, the amount of what was due from me for that period, that the officer when he called again, might have occasion to stay as short of time as possible in my house. No application of any kind has since that time been made to be by any excise officer, and I found upon enquiry, that I could not procure a permit to remove whiskey, which I had distilled between June 1794 and June 1795, owing to the want of an officer in the county. I have very lately been obliged to apply personally to the officer who is at this time acting in this county, to receive the taxes due from me for that period, and from June 1795 to June 1796.

"From this statement of facts, the public will find that your assertion, as far as it concerns me, is false; and I believe it to be equally groundless, as far as it concerns the distillers in general within this State. I have no doubt but that it will be found upon an impartial enquiry, that the distillers have paid considerable sums on account of the excise; and that it had been owing to the neglect or misconduct of the officers of Government, that the duties have not been universally collected from June 1791.

"It is a matter of indifference to me, whether you fabricated your false statement yourself, or received it from others; having made it, you are responsible for the truth of it: but, as the distance between us renders a personal application to you impracticable, I shall upon this, and all future

occasions where you may use my name improperly, take the liberty of
assuring you in this public manner, that I despise you most heartily.

ISAAC SHELBY.

"Kentucky, October 15, 1796."[468]

On the 4th day of January 1797, The proposition for publishing the
Kentucky Gazette twice a week, was carried into effect. The reasons
assigned for this change, will be best understood, by examining the
printer's address in the first number, which is as follows:

"To the Patrons of the Kentucky Gazette.

"FELLOW CITIZENS:

"It is with peculiar pleasure that I now present you with the first number
of the KENTUCKY GAZETTE, on the plan lately proposed. As the circumstances which at first gave birth to this paper, are unknown to the greater
part of its present patrons, it may not be disagreeable to any of them, to
take a retrospective view of its origin and progress, as well as the motives
that first induced me to undertake the business of a Printer.

"In the year 1786, whilst a convention of the Citizens of Kentucky by
their Delegates, were deliberating on the propriety of separating from the
State of Virginia, the want of a proper channel through which to communicate to the people at large, political sentiments on a subject so extremely
interesting to them, and in which unanimity was so very necessary,
induced them to appoint a committee of their own body to encourage a
Printer to settle in the District. The critical situation in which the District
of Kentucky as at that time placed, by being surrounded on every side by
a cruel and savage foe; and which almost put an entire stop to immigration, consequently to the influx of a sufficient circulating medium, occasioned a belief, that no encouragement *could* be given by the committee,
that would induce a Printer to remove to Kentucky; this belief was much
strengthened, by an unsuccessful attempt which had been made to
prevail on a Mr. Miles Hunter (a Printer) to settle in this country, who
refused, unless he could have secured to him, certain stipulated emolu-
ments, to continue for a given time, which they would not venture to
promise.

"Having duly weighed all the circumstances, and from a confidence
in my own mechanical talents, (notwithstanding I had not the least
knowledge of the printing business,) together with a belief that I could
execute the business on a small scale, until I should be able to instruct my
sons, (of whom I had five,) added to a prospect of future advantages to
them and myself, I was prompted to make a tender of my services to the
committee—they accepted them and made report thereof to the Convention, who concurred with their committee; and as the highest mark of
approbation, gave me their unanimous promise of patronage.

"Satisfied of having obtained every encouragement that I had a right to expect, or that they as a body had power to grant, and in which I had the fullest confidence, employing every possible means in my power to perform the engagements made on my part, and on the 11th day of August 1787, presented to the world, the first number of the KENTUCKY GAZETTE. It is impossible to express the grateful sensations I experienced at the approbation with which it was received by its patrons, notwithstanding its almost innumerable imperfections.—What a striking difference between that paper, and the one now before you!

"From the great scarcity of money, and low state of population at that time, I was enabled to procure about one hundred and eighty subscribers only; notwithstanding which, and the high prices of every article used in the prosecution of the business, I was determined to persevere, if possible; and from the friendly assistance which I received from the merchants of Lexington, I was enabled to continue the paper on that small scale, until the 17th of Sept. 1791.

"Two important events which took place about that time, gave birth to that of a remarkable change in the KENTUCKY GAZETTE: one of which was, permission from Congress to the citizens of Kentucky, to carry volunteer expeditions against the Indians at the expense of the Union, which before had been forbidden at any rate: The other, a separation of the District of Kentucky from the State of Virginia, its admission into the Federal Union as an independent State, and the electing of members to a Convention to form a Constitution. These expeditions occasioned an influx of money into the District; and the admission of Kentucky into the Federal Union as an independent State, together with the framing a constitution for its government, presented a new field for political disquisitions, in which every citizen was deeply interested, and for which purpose the paper was enlarged from a half sheet to a sheet. What effect the free circulation of thoughts and opinions through this paper had, in producing these events, I shall not pretend to determine; the events were produced, the paper enlarged, and within a few weeks after, the number of subscribers to it doubled. For whilst one of these events placed in the hands of the citizens the means of procuring, the other created the necessity of acquiring political information. No person unless he has been in a similar situation can conceive the heartfelt satisfaction which I at that time experienced, from so pleasing a prospect, as that of having it in my power, to discharge those debts necessarily contracted for the support of the paper, and which had been increasing from its commencement; nor was I deceived in my expectations, for the liberal encouragement then given it, enabled me in the course of two years, not only to defray the expense there of, but also to discharge those debts, contracted for its support in the four preceding ones, and prevented me from abandoning it, as a ruinous project; which at that time I had serious thoughts of doing.

If a knowledge of past events, is a good criterion by which we can judge of the future, there can be no doubt of the success that will attend the alteration made in this paper; for the critical situation in which the United States are at this time placed in consequence of their treaties with France and England, and the later conduct of those two nations towards them, must be interesting, and awaken an anxiety of the first magnitude in the minds of every description of citizens; to relieve which, demands more room than my former plan afforded; especially when we consider that our interests are so interwoven with the policy of the European world, as to make it necessary to pay particular attention to all their transactions, as well as to the conduct of the American Government.

"More than nine years experience has convinced me, that strict *impartiality* forms one of the most valuable traits in the character of a Newspaper Printer; and notwithstanding it has sometimes operated as a partial disadvantage, duty and interest have continually prompted me unalterably to pursue it. The discussion of political questions, is an advantage of importance to society, (especially when the object is the public good,) and ought to be encouraged; but when the object is mere party purposes or personal aggrandisement, it ought to be discountenanced.

"I feel it is my indispensable duty to return my sincere thanks, to all who have encouraged this paper, and more especially those who were its first patrons; few of whom have failed to continue its constant supporters. To you it is that the public are indebted, not only for the birth of the First *Newspaper* ever printed in Kentucky, but for all the advantages the community have derived from a free and impartial circulation of political opinions, at the time when deemed most proper, for the interest and happiness of this part of the Western World. Under the auspices of your patronage, you have seen the progress of the KENTUCKY GAZETTE until it has acquired a rank of equality with most papers published in the United States, and perhaps superior to almost any paper in the world, whose origin and progress has been marked with as many disadvantages. As I ever have, I shall still continue, to use my best abilities to contribute to its usefulness, which can only succeed under your approbation; to gain which shall be the constant study of

"The public's most obedient Humble servant,   J. BRADFORD.
"Lexington, January 4th, 1797."[469]

Open the Great Mississippi

[February 23, 1829]

On the 17th of May 1797, the following interesting information respecting the conduct of Spain relative to the Mississippi, was received in Kentucky by a gentleman who left Natches on the 20th April. The gentleman, in whom the utmost confidence was placed, states, "That the Governor of Natches (Gayoso) had issued his proclamation, informing the inhabitants of that district, that the Spanish posts on the Mississippi, (claimed by the United States,) will not be delivered into the possession of the United States. That Mr. Ellicott will not be permitted to run the line between the United States and the Spanish territory.—That the Spaniards are repairing their fortifications at the different posts on the Mississippi, except at the Chickasaw Bluff, which they have evacuated and demolished—That an embargo is laid on all the shipping at New Orleans.—That a large body of French troops, are on the island of Cuba, supposed to be destined for the Mississippi.—That Mr. Elliott [Ellicott] has pitched his Markee within about 600 yards of the garrison at Natchez, at which place the American standard was hoisted; that the Governor had ordered it to be taken down, which order was not attended to; in consequence of which, a piece of artillery was levelled at the Markee every evening—That Mr. Ellicott has forwarded despatches to the Executive of the United States by a Mr. Knox, (in whose company the gentleman who gave this information travelled from Natchez.)—That the Governor of Natchez, sent men to waylay the road in order to intercept these despatches; but having previous information thereof, they avoided them by travelling through the woods.—That a war is likely to take place between the Creek and Chickasaw Indians; the former having lately stolen a number of horses from the latter, who are busily employed at present in fortifying themselves."

Correspondence between Mr. Ellicott, who was appointed to run the Boundary line between the United States and East and West Floridas, and the Spanish Governor *Manuel Gayoso de Lemos* and the *Baron de Carondelet*.[470]

No. 1

Manuel Gayoso de Lemos, to Andrew Elliot [Ellicott].
"Sir—Some gentlemen that left you at the mouth of the Ohio, have informed me of your approaching arrival here, and that to attend you in your commissions you bring a military guard and some woodsmen.

"It is with pleasure that I propose myself the satisfaction of seeing you here, and to make your acquaintance. Though I do not conceive that the least difficulty will arise respecting the execution of the part of the treaty in which you are an acting person; yet, as we are not prepared to evacuate the posts immediately; for want of the vessels that I expect will arrive soon, I find it indispensible to request you to leave the troops about the mouth of Bayou Pierre, where they may be provided with all their necessaries, which you can regulate on your arrival here. By this means every unforeseen misunderstanding will be prevented between his majesty's troops and those of the United States; besides, it is necessary to make some arrangements previous to the arrival of the troops, on which subject I shall have the honour of entertaining you when we meet.

"I embrace this opportunity to assure you of the satisfaction I feel in being appointed to act in concert with you, though your first interview is to be with the general in chief of the province.

"I have the honour to be, with the highest consideration, Sir, your most humble, obedient servant,   MANUEL GAYOSO DE LEMOS.
"Natchez, February 17th, 1797.
The Honourable A. Elliott [Ellicott]."[471]

No. 2.

Natchez, 24th February, 1797

"SIR:—By your favour of this day, delivered to me by Mr. Nolan, I learn with pleasure, your arrival at this post, in the character of Commissioner in behalf of the United States to ascertain the boundaries between the territories of his most Catholic Majesty and the said United States.

"I have the honour to be, with the highest respect, Sir, your most humble servant,   MANUEL GAYOSO DE LEMOS.
"The Honourable ANDREW ELLIOTT [Ellicott]."[472]

No. 3.

"Natchez, February 17th, 1797.

"SIR:—It is with pleasure I embrace this opportunity of informing you of my safe arrival at this place, as Commissioner on behalf of the United States, for ascertaining the boundaries between the territories of his most Catholic Majesty, and those of the United States.

"The polite manner in which I have been received at the posts on the Mississippi, and in possession of his most Catholic Majesty; demands my thanks and gratitude, and am in hopes, that a similar conduct will be observed on our part.

"I have the honor to be, &c. &c. &c.   ANDREW ELLICOTT.
"The Baron de CARONDILETT [Carondelet]."[473]

[Translation.]
No. 4.
"New Orleans, March 1st, 1797.

"MY DEAR SIR: I have received with great satisfaction, your friendly letter of the 27th of February last; in consequence of which, I congratulate you on your arrival in this country in the character of a commissioner on the part of the United States, to run the dividing line between the territories of his most Catholic Majesty and the United States. You likewise did me the favour to mention with what kindness and attention you were received at the different posts, as well as by the whole government under my direction; and from the general principles of your nation, I have no doubt but the same conduct will be observed on the part of the United States.

"God guard you most excellent sir,   BARON DE CARONDELET.
"ANDREW ELLICOTT, Esq."[474]

No 5.
Hon. A. Ellicott, to Manuel Gayoso de Lemos.
"Natchez, March 11th, 1787 [1797].

"MY DEAR SIR: The conduct of the Indians yesterday and last night, owing principally to their constant state of intoxication, renders it absolutely necessary, in my opinion, to have recourse to my military escort for protection. The discipline of our army is such, that you may rest assured, none of the inconveniences mentioned in your first communication to me, are to be apprehended from the escort's being stationed at this place on our part. And as the attendance of the guard forms a part of the treaty now carrying into effect between his most Catholic Majesty and the United States, which I am authorized to declare will be observed by the nation I have the honor to represent, with good faith and punctuality, I must request the favor of you to withdraw your objections against my escorts' joining me at this place as soon as possible.

"I am, &c. &c.   ANDREW ELLICOTT.
"His Excellency, Manuel Gayoso de Lemos."[475]

No. 6.
Manuel Gayoso de Lemos, to the Hon. A. Ellicott.
"Natchez, 11th March, 1797.

"MY DEAR SIR: This morning I had the pleasure to receive your amicable communication, dated yesterday. I give you my sincere thanks for having established this form of intercourse, as it will make our business more easy and indeed, is more comfortable to the sincere friendships we have contracted.

"In answer to your said letter, I will remark, that such conduct of the Indians is not customary here; I foresaw that it would happen, from the

moment you showed a desire of having your colours flying, before all
the transactions were terminated; knowing the Indians as well as I do,
this was the reason of the objections I offered the moment I saw it hoisted.
For otherwise, I know it very well, that it is frequently used by the
representatives of any nation in a foreign country; it is even done in Spain
by foreign Consuls. I am sorry you should have experienced any inconve-
niency from this particular circumstance, and that urged by such effects,
to wish to have by you your effort [escort]. I have not the least objection
that it should be called from its actual station, but as it is my duty, and that
I am answerable for the tranquility of the country, that is entrusted to my
charge, I must propose to you a method that will answer every good and
satisfactory purpose. Had not you been unluckily stopped on your voy-
age to this country, you would have had immediately the general of the
province here, to begin the operation of demarking the divisory line
between the territories of his Catholic Majesty, and those of the United
States of America. He had every necessary preparation to attend to the
business; but since the time he had a right to expect the Commissioners of
the United States, the war with England had taken place, and his cares
thereby increased, yet he expected to have had it in his power to come to
meet you at Daniel Clarke's Esq. which place is near the point of the 31st
degree, but he has found it impossible, as it would oblige him to make too
long an absence from New Orleans; therefore it is myself that will have
the honor to accompany you on that important commission, on behalf of
his Catholic Majesty. This is the moment when I am in want of every
individual thing, both for my person and for the attendance of the
commission, though the geometer and other officers that are to be employed, are already on their way from New Orleans, and will stop at
Clarksville, where I shall go myself as soon as my equippage arrives from
the Capital; but this will inevitably take some time, therefore the plan that
I wished to arrange with you, will be to make Loftus Cliffs our point of
reunion. This place is a short distance from Clarksville, and is a very
healthy situation;—there, I will send every thing concerning the Spanish
commission; and that will be the most convenient place to establish for a
while, your head quarters, under your military escort.—By adopting this
measure, you will have your people together, and the most distant
disagreeable occurrence avoided, as I am positively confident that some
would happen by the conjunction here, as you propose. It is true, that by
the treaty an escort is supposed, and even recommended to each commission, but it is to be on the line and not at a distance from it, where it would
interfere with other business; therefore, I feel sensibly hurt, that it is out
of my power to consent to the landing of the troops in this place, though I
have not the least objection to their going immediately to Loftus' Cliffs.

"I have given the most positive orders to prevent the Indians getting
liquor, and to their interpreter, I have given the strictest charge to be

always in sight, and to morrow, I expect that they will remove to some distance from here.

"I have the honour to be, with the highest respect and esteem, your most affectionate friend, and humble servant,   MANUEL GAYOSO DE LEMOS.

"(A true copy) D. Gillespie, Sec'y.
"The Honourable ANDREW ELLICOTT."[476]

No. 7.
Hon. A. Ellicott, to Manuel Gayoso de Lemos.

"MY DEAR SIR: Your favor of yesterday was handed to me in due time, which would have been answered sooner, had not the storm last night prevented me from writing in my tent.—Your letter, as well as many other circumstances which have come to my knowledge, contain fresh proofs of your desire to promote good order and harmony in this part of the country.—But, sir, I cannot suppose that any inconvenience could possibly arise, or the peace of the settlement be disturbed, by the arrival and landing of the escort which I left at Bayou Pierre; if I did not suppose the contrary, I trust I should be one of the last persons to propose the measure. In my opinion, the escort which accompanied me, is as much bound to observe good order in this country, as the troops of his Catholic Majesty.—This is not an opinion of the day, it has uniformly been mine ever since I left the seat of our government: in consequence of which, immediately upon my entering the Mississippi, I issued a standing order, that when any of our party, the military included, should be at any place where the jurisdiction was exercised by his Catholic Majesty, the laws and usages of that government should be observed and submitted to in the most pointed manner. The escorts by the spirit of the treaty, are intended for our mutual protection against straggling hostile Indians, and the preservation of our stores. This appears to be their whole business.

"As I hope that mere punctilios may never interrupt our friendship, and the conduct of the Indians having become more peaceable since the night before last, I am less anxious for the escort being stationed at my present encampment. I would, therefore, to prevent any disturbance, or misunderstanding, propose that the officer who commands the escort which has accompanied me to Bayo Pierre, be directed to proceed down the river, to Bacon landing, from whence he may come to this place and to procure such necessaries as he may be in want of for the ensuing season.

"As this is the place designated for our meeting, and making our arrangements for carrying on the business, I conceive there would be an impropriety in my leaving it till your excellency is ready to join me in fixing the first point of latitude.

"I am, &c. &c.   ANDREW ELLICOTT"[477]
"Note—The last two paragraphs were added after having had a private conversation with the governor."

No. 8.

Manuel Gayoso de Lemos, to the Hon. A. Ellicott.

"MY DEAR SIR: I do myself the pleasure to acknowledge the reception of your favour dated of yesterday, and am very happy to find that our sentiments uniformly agree in every thing that can combine the mutual interests of our nations, and I pledge you my honor and friendship, that every step of my conduct shall be guided by this principle, impressed on me by my duty, and by the very particular attachment I have for you.

"I have the honor to be, with the greatest esteem and affection, my dear sir, your most obedient servant,   MANUEL GAYOSO DE LEMOS.

"(Copy,) D. Gillespie, Sec'y.
"The Honourable ANDREW ELLICOTT." [478]

No. 9.

Honourable A. Ellicott, to Manuel Gayoso de Lemos.

"Natchez, March 23d, 1797.

"MY DEAR SIR: The remounting of the cannon at this place at the very moment when our troops are daily expected down to take possession of it, the insolent treatment which the citizens of the United States have received at the Walnut Hills, and the delay of the business upon which I came, concur in giving me reason to suppose, that the treaty will not be observed with the same good faith and punctuality by the subjects of his Catholic Majesty, as it will by the citizens of the United States. I hope your excellency will give such an explanation of the above, as to remove my doubts and apprehensions, which I am afraid have been too justly excited.

"I am, &c. &c.   "ANDREW ELLICOTT.
"His Ex. Manuel Gayoso de Lemos." [479]

No. 10

"Mr. Ellicott's compliments to his friend Governor Gayoso, and wishes to be informed, whether the following information which he received this day, "that all the works at the Chickasaw Bluffs, have been either demolished or carried to the opposite side of the river, and that exertion is making at the Walnut Hill, to put that post in a state of defence be correct.

"March 23rd, 1797."

No. 11

From his Excellency Manuel Gayoso de Lemos, to Andrew Ellicott, Esq.

"Natchez, March 23d, 1797.

"MR DEAR SIR: I have just now received your communication of this day, by which I am sorry to find the construction you put on the storing of the ammunition that came from the Walnut Hills, in this fort; I have no other place to put them in, for it would be imprudent to leave them exposed in an insecure place at a time when the Indians might take advantage of us, if they found that in the present circumstances, we acted without the necessary precautions. At the time you see me conducting ammunition to this fort, you will likewise see as many go out of it for the Arkansas, to reinforce that post which will now be exposed to the incursions of the Osage Indians, who in the last season pillaged the white hunters of that country.

"I am entirely unacquainted with any ill treatment that the citizens of the United States should have received at the Walnut Hills, if you mean the execution of the orders of the general in chief of this province to demolish that post, it was in consequence of our treaty with the Indians that they might have no reason to complain of our conduct, but since I have been informed of their unsettled disposition, I have sent counter orders to suspend every thing that might injure the actual state of those fortifications, and in such circumstances shall not move any thing else until the arrival of the American troops that are daily expected.

"The unavoidable detention that has been experienced in beginning the line you know the reasons, but they shall soon be removed, as Lieutenant Colonel Guillemard is far on his way up, and at his arrival, this important business shall be begun.

"I do assure you that there is nothing that can prevent the religious compliance of the treaty, though I might observe, that the conduct of some persons that seem to affect an immediate interest for the United States, is such as to occupy my attention.

"As I was finishing this, Mr. Gillespie brought me your note enquiring if the works at the Bluffs had been destroyed or removed to the opposite side of the river.

"What I have already said concerning our treaty with the Indians, I suppose has guided the general of this province to take that step. I really do not know whether they are destroyed or not. I give you my word that I did not know what was to be done there, and it is only by Baron Easthrop that I learn that that post would seen be evacuated. But this is a thing that only regards the General of the province. I cannot account for it, nor can I say more on the subject, as all the orders proceed from him, that post being entirely out of my jurisdiction.

"My dear sir, your most humble obedient servant and friend.
"MANUEL GAYOSO DE LEMOS.
"The Honourable A. ELLICOTT." [480]

No. 12.
From Andrew Ellicott, Esq. to his Excellency Manuel Gayoso de Lemos.
"*Natchez, March* 24, 1767 [1797].
"MR DEAR SIR: It is with pleasure, I acknowledge the receipt of your Excellency's very satisfactory letter of yesterday. You may rest assured

that I have and shall continue to discountenance every measure, and the propagation of any opinion which may have a tendency to disturb the good order and harmony of this settlement. I shall close this with requesting that the commandant of the Walnut Hills be directed to treat the citizens of the United States with politeness when they stop at that post, as a contrary conduct may be attended with disagreeable consequences on a river which both nations have an equal right to navigate.

"I am with sentiments of real esteem, your sincere and affectionate friend. "ANDREW ELLICOTT.
"His Excellency Manuel Gayoso de Lemos."[481]

No. 13.
From his Excellency Manuel Gayoso de Lemos, to Andrew Ellicott, Esq.
"MY DEAR SIR: By every report you are acquainted with the confirmation of every thing I have told you concerning our business, you know that Lieutenant Colonel Guillemard will be here very soon, and that immediately we shall proceed to the running of the line. But as nothing but friendly arrangements are to guide our conduct, it is necessary to avoid every shadow of compulsion. By the contents of my letter to Captain Pope, you will see my reasons—therefore I request that you will join a couple of lines to avoid any more writing.

"I am surrounded by many people who have business, this being court day, though I have tried to disembarrass myself, but cannot wait upon you.

"I am with the highest esteem and respect, my dear sir,
your most humble servant and friend, MANUEL GAYOSO DE LEMOS.

"The Honorable ANDREW ELLICOTT."[482]

No. 14.
From Andrew Ellicott, Esq. to Lieutenant Pope.
"Natchez, March 25th, 1767 [1797]
"DEAR SIR. This will be handed you by Maj. Minor, a friend of mine, an officer in the service of his Catholic Majesty, your polite attention to him will be considered as a particular favour conferred upon men. By order of Governor Gayoso, his letter to you of this day has been shown to me, his request for you and the troops under your command, to remain for an undetermined time above this place, appears to me a very extraordinary one; sufficient time has already been given by the United States for the evacuation of all the posts of the east side of the Mississippi, above the first degree of North latitude; and from the troops of his Catholic Majesty carrying up and remounting the cannon at this place, I cannot pretend to say that an evacuation is really intended in any reasonable time. From this circumstance, I should conclude, that the sooner you are here the better.

However, as I have no control over the destination of the troops of the United States, except my own escort, I shall take it for granted, that your instructions are sufficiently pointed to direct your conduct. Please to accept my sincere wishes for the safe and speedy arrival of yourself and troops at this place.

"And am dear sir, your friend and humble servant,

ANDREW ELLICOTT.[483]

"Lieutenant POPE."

Notes

Introduction

1. *Kentucky Gazette*, April 2, 1830; *Argus of Western America*, March 31, 1830; *Louisville Public Advertiser*, April 1, 1830; *Biographical Encyclopedia of Kentucky*, 415; James M. Lee, "John Bradford," in *Dictionary of American Biography*, 2:557-58.

2. William H. Perrin, J.H. Battle, and G.C. Kniffen, *Kentucky: A History of the State*, 490-92; Charles R. Staples, "John Bradford and the *Kentucky Gazette*—First Newspaper," *Kentucky Press* 8 (Feb. 1937): 4-6.

3. In assuming the publication of the *Kentucky Gazette* John Bradford more or less obligated himself to know what was happening in the separation conventions. Two corroborative sources on this subject are John Mason Brown, *The Political Beginnings of Kentucky*, and William Littell, *Political Transactions in and Concerning Kentucky*. A modern source is Patricia Watlington, *The Partisan Spirit: Kentucky Politics, 1779-1792*, 79-102.

4. The Bradford collections of both the *Gazette* and his working notes and manuscripts were sold at public auction and were eventually lost, or were carelessly managed by his descendants. In this collection no doubt were notes on the Indian wars made by Allan B. Magruder. Magruder turned his notes over to John Bradford in 1805 when he departed Lexington for Louisiana. *Kentucky Gazette*, Aug. 20, 1805.

5. Joseph Ficklin in an interview with John D. Shane (1853), Draper Collection, Wisconsin State Library, the Kentucky Papers, 11CC156, 16CC257-85. Ficklin revealed an animus toward the Bradfords, and he no doubt was in error in some of his references to Magruder. Magruder apparently did not die a drunkard's death, nor was he collecting notes to write a history of Kentucky.

6. The *Ohio State Journal*, Sept. 28, 1828, said Bradford had in hand notes by or about Daniel Boone, George Rogers Clark, Alexander Bullitt, Isaac Shelby, Levi Todd, M.J. Todorosky, W. Randolph, Major Smith, A.B. Magruder, and others. These may have been the material to which Bradford referred in his introduction to the "Notes" on August 25, 1826.

7. Thomas Jefferson, *Notes on the State of Virginia* (1784, 1785, 1786). The Jefferson notes are not as numerous as Bradford's but are more sophisticated and analytical and contain considerable tabular data. It would have been only natural for John Bradford to read the Master's notes. The loss of the Bradford collection has wiped out any proof that Bradford possessed this book.

8. Samuel L. Metcalf, *A Collection of Some of the Most Interesting Narratives of Indian Warfare in the West*, 138-48. Joseph Ficklin told John D. Shane in his interview (see note 5 above) that John Bradford took exceptions to Metcalf's collection.

9. The accounts of the Indian raids in the "Notes" are almost identical to those that appeared in the *Kentucky Gazette* prior to 1795. Lyman C. Draper copied many of these in his papers on Kentucky.

10. Humphrey Marshall was as much concerned with Indian affairs as John Bradford. Much of volume 1 and at least two chapters of volume 2 of Marshall's *History of Kentucky* seem to have been drawn from accounts of Indian attacks that appeared in the newspaper. Marshall published the first edition of his *History of Kentucky* in 1812 in a single volume. He expanded the text and published it in two volumes in 1824. Bradford was fully aware of the

bitter controversy Marshall stirred up over the so-called Spanish Conspiracy. Both men came from Fauquier County, Virginia. Anderson C. Quisenberry, *The Life and Times of the Honorable Humphrey Marshall*, 119-30. John Mason Brown, in *Political Beginnings*, took issue with Marshall (175-217).

11. John Bradford was throughout the years 1787-1830 a Jeffersonian Republican, and Humphrey Marshall was an equally committed Federalist. Quisenberry, *Humphrey Marshall*, 119-34; E. Merton Coulter, "Humphrey Marshall," in *Dictionary of American Biography*, 12:309-10; Brown, *Political Beginnings*, 158-182; Lowell H. Harrison, *John Breckinridge, Jeffersonian Republican*, 109.

12. The *Kentucky Gazette* carried rather extensive coverage of the St. Clair expedition. This was a matter of vital concern to Kentuckians. Both Henry Clay and John Pope were subscribers to General St. Clair's book. It would be inconceivable that John Bradford had not read it. *American State Papers*, vol. 4 (*Indian Affairs*), 133-37, and vol. 1 (*Military Affairs*), 20-39; Jacob Burnet, *Notes on the Settlement of the North-western Territory*, 108-31; J.D. Richardson, ed., *Messages and Papers of the Presidents, 1789-1908*, 1:113.

13. The *American State Papers*, including the sections *Foreign Affairs, Military Affairs*, and *Indian Affairs*, were published in an extensive edition only after 1830. This is true also of the *Papers of George Rogers Clark*; Charles J. Kappler's *Indian Affairs, Laws, and Treaties*; Temple Bodley, ed., *Littell's Political Transactions in and Concerning Kentucky*; Jacob Burnet's *Notes on the Early Settlement of the North-western Territory*; John A. McClung's *Sketches of Western Adventure*; and Mann Butler's *History of the Commonwealth of Kentucky*. All of these sources pertain to the central objectives of the "Notes."

14. Ficklin interview by Shane, Draper Mss., Kentucky Papers, 16CC257-85, 11CC156.

15. John Bradford quoted in the *Kentucky Gazette* information from any newspaper which came to hand. See specifically a Baltimore paper of July 26, 1788; the *Pennsylvania Mercury*, Sept. 19, 1789; the *New York Daily Advertiser*, Sept. 26, 1789; the *Massachusetts Sentinel*, Feb. 27, 1790; and the *National Gazette*, May 18, 1793. See also Samuel M. Wilson, *The First Land Court of Kentucky, 1779-1780*, 60-94.

16. John Bradford published the first five volumes of the *Acts* of the Kentucky General Assembly. In 1788 he published the first *Kentucky Almanac*. He also was the printer for the Fayette County government. The work of the *Gazette* printers was of unusually good graphic quality.

17. William W. Hening, *The Statutes at Large; Being a Collection of all the Laws of Virginia*, vol. 6 (Feb. 1759): 311-12.

18. John Bradford arrived in Kentucky as a deputy land surveyor in 1779 or 1780; the precise date is uncertain. Staples, "Bradford and the *Kentucky Gazette*," 2

19. As well as dealing with mathematical problems in surveying land, John Bradford was interested in astronomy. His writing in both the *Gazette* and the "Notes" was of a lean narrative style, with no more than a few flashes of color or rhetorical flights.

20. James Melvin Lee, "John Bradford," *Dictionary of American Biography*, 2:557-58; Dwight Mikkelson, "The *Kentucky Gazette*: Herald to a Noisy World," Ph.D. diss., Univ. of Kentucky, 1963.

21. Staples, "Bradford and the *Kentucky Gazette*," 2. Amazingly, there is no full biography of John Bradford, and some of the materials about him are contradictory. See also the voluminous notes on Bradford in the papers of Samuel M. Wilson, Special Collections, Margaret I. King Library, Univ. of Kentucky.

22. Leland A. Brown, "The Family of John Bradford," *Kentucky Press* 8 (Sept. 1937): 2; Wilson, Address to the American Bibliographical Society, 1937, Wilson Collection, Univ. of Kentucky.

23. This year is disputed; some sources say 1785, others 1784.

24. Nelle Rhea White, *The Bradfords of Virginia in the Revolutionary War and Their Kin*, passim; Brown, "The Family of John Bradford," 2.

25. Quisenberry, *Humphrey Marshall*, 7-20; Albert J. Beveridge, *The Life of John Mar-*

shall, 1:2-32; Maude H. Woodfin, "Thomas Marshall," *Dictionary of American Biography*, 12:328-29.

26. Staples, "Bradford and the *Kentucky Gazette*," 2. Bradford was a major landholder. He recorded numerous land transactions in Fayette County, Kentucky. Deed Books A, B, C, D, F, H, K, L, M, N, P, and Q list sixty-five land transactions. Many of the deeds were made for property on Cane Run and David Fork creeks. He also owned numerous lots in the town of Lexington, including five acres on Limestone Street between Third and Fourth streets.

27. "Notes on Kentucky," section 7 (Oct. 6, 1826); Charles G. Talbert, *Benjamin Logan, Kentucky Frontiersman*, 75-81; Lewis Collins and Richard H. Collins, *History of Kentucky*, 2: 425-27.

28. "Notes on Kentucky," section 7 (Oct. 6, 1826).

29. The Democratic Society, patterned after the one in Philadelphia, was organized largely to protest the prospective closing of the Mississippi River to free access by Kentucky farmer-flatboatmen. The ire of Kentuckians was raised by Jay's proposed treaty with Spain. Throughout both the *Gazette* and in the "Notes on Kentucky" John Bradford kept the issue before his readers: *Kentucky Gazette*, Nov. 2 and 16, 1793, May 17, 1794; "Notes on Kentucky," section 48. See also E.M. Coulter, "The Efforts of the Democratic Societies of the West to Open the Navigation of the Mississippi River," *Mississippi Valley Historical Review* 11 (1924-25): 376-89; Samuel Flagg Bemis, *Jay's Treaty: A Study in Commerce and Diplomacy*, 17-18; Arthur P. Whitaker, *The Mississippi Question, 1795-1803*, 3-29.

30. Staples, "Bradford and the *Kentucky Gazette*," 2; Brown, "Family of John Bradford," 2; Charles R. Staples, *History of Pioneer Lexington*, 29; *Manson v. Craig*, Complete Record Book E, p. 338, Fayette Circuit Court, Lexington.

31. Among safe places for camp sites were Cumberland Gap, Cumberland Ford, Raccoon Spring, Wood's Blockhouse, the Hazel Patch, Rockcastle Crossing, and Big Hill. Robert L. Kincaid, *The Wilderness Road*, 127-95; William Calk's Journal, 1775, original in possession of the Calk family, Mount Sterling, Ky.; William Ayers, *Historical Sketches*, 174-96; "William Fleming's Journal," in Newton D. Mereness, ed., *Travels in the American Colonies*, 636-37.

32. *Kentucky Gazette*, March 22 and 29, July 19, 1794; Oct. 11, 18, and 25, 1798; Talbert, *Benjamin Logan*, 13, 277-81.

33. *Kentucky Gazette*, April 6, 1787, Feb. 28, 1789, March 26, 1791, April 6, 1793.

34. Bemis, *Jay's Treaty*, 7-20; Maj. Arent de Peyster to Lt. Col. Mason Bolton (March 10, 1780), and McKee to Maj. Arent de Peyster (June 4, 1780), "Haldimand Papers," 19 (1911): 501-2, 530-31; J. Winston Coleman, *The British Invasion of Kentucky*, 1-25.

35. Prime examples of such attacks were those on the Davis family in 1779; William Fleming, "Journal," 625-26. See also *The Journal of the Rev. Francis Asbury*, 2:74; Kincaid, *Wilderness Road*, 177.

36. Marshall, *History of Kentucky*, 1:220-22.

37. Ibid., 252; J.J. Dickey, "McNitt's Defeat," in Russell Dyche, *History of Laurel County*, 17-18.

38. *Kentucky Gazette*, March 22 and 29, July 19, 1794; Talbert, *Benjamin Logan*, 217; J.G.M. Ramsey, *Annals of Tennessee to the End of the Eighteenth Century*, 394-423; "Notes on Kentucky," section 60 (Dec. 12, 1828).

39. James Rood Robertson, *Petitions of the Early Inhabitants of Kentucky to the General Assembly of Virginia, 1769-1792*, 68; Marshall, *History of Kentucky*, 1:268-81.

40. Robertson, *Petitions of the Early Inhabitants*, 41-42, 63-65.

41. Ibid., 45-47, 62, 78-79.

42. *American State Papers*, vol. 1 (*Foreign Relations*), 248-57; "Notes on Kentucky," section 62 (Jan. 2 and 9, 1829); Marshall, *History of Kentucky*, 1:258-69; "Wilkinson's Memorial and Expatriation Declaration," Bodley, ed., *Littell's Political Transactions*, 63-64; Coulter, "Efforts of the Democratic Societies," 376-89.

43. *Kentucky Gazette*, May 17, Nov. 2 and 16, 1793, May 17, 1794.

44. Robertson, *Petitions of the Early Inhabitants*, 45-47, 62-65, 141-42; Marshall, *History of Kentucky*, 1:260-80; Brown, *Political Beginnings*, 60-88; Watlington, *Partisan Spirit*, 98-132.

45. Marshall, *History of Kentucky*, 1:196-99; Brown, *Political Beginnings*, 58.

46. Marshall, *History of Kentucky*, 1:192.

47. Temple Bodley, "Introduction," *Littell's Political Transactions*, x-xx; Brown, *Political Beginnings*, 57-69; Marshall, *History of Kentucky*, 1:200-226.

48. William H. Perrin, *The Pioneer Press of Kentucky*, 9.

49. Brown, *Political Beginnings*, 60-70; Marshall, *History of Kentucky*, 1:201, 204.

50. Perrin, *Pioneer Press*, 9; "Notes on Kentucky," section 24 (March 2, 1827).

51. "Notes on Kentucky," section 24 (March 2, 1827)

52. Ibid.; Staples, "Bradford and The *Kentucky Gazette*," 2-6.

53. "Notes on Kentucky," section 24 (March 2, 1827).

54. The *Gazette* office printed the *Acts* of the Kentucky General Assembly, 1792-98. In 1788 it produced the first *Kentucky Almanac*, the *Instructions to Magistrates and Constables*, and other publications.

55. Among those who acquired experience at Bradford's shop was Joseph Charless, the pioneer Louisville and St. Louis editor; James H. Stewart of the *Kentucky Herald*; William Hunter, state printer and publisher, of Frankfort; and Fielding Bradford.

56. "Notes on Kentucky," section 24 (March 2, 1827).

57. Mikkelson, *"The Kentucky Gazette"*; Wilson, "Address to the Bibliographical Society of America, 1937," 19-20, Wilson Collection, Univ. of Kentucky.

58. Perrin, *Pioneer Press*, 9.

59. Staples, "Bradford and the *Kentucky Gazette*," 2.

60. *Kentucky Gazette*, Aug. 30, Sept. 12, 1788, and Jan. 17, 1789.

61. There are some differences in the records regarding the year John Bradford's second stint as editor of the *Kentucky Gazette* began. Staples' article (*Kentucky Press*, 5), says 1823. A note in the Wilson Collection at the University of Kentucky cites 1825. Undoubtedly the latter date is correct.

62. Frances L.S. Dugan and Jacqueline P. Bull, *Bluegrass Craftsman*, 86-87, 211-17. Earlier, Jacob Meyers operated a paper mill on the Dick's River.

63. Ibid., 211-17.

64. John Bradford published the text of the Constitution in the *Gazette* and offered copies of it for sale; *Kentucky Gazette*, May 12, 1792.

65. Ibid.

66. Ibid.

67. Wilson, "Address to the Bibliographical Society," 14.

68. Ibid., 14, 25. Also Bradford's "Notes on Kentucky" constitutes in many cases a true primary source of information concerning the pioneer era in Kentucky.

69. The *Kentucky Gazette* seems to have printed a brief notice of every Indian attack and raid. John Bradford said that not all reports of such incidents were factual. For examples, see April 9 and 16, 1791, Sept. 1, 1792, Oct. 26, Nov. 23 and 30, 1793, and Feb. 22, March 8 and 22, 1794.

70. *Kentucky Gazette*, Sept. 24 and Oct. 8, 1794; Marshall, *History of Kentucky*, 1:220-24; Collins, *History of Kentucky*, 2:760-61; Kincaid, *Wilderness Road*, 173-79; Russell Dyche, *History of Laurel County*, 11-18.

71. The time lag varied from a week to three months. Occasionally in reporting local Kentucky news there was an indication that it had been gathered by word of mouth or in conversation with travelers.

72. Bradford had no regional newspapers to excerpt in the early years of publication of the *Gazette*. Travelers brought news on happenings outside Lexington, and stories, especially of Indian attacks, were brought into the office. The advertisements gave a more precise view of the local scene than the news accounts.

73. "Notes on Kentucky," section 33 (May 4, 1827): Marshall, *History of Kentucky*, 1:42-77.

74. George W. Ranck, "The Traveling Church: An Account of the Baptist Move from Virginia in 1781," *Register of the Kentucky Historical Society* 79 (Summer 1981): 240-65: Thomas D. Clark, *Kentucky, Land of Contrast*, 40-68.

75. Reuben T. Durrett, ed., *Bryant's Station and the Memorial Proceedings*, 49-52; Robert S. Cotterill, *History of Pioneer Kentucky*, 184; Marshall, *History of Kentucky*, 1:134-38.

76. *Kentucky Gazette*, Aug. 10, 1793, "Notes on Kentucky," sections 62, 63, 64.

77. William E. Connelley and E.M. Coulter, *A History of Kentucky*, 1:403-6; Robertson, *Petitions of the Early Inhabitants*, 48-52, 62-65, 76-77; Hening, *Statutes at Large*, 10 (May 1779): 35-50.

78. *Kentucky Gazette*, April 16, 1791; "Notes on Kentucky," sections 26, 27, 33, 35, 44, 45 (March 16 and 23, May 4 and 18, Nov. 9 and 16, 1827).

79. "Notes on Kentucky," sections 25, 28, 29, 48, 50, 51, 56 (March 9 and 30, April 6, Dec. 14, 1827; Jan. 4 and 11, Nov. 7, 1828).

80. James A. James, *The Life of George Rogers Clark*, 109-46; Durrett, *Bryant's Station*, 87-120.

81. James A. James, ed., *George Rogers Clark Papers*, 4:xvii, xxiii; Temple Bodley, *Our First Great West*, 201-2; Gen. Haldimand to Major de Peyster (July 6, 1780), "Haldimand Papers," 10:408-10; Coleman, *British Invasion of Kentucky*, 4-24; Marshall, *History of Kentucky*, 1:106-9.

82. *Kentucky Gazette*, Oct. 4, 11, 18, 25, 1794; Talbert, *Benjamin Logan*, 277; Ramsey, *Annals of Tennessee*, 576, 616-18.

83. *Kentucky Gazette*, Oct. 8 and 12, 1791, March 17, 1792, Oct. 26 and Nov. 23, 1793, March 8, 1794.

84. "Notes on Kentucky," sections 11 and 26 (Nov. 3, 1826, March 16, 1827).

85. McClung, *Sketches of Western Adventure*, 148-51.

86. "Notes on Kentucky," section 11 (Nov. 3, 1826); McClung, *Sketches of Western Adventure*, 148-51; James Hughes, *A Report of the Causes Determined by the Late Supreme Court for the District of Kentucky . . .*, 134-69.

87. McClung, 171-73.

88. "Notes on Kentucky," section 23 (Feb. 16, 1827).

89. "Clark's Diary" in William Hayden English, *Conquest of the Country Northwest of the River Ohio, 1778-1783*; James, *Life of George Rogers Clark*, 1:579-83.

90. "Notes on Kentucky," section 26 (March 16, 1827; McClung, *Sketches of Western Adventure*, 179-87.

91. McClung, 183-87.

92. Ironically, the rifle played a major role on the frontier for settler and Indian alike. Indians used cheap English trade guns. Powder was scarce and lead was difficult to melt and mold into bullets. See Merrill Lindsay, *The Kentucky Rifle*, first 6 unnumbered pages; John Bakeless, *Daniel Boone, Master of the Wilderness*, 39-40; Memorandum to Col. A.S. de Peyster, "Haldimand Papers," 20:28.

93. Marshall, *History of Kentucky*, 1:32-35; Benjamin O. Casseday, *The History of Louisville from Its Earliest Settlement till the Year 1852*, 16-21.

94. Three reports support the vengeful attitude toward the Indian raiders and their villages: "Report of Brigadier Charles Scott, June 28, 1791," "Lieut. Colonel-commandant Wilkinson's Report, August 24, 1791," and "H. Knox, Summary Statement of Facts, December 26, 1791," *American State Papers*, vol. 4 (*Indian Affairs*), 131-32, 133-35, 139-40. See also Marshall, *History of Kentucky*, 1:91-95. John Braddock was with Bowman's militia.

95. Kappler, *Indian Affairs*, 1:18-22, 32-34, 38-45.

96. The annals of white settler pressures against the Indians are numerous and full relating to the raids of John Bowman, George Rogers Clark, Benjamin Logan, and William Whitley, and even to the British Henry Bird and Henry Hamilton, but the record of Indian reactions is skimpy.

97. More than a third of the sections of the "Notes of Kentucky" deal with Indian raids and incidents. See sections 7, 9, 11, 13, 21, 26, 27, 32, 33, 34, 35, 44, 45, and 47.

98. Marshall, *History of Kentucky*, 1:252-54, 357-89; McClung, *Sketches of Western Adventure*, 148-54, 171-87; *Western Review and Miscellaneous Magazine*, 1:253-59; Alexander Scott Withers, *Chronicles of Border Warfare*, 143-51, 193-97; Metcalf, *Narratives of Indian Warfare*, 149-58.

99. Robertson, *Petitions of the Early Inhabitants*, 41-42, 62-66, 78-79.

100. Marshall, *History of Kentucky*, 1:200-215; Brown, *Political Beginnings*, 57-69.

101. Perrin, *Pioneer Press*, 11; "Notes on Kentucky," section 24 (March 2, 1827).

102. The *Kentucky Gazette* published the proceedings of the Danville conventions on July 28, Aug. 9 and 30, 1788, and July 24, 1791.

103. Hening, *Statute Laws*, 12 (Oct. 10, 1786): 37-40.

104. William O. Hubbard and Dennis Lee Taulbee, *Kentucky's Ohio River Boundary from the Great Miami to the Wabash*, 3-22.

105. Brown, *Political Beginnings*, 222-34.

106. "Notes on Kentucky," section 20 (Jan. 19, 1827); James, *George Rogers Clark*, 109-46.

107. Brown, *Political Beginnings*, 58-69.

108. Including "Valerius," "Nicatus," "Aristides," "Brutus," "Plicoa," "Quericus," and "Theologues."

109. "Notes on Kentucky," section 20 (Jan. 19, 1827); Ware Interview, Draper Collection, 11CC166; Staples, *History of Pioneer Lexington*, 297-98.

110. Brown, *Political Beginnings*, 78-83.

111. Marshall, *History of Kentucky*, 1:258-67; Samuel Flagg Bemis, *Pinckney's Treaty*, 17-20; Arthur P. Whitaker, *The Spanish-American Frontier, 1783-1795*, 63-77; *The Mississippi Question, 1795-1803*, 79-85.

112. "Wilkinson's Memorial and Expatriation Declaration," in Temple Bodley, ed., *Littell's Political Transactions*, cxix-cxxxvii, 72-76; Brown, *Political Beginnings of Kentucky*, 200-202.

113. Connelley and Coulter, *History of Kentucky*, 1:242-59; Watlington, *Partisan Spirit*, 128-56; Bodley, ed., *Littell's Political Transactions*, 19-20; *Kentucky Gazette*, Jan. 26, 1788.

114. It is true that this issue had culminated by the time the first issue of the *Kentucky Gazette* appeared on August 11, 1787.

115. Benjamin Logan was the true trail-breaking pioneer who played an active role in the separation from Virginia and the formation of the Commonwealth of Kentucky: Talbert, *Benjamin Logan*, 222-67.

116. Brown, *Political Beginnings*, passim; Richard H. Caldemeyer, "The Career of George Nicholas," master's thesis, Indiana Univ., 1951, 75-77; Thomas Speed, *The Political Club of Danville, Kentucky, 1786-1790*, 100-101; Connelley and Coulter, *History of Kentucky*, 1:279-85.

117. "Notes on Kentucky," section 25 (March 9, 1827), quotes this statement in one form, and Marshall, *History of Kentucky*, 1:253, quotes it with slightly different wording.

118. "Notes on Kentucky," sections 28 (March 30, 1827) and 36 (May 25, 1827); Richard Peters, ed., *The Public Statutes-at-Large of the United States of America*, 1:189; Brown, *Political Beginnings of Kentucky*, 150-55.

119. "Notes on Kentucky," sections 27 and 28 (March 23 and 30, 1827). John Bradford was mistaken in his assessment of Nathan Dane's role in the delay in admitting Kentucky to the Union. Brown, *Political Beginnings*, 90-98: Littell, *Political Transactions*, 32-35.

120. "Notes on Kentucky," section 27 (March 23, 1827).

121. *Kentucky Gazette*, March 5, 12, Oct. 8, 15, 29, Nov. 26, 1791, Jan. 25 and 28, 1792.

122. This may not be a singular matter. Nicholas's name does not appear in Humphrey Marshall's *History*. John Mason Brown in *Political Beginnings*, 227-28, notes Nicholas's arrival in the Kentucky District.

123. The report of the event in the *Kentucky Gazette* was matter-of-fact, and there is no

substantial official report. See Ranck, *History of Lexington*, 171-75; idem, "How Kentucky Became a State."

124. *Kentucky Gazette*, Aug. 25, 1826; "Notes on Kentucky," sections 29, 37, and 48 (April 6, June 1, and Dec. 14, 1827).

125. Samuel M. Wilson, typescript note, Sept. 8, 1932, Bradford Papers, Wilson Collection, Univ. of Kentucky.

126. Draper apparently saw only twenty-three sections, the ones published in G.W. Stipp's *Western Miscellany*. Draper made revisions, some typographical in nature and others corroborative or corrective of facts as stated.

127. The number sixty-two appeared in several other sources, largely because of the widely scattered files of the *Kentucky Gazette*. See J. Winston Coleman, *A Bibliography of Kentucky History*, no. 2247; manuscript listing of the "Notes" by Samuel M. Wilson (Sept. 8, 1932), Bradford Papers, Wilson Collection. See also James M. Lee, "John Bradford," *Dictionary of American Biography*, 2:557-58.

128. Such scholars include Thomas Perkins Abernethy, E.M. Coulter, Charles G. Talbert, John D. Barnhart, J. Winston Coleman, John Mason Brown, Patricia Watlington, Robert S. Cotterill, Theodore Roosevelt, and John Bakeless.

129. Shelby's Governor's Papers in the Kentucky State Archives, Frankfort, pertain largely to appointments of local and state officials, principally magistrates. They are disappointing in their contents.

130. For Clark's papers, see James A. James, ed., *George Rogers Clark Papers*. For St. Clair's, see Henry William Smith, ed., *The St. Clair Papers*. For Wayne's, see Richard C. Knopf, *Anthony Wayne: A Name in Arms*.

131. The original land records are on file in the Kentucky secretary of state's office in Frankfort. The entries of land claims were copied and published from the originals by Willard Rouse Jillson in *The Kentucky Land Grants*.

132. *American State Papers*, vol. 4, (*Indian Affairs*), 58-59, 84-85, 127-47; Clarence E. Carter, ed., *The Territorial Papers of the United States*, 2:31-35, 255; 3:454-61; 4:354-61.

John Bradford's "Notes on Kentucky"

1. John Bradford made a note of Dr. Thomas Walker telling Isaac Shelby in 1779 about cutting his initials on the beech tree on the side of the "Indian Road." He recorded in his journal, April 13, 1750, that "A beech tree stands on the left hand, on which I cut my name." J. Stoddard Johnston, *First Explorations of Kentucky: Journals of Dr. Thomas Walker and Christopher Gist*, 48-49. No doubt Walker's conversation with Shelby pertained to details of extending the Walker-Henderson survey of the Virginia-North Carolina boundary westward. "The Journal of General Daniel Smith, August 1779 to July 1780," quoted in James W. Sames, III, *Four Steps West*, 26-42.

2. Johnston, *First Explorations*, 49: 54-56.

3. Marshall, *History of Kentucky*, 1:39; Collins, *History of Kentucky*, 1:16.

4. James Hall, *Sketches of History, Life and Manners in the West*, 1:244; Collins, *History of Kentucky*, 1:16; John Filson, *The Discovery, Settlement and Present State of Kentucke*, 50-56; William Stewart Lester, *The Transylvania Colony*, 50-51. It is interesting that Bradford used the term "Dark and Bloody Ground" for a date prior to 1775.

5. Lucian Beckner, "John Findley," *Filson Club History Quarterly* 2 (April 1927): 119; Lester, *Transylvania Colony*, 52; Filson, *Discovery*, 51; Collins, *History of Kentucky*, 2:167.

6. Filson, *Discovery*, 51.

7. Ibid., 52.

8. Ibid., 54.

9. Ibid., 53.

10. Bakeless, *Daniel Boone*, 63-65.

11. Marshall, *History of Kentucky*, 1:38; Collins, *History of Kentucky*, 1:16, 256.

12. William Ayers, *Historical Sketches*, 95-99; Marshall, *History*, 1:8-9.

13. Collins, *History of Kentucky*, 1:16, 256.

14. Filson, *Discovery*, 57-58; Bakeless, *Daniel Boone*, 67-79; Kincaid, *Wilderness Road*, 78-81.

15. Hening, *Statutes at Large*, May 1779, 9:3-4, 50; 10:431-32; Samuel M. Wilson, *The First Land Court of Kentucky, 1779-1780*, 14-17; Clarence W. Alvord, *The Mississippi Valley in British Politics*.

16. Marshall, *History of Kentucky*, 1:32-35; Casseday, *History of Louisville*, 16-21.

17. Collins, *History of Kentucky*, 2:18, 20, 358.

18. Marshall, *History of Kentucky*, 1:26.

19. Ibid., 1:12; Collins, *History of Kentucky*, 2:619-20; *Biographical Encyclopedia of Kentucky*, 94-95; Katherine Mason Harrod, *James Harrod of Kentucky*, 94-95.

20. Marshall, *History of Kentucky*, 1:38.

21. Withers, *Chronicles of Border Warfare*, 121-38; Reuben Gold Thwaites and Louise Phelps Kellogg, *Documentary History of Dunmore's War, 1774*, 302-7.

22. W.P. Palmer, comp. and ed., *Calendar of Virginia State Papers*, 1:165; Archibald Henderson, *The Conquest of the Old Southwest*, 216-52; Lester, *Transylvania Colony*, 31-36.

23. Hening, *Statutes at Large*, 10:35-50; Lester, *Transylvania Colony*, 275.

24. Filson, *Discovery*, 60; Lester, *Transylvania Colony*, 58-62; George W. Ranck, *Boonesborough*, 9-12, 24-27, 37-41; Felix Walker, "Narrative of His Trip with Boone from Long Island to Boonesborough in 1775," *DeBow's Review* 16 (1854): 150-55.

25. Filson, *Discovery*, 59; Lester, *Transylvania Colony*, 65; Ranck, *Boonesborough*, 20; William Calk, Journal, April 20, 1775.

26. Talbert, *Benjamin Logan*, 15-17; Marshall, *History of Kentucky*, 1:42.

27. Marshall, 1:42.

28. Filson, *Discovery*, 60; Ranck, *Boonesborough*, 49-51.

29. James, *Life of George Rogers Clark*, 20-21; Collins, *History of Kentucky*, 1:18.

30. Collins, 1:17.

31. Lester, *Transylvania Colony*, 22-23.

32. Ibid., 114-18.

33. Collins, *History of Kentucky*, 1:19; "Diary of George Rogers Clark from December 25, 1776 to November 22, 1777," in English, *Conquest*, 1:579-83.

34. B.O. Gaines, *The B.O. Gaines History of Scott County*, 1:13; "Diary of George Rogers Clark," English, *Conquest*, 1:579.

35. Gaines, 1:13.

36. Lester, *Transylvania Colony*, 173; Draper Mss. MSS48J12; "Diary of George Rogers Clark," English, *Conquest* 1:579.

37. James, *Life of George Rogers Clark*, 56; "Diary of George Rogers Clark," April 20, June 22, 1777, James, ed., *Clark Papers*, 3:lvii, 21-22; Clark Journal, Draper Mss. 4B111-12; Talbert, *Benjamin Logan*, 33.

38. Hening, *Statutes at Large*, Oct. 1776, 9:257-61.

39. "Diary of George Rogers Clark," April 20, June 22, 1777, James, ed., *Clark Papers*, 3:lvii, 21-22; Collins, *History of Kentucky*, 1:19; Connelley and Coulter, *History of Kentucky*, 1:176; "Clark's Memoir, 1773-1779," James, ed., *Clark Papers*, 3:218.

40. Talbert, *Benjamin Logan*, 36-41.

41. "Diary of George Rogers Clark," English, *Conquest*, 1:580; Ranck, *Boonesborough*, 58-60.

42. Talbert, *Benjamin Logan*, 42-44.

43. Ibid., 44-45.

44. Collins, *History of Kentucky*, 2:611; Draper Mss. 12CC136, 12C15, 4B118, 26CC55; Harrod, *James Harrod*, 114-15; Bakeless, *Daniel Boone*, 146-49.

45. Bakeless, 149-51.

46. Littell, *Political Transactions*, 8-14; Talbert, *Benjamin Logan*, 36-40.

47. James, ed., *Clark Papers*, 4:xxii-xxv; *Michigan Pioneer Historical Collections*, 11:326-28, 347-49; Marshall, *History of Kentucky*, 1:68-70.

48. "Diary of George Rogers Clark," English, *Conquest*, 1:580.

49. Filson, *Discovery*, 69-70; Bakeless, *Daniel Boone*, 192-94.

50. McClung, *Western Adventure*, 51-57; Collins, in *History of Kentucky*, 2:528, quotes the "Notes on Kentucky" concerning this incident.

51. Filson, *Discovery*, 67-69.

52. Ibid., 69.

53. Ibid., 69-70; Chester Young, ed., *Westward into Kentucky*, 59; Lester, *Transylvania Colony*, 220-21.

54. English, *Conquest*, 1:158-65; James, ed., *Clark Papers*, 3:lvii-lxi.

55. English, 1:159; James, ed., *Clark Papers*, 3:141.

56. English, *Conquest*, 3:50-54; James, ed., *Clark Papers*, 1:194-200.

57. "Bowman's Letter to Mason, Nov. 19, 1779," English, *Conquest*, 1:420-26.

58. English, *Conquest*, 1:420-26; James, ed., *Clark papers*, 3:50-54.

59. English, 1:211; Clark to George Mason, Nov. 19, 1779, James, ed., *Clark Papers*, 3:123-24.

60. "Bowman's Letter to Brinker, July 30, 1778," English, *Conquest*, 1:560.

61. "Bowman's Letter to Hite, Dec. 29, 1778," ibid., 564-66.

62. English, *Conquest*, 1:354-55; James, ed., *Clark Papers*, 3:lxxx-lxxxvi.

63. Haldimand to de Peyster, "Haldimand Papers," 1:92.

64. Marshall, *History of Kentucky*, 1:91-96; Young, ed., *Westward*, 65; Collins, *History of Kentucky*, 1:253, 2:175-80.

65. McClung, *Western Adventure*, 149-51.

66. Mereness, ed., *Travels*, 636-37.

67. Hening, *Statutes at Large*, 10:35-49, 50-54.

68. Wilson, *First Land Court*, 27-58. Wilson's Station was located about two miles southwest of Harrodsburg.

69. Mereness, *Travels*, 636-37.

70. Bodley, *First Great West*, 202-20.

71. James, ed., *Clark Papers*, 3:364-65; English, *Conquest*, 2:667-75.

72. English, 1:209-14.

73. James, ed., *Clark Papers*, 4:xix.

74. Ibid., xxi-xxiv.

75. Ibid., 350.

76. Bird to de Peyster, June 3 and 11, 1780, "Haldimand Papers," 19:528-29, 533-34.

77. James, ed., *Clark Papers*, 4:12.

78. James, *Life of George Rogers Clark*, 276-77; James, ed., *Clark Papers*, 3:46-49; Talbert, *Benjamin Logan*, 108-14.

79. Bird to de Peyster, May 21, 1780, "Haldimand Papers," 19:524; Coleman, *British Invasion of Kentucky*, 6-25; Collins, *History of Kentucky*, 2:327; Marshall, *History of Kentucky*, 1:107-8.

80. Collins, *History of Kentucky*, 2:329; Young, *Westward*, 80-81; Milo M. Quaife, "When Detroit Invaded Kentucky."

81. James, ed., *Clark Papers*, 3:476-83; Talbert, *Benjamin Logan*, 108-14.

82. Talbert, 113-14.

83. James, ed., *Clark Papers*, 3:478, 4:xxvi-xxviii; Talbert, *Benjamin Logan*, 171-81.

84. English, *Conquest*, 2:681-87; James, ed., *Clark Papers*, 4:xxiv; Talbert, *Benjamin Logan*, 10.

85. James, ed., *Clark Papers*, 3:482; Talbert, 114; English, *Conquest*, 2:683-87.

86. James, ed., *Clark Papers*, 4:liv-lxi.

87. Talbert, *Benjamin Logan*, 114; Marshall, *History of Kentucky*, 1:146-49.

88. James, *Life of George Rogers Clark*, 278-79; Haldimand to Thomas Townsend, Nov. 9, 1782, "Haldimand Papers," 1:320-21; Marshall, *History of Kentucky*, 1:109-10.

89. Marshall, 1:110-11; Connelley and Coulter, *History of Kentucky*, 1:184; James A. James, "Significant Events during the Last Year of the Revolution in the West," 251-53.

90. *Pennsylvania Gazette*, March 29, 1787, quoted in John Bach McMaster, *History of the People of the United States*, 1:149; Connelley and Coulter, *History of Kentucky*, 1:288; Collins, *History of Kentucky*, 2:238-39; Ranck, *History of Lexington*, 28.

91. Marshall, *History of Kentucky*, 1:115-16.

92. Ibid.

93. McClung, *Western Adventure*, 154-55; Collins, *History of Kentucky*, 2:618; Talbert, *Benjamin Logan*, 124.

94. Marshall, *History of Kentucky*, 1:114-15.

95. Collins, *History of Kentucky*, 2:472; Marshall, 1:121.

96. Collins, 2:657.

97. McConnell's adventure was a popular one that was often described. See McClung, *Western Adventure*, 151-57; Ranck, *History of Lexington*, 65-68.

98. McClung, 153-54; George W. Ranck, "The Story of Bryan's Station," in Reuben T. Durrett, ed., *Bryant's Station and the Memorial Proceedings*, 76-107.

99. Ranck, "Bryan's Station," in Durrett, 70-72; Bakeless, *Daniel Boone*, 28.

100. Marshall, *History of Kentucky*, 1:124-35; Ranck, *Boonesborough*, 77-85; Collins, *History of Kentucky*, 2:186-87; McClung, *Western Adventure*, 156-57; Samuel M. Wilson, *Battle of the Blue Licks*, 23-24, 156-57.

101. McClung, *Western Adventure*, 158.

102. Filson, *Discovery*, 78; Bakeless, *Daniel Boone*, 256-57.

103. Marshall, *History of Kentucky* (1812 ed.), 157-60; Bakeless, 273-74.

104. Ranck, "Bryan's Station," Durrett, ed., *Bryant's Station*, 94-98; Collins, *History of Kentucky*, 2:188-91.

105. Marshall, *History of Kentucky* (1812 ed.), 189-90; *Biographical Encyclopedia of Kentucky*, 297-98; Leland Winfield Meyer, *The Life and Times of Colonel Richard M. Johnson of Kentucky*, 2.

106. Ranck, "Bryan's Station," Durrett, ed., 87-88.

107. Ibid., 94-101; Marshall, *History of Kentucky* (1812 ed.), 160-61; Wilson, *Battle of the Blue Licks*, 32-36.

108. Ranck, "Bryan's Station," Durrett, ed., 98-110.

109. Ibid.

110. Ibid., 119.

111. James R. Albach, *Annals of the West*, 332-33; Marshall, *History of Kentucky* (1812 ed.), 160-72; Wilson, *Battle of the Blue Licks*, 32-113.

112. Wilson, 55-77; McClung, *Western Adventure*, 68-73; Collins, *History of Kentucky*, 2:657-63.

113. Bakeless, *Daniel Boone*, 294-95; Wilson, *Battle of the Blue Licks*, 48-58.

114. Filson, *Discovery*, 75-77; Wilson, *Battle of the Blue Licks*, 68.

115. Bakeless, *Daniel Boone*, 75-77; Wilson, 48-58.

116. Robert Patterson described the Battle of the Blue Licks and the generosity of Aaron Reynolds. Wilson, *Battle of the Blue Licks*, 51-52; Marshall, *History of Kentucky* (1812 ed.), 161.

117. Talbert, *Benjamin Logan*, 156-60; Draper Mss., 17CC143-44.

118. Wilson, *Battle of the Blue Licks*, 91-93.

119. Marshall, *History of Kentucky*, 1:109-10; James, *Life of George Rogers Clark*, 276-78; James, ed., *Clark Papers*, 3:476-84; Bodley, *History of Kentucky*, 1:316-17.

120. Albach, *Annals of the West*, 394-98.

121. "Fleming's Journal, 1782-1783" in Mereness, ed., *Travels*, 2; Draper Mss., 2ZZ69 (22).

122. Littell, *Political Transactions*, Appendix V, 12-13.

123. Marshall, *History of Kentucky*, 1:145-46.

124. Littell, *Political Transactions*, Appendices I, II, 61-63.

125. Ibid., 15-16.

126. Ibid.

127. Ibid., 16.

128. Ibid.

129. Ibid., 16-17.

130. Ibid.

131. Ibid.

132. Ibid.

133. Littell, *Political Transactions*, Appendix III, 7-9; Brown, *Political Beginnings*, 69-73; Marshall, *History of Kentucky*, 1:220-21.

134. Littell, Appendix V, 12-13.

135. Marshall, *History of Kentucky*, 1:220-21.

136. Ibid., 221.

137. Ibid., 1:109-10; Talbert, *Benjamin Logan*, 108-16; James, *Life of George Rogers Clark*, 270-78.

138. Talbert, *Benjamin Logan*, 204-13.

139. Littell, *Political Transactions*, 12.

140. Ibid., 13.

141. Ibid.

142. Ibid.

143. Hening, *Statutes at Large*, 12 (Oct. 1780): 37.

144. Ibid., 12 (Jan. 10, 1786): 37-40.

145. McClung, *Western Adventure*, 171-72.

146. Palmer, comp., *Calendar of Virginia State Papers*, 4:120; Talbert, *Benjamin Logan*, 205.

147. James, *Life of George Rogers Clark*, 354-58; Marshall, *History of Kentucky*, 1:247-49; Littell, *Political Transactions*, 21.

148. Brown, *Political Beginnings*, 73-78; John Marshall to Thomas Marshall, in Littell, *Political Transactions*, Appendices I, II, 1, 15-19; Marshall, *History of Kentucky*, 1:253-55.

149. Littell, 16-19.

150. Ibid.

151. Staples, *History of Pioneer Lexington*, 297-98; McClung, *Western Adventure*, 158-60; interview with Ware, Draper Mss. 11CG166, 11CGw1.

152. McClung, *Western Adventure*, 160.

153. Ibid.

154. Ibid., 177-79.

155. Ibid.

156. Ibid.

157. The latter part of the Downing story was no doubt conveyed orally to John Bradford. Francis Downing moved to Lexington and became a house painter; *Kentucky Gazette*, June 5, 1805.

158. John Strode, founder of Strode's Station in Clark County. Bradford must have gotten the rest of the Downing story from either Strode or Downing, or both. No other source seems to contain this material. *Kentucky Gazette*, Aug. 20, 1805.

159. Downing to Bradford, possibly in 1805.

160. *Biographical Encyclopedia of Kentucky*, 77-78; Collins, *History of Kentucky*, 2:127; James, *Life of George Rogers Clark*, 345.

161. Marshall, *History of Kentucky*, 1:252; John J. Dickey, "McNitt's Defeat," in Dyche, *History of Laurel County*, 17-18.

162. Marshall, *History of Kentucky*, 1:252; Collins, *History of Kentucky*, 2:97.

163. Marshall, 1:252.

164. Ibid., 258-59; *Kentucky Gazette*, Jan. 26, 1787; Littell, *Political Transactions*, Appendix VIII, 19-20.

165. Marshall, *History of Kentucky*, 1:262-63; Littell, *Political Transactions*, Appendix XXXII, 65-66.

166. Marshall, 1:269-70.

167. Palmer, comp., *Calendar of Virginia State Papers*, 4:261; Draper Mss., 12S-131-132; Talbert, *Benjamin Logan*, 226.

168. Marshall, *History of Kentucky*, 1:271.

169. Harry Innes to Governor Edmund Randolph, July 21, 1787, in Littell, *Political Transactions*, Appendix X, 22-24.

170. Robert Patterson was born March 15, 1753, in Cave Mountain, Pennsylvania. In 1775 he was second in command in the famous Bowman's Raid against the Shawnees, was at the Battle of the Blue Licks, and was wounded in Logan's raid against Chillicothe. He was one of the founders of Lexington (Ranck, *History of Lexington*, 26). He moved to Dayton, Ohio, in 1804.

171. John W. Cleve, "Colonel Robert Patterson," *American Pioneer* 2:343-47.

172. No doubt Robert Patterson made available to John Bradford a copy of the *Ohio National Journal*. This account was republished by Henry Howe in *Historical Collections of Ohio, and Encyclopedia of the State*, 2:270-73.

173. Kentuckians first reacted against the Jay-Spanish negotiations purely on rumor; Marshall, *History of Kentucky*, 1:258-69. In this instance John Bradford was editorializing. He was correct in February 1827 in saying the "treaty" was only a proposition which had considerable reluctant discussion on the part of John Jay and others behind it. Richard B. Morris, ed., *John Jay: The Making of a Revolutionary*, vol. 1, *Unpublished Papers, 1745-1780*, 649-834.

174. Hening, *Statutes at Large*, 10:537-38.

175. Morris, ed., *John Jay*, 1:650, 715.

176. Morris, 1:717; Marshall, *History of Kentucky*, 1:258-83; Hening, *Statutes at Large*, 10:237-38.

177. Littell, *Political Transactions*, Appendix VIII, 19-21; Marshall, *History of Kentucky*, 1:285-86; *Kentucky Gazette*, Jan. 26, 1788.

178. William H. Perrin, J.H. Battle, and G.C. Kniffen, *Kentucky: A History of the State*, 490-91.

179. Staples, "John Bradford and the *Kentucky Gazette*," *Kentucky Press* 8 (Feb. 1937): 2.

180. Staples, 2; Samuel M. Wilson, Address to the Bibliographical Society of America, 1937, Wilson Collection, Univ. of Kentucky.

181. Perrin, *Pioneer Press*, 9.

182. Littell, *Political Transactions*, 82-83.

183. Ibid., 78-84.

184. Ibid., 83.

185. Ibid., 84.

186. Ibid., 84-93.

187. Marshall, *History of Kentucky*, 1:258-69; Littell, *Political Transactions*, Appendices XIII, XIV, 26-30.

188. Littell, Appendix XIII, 27-28.

189. Ibid.

190. *Kentucky Gazette*, Feb. 22, 1788.

191. Ibid., Aug. 16, 1788.

192. John Bradford was mistaken. The widow was named Skaggs, not Shanks. McClung, *Western Adventure*, 179-83; Collins, *History of Kentucky*, 2:72-74.

193. McClung, *Western Adventure*, 182-83.

194. Ibid., 185-86.

195. Ibid., 91-98.

196. Perrin, Battle, and Kniffen, *Kentucky: A History,* 244; Marshall, *History of Kentucky,* 1:269.

197. Gaines, *History of Scott County,* 1:5.

198. *Kentucky Gazette,* Nov. 15, 1787.

199. Gaines, *History of Scott County,* 1:5; *Kentucky Gazette,* Feb. 9, 1788.

200. *Kentucky Gazette,* March 8, 1788; Marshall, *History of Kentucky,* 1:282.

201. *Kentucky Gazette,* Feb. 24, May 23, 1788; Marshall, *History of Kentucky,* 1:282.

202. *Kentucky Gazette,* Feb. 23, 1788. Bradford in his "Notes" cited the wrong date.

203. Ibid., Nov. 8, 1788.

204. *Biographical Encyclopedia of Kentucky,* 14; Marshall, *History of Kentucky,* 1:279.

205. "Proceedings," Danville Convention, Nov. 17, 1787, Feb. 23, Aug. 16, 1788.

206. "Proceedings," Danville Convention, July 28, 1788; *Kentucky Gazette,* Aug. 31, 1788; Littell, *Political Transactions,* Appendix XV, 30-35.

207. In this case, however, John Bradford did some editorializing. The convention did ask Congress to give attention to the issue of access to Mississippi River, but in not quite the same language.

208. *Journal of Congress* (House of Representatives, 1st Cong.), 1:17, 331: Littell, *Political Transactions,* Appendix XV, 35-37.

209. Jonathan Elliott, *The Debates on the Adoption of the Federal Constitution,* 3:340-43, 349-57, 365-66.

210. *Kentucky Gazette,* Sept. 6, 1788.

211. Littell, *Political Transactions,* Appendix XVI, 36-37; "Proceedings," Danville Convention, July 31, 1788, 3.

212. "Proceedings," Danville Convention, Nov. 10, 1788, 7-15.

213. Ibid.

214. Ibid.

215. Ibid.

216. *Kentucky Gazette,* Jan. 30, Feb. 5, 1789.

217. "Proceedings," Danville Convention, Nov. 10, 1788, 15.

218. Marshall, *History of Kentucky,* 1:300-306.

219. Clarence E. Carter, ed., *Territorial Papers of the United States,* vol. 4, *The Territory South of the River Ohio, 1790-1796* (Oct. 6, 1794), 358-59; Ramsay, *Annals of Tennessee,* 610-19.

220. *Kentucky Gazette,* Aug. 25, 1787; Talbert, *Benjamin Logan,* 219-21.

221. *Kentucky Gazette,* Aug. 25, 1787.

222. Ibid.; Palmer, comp., *Calendar of Virginia State Papers,* 4:344.

223. *Kentucky Gazette,* Sept. 18, 1787.

224. Ibid., May 24, 1788.

225. Ibid.

226. "Proceedings," Danville Convention, Nov. 10, 1788, 15.

227. Ibid.

228. Ibid.

229. Ibid.

230. John Bradford was perhaps editorializing in this area. Indian raids had become an obsession for Kentucky pioneers. As long as there were British posts in the Northwest, this no doubt would be the case. The Virginia General Assembly responded to the Kentucky resolutions by enacting the so-called Virginia Compact Bill of 1788. Hening, *Statutes at Large,* 12 (Dec. 18, 1788): 240-43.

231. Littell, *Political Transactions,* Appendix XXI, 51-54.

232. Marshall, *History of Kentucky,* 1:282-86.

233. Ibid., 285.

234. *Kentucky Gazette,* Feb. 23, March 8, 9, April 12, Nov. 8, Dec. 19, 1788.

235. "Proceedings," Danville Convention, July 26, 1790, 6-10.

236. Ibid., July 28, 1790, pp. 5-8.

237. Ibid.

238. Ibid., July 30, 1790.

239. Littell, *Political Transactions,* Appendix XXIV, 59.

240. Ibid.

241. Ibid.

242. *Kentucky Gazette,* March 28, June 25, July 16, 1791.

243. Indian raids in late 1789 and 1790 grew numerous and irksome. See *Kentucky Gazette,* Dec. 3, 1789, and Jan. 22, 1790; Marshall, *History of Kentucky,* 1:358, 363-76; *American State Papers,* vol. 4 *(Indian Affairs),* 84, 171-98; Jacob Burnet, *Notes on the Settlement of the Northwestern Territory,* 83-107; Samuel Metcalf, *A Collection of Some of the Most Interesting Narratives of Indian Warfare in the West,* 184-87.

244. *Kentucky Gazette,* March 26, 1791; *Western Review,* 2:48-53.

245. Peters, ed., *Public Statutes at Large of the United States,* 1:189.

246. Ibid.; *Kentucky Gazette,* April 26, Dec. 6, 1790.

247. Bradford touched on a sensitive question without attempting to answer it: the Mississippi question, Indian raids, floundering in the Danville conventions, solving differences between the Western District and the Virginia General Assembly, bad timing in Congress, and failure to have a constitutional draft in hand earlier.

248. *Kentucky Gazette,* June 25, 1791; "Report of Brigadier General Scott, June 28, 1791," *American State Papers,* vol. 4 *(Indian Affairs),* 131-32.

249. Littell, *Political Transactions,* Appendix XXVII, 60-61.

250. Ibid., 62.

251. *Kentucky Gazette,* July 16, 1791.

252. The campaign against the Wabash Indians was a complex one. See *American State Papers,* vol. 4 *(Indian Affairs),* 129-36.

253. Ibid.

254. "Lieutenant Commandant Wilkinson's Report, August 24, 1791," *American State Papers,* vol. 4 *(Indian Affairs),* 133-35. Humphrey Marshall was correct in his observation that "the year 1791 is more than usually crowded with accounts of depredations, incursions, and expeditions." *History of Kentucky,* 1:370. Accounts of such occurred frequently in the *Kentucky Gazette:* see April 16, June 4, 1791.

255. *Kentucky Gazette,* July 25, 1791.

256. Ibid.

257. Ibid., Oct. 8, 1791.

258. Ibid.

259. *American State Papers,* vol. 4 *(Indian Affairs),* 138.

260. Metcalf, *Indian Wars,* 144-45.

261. *Kentucky Gazette,* Nov. 12, 1791.

262. Ibid., Dec. 10, 1791.

263. Ibid.

264. Ibid., Oct. 6, 1791.

265. Ibid.

266. Ibid., Nov. 10, 1791.

267. Ibid., Feb. 25, 1792.

268. Ibid. A series of St. Clair letters appeared in the issues of Nov. 6 and 9, 1791, and Jan. 29, 1792.

269. Ibid., April 7, May 12, June 2, 1792.

270. "Proceedings," Danville Convention, April 1792, 4-7.

271. *Kentucky Gazette,* June 9, 1792.

272. Ibid.

273. Ibid.

274. Ibid.

275. Ibid.

276. Ibid., June 23, 1792.

277. Ibid.

278. *American State Papers*, vol. 4, (*Indian Affairs*), 197-98.

279. Ibid.

280. Ibid., 197.

281. Ibid.; Albach, *Annals of the War,* 522-23.

282. John Bradford covered several subjects in this section. Some of the material he apparently injected editorially. The subjects covered here involved extensive correspondence. *State Papers and Publick Documents of the United States from the Accession of George Washington to the Presidency, Exhibiting a Complete View of Our Foreign Relations since that Time,* 10:115-397; *American State Papers,* vol. 4 (*Indian Affairs*), 139-147; vol. 1 (Foreign Relations), 247, 252-61.

283. *Kentucky Gazette,* March 14, 1790; *American State Papers,* vol. 4 (*Indian Affairs*), 197-98.

284. *Kentucky Gazette,* June 30, 1792.

285. Hugh Henry Brackenridge was a political and literary personality on the upper Ohio Valley frontier. A native Scotsman, he was educated at Princeton College, where he was a classmate of James Madison and Philip Freneau. He taught school and was an editor, author, and lawyer. As a pioneer bookstore operator in Pittsburgh he contributed materially to the cultural beginnings of that town. As his essay indicates, he had decided views on the Indian problem, especially in connection with British incitement of raids and commission of atrocities. See C.M. Newling, "Hugh Henry Brackenridge," *Dictionary of American Biography,* 2:644-46. The first part of the essay appeared in the *Kentucky Gazette,* May 12, 1792.

286. *Kentucky Gazette,* May 19, 1792.

287. Ibid., July 7, 1792.

288. Ibid., July 21, 1788.

289. Ibid., July 28, 1792.

290. Ibid., Sept. 9, 1792.

291. Ibid., Sept. 11, 1792.

292. Ibid.

293. Ibid.

294. Ibid.

295. Ibid.

296. Ibid.

297. Ibid., Jan. 26, March 16, April 26, May 11, Dec. 7, 1793.

298. Ibid., March 8, 1794.

299. Ibid., Feb. 15, 1792.

300. Ibid., March 30, 1792.

301. Ibid., April 6, 1793.

302. Ibid.

303. Ibid., April 13, 1793.

304. Ibid.

305. Ibid., April 20, 1792.

306. Ibid., March 3, April 29, May 11 and 25, 1792.

307. Ibid., July 27, 1792.

308. Ibid., Aug. 17, 1793.

309. Ibid., Aug. 24, Sept. 14, 1792.

310. Ibid., Aug. 31, 1792.

311. Ibid.

312. *American State Papers,* vol. 4 (*Indian Affairs*), 359. The entire correspondence is on 340-61.

313. Ibid., 359.

314. *Kentucky Gazette,* July 7, 1793.

315. Ibid., Oct. 5, 1793.

316. Ibid.

317. Ibid.

318. Ibid., Oct. 12, 1793.

319. Ibid., Oct. 19, 1793.

320. Ibid., Oct. 26, 1793.

321. Ibid., Nov. 16, 1793.

322. Reaction to the Monroe speech in the Virginia ratification convention revealed the extreme sensitivity of the West on the Spanish-Mississippi issue. Elliott, *The Debates on the Adoption of the Federal Constitution*, 3:214-16, 331-40.

323. *Kentucky Gazette*, Nov. 2, 1793.

324. Ibid.

325. Ibid., Jan. 4, 1794.

326. Ibid., March 17, 1792; D.R. Dewey, *Financial History of the United States*, 105-6; Leland D. Baldwin, *Whiskey Rebels*, 16-28, 67-75.

327. The name John Jay stirred anger in the western country because of the phantom Spanish treaty. At the time (1793) he was serving as chief justice of the United States. He was chosen to negotiate with England when the issue of the Northwest Posts was hottest.

328. *Kentucky Gazette*, Jan. 24, May 17, 1794.

329. Ibid., Jan. 11, Feb. 9, 1794.

330. Ibid., Feb. 8, March 22, 1794; James, *George Rogers Clark*, 426-27.

331. *Kentucky Gazette*, Feb. 8, 1794.

332. Ibid.

333. Ibid., March 15 and 22, April 5 and 26, 1794.

334. Ibid., May 3, 1794.

335. Ibid., May 17, 1794.

336. Albach, *Annals of the West*, 333-35.

337. Hening, *Statutes at Large*, 10 (May 5, 1780): 287-88.

338. Ibid., 11 (May 5, 1782): 282-87.

339. Minutes, Transylvania Board of Trustees, Nov. 4, 1784, 3.

340. Ibid., May 24, 1785.

341. Ibid., July 21, 1786, Oct. 13, 1788.

342. Ibid., July 21, 1788, Oct. 13 and 17, 1788.

343. There are no entries for this date in the proceedings of the Transylvania Board of Trustees. A full financial report was made April 12, 1791, p. XXXI.

344. Hening, *Statutes at Large*, 13 (Dec. 30, 1790): 173.

345. Minutes, Transylvania Board of Trustees, April 12, 1791, 36.

346. Ibid., Oct. 11, 1791, 38-39.

347. Ibid., April 10, 1792, 40.

348. Ibid., April 8, 1793, 51.

349. Ibid., April 8 and 10, 1793, 51-55.

350. Ibid.

351. Ibid., April 10, 1794, 55. The date October 19, 1794, is a Bradford error. It should read "9th of October 1793." Minutes, Transylvania Board of Trustees, Oct. 9, 1793. Harry Toulmin was sworn in as president of Transylvania on June 30, 1794.

352. Ibid., Oct. 26, 1795, 96.

353. Ibid., April 4, 1796, 108.

354. Harry Toulmin resigned the presidency of Transylvania on April 4, 1796. See Minutes, Transylvania Board of Trustees, 106, Oct. 3, 1796, 112-16.

355. Ibid., Jan. 8, 1799, 1-4.

356. Ibid., Oct. 18, 1799, 31-32.

357. Bradford misstated the date; it was Oct. 25, 1799. See Minutes for that date, 33.

358. *Acts*, Kentucky General Assembly, Dec. 22, 1798, 43-46; Minutes, Transylvania Board of Trustees, April 1, 1801, 74; July 1, 1801, 88-99.

359. Minutes, Transylvania Board of Trustees, July 16, 1801, 96. James Welsh, a Presbyterian minister, was appointed professor of languages in December 1799. He served churches in Lexington and Georgetown. His dispute with students was a celebrated incident in the early history of Transylvania. Robert Peter and Johana Peter, *Transylvania University*, 82-84.

360. Minutes, Board of Trustees, June 23, 1801, 82-98.

361. Ibid., Oct. 7, 1802, 323.

362. Ibid., Oct. 6, 1802, 225.

363. Ibid., Oct. 7, 1802, 225-26.

364. Ibid., April 2, 1804, 262.

365. Ibid., Oct. 18, 1803, 260.

366. Ibid., Oct. 1, 1804, 273.

367. Ibid., Nov. 1, 1804, 282.

368. John Wright, *Transylvania: Tutor to the West*, 52.

369. Minutes, Transylvania Board of Trustees, Oct. 16, 1807, 329.

370. Ibid., Nov. 16, 1808, 348.

371. John Bradford spoke from first-hand experience as a trustee. There could not have been much excitement in this period, as there were only thirty students in 1801 and thirty-nine in 1810.

372. There is a note regarding Horace Holley's appointment in the Holley Scrapbook, dated Nov. 11, 1815. See Minutes, Transylvania Board of Trustees, Oct. 6, 1815, 198, and Nov. 11, 1815, 205.

373. Ibid., 205.

374. Ibid., March 12, 1816, 224.

375. Ibid., March 13, 1816, 233.

376. Ibid., Feb. 28, 1817, 281.

377. *Acts*, Kentucky General Assembly, Feb. 3, 1818, 554-55.

378. The minutes of the Board of Trustees for 1816-1827 have been lost. The *Kentucky Gazette* and the *Lexington Reporter* gave abbreviated coverage to the news of Transylvania. Obviously John Bradford, as a member of the Board of Trustees, had access to the minutes and had before him the volume that is now missing. He cited here the minutes of the Board Meeting on May 2, 1818, without a page number.

379. Minutes, May 2, 1818. On November 28, 1825, John Bradford submitted a full report of Transylvania affairs, including land transactions, to the Kentucky General Assembly. See *Journal* of the Kentucky Senate, Nov. 29-30, 1818, 140-59.

380. Minutes, Transylvania Board of Trustees, March 14, 1818. Robert Wickliffe, Kentucky's largest land- and slaveholder, was a member of the Kentucky General Assembly and a major political figure in central Kentucky. J. Winston Coleman, *Slavery Times in Kentucky*, 140-59.

381. The minutes of the Board of Trustees for November 11, 1815, indicate that Horace Holley was employed on that date. He did not arrive in Lexington, however, until May 25, 1818. See *Lexington Reporter*, May 27, 1818; also, Henry Clay to Horace Holley, Sept. 8, 1818, in James F. Hopkins and Mary W.M. Hargreaves, ed., *The Papers of Henry Clay*, vol. 2, *The Rising Statesman, 1815-1820*, 597-98.

382. Robert Peter, *The History of the Medical Department of Transylvania University*, 33-35, 41, 157.

383. Minutes, Transylvania Board of Trustees, Dec. 19, 1818; the *Kentucky Gazette*, on May 29, 1818, reported that President Holley had addressed the students.

384. Peter, *History of the Medical Department*, 6-7, 41-57.

385. Ibid., 12.

386. Daniel Bradford was the son of John Bradford. In 1802 he served as editor of the *Kentucky Gazette* for a time. He was quite active in public affairs in Lexington. He served as tutor at Transylvania and in 1822-23 as steward of the university. Leland Brown, "The Family of John Bradford," *Kentucky Press*, Sept. 1937, 3.

387. Thomas Caldwell was a naturalist. Later he became director of the local botanical garden. Peter, *History of the Medical Department*, 38.

388. Ibid., 31. See also Niels Henry Sonne, *Liberal Kentucky*, 75.

389. *Lexington Reporter*, May 5, 1823; *Kentucky Gazette*, May 15, 1823.

390. James Morrison died in Washington, D.C., on April 20, 1823. His funeral in Lexington was not held until after May 5.

391. Horace Holley's memorial address became a source of bitter and bigoted criticism. Peter and Peter, *Transylvania University*, 34-37; Horace Holley, *A Discourse Occasioned by the Death of Col. James Morrison;* Sonne, *Liberal Kentucky*, 193-223.

392. *Lexington Reporter*, June 30, 1823; Hopkins and Hargreaves, eds., *Papers of Henry Clay*, 3:424-26; Peter and Peter, *Transylvania University*, 138-39; *Biographical Encyclopedia of Kentucky*, 108.

393. *Lexington Reporter*, June 30, 1823; Minutes, Transylvania Board of Trustees, July 10 and 18, 1823.

394. Settlement of the Morrison estate became a somewhat complicated affair, dragging on for several years. Hopkins and Hargreaves, eds., *Papers on Henry Clay*, 5 (March 16, May 10, July 12, 1826): 173, 158-59, 543; Peter and Peter, *Transylvania University*, 154-57.

395. John McFarland, a Presbyterian minister who served as pastor to several central Kentucky churches, was a persistent critic of Horace Holley. In 1823 McFarland was a member of a group of Presbyterian ministers who sought to depose Holley. *The Literary Pamphleteer*, 1823-24, outlined the basics of this issue. See also *Lexington Reporter*, Dec. 8, 1823; Robert Davidson, *History of the Presbyterian Church in the State of Kentucky*, 310-18; Sonne, *Liberal Kentucky*, 196-99, 219-23.

396. *Lexington Reporter*, April 12, 1824.

397. Ibid.; Sonne, *Liberal Kentucky*, 196-202.

398. *Lexington Reporter*, April 12, 1824.

399. Ibid.

400. Holley File A-Z (May 28, 1824), Special Collections, Transylvania University.

401. *Lexington Reporter*, June 14, 1824.

402. Charles Caldwell, *A Discourse on the Genius and Character of the Reverend Horace Holley*, 207-15.

403. Holley Scrapbook, March 24, 1827.

404. Ibid.

405. *Kentucky Gazette*, May 31, 1794.

406. Ibid.

407. Ibid.

408. Ibid, June 14, 1794.

409. Ibid., June 29, 1794.

410. Ibid.

411. Ibid.

412. Ibid.

413. Ibid.

414. Ibid., June 12, 1794.

415. Ibid., June 19, 1794.

416. Ibid.

417. Ibid.

418. Ibid.

419. Ibid., June 14, 1794.

420. Ibid., Nov. 1, 1794.

421. Ibid.

422. Ibid.

423. Ibid.

424. Ibid.

425. Ibid.

426. Ibid., Oct. 4, 1794.

427. Ibid.

428. Ibid., Oct. 11, 1794. A letter from Edmund Randolph, dated September 1, 1794, contained the quotation from one from R.H. Sheaffe, lieutenant, 5th Reg. and Qr. Maj. Gen. Dept. The letter was addressed to George Hammond, British minister plenipotentiary.

429. *Kentucky Gazette*, Oct. 4, 1794.

430. Ibid., Oct. 11 and 25, 1794.

431. Ibid.

432. Ibid.

433. Ibid., Jan. 10, 1795.

434. Ibid.

435. Ibid.

436. Ibid.

437. Ibid.

438. Ibid.

439. Ibid., Jan. 17, 1794.

440. Ibid.

441. Ibid.

442. Ibid.

443. Ibid., Feb. 28, 1795.

444. Ibid., Jan. 24, 1795. Bradford no doubt was editorializing, as no newspapers had arrived in Lexington after Dec. 10, 1794.

445. Ibid., March 14, 1795.

446. Ibid.

447. Ibid.

448. Ibid.

449. Ibid.

450. Ibid.

451. Ibid.

452. Ibid., March 21 and 28, April 4, May 9 and 23, June 6, 1795.

453. Ibid., July 11, 1795.

454. Ibid.

455. Ibid.

456. *American State Papers*, vol. 1 (*Foreign Relations*), 252-61.

457. Kappler, *Indian Affairs*, 2:18, 39, 45.

458. *Kentucky Gazette*, March 26, 1796.

459. The text of the proclamation does not appear among Governor Shelby's papers in the Kentucky State Archives. On November 5, 1795, he informed members of the Kentucky Senate and House that negotiations were under way for the formation of the Pinckney Treaty, the Jay Treaty with Great Britain was concluded, and so was the Treaty of Greenville. Regarding the latter he wrote, "I flatter myself that no interruption will be given to that peace by any improper conduct of any citizen of this state." *Journal*, Kentucky Senate, 1795, p. 5; *Kentucky Gazette*, Oct. 31, Nov. 2, and 28, 1795.

460. *Kentucky Gazette*, Feb. 20, 1796.

461. John Bradford may have had a copy of this proclamation among his notes. He published the Kentucky House and Senate *Journals*.

462. *Kentucky Gazette*, April 23, 1796.

463. "Proceedings," Danville Convention, April 18, 1792, 21-53.

464. *Kentucky Gazette*, May 14 and 28, 1796.

465. Ibid.

466. Ibid.

467. Ibid., March 12, 1796.

468. Ibid.
469. Ibid., Jan. 4, 1797.
470. *American State Papers,* vol. 2 (*Foreign Relations*), 22-44.
471. Ibid.
472. Ibid.
473. Ibid.
474. Ibid.
475. Ibid.
476. Ibid.
477. Ibid.
478. Ibid.
479. Ibid.
480. Ibid.
481. Ibid.
482. Ibid.
483. Ibid.

Bibliography

In the publication of the *Kentucky Gazette* and later the "Notes on Kentucky," John Bradford had only a limited amount of source material from which to extract information. Fortunately he had immediate access to much of the information relating to military activities, to the proceedings of the separation conventions in Danville, to some federal government documents, and to all those of the Kentucky state government after 1792.

News accounts to be published in the *Kentucky Gazette* were often gathered from word-of-mouth information supplied by travelers and persons engaged in various contemporary activities. In 1826 Bradford began the process of publishing his "Notes on Kentucky." He perhaps had no notion at the outset as to how many there would be in the end. At that date he had available to him a complete file of the *Kentucky Gazette*, some government documents, and some published histories. Too, he had first-hand knowledge of the proceedings of the Lexington Democratic Society, the Lexington town trustees, and the board of trustees of Transylvania University.

John Bradford no doubt intended his "Notes on Kentucky" to be basic sources from which future historians of Kentucky and the westward movement would draw information. In this he was amply rewarded. Lyman Copeland Draper drew a good portion of his information about Kentucky either from the *Gazette* or from Bradford's "Notes." Formulating this bibliography has been an exercise in sifting through a considerable mass of incestuous historical documentation to locate either primary sources or corroborative ones. About the only published historical relating to the early history of Kentucky and the westward movement which did not use Bradford's "Notes" was John Filson's so-called history of Kentucky, whose publication antedated that of the *Gazette*.

Manuscripts and Papers

Asbury, Francis. *The Journal of the Rev. Francis Asbury, Bishop of the Methodist Church, from August 7, 1771 to December 7, 1815.* 3 vols. New York, 1821.

Calk, William. Journal (1775). Calk Family Papers Collection. Mount Sterling.

Fleming, William. "Journal." In Newton D. Mereness, ed., *Travels in the American Colonies.* New York, 1916.

"Haldimand Papers." *Historical Collections Made by the Michigan Pioneer and Historical Society*, vols. 1, 9, 10, 11, 19, and 20.

Holley, Horace. Letter and Paper File, 1815-1827, A-Z. Special Collections File, Transylvania University.

Holley Scrapbook, 1815-1827. Special Collections, Transylvania University.

Hopkins, James F., and Mary W.M. Hargreaves, eds. *The Papers of Henry Clay*, vol.

2 (*The Rising Statesman, 1815-1820*); vol. 3 (*Presidential Candidate, 1821-1824*). Lexington, 1961, 1963.

Minutes, Transylvania Board of Trustees, 1792-1817, 1827-1830. Special Collections, Transylvania University.

Proceedings, Kentucky Separation Conventions, 1787-1792. Kentucky Historical Society Collection, Frankfort.

Smith, William Henry. *The St. Clair Papers: The Life and Public Services of the Revolutionary War President of the Continental Congress, the Governor of the Northwestern Territory; with His Correspondence and Other Papers, arranged and annotated.* 2 vols. Cincinnati, 1882.

Weeks, Mabel Clara. *Calendar of the Kentucky Papers of the Draper Collection of Manuscripts.* Madison, Wisc., 1925.

White, David, Sr. Application for a Revolutionary War Pension, March 4, 1831. Pension Rolls, Commonwealth of Kentucky, Book 2C, 7:57. Kentucky Archives, Frankfort.

Wilson, Samuel M. John Bradford Papers. Wilson Collection. Special Collections, Margaret I. King Library, University of Kentucky.

Unpublished Theses

Beasley, Paul W. "The Life and Times of Isaac Shelby." University of Kentucky, 1956.

Caldemeyer, Richard H. "The Career of George Nicholas." Indiana University, 1951.

Mikkelson, Dwight. "*The Kentucky Gazette:* Herald to a Noisy World." University of Kentucky, 1963.

Public Records

Fayette Circuit Court. Record Books. Lexington-Fayette County Archives.

Fayette County Deed Books. Lexington-Fayette County Archives.

Minute Book, Town Trustees, 1781-1817. Lexington-Fayette County Archives.

The Papers of Governor Isaac Shelby, 1792-1798, Kentucky State Archives, Frankfort.

Town Assessor's Book, 1815. Lexington-Fayette County Archives.

Town Ledger Book C, 1803, 1814, 1819. Lexington-Fayette County Archives.

Public Laws, Documents, and Collected Papers

Acts. Kentucky General Assembly. Frankfort, 1792-1830.

Alvord, Clarence W., ed. *Cahokia Records, 1778-1790.* Collections of the Illinois State Historical Library. Virginia Series. Springfield, Ill., 1907.

———, ed. *Kaskia Records, 1778-1790.* Collections of the Illinois State Historical Library. Virginia Series. Springfield, Ill., 1909.

American State Papers. Foreign Relations, 6 vols. Vols. 1 and 2, ed. Walter Lowrie and Matthew St. Clair Clarke. Washington, D.C., 1833. *Indian Affairs,* 2 vols. Vol. 4 [sic] (March 3, 1789-March 3, 1815), ed. Walter Lowrie and Matthew St. Clair Clarke. Washington, D.C., 1832.

Carter, Clarence E., comp. and ed. *The Territorial Papers of the United States*. Vols. 2-3, *The Territory Northwest of the River Ohio, 1787-1803*. Washington, D.C., 1934. Vol. 4, *The Territory South of the River Ohio, 1790-1796*. Washington, D.C., 1936.

Constitution. A Form of Government for the State of Kentucky. Lexington, 1792.

Diplomatic Correspondence of the United States of America from the Beginning of the Definitive Treaty of Peace, 10th of September 1783. 3 vols. Washington, D.C., 1837.

Elliott, Jonathan. *The Debates on the Adoption of the Federal Constitution in the Convention held at Philadelphia in 1787*. 5 vols. New York, 1888.

Hening, William W. *The Statutes at Large; Being a Collection of all the Laws of Virginia from the First Session of The Legislature in the Year 1619*. Richmond, Va., 1823.

Hughes, James, comp. *A Report of the Causes Determined by the Late Supreme Court for the District of Kentucky, and by the Court of Appeals, in which Titles to Land were in Dispute*. Lexington, 1803.

James, James A., ed. *George Rogers Clark Papers*. 8 vols. Collections of the Illinois State Historical Library. Virginia Series, Vols. 3-4. Springfield, Ill., 1912, 1926.

Journal of the First Constitutional Convention of Kentucky. Held in Danville, Kentucky, April 2 to 18, 1792. Lexington, 1942.

Journals, House of Representatives, Commonwealth of Kentucky. Frankfort, 1792-1830.

Journal of the House of Representatives of the United States, being the First Session of the First Congress being held in the City of New York, March 4, 1789. Washington, D.C., 1826.

Journal of the Senate of the Commonwealth of Kentucky. Frankfort, 1792-1830.

Kappler, Charles J., comp. *Indian Affairs, Laws, and Treaties*. 2 vols., Washington, D.C., 1904.

Littell, William. *The Statute Law of Kentucky, with Notes, Praelections, and Observations on the Public Act*. 5 vols. Frankfort, 1809-1819.

Morris, Richard. *John Jay: The Making of a Revolutionary: Unpublished Papers, 1745-1780*. New York, 1975.

Palmer, W.P., comp. and ed. *Calendar of Virginia State Papers*. 11 vols. Richmond, 1875-1893.

Peters, Richard, ed. *The Public Statutes-at-Large of the United States of America from the Organization of the Government in 1789, to March 3, 1845*. vol. 1. Boston, 1845.

Richardson, James D., comp. *A Compilation of the Messages and Papers of the Presidents of the United States, 1789-1908*. 10 vols. Washington, 1908.

State Papers and Publick Documents of the United States from the Accession of George Washington to the Presidency, Exhibiting a Complete View of Our Foreign Relations since that Time. 10 vols. Boston, 1817.

Periodical and Special Articles

Abernethy, Thomas Perkins, ed. "Journal of the First Kentucky Conventions, December 27, 1784-January 5, 1785." *Journal of Southern History* 1 (Feb.-Nov. 1935): 67-78.

Alvord, Clarence W. "Virginia and the West." *Mississippi Valley Historical Review* 3 (1916-1917): 19-38.

Attack of "Dunlap's Station." *American Pioneer* 2 (April 1843): 148-49.

Brickell, John. "John Brickell's Narrative." *American Pioneer* 1 (Jan. 1842): 43-56.

Brown, Leland A. "The Family of John Bradford." *Kentucky Press* 8 (Sept. 1937): 2.

Bryan, Edward. "Bryan, a Pioneer Family." *Register of the Kentucky Historical Society* 40 (July 1942): 318-22.

Byrd, Pratt. "The Kentucky Frontier, 1792." *Filson Club History Quarterly* 25 (July 1951): 286-94.

Collins, Richard H., "The Siege of Bryan's Station, ed. by Willard Rouse Jillson." *Register of the Kentucky Historical Society* 36 (Jan. 1938): 15-25.

Coulter, E. Merton, "The Efforts of the Democratic Societies of the West to Open the Navigation of the Mississippi River." *Mississippi Valley Historical Review* 11 (1924-1925): 376-89.

"Daily Journal of Wayne's Campaign from July 28th 1794, Including an Account of the Memorable Battle of 20th August." *American Pioneer* 1 (Aug. 1842): 315-22, 351-57.

Donalson, Israel. "Captivity of Israel Donalson (and Timothy Downing)." *American Pioneer* 1 (Nov. 1842): 425-33.

Farnham, Thomas J. "Kentucky and Washington's Mississippi Policy of Patience and Persuasion." *Register of the Kentucky Historical Society* 64 (Jan. 1966): 14-28.

Hadsell, Richard Miller. "John Bradford and His Contributions to the Culture and the Life of Early Lexington and Kentucky." *Register of the Kentucky Historical Society* 42 (Oct. 1964): 265-77.

Ham, F. Gerald. "Central Kentucky Broadsides and Newspapers, 1793-1846, in the John M. McCalla Papers, West Virginia University." *Register of the Kentucky Historical Society* 58 (Oct. 1960): 322-52; 59 (Jan. 1961): 47-78.

Harden, Bayless H., ed. "Whitley Papers." *Register of the Kentucky Historical Society* 36 (July 1938): 189-209.

Henderson, Archibald. "Dr. Thomas Walker and the Loyal Land Company." *Proceedings, American Antiquarian Society* (April 1931).

James, James A. "Significant Events during the Last Year of the Revolution in the West." *Proceedings of the Mississippi Valley Historical Association for the Year 1912-1913* 6: 238-57.

"Journal of the Proceedings of General St. Clair's Army, Defeated at Fort Recovery 4th November 1791." *American Pioneer* 2 (March 1843): 135-38.

"Letters of General James Wilkinson." *Register of the Kentucky Historical Society* 24 (Sept. 1926): 259-67.

McMurtry, Douglas C. "Notes on Printing in Kentucky in the Eighteenth Century." *Filson Club History Quarterly* 10 (1936): 261-66.

Paxson, W.M. "The Marshall Family." *Register of the Kentucky Historical Society* (June 1921): 93-96.

Quaife, Milo M. "When Detroit Invaded Kentucky." *Filson Club History Quarterly* 1 (1926-27): 53-57.

Ranck, George W. "How Kentucky Became a State." *Harper's Magazine* 86 (June 23, 1892): 46-49.

———. "The Traveling Church: An Account of the Baptist Exodus from Virginia in 1781." *Register of the Kentucky Historical Society* 79 (Summer 1981): 240-65.

Reeves, Charlotte. "Colonel Robert Patterson." *Yearbook 1913, Kentucky Society, Sons of the Revolution*, 131-33.

Robertson, James Rood. "New Light on Early Kentucky." *Proceedings of the Mississippi Valley Historical Association* 9 (1915-1918): 90-98.

Rothert, Otto A. "Shane, the Western Collector." *Filson Club History Quarterly* 4 (Jan. 1936): 1-16.

Schuyler, Dean Haslet. "Some Notes on British Intrigue in Kentucky, 1788-1791." *Register of the Kentucky Historical Society* 38 (Jan. 1940): 54-56.

Speed, Thomas. "Kinchloe's or the Burnt Station." *Register of the Kentucky Historical Society* 32 (Jan. 1934): 169-77.

"Sketch of the Virginia Bounty Land System." *Yearbook 1913, Kentucky Society, Sons of the Revolution*, 164-272.

Staples, Charles R. "John Bradford and the *Kentucky Gazette*—First Newspaper." *Kentucky Press* 8 (Feb. 1937): 2-6.

Talbert, Charles G. "Kentucky Invades Ohio." *Register of the Kentucky Historical Society* 53 (Oct. 1955): 288-97.

Threlkeld, Marguerite. "Mann's Lick." *Filson Club History Quarterly* 1 (July 1927): 174.

Van Cleve, John Walter. "Early Recollections of the West." *American Pioneer* 2 (May 1843): 203-24, 269-73.

———. "Colonel Robert Patterson." *American Pioneer* 2 (Aug. 1843): 343-47.

Walker, Felix. "Narrative of His Trip with Boone from Long Island to Boonesborough in 1775." *DeBow's Review* 16 (1854): 150-55.

Wilson, Samuel M. "Kentucky's Part in the Revolution." *Yearbook 1913, Kentucky Society, Sons of the Revolution*, 139-50.

———. "Catalogue of Revolutionary Soldiers and Sailors of the Commonwealth of Virginia to Whom Land Bounty Warrants Were Granted for Military Service in the War for Independence." *Yearbook 1913, Kentucky Society, Sons of the Revolution*, 190-272.

———. "The Ohio Valley in the Revolutions." *Yearbook 1913, Kentucky Society, Sons of the Revolution*, 153-63.

Yanchisin, Daniel A. "John Bradford, Public Servant." *Register of the Kentucky Historical Society* 68 (Jan. 1978): 61-69.

General Works

Abernethy, Thomas Perkins. *Three Virginia Frontiers*. Baton Rouge, La., 1940.

———. *Western Lands and the American Revolution*. New York, 1959.

Albach, James R. *Annals of the West Embracing a Complete Account of Principal Events which have Occurred in the Western States and Territories*. Pittsburgh, 1857.

Alvord, Clarence W. *The Mississippi Valley in British Politics*. Cleveland, 1917.

Alvord, Clarence Walworth, and Lee Bidgood. *The First Explorations of the Trans-Allegheny Region by Virginians, 1650-1674*. Cleveland, 1912.

Ayers, William. *Historical Sketches*. Pineville, Ky., 1930.

Bakeless, John. *Daniel Boone, Master of the Wilderness*. New York, 1939.

Baldwin, Leland D. *Whiskey Rebels: The Story of a Frontier Uprising*. Pittsburgh, 1939.

Barnhart, John D. *Valley of Democracy*. Bloomington, Ind., 1953.

Bemis, Samuel Flagg. *Jay's Treaty: A Study in Commerce and Diplomacy*. New York, 1923.

———. *Pinckney's Treaty: America's Advantage from Europe's Distress, 1783-1800*. New Haven, Conn., 1960.

Biographical Encyclopedia of Kentucky. Cincinnati, 1878.

Bodley, Temple. *History of Kentucky before the Louisiana Purchase.* 2 vols. Chicago, 1928.

———. *Our First Great West in Revolutionary War, Diplomacy and Politics.* Louisville, 1938.

Bodley, Temple, ed. *Littell's Political Transactions In and Concerning Kentucky.* Filson Club Publication No. 31. Louisville, 1926.

Brown, John Mason. *The Political Beginnings of Kentucky.* Louisville, 1889.

Burnet, Jacob. *Notes on the Settlement of the North-western Territory.* Cincinnati, 1847.

Butler, Mann. *History of the Commonwealth of Kentucky.* Louisville, 1834.

Caldwell, Charles. *A Discourse on the Genius and Character of the Rev. Horace Holley, LL.D., Late President of Transylvania University.* Boston, 1828.

Casseday, Benjamin O. *The History of Louisville from Its Earliest Settlement til the Year 1852.* Louisville, 1852.

Clark, Thomas D. *Kentucky, Land of Contrast.* New York, 1968.

Coleman, J. Winston. *A Bibliography of Kentucky History.* Lexington, 1949.

———. *The British Invasion of Kentucky.* Lexington, 1951.

———. *Slavery Times in Kentucky.* Chapel Hill, N.C., 1940.

Collins, Lewis, and Richard H. Collins. *History of Kentucky.* 2 vols. Covington, Ky. 1874.

Connelley, William E., and E. Merton Coulter. *A History of Kentucky.* 2 vols. Chicago, 1922.

Cotterill, Robert S. *History of Pioneer Kentucky.* Cincinnati, 1917.

Coward, Joan Wells. *Kentucky in the New Republic: The Process of Constitution Making.* Lexington, 1979.

Davidson, Robert. *History of the Presbyterian Church in the State of Kentucky: with a Preliminary Sketch of the Churches in the Valley of Virginia.* New York, 1847.

Dewey, Davis Rich. *Financial History of the United States.* New York, 1939.

Doddridge, Joseph. *Notes on the Settlement and Indian Wars of the Western Parts of Virginia and Pennsylvania, from the Year 1763 until the year 1783 Inclusive.* Wellsburg, Va., 1824.

Dugan, Frances L.S., and Jacqueline P. Bull. *Bluegrass Craftsman; Being the Reminiscences of Ebenezer Hiram Stedman, Papermaker, 1808-1885.* Lexington, 1959.

Durrett, Reuben T., comp. *Bryant's Station and the Memorial Proceedings Held on Its Site Under the Auspices of the Lexington Chapter, D.A.R., August the 18th, 1896, in Honor of Its Heroic Mothers and Daughters.* Filson Club Publication No. 12. Louisville, 1897.

Dyche, Russell. *History of Laurel County.* London, Ky., n.d.

Ellis, William, H.E. Everman, and Richard Sears. *Madison County: 200 Years in Retrospect.* Richmond, Ky. 1985.

English, William Hayden. *Conquest of the Country Northwest of the River Ohio, 1778-1783.* 4 vols. Indianapolis, 1897.

Filson, John. *The Discovery, Settlement and Present State of Kentucke.* Wilmington, Del., 1784.

Gaines, B.O. *B.O. Gaines History of Scott County.* 2 vols. Georgetown, Ky., 1904.

Green, Thomas M. *The Spanish Conspiracy: A Review of Early Spanish Movements in the Southwest.* Cincinnati, 1891.

Hall, James. *Sketches of History, Life and Manners in the West.* 2 vols. Philadelphia, 1835.

Harrison, Lowell H., *John Breckinridge: Jeffersonian Republican,* Louisville, 1969.

———. *Kentucky's Governors, 1792-1985.* Lexington, 1985.

———. *Kentucky's Road to Statehood.* Lexington, 1992.

Hay, Thomas Robson, and M.R. Werner. *The Admirable Trumpeter.* New York, 1941.

Haywood, John. *The Civil and Political History of the State of Tennessee Up to the Year 1796.* Knoxville, 1823.

Henderson, Archibald. *The Conquest of the Old Southwest.* New York, 1920.

Holley, Horace A. *A Discourse Occasioned by the Death of Colonel James Morrison. Delivered in the Episcopal Church, Lexington, Kentucky, February 3, 1822.* Lexington, 1823.

Howe, Henry. *Historical Collections of Ohio: An Encyclopedia of the State.* 2 vols. Cincinnati, 1908.

Hubbard, William O., and Joe Johnson. *Kentucky's Ohio River Boundary: From the Big Sandy to the Great Miami.* Information Bulletin No. 81. Frankfort: Legislative Research Commission, 1969.

Hubbard, William O., and Dennis Lee Taulbee. *Kentucky's Ohio River Boundary: From the Great Miami to the Wabash.* Information Bulletin No. 83. Frankfort: Legislative Research Commission, 1972.

James, James Alton. *The Life of George Rogers Clark.* Chicago, 1928.

Jefferson, Thomas. *Notes on the State of Virginia.* 1787; Richmond, Va., 1853.

Jennings, William Walter. *Transylvania: Pioneer University of the West.* New York, 1955.

Jillson, Willard Rouse. *The First Printing in Kentucky: Some Account of Thomas Parvin and John Bradford and the Establishment of the* Kentucky Gazette *in the year 1787.* Louisville, 1936.

———. *The Kentucky Land Grants.* Louisville, 1925.

———. *Old Kentucky Entries and Deeds.* Louisville, 1926.

Johnston, J. Stoddard, ed. *First Explorations of Kentucky: Journals of Dr. Thomas Walker and Christopher Gist.* Chicago, 1896.

Kappler, Charles J. *Indian Affairs: Laws and Treaties.* 2 vols. Washington, D.C., 1904.

Kincaid, Robert L. *The Wilderness Road.* Indianapolis, 1947.

Knopf, Richard C. *Anthony Wayne: A Name in Arms, Soldier, Diplomat, Defender of Expansion Westward of a Nation.* Pittsburgh, 1960.

Lee, Rebecca Smith. *Mary Austin Holley: A Biography.* Austin, Tex., 1962.

Lester, William Stewart. *The Transylvania Colony.* Spencer, Ind., 1935.

Lindsay, Merrill. *The Kentucky Rifle.* New York, 1972.

Littell, William. *Political Transactions in and Concerning Kentucky.* Frankfort, 1806.

Lofaro, Michael A. *The Life and Adventures of Daniel Boone.* Lexington, 1978.

McClung, John A. *Sketches of Western Adventure, Containing an Account of the Most Interesting Incidents in the Settlement of the West.* Dayton, Ohio, 1847.

McDonald, John. *Biographical Sketches of General Nathaniel Massie, General Duncan McArthur, Captain William Wells, and General Simon Kenton.* Dayton, Ohio, 1852.

Marshall, Humphrey. *The History of Kentucky including an Account of the Discovery—*

Settlement—Progressive Improvement—Political and Literary Events—and Present State of the Country. Frankfort, 1812.

————. *The History of Kentucky.* 2 vols. Frankfort, 1824.

Mason, Kathryn Harrod. *James Harrod of Kentucky.* Baton Rouge, La., 1951.

Mereness, Newton D., ed. *Travels in the American Colonies.* New York, 1916.

Metcalf, Samuel L. *A Collection of Some of the Most Interesting Narratives of Indian Warfare in the West, Containing an Account of the Adventures of Colonel Daniel Boone, One of the First Settlers of Kentucky.* Lexington, 1821.

Meyer, Leland Winfield. *The Life and Times of Colonel Richard M. Johnson of Kentucky.* New York, 1932.

Nevins, Allan. *The American States during and after the Revolution, 1775-1789.* New York, 1924.

Perrin, William H. *The Pioneer Press of Kentucky.* Louisville, 1888.

————, J.H. Battle, and G.C. Kniffen. *Kentucky: A History of the State.* Louisville, 1888.

Peter, Robert. *The History of the Medical Department of Transylvania University.* Louisville, 1905.

————, and Peter, Johana. *Transylvania University: Its Origins, Rise, Decline, and Fall.* Louisville, 1896.

Quisenberry, Anderson C. *The Life and Times of the Honorable Humphrey Marshall.* Winchester, Ky., 1892.

Ramsey, J.G.M., *The Annals of Tennessee to the End of the Eighteenth Century.* Charleston, 1853.

Ranck, George W. *Boonesborough: Its Founding, Pioneer Struggle, Indian Experiences, Transylvania Days, and Revolutionary Annals.* Louisville, 1901.

————. *History of Lexington, Kentucky: Its Early Annals and Recent Progress.* Cincinnati, 1872.

————. *The Story of Bryan's Station.* Lexington, 1896.

————. *The Traveling Church.* Louisville, 1891.

Robertson, James Rood. *Petitions of the Early Inhabitants of Kentucky to the General Assembly of Virginia, 1769-1792.* Louisville, 1914.

Rodabaugh, James H. *Robert Hamilton Bishop.* Columbus, Ohio, 1935.

Sames, James W., III, comp. *Four Steps West.* Frankfort, 1971.

Sonne, Niels Henry. *Liberal Kentucky, 1780-1828.* New York, 1939.

Speed, Thomas. *The Political Club of Danville, Kentucky, 1786-1790.* Louisville, 1894.

Staples, Charles R. *The History of Pioneer Lexington, 1779-1806.* Lexington, 1959.

Stipp, G.W., *John Bradford's Historical &c. Notes on Kentucky from the Western Miscellany.* San Francisco, 1932.

————. *The Western Miscellany, or, Accounts Historical, Biographical, and Amusing.* Xenia, Ohio, 1827.

Talbert, Charles Gano. *Benjamin Logan, Kentucky Frontiersman.* Lexington, 1962.

Thwaites, Reuben Gold, and Louise Phelps Kellogg. *Documentary History of Dunmore's War, 1774.* Madison: Wisconsin Historical Society, 1905.

Volwiler, A.T. *George Croghan and the Westward Movement, 1741-1748.* Cleveland, 1926.

Watlington, Patricia. *The Partisan Spirit: Kentucky Politics, 1779-1792.* New York, 1972.

Whitaker, Arthur Preston. *The Mississippi Question, 1795-1803: A Study in Trade, Politics, and Diplomacy.* New York, 1934.

————. *The Spanish-American Frontier, 1783-1795: The Westward Movement and the Spanish Retreat in the Mississippi Valley.* Boston, 1927.

White, Nelle Rhea. *The Bradfords of Virginia in the Revolutionary War and Their Kin.* Richmond, Va., 1932.

Withers, Alexander Scott. *Chronicles of Border Warfare, or a History of the Settlement of the Whites of Northwestern Virginia and the Indian Wars and Massacres.* Clarksburg, Va., 1831.

Wilson, Samuel M. *Battle of the Blue Licks.* Louisville, 1927.

————. *The First Land Court of Kentucky, 1779-1780.* Lexington, 1923.

Young, Chester R., ed. *Westward into Kentucky: The Narrative of Daniel Trabue.* Lexington, 1981.

Wright, John D., Jr. *Transylvania: Tutor to the West.* Lexington, 1975.

Index

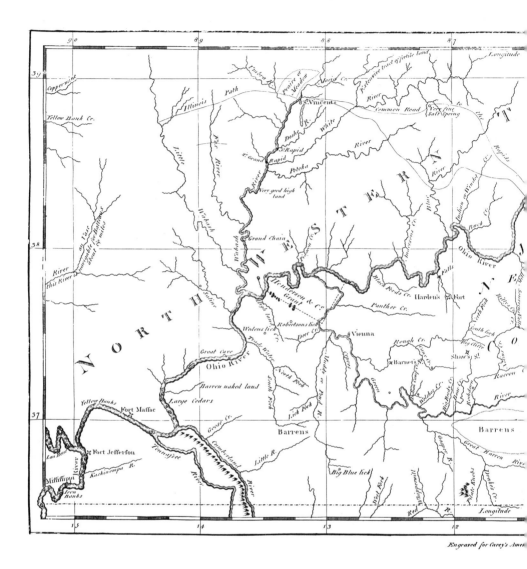

"Kentucky, Reduced from Elihu Barker's Large Map. W. Barker Sculp." From William
Guthrie, *A New System of Modern Geography* (Philadelphia, 1794-95). Courtesy of
Special Collections, Margaret I. King Library, University of Kentucky.